CONTROLLING IMMIGRATION THROUGH CRIMINAL LAW

This book provides a systematic and comprehensive overview of the increased role of criminal law in managing migration, from a European, domestic and comparative law perspective.

The contributors critically engage with the current trends leading to the criminalisation of irregular migrants, asylum seekers and those who engage in 'humanitarian smuggling', and the national and common policies calling for a broader use of criminal law measures.

The chapters explore the measures used to protect borders, their impact in terms of effectiveness and their ability to strike a fair balance between security and the protection of human rights. The contributors to the book cover a range of disciplines within law, human rights and criminology resulting in a broad understanding of the issues at play.

Volume 12 in the series Hart Studies in European Criminal Law

Hart Studies in European Criminal Law

Series Editors: Professor Katalin Ligeti, University of Luxembourg;
Professor Valsamis Mitsilegas, Queen Mary University of London;
Professor Anne Weyembergh, Brussels Free University

Since the Lisbon Treaty, European criminal law has become an increasingly important field of research and debate. Working with the European Criminal Law Academic Network (ECLAN), the series will publish works of the highest intellectual rigour and cutting edge scholarship which will be required reading for all European criminal lawyers.

The series is happy to consider both edited and single authored titles. The series defines 'European' and 'criminal law' in the broadest sense, so books on European criminal law, justice and policy will be considered. The series also welcomes books which offer different methodological approaches.

Volume 1: *EU Criminal Law after Lisbon: Rights, Trust and the Transformation of Justice in Europe*
by Valsamis Mitsilegas

Volume 2: *Challenges in the Field of Economic and Financial Crime in Europe and the US*
Edited by Vanessa Franssen and Katalin Ligeti

Volume 3: *Chasing Criminal Money: Challenges and Perspectives On Asset Recovery in the EU*
Edited by Katalin Ligeti and Michele Simonato

Volume 4: *Limits to EU Powers: A Case Study of EU Regulatory Criminal Law*
by Jacob Öberg

Volume 5: *The Needed Balances in EU Criminal Law: Past, Present and Future*
Edited by Chloé Brière and Anne Weyembergh

Volume 6: *Redefining Organised Crime: A Challenge for the European Union?*
Edited by Stefania Carnevale, Serena Forlati and Orsetta Giolo

Volume 7: *White Collar Crime: A Comparative Perspective*
Edited by Katalin Ligeti and Stanislaw Tosza

Volume 8: *Criminal Liability of Managers in Europe: Punishing Excessive Risk*
Stanisław Tosza

Volume 9: *The European Union and Deprivation of Liberty: A Legislative and Judicial Analysis from the Perspective of the Individual*
Leandro Mancano

Volume 10: *The Legitimacy of EU Criminal Law*
Irene Wieczorek

Volume 11: *The Fight Against Impunity in EU Law*
Edited by Luisa Marin and Stefano Montaldo

Volume 12: *Controlling Immigration Through Criminal Law: European and Comparative Perspectives on 'Crimmigration'*
Edited by Gian Luigi Gatta, Valsamis Mitsilegas, and Stefano Zirulia

Controlling Immigration Through Criminal Law

European and Comparative Perspectives on "Crimmigration"

Edited by
Gian Luigi Gatta,
Valsamis Mitsilegas
and
Stefano Zirulia

•HART•
OXFORD • LONDON • NEW YORK • NEW DELHI • SYDNEY

HART PUBLISHING

Bloomsbury Publishing Plc

Kemp House, Chawley Park, Cumnor Hill, Oxford, OX2 9PH, UK

1385 Broadway, New York, NY 10018, USA

HART PUBLISHING, the Hart/Stag logo, BLOOMSBURY and the Diana logo are trademarks of Bloomsbury Publishing Plc

First published in Great Britain 2021

A catalogue record for this book is available from the British Library.

Library of Congress Cataloging-in-Publication data

Names: Gatta, Gian Luigi, editor. | Mitsilegas, Valsamis, 1971- editor. | Zirulia, Stefano, editor.

Title: Controlling immigration through criminal law : European and comparative perspectives on "crimmigration" / edited by Gian Luigi Gatta, Valsamis Mitsilegas and Stefano Zirulia.

Description: Oxford, UK ; New York, NY : Hart Publishing, an imprint of Bloomsbury Publishing, 2021. | Series: Hart studies in European criminal law; volume 12 | Includes bibliographical references and index.

Identifiers: LCCN 2020035595 (print) | LCCN 2020035596 (ebook) | ISBN 9781509933921 (hardback) | ISBN 9781509942756 (paperback) | ISBN 9781509933938 (Epub) | ISBN 9781509933945 (pdf)

Subjects: LCSH: Emigration and immigration law—European Union countries—Criminal provisions. | Emigration and immigration law—Criminal provisions. | Human smuggling—Law and legislation—European Union countries | Illegal aliens.

Classification: LCC KJE6044 .C668 2020 (print) | LCC KJE6044 (ebook) | DDC 345.4/0237—dc23

LC record available at https://lccn.loc.gov/2020035595

LC ebook record available at https://lccn.loc.gov/2020035596

ISBN: HB: 978-1-50993-392-1
ePDF: 978-1-50993-394-5
ePub: 978-1-50993-393-8

Typeset by Compuscript Ltd, Shannon

To find out more about our authors and books visit www.hartpublishing.co.uk. Here you will find extracts, author information, details of forthcoming events and the option to sign up for our newsletters.

CONTENTS

List of Contributors .... *vii*

Introduction *1*
Gian Luigi Gatta, Valsamis Mitsilegas and Stefano Zirulia

PART I
THE CRIMINALISATION OF MIGRATION:
FRAMING THE DEBATE

1. *Assessing Migration Management and the Role of Criminal Law* *9*
Elspeth Guild

2. *The Criminalisation of Migration in the Law of the European Union: Challenging the Preventive Paradigm* *25*
Valsamis Mitsilegas

3. *Global Trends in 'Crimmigration' Policies: From the EU to the USA* *47*
Gian Luigi Gatta

4. *The Connections between Migration, Crime and Punishment: Historical and Sociological Questions* *81*
Dario Melossi

5. *Current Trends, Numbers and Routes in EU Migrations: Is Existing Legislation Creating More Irregularity?* *101*
Maria Giovanna Manieri

PART II
THE CRIMINALISATION OF MIGRATION:
NATIONAL, EUROPEAN AND COMPARATIVE PERSPECTIVES

6. *Crimmigration in Spain* *119*
José A Brandariz

7. *Ethnicity Based Immigration Checks: Crimmigration and the* How *of Immigration and Border Control* *141*
Maartje van der Woude

8. *Crimmigration in Greece: A Story of Exceptional Derogations from the Rule of Law within a Permanent Situation of Emergency*................165
Nikolaos Chatzinikolaou

9. *Immigration Detention between Law and Practice in Italy: Managing the Border Through Arbitrary Detention*..193
Francesca Cancellaro

10. *Detention as a Tool of Immigration and Asylum Enforcement in the EU*..211
Justine N Stefanelli

PART III
WHO IS TO BLAME? SMUGGLING, HUMANITARIAN ASSISTANCE AND HUMAN RIGHTS VIOLATIONS IN THE MEDITERRANEAN AREA

11. *Is that a Smuggler?: The Blurring Line between Facilitating Illegal Immigration and Providing Humanitarian Assistance at the European Borders*..235
Stefano Zirulia

12. *Reversing the Perspective: Criminal Responsibility of Italian Authorities for Human Rights Violations in Libya?*..267
Luca Masera

Index..281

LIST OF CONTRIBUTORS

José A Brandariz, Associate Professor of Criminal Law and Criminology at the University of A Coruña, Spain

Francesca Cancellaro, PhD (Università di Bologna), Post-doc Researcher, Università della Tuscia; Lawyer specialising in Criminal law and Human Rights law

Nikolaos Chatzinikolaou, PhD (Aristotle University of Thessaloniki), Lawyer specialising in Criminal Law, Thessaloniki

Gian Luigi Gatta, Professor of Criminal Law, Department of Law 'Cesare Beccaria', Università degli Studi di Milano

Elspeth Guild, Jean Monnet Professor ad personam at Queen Mary University of London and Radboud University Nijmegen, Netherlands

Maria Giovanna Manieri, Political Advisor on Civil Liberties, Justice and Home Affairs for the Greens/EFA in the European Parliament

Luca Masera, Associate Professor of Criminal Law at the Università di Brescia, vice-president of the ASGI (Associazione per gli Studi Giuridici sull'Immigrazione)

Dario Melossi, Professor of Criminology, Università di Bologna

Valsamis Mitsilegas, Professor of European Criminal Law and Global Security and Deputy Dean for Global Engagement (Europe) at Queen Mary University of London

Justine N Stefanelli, Director of Publications and Research, American Society of International Law, Washington, DC

Maartje Van Der Woude, Professor of Law & Society, Van Vollenhoven Institute for Law, Governance & Society, Leiden University

Stefano Zirulia, Assistant Professor of Criminal Law, Department of Law 'Cesare Beccaria', Università degli Studi di Milano

Introduction

GIAN LUIGI GATTA, VALSAMIS MITSILEGAS
AND STEFANO ZIRULIA

Over the last 20 years, increasingly securitised and repressive measures have been the main feature of the EU common immigration policy. More and more restrictive conditions for entry and constant reinforcement of border surveillance are just the tip of the iceberg in a complex system characterised by the criminalisation of both undocumented migrants and those facilitating their entry or permanence, even when assistance is provided due to family or humanitarian reasons alone. Legal, sociological and criminological literature have dealt with this approach to immigration control extensively. Although authors differ in compiling their thoughts and proposing solutions, a wide consensus has emerged as to the current system of European immigration law being far from transparent, humane and sustainable. Despite this chorus of criticism, the European Union and the Member States continue to face the migratory phenomenon in a contradictory manner that has been perpetuated since the Tampere European Council of 1999, where policy statements are in stark contrast with the way the migratory phenomenon is managed in practice: while declarations abound in commitments to develop migration and asylum policies based on creating legal access routes, protecting vulnerable individuals, and integrating foreigners (see, in addition to the Tampere Conclusion, the European Agenda on Migration 2015), the practice has so far contributed to building a system that moves in the opposite direction. Devastating ongoing reports from the Mediterranean Routes, the Balkan Route and the Greek hotspots, among others, show a different side of Europe, steadily closing up at the mercy of populist anti-immigration rhetoric, incapable of drawing up a policy of incoming mobility consistent with the principles it claims to be inspired by.

In this context, the inability to come up with an approach towards the migratory phenomenon disengaged from a public-order frame of reference, where migration is only perceived as a threat to the internal security of the Schengen area, represents one of the aspects heavily affecting European action. This has resulted in an increasing contamination of immigration law and refugee law with preventive and repressive measures traditionally falling within the purview of criminal law, out of which a hybrid, substantially criminal-type system was established, where administrative law borrows enforcement agencies and tools from criminal law, and the latter provides an array of sanctioning options beyond the scope of the former.

The multifaceted intersections between criminal justice and immigration control were amply addressed in the context of an international conference which took place at Università degli Studi di Milano, Department of Law Cesare Beccaria on 3 and 4 December 2018. The conference panels comprised experts from all over Europe and different fields: legal and criminological scholars, members of public institutions and law practitioners. Sessions involving the above experts were held over a day and a half, aimed at achieving a holistic understanding of the state of the art of 'crimmigration' policies in the EU and beyond, and discussing the remedies available to ensure the protection of fundamental guarantees and human rights in the current migratory crisis.

This book collects original chapters reproducing the presentations given by the speakers at the conference, updated and supplemented with bibliographic references, and including additional contributions from preeminent immigration-law scholars. Contributions also take into account the latest relevant developments between 2018 and early 2020, in terms of legal reforms, case-law and practices related to detention, deportation, and in general the criminalisation of undocumented migrants and those who assist them in their journeys.

From the editors' standpoint, *Controlling Immigration Through Criminal Law* is an umbrella concept covering the manifold instances of the security-oriented approach to migration management that contemporary Western policy-makers essentially take for granted when dealing with incoming flows of people from underprivileged countries. The purpose of the book is to provide a critical analysis of the legislation, case-law and practices of a number of transit and destination states where the intersection between criminal and migration law is concerned. The aim is to cast light on the lack of consistency, effectiveness and fundamental rights deficit that these systems display.

The reference to 'criminal law' sums up in an all-encompassing way the entire arsenal of coercive measures currently available for immigration enforcement purposes, each of which has traceable origins within the criminal law system (detention, arrest, police control, removal from a given territory). Moreover, it shows that the coercive measures in question ought to be imposed in compliance with the guarantees provided for (e.g., those established within the criminal justice system), which instead have been reduced or removed for the sake of efficiency. Against this backdrop, the chapters included in this book suggest reassessing the undiscerning criminalisation of migration by national and supranational institutions, an attitude that combines an approach to criminal law construed as a central feature of state sovereignty with the policy-making tendency to look at global mobility of people as a mere threat to border integrity, as opposed to being intrinsic to human nature, and possibly a resource for the State. Indeed, it is no coincidence that the securitised approach goes hand in hand with a management of flows marked by recurrent 'emergencies', inadequate reception facilities and integration programmes, reduction of legal grounds to enter and stay.

All of the above-mentioned aspects worsen the marginalisation of migrants and asylum seekers, and thus fuel public demand for increased security, which – paradoxically – constitutes one of the root causes of the issues it seeks to address. Given the above premises, the book seeks to challenge immigration enforcement through criminal law and criminal-law tools by both pointing out its political unsustainability and singling out the limits to such criminalisation arising from a plethora of sources: domestic constitutional law, human rights law, EU law and international law.

So far, a number of crimmigration scholars have focused on the increasing overlapping between immigration law and criminal law, providing references that are also essential to the chapters included in this book. At the same time, a renewed attention to the subject matter is justified by the dynamic nature of the phenomena under consideration, due to a fast-changing regulatory framework; the unpredictable and not always consistent case-law developments; as well as practices implemented by law enforcement, perilously flirting with the boundaries of legality, if not disregarding them altogether. This backdrop provides the inspiration for placing several works within a single book, works that while being scientifically independent, insofar as each of them comprehensively addresses a well-identified selected topic, all seek the common aim of addressing the most significant demonstrations of immigration control through criminal law in the above-explained sense. The leading cross-cutting issues dealt with in this book are summarily outlined below.

Undocumented migrants are, of course, the main targets of immigration enforcement measures. Here the use of criminal law is all the more apparent, first and foremost, in the provision of 'status crimes', i.e. criminal offences based on administrative non-compliance alone, without punishment ensuring a more effective protection of the interests at stake, in breach of the *ultima ratio* principle (Gatta, chapter three). With respect to this use of criminal law, EU law has had a protective function through the case-law of the Court of Justice in and following *El Dridi*, although not all its implications are fully satisfactory: indeed, the *Celaj* ruling – authorising a custodial sentence in the event of violation of re-entry bans – lends itself to criticism to the extent that 'the interests protected by national law criminalising re-entry or the harm in re-entry are difficult to pin down unless re-entry is viewed as an additional affront to state sovereignty as translated in its capacity to guard the border effectively' (Mitsilegas, chapter two). On a closer inspection, 'status crimes' may also be defined as a 'doubly artificial offences': not only are they *mala quia prohibita* (i.e., unlawful only due to contingent criminal policy), but it is the very legal system which, by reducing grounds for regular entry and making the status of regular migrants and refugees precarious (Manieri, chapter five), lays down the conditions for these criminal offences to be committed. This is a circumstance in which we are confronted with 'a legislation and a society that punish people for having become which society has helped them to become' (Melossi, chapter four). Migrants' higher exposure to criminalisation is also closely linked to the issue of ethnic or racial profiling by law enforcement.

This form of discrimination has many different causes, including the type of offence the police are concerned with, the type of guidance that the police receive from politicians, media pressure (Melossi, chapter four), as well as the wide discretionary power that street-level border patrol officers enjoy, which 'creates room for 'crimmigrant' stereotypes to roam freely' (Van Der Woude, chapter seven).

Another instance of immigration control through criminal law is coercive removal from the EU territory. Indeed, this is not just a typical measure to enforce deportation orders, as it is widely used to ensure public order and punish undocumented migrants, both in the USA and in the EU (Gatta, chapter three). In Spain, for instance, in order to fill the 'deportation gap' (i.e., the difference between deportation orders issued and those actually enforced), criminal deportations and administrative removals based on criminal records were increased, and at the same time political narratives seeking to portray deported migrants as 'criminal aliens' were put in place. Even removals based on immigration-law breaches cannot be set apart from the 'crimmigration' pattern in that country, as they 'operate as a cost-effective – albeit, highly questionable – strategy to cope with minor criminal activities, circumventing the lengthy, resource-consuming, and evidently more rights-based criminal adjudication processes' (Brandariz, chapter six).

Similarly, an ambiguity in the rationale of the measures (immigration enforcement, removal efficiency and punishment) can also be found in immigration-detention laws and practices. The expansive tendency of immigration detention, albeit partially curbed by the Court of Justice (see, e.g., the rulings in *Al Chodor*, *J.N.* and *Kadzoev*), seems to have regained momentum through the recent proposal for a recast Return Directive (Stefanelli, chapter ten). Moreover, deprivation of personal liberty represents one of the areas in which immigration enforcement is carried out in systemic breach of the fundamental rights of migrants. The effort to contain flows at the external borders at all costs has in fact led to legal-limbo areas, where *habeas corpus* is suspended and people risk being 'trapped' and having no judicial recourse, as is frequently the case at the Italian border, inside reception centres and hotspots or aboard ships (Cancellaro, chapter nine).

In addition to coercive measures applied in relation to asylum seekers and undocumented migrants, the crackdown on entry flows is also carried out through the fight against humanitarian assistance activities provided by NGOs and civilian aid in favour of vulnerable people. In this field, criminalisation in the narrower sense, i.e., sanctions of a criminal nature, mainly occurs through instruments of international and EU law originally intended to combat the phenomena of migrant smuggling and human trafficking (Guild, chapter one, Mitsilegas, chapter two). However, these instruments, coupled with the absence of grounds for regular entry, have substantially fed a flourishing mobility black market, where migrants pay ever higher fees for increasingly dangerous transfers: so far, 'the insertion of transnational criminal law into the field of migration has done more harm than good in respect of the objectives espoused – diminishing irregular border crossing and exploitation of labour', as the approach in question has actually 'resulted in increasing amounts of unsafe, disorderly and irregular migration' (Guild, chapter one). With particular regard to EU obligations to criminalise the facilitation of illegal entry of third-country nationals, the so-called Facilitators Package of 2002 still imposes upon Member States the obligation to criminalise any form of assistance to undocumented migrants, including cases where no financial gain is pursued, and leaves to national legislatures the choice whether to establish a humanitarian clause to justify or excuse humanitarian assistance – or not. This results in a supranational legal framework fraught with 'adverse impact on the functioning of civil society and on compliance with fundamental obligations under international and EU human rights, humanitarian and refugee law' (Mitsilegas, chapter two). At the national level, the implementation of such a framework results, in turn, in criminal offences that go so far as to target with severe penalties humanitarian assistance provided by NGOs and civilian aid (Chatzinikolaou, chapter eight, Zirulia, chapter eleven). Notwithstanding sustained calls for reform and de-criminalisation, the persistent imperviousness of EU law to the issue at hand suggests that the way might consist in challenging the Facilitators Package's lawfulness before the Court of Justice, in light of the EU Charter of Fundamental Rights (Zirulia, chapter eleven).

Strikingly, the current European and Mediterranean scenarios show the indifferent approach that national and supranational rules and practices, promoted and tolerated by governments, and sometimes even courts, take with respect to the protection of migrants' fundamental rights. As if these were 'minor' fundamental rights, designed to perish, or in any case to have a marginal weight, when offset with the interest of protecting the external borders. Human rights that we, as European citizens, are used to taking for granted in ordinary circumstances – such as personal liberty, physical integrity and even life – are on the contrary under systematic threat when ascribable to migrants, both within the European territory (in detention facilities or during dangerous attempts of secondary movements) and, above all, in transit countries, such as Libya. This situation cannot be justified by invoking the need to face the migratory 'emergencies' that periodically affect the European continent: aside from the fact that some of the human rights at stake are inviolable, the reference to an emergency often seems a pretext for further crackdowns on immigration (Van der Woude, chapter seven). Faced with such blatant and well-known violations of human rights, the issue of a potential contributory criminal liability of public authorities complicit in such infringements cannot be ignored. This is already being tackled in Italy, where the former Minister of the Interior is currently subject to criminal proceedings for the criminal offence of kidnapping, having on different occasions unjustifiably denied the disembarkation of rescued migrants (Cancellaro, chapter nine). Moreover, legal scholars and human-rights lawyers now envision liability on the part of Italian and European authorities for complicity in the crimes against humanity perpetrated at sea and in the Libyan detention camps (Masera, chapter twelve).

Compared to the current situation, only a part of the recent European initiatives in the field of immigration control offers room for improvement: on the one hand, 'it could be argued that a number of provisions in the proposed reform of the Common European Asylum System and recast Return Directive point to a risk of creating more irregularity, including precariousness and loss of status in a number of ways' (Manieri, chapter five); on the other hand, the policy lines of the UN Global Compact for Safe, Orderly and Regular Migration steer towards a cautiously positive assessment. In this regard, it has been noted that 'while the progress towards a more human rights oriented approach to smuggling and trafficking of people across borders is only minor in the Compact, nonetheless, the more coercive of the provisions of the Protocols are tempered by a more human rights compliant approach and respect of international labour standards' (Guild, chapter one). The hope is that this is not yet another instance, as the past would suggest, of soft law documents not being matched by initiatives actually capable of bringing about change to the current regulation of immigration flows and its implementation at the border and within the European space. The objective of striking a fair balance between border control and the protection of fundamental rights of all those involved, including natives, will only be reached when legality and solidarity will no longer be perceived as conflicting values, but rather as complementing each other.

By exploring the commixture of immigration and criminal law, specifically within the European and Mediterranean area, taking into account its political and historical roots, its normative foundations, its developments and current 'state of the art' in some benchmark EU Member States, this book aims to fill a knowledge gap in the field of immigration control via criminal law and criminal-law-type measures, hopefully providing academics and practitioners operating in the fields of criminal law, immigration law, criminology, EU law and human rights with an instrument that has been lacking from their shelves up until now.

PART I

The Criminalisation of Migration: Framing the Debate

1

Assessing Migration Management and the Role of Criminal Law

ELSPETH GUILD

I. Introduction

In December 2018 the international community, meeting at the UN General Assembly, acknowledged that no state can address migration alone, and while upholding the sovereignty of states and their obligations under international law, and it stated that international cooperation among all relevant actors on migration is necessary.[1] This statement is important because migration policy has been a source of substantial friction among states in the late twentieth and twenty-first centuries in particular as regards the entitlement of states to take action regarding border controls and migration without consultation with their neighbours. This is in some ways a paradoxical situation as this period also includes the development of increasingly complete free travel areas among regional groups of states.[2]

International debates and controversies on the subject of borders and migration have been myriad (including within the UN), but appetite to develop new international instruments has waxed and waned over the twentieth and twenty-first centuries. A short overview of the international community's treatment of the reality of migration is worth setting out as it reveals the rapidity and flexibility of approaches over fairly short periods of time. It is also worth bearing in mind that the second half of the twentieth century saw a rapid decline in colonial occupation which resulted in new states and new borders appearing across the world. Similarly the end of the Soviet Union at the end of the twentieth century brought into existence a substantial number of new states with border claims.

The International Labour Office was the standard bearer in the post-World War II period, addressing migration from the perspective of states' obligations

[1] UN Global Compact for Safe, Orderly and Regular Migration (19 December 2018).

[2] DA Arcarazo and A Wiesbrock (eds), *Global Migration: Old Assumptions, New Dynamics* (Westport, CT, Praeger, 2015).

to protect migrant workers' rights. The 1949 ILO Convention 97 on the subject of recruitment of migrant workers is the most widely ratified.[3] A second effort by the ILO to promote migrant workers' rights more extensively in 1975 did not attract substantial state enthusiasm.[4] In parallel to the ILO activities, the international community was developing its international human rights acquis out of the Universal Declaration of Human Rights.[5] Starting with the two Covenants of 1966,[6] these international instruments were framed as applicable to everyone, irrespective of their nationality or immigration status, thus providing a foundation of human rights which embrace also migrants.[7] Of all migrants, only refugees were covered by a specific instrument, the Refugee Convention adopted in 1951,[8] and at that time both limited in time and geography. These limitations were lifted in 1967.[9] A minor encounter between refugee protection and human rights took place in 1984 with the inclusion in the Convention against Torture 1984[10] of the core refugee protection principle of non-refoulement.[11] The non-refoulement principle prohibits states from sending a person to a state where he or she would be persecuted.[12] The inclusion of the non-refoulement prohibition in the Convention against Torture widened substantially the class of persons entitled to international protection but from within a human rights instrument rather than a refugee protection one.[13] The link between human rights and migration was seen as potentially fruitful and led to the UN opening for signature the Convention on the rights of migrant workers and their families in 1990.[14] However, by October 2019, only 55 states have ratified it and another 13 have signed it. For a convention

[3] International Labour Organization (ILO), Migration for Employment Convention (Revised) (1 July 1949, C97).

[4] International Labour Organization (ILO), Migrant Workers (Supplementary Provisions) Convention (24 June 1975, C143).

[5] UN General Assembly, Universal Declaration of Human Rights (10 December 1948), 217 A (III).

[6] UN General Assembly, International Covenant on Civil and Political Rights (16 December 1966), United Nations, Treaty Series, vol. 999, 171; UN General Assembly, International Covenant on Economic, Social and Cultural Rights (16 December 1966), United Nations, Treaty Series, vol. 993, 3.

[7] UN Human Rights Committee (HRC), CCPR General Comment No. 15: *The Position of Aliens Under the Covenant* (11 April 1986), available at: www.refworld.org/docid/45139acfc.html.

[8] UN General Assembly, Convention Relating to the Status of Refugees (28 July 1951), United Nations, Treaty Series, vol. 189, 137.

[9] UN General Assembly, Protocol Relating to the Status of Refugees (31 January 1967), United Nations, Treaty Series, vol. 606, 267.

[10] UN General Assembly, Convention Against Torture and Other Cruel, Inhuman or Degrading Treatment or Punishment, 10 December 1984, United Nations, Treaty Series, vol. 1465, 85.

[11] C Costello and F Michelle, 'Non-Refoulement as Custom and *Jus Cogens*? Putting the Prohibition to the Test' in Maarten den Heijer and Harmen van der Wilt (eds), *Netherlands Yearbook of International Law 2015* (The Hague, TMC Asser Press, 2016) 273–327.

[12] MT Gil-Bazo, 'Refugee Protection under International Human Rights Law: From Non-Refoulement to Residence and Citizenship' (2015) 34 (1) *Refugee Survey Quarterly* 11–42.

[13] M Nowak, E McArthur and K Buchinger, *The United Nations Convention Against Torture: a Commentary* (Oxford, Oxford University Press, 2008).

[14] UN General Assembly, International Convention on the Protection of the Rights of All Migrant Workers and Members of their Families (18 December 1990), A/RES/45/158.

which is almost 30 years old (at the time of writing), this is not an impressive demonstration of support.[15]

Instead, in 2000, the international community moved in another direction relating to migration (which would also have a substantial impact on refugee protection): criminalisation. It is important to remember that this pre-dates the terrorist attacks in the USA of 2001. In 2000, the UN negotiated a convention against transnational organised crime.[16] Two protocols were attached to the convention – the Palermo Protocols – which require states to create crimes of smuggling[17] and trafficking of human beings.[18] This approach of criminalisation in a transnational framework was very successful with states, the Smuggling Protocol has 112 signatory states and its Trafficking counterpart 117. Since then, in the form of international law there have been few developments. In 2011, the ILO opened for signature a convention to protect domestic workers which indirectly acknowledges that many of the people it is designed to protect are migrants as well as domestic workers.[19] So far 29 countries have ratified it which is fairly respectable for such a young convention. But this convention does not specifically address migration. It is rather sectoral. Instead, the issue of border controls and migration management has been the subject of international discussion but not international legal instruments.[20] Yet, world developments in 2015 and beyond, led to a reconsideration of the role of the international community in this field.

Between 2016 and 2018 the international community within the UN again focused on the question of migration resulting in two new instruments, a Global Compact for Safe, Orderly and Regular Migration and a Global Compact for Refugees.[21] While at the outset of the process, following the UN General Assembly Resolution of 19 September 2016,[22] it was unclear whether the process would lead to a legally binding document or not, in the end there was insufficient international appetite for a legally binding instrument. Both Compacts are explicitly stated to be

[15] R Cholewinski, P de Guchteneire and A Pecoud (eds), *Migration and Human Rights. The United Nations Convention on Migrant Workers' Rights* (Cambridge, Cambridge University Press, 2009).

[16] UN General Assembly, United Nations Convention against Transnational Organized Crime (8 January 2001), A/RES/55/25.

[17] UN General Assembly, Protocol against the Smuggling of Migrants by Land, Sea and Air, Supplementing the United Nations Convention against Transnational Organized Crime (15 November 2000).

[18] UN General Assembly, Protocol to Prevent, Suppress and Punish Trafficking in Persons, Especially Women and Children, Supplementing the United Nations Convention against Transnational Organized Crime (15 November 2000).

[19] International Labour Organization (ILO), Convention Concerning Decent Work for Domestic Workers (16 June 2011), PRNo.15A.

[20] S Lavenex, TE Givens, F Jurje and R Buchanan, 'Regional Migration Governance', in TA Börzel and T Risse (eds), *The Oxford Handbook of Comparative Regionalism* (Oxford, Oxford University Press 2016) 457–85.

[21] E Guild and S Grant, 'Migration Governance in the UN: What is the Global Compact and What does it Mean?' (2017) *Queen Mary School of Law Legal Studies Research Paper* 252.

[22] UN General Assembly, *New York Declaration for Refugees and Migrants* (3 October 2016) A/RES/71/1.

non-legally binding, though they are clearly politically binding. A new approach is apparent in the Compacts which returns to an insistence on embracing migration in a human rights framework and limiting its exposure to criminal law.

In this chapter I will examine the insertion of transnational criminal law into the field of migration in 2000 and its marginalisation in 2018. To do so I will look at three aspects:

- The Palermo Protocols: their relationship with migration;
- the Palermo Protocols: what role for human rights;
- the Global Compact Migration: Safe Travel and the Palermo Protocols.

My argument is that the insertion of transnational criminal law into the field of migration has done more harm than good in respect of the objectives espoused – diminishing irregular border crossing and exploitation of labour. It has resulted in increasing amounts of unsafe, disorderly and irregular migration – the three failures which the Global Compact on Migration seeks to remedy. The international community's 2018 decision to seek to address these ills has resulted in a diminution of the space for the Palermo Protocols and its insistence on a 'solution' through transnational criminal law. Part of the reason for this is very simple – one country's migrant is another country's citizen. When states take actions which result in migrants being made vulnerable they make vulnerable the citizens of other states.[23] Those states of citizenship are generally bound by their constitutions to aid their citizens, including against the actions of other states which place them in situations of vulnerability. This is the foundation of the principle of consular protection. The transformation of the language of people from citizens/foreigners to citizens/migrants disguises the link of rights of migrants with their home states (because they are citizens there) but does not extinguish it. The resurgence of states' concerns to protect their citizens when they travel to other states has also spilled over into the field of anti-smuggling and trafficking criminalisation. The expansionism of the anti-smuggling and trafficking advocates has entered into friction with states duties towards their citizens for reasons which I will explain below.

II. The Palermo Protocols and their Relationship with Migration

Elsewhere in this volume there are chapters which examine in depth these two protocols so I will not repeat this here. The core objective of the two protocols

[23] I Atak, D Nakache, E Guild and F Crépeau, '"Migrants in Vulnerable Situations" and the Global Compact for Safe Orderly and Regular Migration' (2018) *Queen Mary School of Law Legal Studies Research Paper* 273.

is the same – the criminalisation of the provision of means of movement across international borders whether this is for services paid by the traveller directly (smuggling) or through the coercion of the traveller to accept servitude contrary to the labour laws of the destination state as part of the travel plan (trafficking). While supporters of the anti-trafficking protocol often insist that it can also be applied to situations within a state where someone is coerced to move from one place to another to carry out work in conditions of servitude, this is not the objective of the Protocol.[24] Further the anti-trafficking protocol also denies agency to young people and women placing them in a category of people who are specifically and definitionally vulnerable and thus entitling the proponents of anti-trafficking measures to confiscate their voices and claim an entitlement to be their spokespersons.[25] I will not return to this aspect of the Protocol but I wish to express my concern at the utter failure of the entitlement of all persons to equality without discrimination on the basis of gender to be respected by this Protocol. Long have the social sciences examined and analysed the claims of third parties to an entitlement to protect women from dangers (including those which they may themselves embrace) which invariably turn out to constitute new forms of disenfranchisement on the basis of gender.[26]

But here I wish to examine the claim that the use of criminal law in a transnational form (not an international form) is a valuable tool to fight a new form of exploitation – smuggling and trafficking across international borders. The first step in this claim which is inherent in the two Protocols is that there are 'criminals' who run businesses providing services to people who want to travel from one place to another.[27] This is also inherent in state practices to eradicate smuggling and trafficking of persons. For instance, the mandate of the EU's naval operation in the Mediterranean, Operation Sophia, states one of its purposes to be to destroy the business model of people smugglers.[28] The problem with this approach is that it utterly fails to examine the conditions of possibility which have conjured into existence this business. Those states which are highly exercised about smuggling of people are those with well-regulated travel industries. These travel industries comply with national legislation which fines them for bringing to the country

[24] C Brusca and S Carol, 'Palermo Protocol: The First Ten Years after Adoption' (2011) 2 (3) *Global Security Studies* 8–20.

[25] R Andrijasevic and N Mai, 'Trafficking (in) Representations: Understanding the Recurring Appeal of Victimhood and Slavery in Neoliberal Times' (2016) 7 *Anti-Trafficking Review* 1–10; J Doezema, 'Who Gets to Choose? Coercion, Consent, and the UN Trafficking Protocol' (2002) 10 (1) *Gender & Development* 20–27.

[26] J Doezema, 'Now You See Her, Now You Don't: Sex Workers at the UN Trafficking Protocol Negotiation' (2005) 14 *Social & Legal Studies* 61–89.

[27] A Gallagher, 'Trafficking, Smuggling and Human Rights: Tricks and Treaties' (2002) 12 (25) *Forced Migration Review* 8–36.

[28] E Papastavridis, 'EUNAVFOR Operation Sophia and the International Law of the Sea' (2016) 2 *Maritime Safety and Security Law Journal* 57–63.

anyone who does not have the correct documentation for entry. These are called carrier sanctions.[29] The theory behind carrier sanctions is that states can move onto the private sector the obligation of carrying out immigration and border controls on persons while they are still in third countries – the countries of departure. While the laws and regulations of the destination country do not apply until such time as the individual arrives there (they do not have extraterritorial effect) by threatening to punish travel companies which do not carry out document and identity checks on their customers in accordance with the legislation of the country of destination while still in the country of departure (all in accordance only with the law of the destination country not that of departure) these states push the cost of border control onto private companies.[30] Those who are made most vulnerable by these practices are refugees who are frequently unable to obtain the necessary documentation to satisfy travel companies carrying out their control obligations that they are entitled to flee. Companies are not competent to receive claims for international protection. So by obstructing departure through coercion of travel companies, states seek to avoid having to deal with refugee claims. The sanctions also push onto companies liability for irregularities which may occur as regards the laws of the states of departure.[31]

States also insulate themselves against claims that they are preventing people from departure from a country contrary to Article 12(2) International Covenant on Civil and Political Rights (ICCPR).[32] As it is not the destination state directly which is preventing a person from leaving the state of departure, but rather the transport company,[33] the destination state claims to be off the hook for any violation of Article 12(2) ICCPR. They also diminish the possibility that a passenger will be able to seek asylum as according to the Refugee Convention a person must be outside his or her country of origin to be a refugee[34] but it is the travel company which is creating the obstacle not the destination state directly.[35]

So such states have tamed their travel industries, insulated themselves against refugees, diminished the cost of border controls by moving these costs onto the

[29] S Scholten and P Minderhoud, 'Regulating Immigration Control: Carrier Sanctions in the Netherlands' (2008) 10 *European Journal of Migration and Law* 123–47.

[30] T Rodenhäuser, 'Another Brick in the Wall: Carrier Sanctions and the Privatization of Immigration Control' (2014) 26 *International Journal of Refugee Law* 223–47.

[31] LA de Vries and Elspeth Guild, 'Seeking Refuge in Europe: Spaces of Transit and the Violence of Migration Management' (2019) 45 *Journal of Ethnic and Migration Studies* 2156–66.

[32] E Guild and V Stoyanova, 'The Human Right to Leave any Country: A Right to be Delivered' (2018) *European Yearbook on Human Rights* 373–94.

[33] Article 12(2): 'Everyone shall be free to leave any country, including his own'.

[34] Article 1A(2) which states that a refugee is someone who 'As a result of events occurring before 1 January 1951 and owing to well-founded fear of being persecuted for reasons of race, religion, nationality, membership of a particular social group or political opinion, is outside the country of his nationality and is unable or, owing to such fear, is unwilling to avail himself of the protection of that country; or who, not having a nationality and being outside the country of his former habitual residence as a result of such events, is unable or, owing to such fear, is unwilling to return to it'.

[35] T Spijkerboer, 'The Human Costs of Border Control' (2007) 9 *European Journal of Migration and Law* 127.

private sector and threatening the private sector with financial sanctions for any failure and generally tidied up, as they see it, the process of sifting the right kind of travellers, called tourists, from the wrong kind, called irregular migrants. But these processes have negative externalities.[36] People who want to travel and who cannot use the services of the well-regulated and usually unionised official travel industry turn to the unregulated travel industry and conjure into existence this alternative travel industry.[37] This unregulated side of the industry provides transport services often on an occasional basis beside other activities such as fishing, smuggling of goods etc, to those who cannot access the regulated industry.[38] The prices are far higher, the conditions of travel are much inferior and often dangerous but for people who must travel, such as refugees, this part of the industry may be their only option.[39] But this unregulated side of the industry invokes the rage of those state officials who have constructed the whole system of carrier sanctions and privatisation of border controls extraterritorially exactly to prevent these distressed people from arriving at their borders. The reaction is to demonise the smugglers and traffickers (to whom those with no resources turn promising to provide services in conditions of servitude for periods of time in the destination country to pay their travel debt) who disrupt the system. Notwithstanding that the numbers are tiny in comparison with those transported by the authorised travel industry,[40] the fury of state authorities falls heavily on them, including in the form of the Protocols calling for transnational cooperation to criminalise and jail smugglers and traffickers.

A new criminal is created, a transnational one, who hoodwinks people who need to travel but cannot access authorised (and cheap) services into paying large amounts of money for irregular travel (and coercive work at the other end in some cases).[41] The states which have engaged in these policies shift the focus of international and national attention from the plight of the people who use these services because they must travel or suffer persecution, torture or death where they are,

[36] T Last and T Spijkerboer, 'Tracking Deaths in the Mediterranean' in T Brian and F Laczko (eds), *Fatal Journeys. Tracking Lives Lost During Migration* (Geneva, International Organization for Migration, 2014) 85–106.

[37] T Gammeltoft-Hansen and N Nyberg Sorensen (eds), *The Migration Industry and the Commercialization of International Migration* (Abingdon, Routledge, 2013).

[38] D Spener, 'Mexican Migrant-Smuggling: A Cross-Border Cottage Industry' (2004) 5 *Journal of International Migration and Integration/Revue de l'integration et de la migration internationale* 295–320.

[39] V Bilger, M Hofmann and M Jandl, 'Human Smuggling as a Transnational Service Industry: Evidence from Austria' (2006) 44 (4) *International Migration* 59–93.

[40] The UN World Tourism Organisation estimates that 1.4 billion people travel internationally every year (see ourworldindata.org/tourism). There is no reliable international estimate of irregularly present migrants. An example, however, is in the European Union, an area of more than 500 million inhabitants and more than 300 million entries at external borders, 435,786 persons were treated as irregularly present in 2017 (see frontex.europa.eu/assets/Publications/Risk_Analysis/Risk_Analysis/Risk_Analysis_for_2018.pdf).

[41] A Aziz, P Monzini and F Pastore, *The Changing Dynamics of Cross-Border Human Smuggling and Trafficking in the Mediterranean* (Rome, Istituto Affari Internazionali, 2015).

to the evils of the smugglers and traffickers who profit from the woes of their customers. Instead of acknowledging that it is the extraterritorialisation of their own border policies which has driven these people into the arms of smugglers and traffickers and indeed created the conditions for the development of this unauthorised travel sector, these state authorities drill down on the 'criminal' behaviour of the smugglers and traffickers.[42] It is self-evident that as long as people must travel or die, someone will provide them with the possibility to move, making it dangerous for smugglers and traffickers to transport desperate people only drives up the cost of journey. In so far as this may be the objective of the measures against smugglers and traffickers it is of a callousness and cynicism unworthy of liberal democracies.

The two Protocols conjure into existence a new evil of smuggling and trafficking of persons across international borders. Yet these economic activities are simply the result of the policies of those states which try to enforce a monopoly over legitimate travel across borders and punish all those who do not respect it.[43] They then designate the activity of the unauthorised travel business as criminal and oblige states to pass criminal law to bolster this designation. But these criminal laws will rarely be enforced if at all in most countries as there is no incentive to do so. Most countries do not invest state sovereignty in border controls and so do not claim a monopoly over legitimate travel to their state.[44]

III. The Palermo Protocols: What Role for Human Rights?

There is no obvious place for human rights in the Palermo Protocols. In the Trafficking Protocol there is one reference to human rights in the preamble:

> Declaring that effective action to prevent and combat trafficking in persons, especially women and children, requires a comprehensive international approach in the countries of origin, transit and destination that includes measures to prevent such trafficking, to punish the traffickers and to protect the victims of such trafficking, including by protecting their internationally recognized human rights …

There is also one reference in the statement of purpose: Article 2 '(b) To protect and assist the victims of such trafficking, with full respect for their human rights',

[42] Andrijasevic and Mai, above n 25.

[43] JC Torpey, *The Invention of the Passport: Surveillance, Citizenship and the State* (Cambridge, Cambridge University Press, 2018).

[44] D Acosta and LF Freier, 'Regional Governance of Migration in South America' in A Triandafyllidou (ed), *Handbook of Migration and Globalisation* (Cheltenham, Edward Elgar Publishing, 2018) 69–85; DA Arcarazo and A Wiesbrock, *Global Migration Issues. Myths and Realities* (May 1, 2015), introductory chapter to our edited collection entitled *Global Migration: Old Assumptions, New Dynamics* (Santa Barbara, Praeger, 2015), available at SSRN: https://ssrn.com/abstract=2604184.

one reference in Article 10 regarding training of officials carrying out anti-trafficking activities[45] and one reference at the end of the Protocol which is in the saving provision.[46] In the Smuggling Protocol there is only one reference in total to human rights in the saving provision.[47] But human rights belong to everyone including smugglers and traffickers. They too are entitled to the human rights to fair trial and presumption of innocence.[48] The human rights of victims of traffickers are generally the prohibitions on torture and inhuman or degrading treatment[49] or forced labour or servitude[50] (it is generally inappropriate to call those using smugglers 'victims' as they are paying for a service, even if the price is exorbitant, it is the measures of states to prevent the customer from accessing safe and regulated travel options which drives up the price). The duties of states to prosecute those who torture others are fully set out in the Convention against Torture. Forced labour and servitude are the subject for two ILO conventions[51] and a Protocol[52] which provide detailed rules for states to counter these activities. Yet this multitude of human rights and labour standards instruments is either ignored or glossed over in the Protocols.

Instead of using these tools which address the human rights and labour exploitation issues, the international community, pushed by a small number of states with embedded investments of state sovereignty in their border control claims, did not consider it relevant to the criminalisation of smugglers and traffickers to ensure their human rights nor to specify the human rights or fair labour requirements to which their victims are entitled. The dominant approach is a criminal justice one, engaging police and prosecutors, not a human rights and labour standards one.

[45] Article 10(2): 'States Parties shall provide or strengthen training for law enforcement, immigration and other relevant officials in the prevention of trafficking in 47 persons. The training should focus on methods used in preventing such trafficking, prosecuting the traffickers and protecting the rights of the victims, including protecting the victims from the traffickers. The training should also take into account the need to consider human rights and child- and gender-sensitive issues and it should encourage cooperation with nongovernmental organizations, other relevant organizations and other elements of civil society'.

[46] Article 14(1): 'Nothing in this Protocol shall affect the rights, obligations and responsibilities of States and individuals under international law, including international humanitarian law and international human rights law and, in particular, where applicable, the 1951 Convention1 and the 1967 Protocol2 relating to the Status of Refugees and the principle of non-refoulement as contained therein'.

[47] Article 19(1): 'Nothing in this Protocol shall affect the other rights, obligations and responsibilities of States and individuals under international law, including international humanitarian law and international human rights law and, in particular, where applicable, the 1951 Convention2 and the 1967 Protocol3 relating to the Status of Refugees and the principle of non-refoulement as contained therein'.

[48] Articles 14–16 ICCPR.

[49] Article 7 ICCPR and ICAT.

[50] Article 8 ICCPR.

[51] International Labour Organization (ILO), Forced Labour Convention (28 June 1930) C29; International Labour Organization (ILO), Abolition of Forced Labour Convention (25 June 1957) C105.

[52] Protocol of 2014 to the Forced Labour Convention, 1930 (Entry into force: 09 Nov 2016).

The big concern was to push what were and continue to be seen as states of origin of smugglers and traffickers (or at least of their operations) to prosecute them, give them lengthy sentences to act as a deterrent to this pesky unauthorised travel industry. Prosecution and incarceration are expensive state commodities usually reserved for persons who have harmed people or interests within the state. Prosecuting people for actions which they might commit in another state is not terribly popular with police and prosecutors whose time is limited and on whom social pressure for local results are great.

The interest of the Protocols in the people who are providing transport services is even more limited. What these people want, as everyone who engages in the field knows, is work and residence permits. That is why they have paid substantial amounts of money to unauthorised transporters to bring them to where they are. No one who can use the cheaper, regular travel industry would dream of using the very expensive unregulated sector. But that is also because people who can use the regulated travel industry will be admitted at external borders by the border officials.[53] They may overstay the permitted duration of the visit or work in breach of conditions but they are already within the state where they want to be. They are not touched by the Protocols, nor do they need to look to them for help. Instead it is those who have travelled with the smugglers or traffickers who arrive generally without having been authorised entry. There are exceptions where smugglers or traffickers provide their customers with such good quality documentation that they can make use of the authorised travel industry but these persons are not the main targets of the Protocols. The Protocols provide next to nothing to the people who they designated as the victims in terms of human rights. There is no reference to their human right to basic services,[54] no reference to their right to seek asylum, no obligations at all regarding the conditions of their residence or protection from expulsion.[55] There are only the vaguest of references to the possibility open to

[53] For example, in the European Union, according to the EU external border agency, Frontex, out of the over 300 million entries at the external borders of the EU (of which 60 million are EU citizens) 183,548 persons were refused entry in 2017. That is approximately 0.005 per cent.

[54] Articles 9–15 ICESCR 1966.

[55] Article 6(3) Trafficking Protocol: 'Each State Party shall consider implementing measures to provide for the physical, psychological and social recovery of victims of trafficking in persons, including, in appropriate cases, in cooperation with non-governmental organizations, other relevant organizations and other elements of civil society, and, in particular, the provision of:

(a) Appropriate housing;
(b) Counselling and information, in particular as regards their legal rights, in a language that the victims of trafficking in persons can understand;
(c) Medical, psychological and material assistance; and
(d) Employment, educational and training opportunities.

4. Each State Party shall take into account, in applying the provisions of this article, the age, gender and special needs of victims of trafficking in persons, in particular the special needs of children, including appropriate housing, education and care.

5. Each State Party shall endeavour to provide for the physical safety of victims of trafficking in persons while they are within its territory'.

states to provide temporary residence permits for victims if they are necessary to criminal proceedings and willing to participate in them against their smuggler or trafficker.[56] There is no protection against expulsion – the biggest fear of these people who have paid so much to arrive somewhere safe.

Further, for trafficking victims, it is the threat of expulsion which the state wields which keeps them from denouncing their traffickers. Forcing people to work in conditions which do not conform to labour standards of a state only works if there is a credible threat which the person exercising the coercion can use. In the case of trafficking victims under the Protocol, it is the threat of denunciation to state authorities which will result in expulsion. Thus it is the state itself which creates the conditions of possibility for trafficking. If trafficking victims could go to labour inspectorates and claim their rights as workers without fearing denunciation to the immigration authorities for expulsion purposes, they would not put up with bad working conditions. This is not rocket science. It is the state's own obsession with 'illegal' migration which creates the business model for traffickers. It also is the enforcer for traffickers and makes real their threats. The system is designed to prevent people including the victims of traffickers from ever being able to claim their human rights. Even the right to seek asylum is silenced by the state's expulsion machinery.

IV. The Global Compact Migration: Safe Travel and the Palermo Protocols

The UN Global Compact for Safe, Orderly and Regular Migration was adopted by 152 states voting at the General Assembly on 19 December 2018. It was not without controversy as a very small number of states, led by the USA, voted against it, considering that the Compact was problematic for their conception of state sovereignty.[57] The objective of safe migration means that people are not to be required to put their lives at risk when moving from one country to another. This objective runs counter to the policies of those states which have put in place complex systems of extraterritorialisation and privatisation of their border controls. For these states, unsafe travel is the only option available to people to

[56] Article 7 Trafficking Protocol: 'Status of victims of trafficking in persons in receiving States: 1. In addition to taking measures pursuant to article 6 of this Protocol, each State Party shall consider adopting legislative or other appropriate measures that permit victims of trafficking in persons to remain in its territory, temporarily or permanently, in appropriate cases. 2. In implementing the provision contained in paragraph 1 of this article, each State Party shall give appropriate consideration to humanitarian and compassionate factors'.

[57] E Guild, T Basaran and K Allinson, 'From Zero to Hero? An analysis of the human rights protections within the Global Compact for Safe, Orderly and Regular Migration (GCM)' [2019] *International Migration* 43–59.

whom they seek to deny movement. Access to that unsafe travel is made more precarious by the criminalisation of those providing it (the Palermo Protocols). Yet, in the preamble of the Compact it is stated that it rests on the two Protocols which are listed among the UN human rights conventions. This is a clear indication of the strength of the anti-smuggling and trafficking industry in inserting its objectives even in UN instruments which are human rights oriented.

The Compact is based on a Common Understanding that migration is a defining feature of our globalised world (paragraph 10). It is also founded on a Shared Responsibility which incorporates human rights at its core.[58] Unity of Purpose is the third basis of the Compact: 'This Global Compact recognizes that safe, orderly and regular migration works for all when it takes place in a well-informed, planned and consensual manner. Migration should never be an act of desperation' (paragraph 13). There are 10 cross-cutting and interdependent guiding principles: (1) people-centred; (2) international cooperation; (3) national sovereignty; (4) rule of law and due process; (5) sustainable development; (6) human rights; (7) gender responsiveness; (8) child sensitive; (9) whole of government and (10) whole of society. Thereafter, the Compact sets out 23 Objectives, each of which commences with a subject and the general outline of the approach to be followed by something of a menu of actions which states could take to seek to achieve the objective. As mentioned above, the Compact is not legally binding, but as its foundations are not only in the Sustainable Development Goals but also in human rights obligations of states, it may well be capable of providing useful guidance for states on how best to achieve some of their human rights commitments in the field of border control and migration management.[59]

Of the 23 Objectives, two are devoted to preventing smuggling and to prevent, combat and eradicate trafficking in persons in the context of international migration to which I will return shortly (numbers 9 and 10). However, a reference to trafficking victims is included in Objective 7, which has as a goal reducing the vulnerabilities which victims of trafficking in persons, and migrants may be subject including exploitation and abuse in the context of smuggling of migrants. Proposed actions are included for state action plans.[60] This objective includes in its

[58] Paragraph 11: 'We acknowledge our shared responsibilities to one another as Member States of the United Nations to address each other's needs and concerns over migration, and an overarching obligation to respect, protect and fulfil the human rights of all migrants, regardless of their migration status, while promoting the security and prosperity of all our communities.'

[59] T Gammeltoft-Hansen et al, 'What is a Compact? Migrants' Rights and State Responsibilities Regarding the Design of the UN Global Compact for Safe, Orderly and Regular Migration' (Raoul Wallenberg Institute, 2017).

[60] Paragraph 23(b): 'Establish comprehensive policies and develop partnerships that provide migrants in a situation of vulnerability, regardless of their migration status, with necessary support at all stages of migration, through identification and assistance, as well as protection of their human rights, in particular in cases related to women at risk, children, especially those unaccompanied or separated from their families, members of ethnic and religious minorities, victims of violence, including sexual and gender-based violence, older persons, persons with disabilities, persons who are discriminated against on any basis, indigenous peoples, workers facing exploitation and abuse, domestic workers, victims of trafficking in persons, and migrants subject to exploitation and abuse in the context of smuggling of migrants.'

menu of measures, regularisation of migrants and access to services. It is strongly based in human rights, unlike the Protocols, and trafficking victims are only one group identified as vulnerable. It also calls for the implementation of labour standards for all migrants. Brief references are made to trafficking victims in particular under screening, assessment and referral (Objective 12) and consular protection (Objective 14).

Turning then, to the smuggling and trafficking objectives, Objective 9 commits the international community to:

> intensify joint efforts to prevent and counter smuggling of migrants by strengthening capacities and international cooperation to prevent, investigate, prosecute and penalize the smuggling of migrants in order to end the impunity of smuggling networks. We further commit to ensure that migrants shall not become liable to criminal prosecution for the fact of having been the object of smuggling, notwithstanding potential prosecution for other violations of national law. We also commit to identify smuggled migrants to protect their human rights, taking into consideration the special needs of women and children, and assisting in particular those migrants subject to smuggling under aggravating circumstances, in accordance with international law.

Six options are proposed to achieve this objective. These include (1) ratification of the Protocols – this is seen as part of the process; (2) sharing of information on smugglers and their operations as well as on the vulnerabilities faced by smuggled migrants; (3) establishment of gender-responsive and child-sensitive cooperation protocols to end impunity for smugglers and prevent irregular migration, while ensuring that counter-smuggling measures are in full respect of human rights; (4) criminalisation of migrant smuggling; (5) enacting clarifications which make distinctions between smuggling and trafficking; and (6) prevention of smuggling of migrants along the migration cycle in partnership with other States and relevant stakeholders. This menu of actions is clearly much influenced by the Smuggling Protocol (indeed calling for its ratification). But it nevertheless places greater emphasis on the human rights of smuggled migrants than the Protocol.[61]

Objective 10 calls for

> legislative or other measures to prevent, combat and eradicate trafficking in persons in the context of international migration by strengthening capacities and international cooperation to investigate, prosecute and penalize trafficking in persons, discouraging demand that fosters exploitation leading to trafficking, and ending impunity of trafficking networks. We further commit to enhance the identification and protection of, and assistance to migrants who have become victims of trafficking, paying particular attention to women and children.[62]

[61] JP Gauci and FR Partipilo, *GCM Indicators: Objective 9: Strengthen the transnational response to smuggling of migrants*, available at https://rli.blogs.sas.ac.uk/themed-content/global-compact-for-migration/.

[62] Dr Jean-Pierre Gauci and Francesca Romana Partipilo, *GCM Indicators: Objective 10: Prevent, combat and eradicate trafficking in persons in the context of international migration*, available at https://rli.blogs.sas.ac.uk/themed-content/global-compact-for-migration/.

Here nine options are set out: (1) once again it calls for ratification of the Trafficking Protocol – the main push in the field; (2) promotion of the Global Plan of Action to Combat Trafficking;[63] (3) monitoring of irregular migration routes – presumably any travel route is capable of fulfilling this definition; (4) information and intelligence sharing, including on financial transactions which may be related to trafficking with no reference to the human right to privacy or data protection; (5) addressing vulnerabilities of women, men and children who are victims of trafficking; here there is a safeguard that states should facilitate access to justice and safe reporting without fear of detention, deportation or penalty for the victims. This is very important for victims as only in this way can the link between state coercion and exploitation in labour conditions be broken; (6) ensure that the legal definition of smuggling and trafficking are clear and separate; (7) enhance prosecution of traffickers (this is the focus on the provider of services discussed above) while avoiding the criminalisation of migrants and ensure that victims receive protection and assistance which is not conditional on cooperation with the authorities against suspected traffickers. Here the Compact moves away from the instrumental approach to protection of victims, exclusively as possible witnesses in criminal trials, and calls on states to provide wider protection which is independent on the criminal prosecution use of the individual; (8) allow migrant victims of trafficking to remain in the state, temporarily or permanently as well as providing assistance for physical, psychological and social recovery as well as redress and compensation; (9) establish information systems and training programmes for citizens, employers and public officials in anti-trafficking measures. This proposed course of action may have the consequence of further stigmatising persons suspected of being trafficking victims.[64]

While the progress towards a more human rights oriented approach to smuggling and trafficking of people across borders is only minor in the Compact, nonetheless, the more coercive of the provisions of the Protocols are tempered by a more human rights compliant approach and respect of international labour standards. The recommendation that states create firewalls to prevent information provided by victims from being used or shared with immigration authorities for expulsion purposes is particularly welcome.

V. Conclusions

In this chapter, I have argued that the linking of migration management with criminal law through international instruments against smuggling and trafficking of people has harmed both international human rights protection and respect

[63] A UN General Assembly Resolution of 2010 A/Res/64/93 of 12 August 2010.

[64] M Capous Desyllas, 'A Critique of the Global Trafficking Discourse and US Policy' (2007) 34 (4) *The Journal of Sociology & Social Welfare* 57.

for international labour standards. To make my argument, I have examined the Palermo Protocols from the perspective of their relationship with migration. I have demonstrated that the role which they play is to demonise the unregulated travel industry which does not comply with some states' extraterritorial border control projects. The result is to make access to refugee protection increasingly difficult as the possibility to cross borders to seek protection is diminished for those without the necessary documents. Second I have looked at the role for human rights in the Palermo Protocols and concluded that it is very limited and vestigial. The focus of the Protocols is not to alleviate the hardship caused to refugees by states' extraterritorial border control activities but rather to reinforce their effectiveness by clamping down on alternative forms of travel which refugees must use to seek international protection. Finally, I have examined the most recent international instrument for global cooperation in the field of migration, the Global Compact for Safe, Orderly and Regular Migration and its relationship with the Palermo Protocols. One can see in the Compact a strong influence of the Protocols but the Compact moderates, at least in part, the highly coercive approach found in the Protocols and brings more human rights back into the field.

2

The Criminalisation of Migration in the Law of the European Union

Challenging the Preventive Paradigm

VALSAMIS MITSILEGAS

I. Introduction

This contribution will attempt to demonstrate how the criminalisation of migration in Europe has been inextricably linked with a preventive rationale, namely to deflect and prevent access by third country nationals to the territory of the European Union. The evolution of this preventive paradigm is linked with a process of securitisation and demonisation of migrants and those who help them, with criminalisation leading to both categories being labelled as dangerous and with migrants being viewed increasingly as undesirable. I will focus here on the preventive dimension of criminalisation as expressed via the adoption and use of substantive criminal law, namely legislation defining criminal offences, imposing criminal sanctions and triggering prosecution. The analysis will examine the continuum of prevention by focusing on both the criminalisation of human smuggling (or facilitation of unauthorised entry, transit and residence) as well as on the criminalisation of irregular entry, transit and residence per se – with the key element of the preventive paradigm centred on the criminalisation of entry and its facilitation. The contribution will examine how this preventive paradigm of criminalisation which rests upon shaky normative foundations and has led to over-criminalisation,[1] can be framed under EU law – to what extent EU law allows and promotes such criminalisation, and to what extent EU law set limits

[1] This contribution expands and builds upon arguments presented in V Mitsilegas, 'The Normative Foundations of the Criminalisation of Human Smuggling. Exploring the Fault Lines between European and International Law' (2019) 10 *New Journal of European Criminal Law* 68–85; and V Mitsilegas, 'The Criminalisation of Human Smuggling as Preventive Justice' in V Militello and A Spena (eds), *Mobilità, Sicurezza e Nuove Frontiere Tecnologiche* (Turin, Giappichelli, 2018) 11–30.

to such criminalisation. The analysis will highlight the complex legal landscape on the criminalisation of migration in this context, with the presence of secondary EU law criminalising smuggling but the absence, at the same time, of EU law criminalising irregular entry, transit and stay per se. A critical evaluation of the evolution and potential of EU law in both fields, as well as of its relationship with national and international law, are key in this context. The analysis will focus on how EU law itself, together with many aspects of international law (ranging from international security law to international refugee law and law of the sea) can provide a framework of challenging an uncritical preventive paradigm of regulating migration flows. The impact of criminalisation on human rights and humanity will underpin this analysis.

II. The Criminalisation of Human Smuggling

The European Union has adopted binding legislation criminalising human smuggling as early as 2002, via two measures reflecting the EU pillar structure at the time (a Directive and a Framework Decision) often called 'the facilitators' package'.[2] The adoption of these measures emerged in the context of the development of the Union's policy on irregular migration and constitute developments of the Schengen *acquis*, repealing the relevant provisions of the Schengen Implementing Convention.[3] This section will evaluate critically the criminalisation of facilitation (or smuggling, with the two terms being used interchangeably) in EU law, by highlighting the move towards over-criminalisation linked with the preventive rationale of the measures, the challenges such over-criminalisation poses on human rights, citizenship and humanitarian and refugee law, and by exploring the potential limits to over-criminalisation evident from a systematic and critical placement of the criminalisation of smuggling within the broader discussion of its normative foundations.

A. The Over-Criminalisation of Smuggling in EU Law

The relevant EU legal framework is set out by a Directive defining what is called in EU law the 'facilitation of unauthorised entry, transit and residence'[4]

[2] Council Directive 2002/90/EC of 28 November 2002 defining the facilitation of unauthorised entry, transit and residence [2002] OJ L328/4 (hereinafter Facilitation Directive); Council Framework Decision 2002/946/JHA of 28 November 2002 on the strengthening of the penal framework to prevent the facilitation of unauthorised entry, transit and residence [2002] OJ L328/1 (hereinafter Facilitation Framework Decision).

[3] Facilitation Directive, art 5; Facilitation Framework Decision, art 10.

[4] Facilitation Directive, see n 2 above.

accompanied – in the light of the first pillar competence limits regarding criminalisation at the time[5] – by a third pillar Framework Decision confirming that the conduct defined as facilitation in the Directive will be treated as a criminal offence.[6] Both instruments of what is rather 'old' law by EU standards predate by far the entry into force of the Lisbon Treaty and, having being proposed not by the Commission but by a Member State (the French Government), they have been negotiated and adopted with minimal scrutiny and debate.[7] The EU Facilitation Directive goes further than the UN Palermo Convention Smuggling Protocol[8] in that it dispenses with the condition of obtaining a financial or other material benefit for the smuggling offence to be established.[9] The Directive calls upon Member States to adopt criminal sanctions for 'any person who intentionally assists a person who is not a national of a Member State to enter, or transit across, the territory of a Member State in breach of the laws of the State concerned on the entry or transit of aliens'.[10] Instigation, complicity and attempt are also criminalised.[11] The Facilitation Framework Decision contains a general obligation for Member States to criminalise such conduct,[12] includes a general provision on sanctions,[13] which may be accompanied by parallel sanctions including confiscation,[14] and imposes specific high levels of sanctions only when certain aggravating circumstances occur.[15]

Notwithstanding the lack of specificity as regards the level of criminal sanctions to be imposed by Member States, it is clear that the scope of criminalisation at EU level is very broad, as it can cover any form of assistance to enter or transit

[5] For an overview, see V Mitsilegas, *EU Criminal Law* (Oxford and Portland, Hart Publishing, 2009) ch 2.

[6] Facilitation Framework Decision, see n 2 above.

[7] For a background, see V Mitsilegas, J Monar and W Rees, *The European Union and Internal Security* (Hampshire and New York, Palgrave/Macmillan, 2003) 106–08.

[8] See section II.C below.

[9] Article 1(1)(a) of the Facilitation Directive.

[10] ibid.

[11] Article 2 of the Facilitation Directive.

[12] According to Article 1(1) of the Framework Decision, each Member State shall take the measures necessary to ensure that the infringements defined in Articles 1 and 2 of the Directive are punishable by effective, proportionate and dissuasive criminal penalties which may entail extradition (Article 1(3)). Article 1(6) of the Facilitation Framework Decision further states that if imperative to preserve the coherence of the national penalty system, the actions defined in paragraph 3 shall be punishable by custodial sentences with a maximum sentence of not less than six years, provided that it is among the most severe maximum sentences available for crimes of comparable gravity.

[13] Article 1(1) of the Framework Decision, infringements shall be punishable by effective, proportionate and dissuasive penalties which entail extradition.

[14] Article 1(2) of the Framework Decision.

[15] According to Article 1(3) of the Facilitation Framework Decision, Member States must ensure that, when committed for financial gain, the infringements defined in Article 1(1)(a) and, to the extent relevant, Article 2(a) of Directive 2002/90/EC are punishable by custodial sentences with a maximum sentence of not less than eight years where they are committed in any of the following circumstances: the offence was committed as an activity of a criminal organization; and the offence was committed while endangering the lives of the persons who are the subject of the offence.

the territory of an EU Member State in breach of what is essentially administrative law (such as cases where the migrant is travelling without travel documents). It is clear that the EU approach aims at preventing entry into EU territory and targets not only the smugglers but also the smuggled. Alessandro Spena makes an insightful point in legal semiotics by drawing our attention to the terminological differences between international law, which defines smuggling as procuring irregular entry, and EU law, which focuses on assistance. Spena notes that 'while assisting denotes an ancillary action, which entails that the principal action is performed by the person who is assisted, "procuring" denotes instead a standalone action, with a meaning of its own'.[16] The negative impact of the EU approach towards criminalisation on third country nationals wishing to apply for asylum is evident. The Directive does attempt to address this issue by granting Member States the discretion not to impose sanctions for human smuggling and instead apply their national law and practice for cases where the aim of the behaviour is to provide humanitarian assistance to the person concerned.[17] However, this provision is discretionary and its value in redressing the balance set out by the broad definition and criminalisation of human smuggling under EU law is questionable. According to a recent Commission Report, only seven Member States specifically include in domestic law an exemption from punishment for facilitation for humanitarian assistance.[18] By using the threat of criminal sanctions, the EU measures on human smuggling essentially aim at deterring individuals and organisations from coming into contact and assisting any third country national wishing to enter the territory of EU Member States. As has been noted in an Issue paper published by the Council of Europe Commissioner for Human Rights, 'the message which is sent is that contact with foreigners can be risky as it may result in criminal charges'.[19] This message is reinforced by the very broad criminalisation of human smuggling in the national law of Member States, with key examples including the criminalisation of any contact with irregular migrants not only at the point of entry but within the territory of the state up to leading to exit,[20] and the, expressly called for by the Facilitation Directive, criminalisation of attempt

[16] A Spena, 'Human Smuggling and Irregular Immigration in the EU: From Complicity to Exploitation?', in S Carrera and E Guild (eds), *Irregular Migration, Trafficking and Smuggling of Human Beings* (Brussels, CEPS, 2016) 37.

[17] Article 1(2) of the Facilitation Directive.

[18] Commission, 'Staff Working Document – REFIT Evaluation of the EU legal framework against facilitation of unauthorised entry, transit and residence' SWD (2017) 117 final, Brussels, 22.3.2017, p 14.

[19] Council of Europe Commissioner for Human Rights, *Criminalisation of Migration in Europe: Human Rights Implications* (Issue paper prepared by Elspeth Guild, 2009), available at rm.coe.int/16806da917.

[20] See the ruling of *Areios Pagos* (the Greek Supreme Court) AP 1344/2016, according to which the terms of transport and onward transfer of irregular migrants are synonymous and apply from the points of entry and internal or external borders to the Greek territory and vice-versa towards the territory of an EU Member State or of a third state. It is not required for criminalisation that the transfer occurs directly from the border – any transfer of the migrant within the country will suffice.

to smuggle. As Spena has noted commenting on Italian law, the fact that this law does not require that the conduct be successful, with smuggling crimes deemed to be committed independently of the attainment of the result, creates a condition teleologically linked to illegal entry.[21] The preventive continuum between the criminalisation of facilitation of irregular entry and the criminalisation of entry per se is thus clearly highlighted.

The 2017 evaluation by the Commission of the EU criminal law framework on human smuggling provided an opportunity for law reform in order to align the EU framework more closely with the approach adopted by the UN Convention on Transnational Organised Crime and to address the human rights concerns arising from the over-criminalisation of the facilitation of unauthorised entry, transit and residence. Yet, the opportunity for law reform along these lines has been markedly and spectacularly missed: in its evaluation, the Commission has come up defending resolutely the status quo.[22] While the Commission appeared to accept an organised crime framing of human smuggling, by noting that the flows of irregular migration across borders are thought to be increasingly controlled by criminal networks,[23] it declined to put forward proposals for law reform to expressly include a requirement for financial gain in the scope of the EU criminal offences on human smuggling. The Commission claimed that to date there is still limited intelligence available on the nature and extent of illicit financial flows associated to migrant smuggling, and noted that

> the cash intensive nature of the payment methods linked to smuggling makes it difficult to trace illicit financial flows and in turn to conduct investigations on the financial nature of the crime … since the time of the adoption of the Facilitators Package and still today, the risks that such difficulties in tracing financial flows connected to migrant smuggling would disproportionately hamper the investigation and prosecution of this crime, affecting states' legitimate interest to control borders and regulate migration flows, have been raised as a reason to avoid including a constituent financial gain element in the offence of facilitating irregular border crossing.[24]

The Commission added that it is difficult to disentangle the effects of the legal framework from the wider array of policy tools and enhanced operational cooperation to counter migrant smuggling, which have been triggered by the crisis'[25] and therefore that 'there is no sufficient evidence to draw firm conclusions about the need for a revision of the Facilitators package at this point in time'.[26]

[21] A Spena, 'Migrant Smuggling: a Normative and Phenomenological View from Italy' in V Militello and A Spena, *Between Criminalization and Protection. The Italian Way of Dealing with Migrant Smuggling and Trafficking within the European and International Context* (Leiden-Boston, Brill Perspectives in Transnational Crime, vol. 2, 2019) 26.

[22] Commission, 'Staff Working Document – REFIT Evaluation' (2017).

[23] ibid, p 4.

[24] ibid, p 9.

[25] ibid, p 34.

[26] ibid, p 35.

The Commission's reasoning for inaction is weak and lop-sided.[27] Rather than examining critically the legality and effectiveness of the current EU substantive criminal law framework on human smuggling, it justifies choices in criminalisation on the grounds of boosting investigatory and prosecutorial interests. In this manner, substantive criminal law becomes a mere tool for prosecutorial efficiency, rather than reflecting normative or societal choices for criminalisation. By declining to adjust EU law, the Commission has missed three opportunities: to align EU law with international law on the criminalisation of human smuggling; to modernise (or 'Lisbonise') – as in the case of the 'parallel' offences of human trafficking[28] – the EU legal framework on human smuggling, by taking more fully into account the human rights obligations of the EU enhanced after the entry into force of the Lisbon Treaty and the constitutionalisation of the EU Charter of Fundamental Rights;[29] and, fundamentally, the Commission missed a first class opportunity for decriminalisation in the field of EU criminal law.[30] This would have been the first time where decriminalisation appeared as a distinct policy choice by the EU legislator, rather than a result of the limitation of national powers to criminalise to EU law.[31] The Commission's reticence regarding law reform is linked with continuing over-criminalisation and arguable abuse of law and prosecution in a number of EU Member States, which have used facilitation offences to target and stigmatise humanitarian efforts to assist migrants and save lives. The Commission's inaction perpetuates the criminalisation of humanitarianism in EU law and sends a very strong preventative signal to anyone inclined to assist migrants.

B. Criminalising Humanitarianism

The Commission's evaluation of the EU anti-smuggling framework states generally and unconvincingly that there is limited evidence that social workers, family members or citizens acting out of compassion have been prosecuted for human smuggling.[32] Yet this assertion is blatantly contradicted by multiple attempts across the EU to criminalise – if not demonise – the humanitarian work of civil

[27] See Mitsilegas, 'The Normative Foundations', above n 1.

[28] V Mitsilegas and N Vavoula, 'Criminal Law: Institutional Rebalancing and Judicialization as Drivers of Policy Change', in F Trauner and A Ripoll Servent (eds), *Policy Change in the Area of Freedom, Security and Justice – How Institutions Matter* (London and New York, Routledge, 2015) 133.

[29] On constitutionalisation, see V Mitsilegas, *EU Criminal Law After Lisbon* (Oxford, Hart Publishing, 2016) ch 2.

[30] For a broader analysis on decriminalisation in EU criminal law see V Mitsilegas, 'From Overcriminalisation to Decriminalisation: The Many Faces of Effectiveness in European Criminal Law' (2014) 5 *New Journal of European Criminal Law* 415–24.

[31] On the relationship between these two processes, see Mitsilegas, above n 29, ch 3.

[32] Commission, 'Staff Working Document – REFIT Evaluation' (2017) 21.

society and to create a 'hostile environment' against humanitarian action.[33] The use of the broad anti-smuggling criminal law framework plays a key part in this process, with a wide range of actors, ranging from individuals to commercial carriers (merchant ships) to NGOs, being targeted.[34] This section will focus on two examples of criminalising humanitarianism, one involving NGOs and the other involving private individuals. In terms of targeting NGOs, developments in recent years related to the criminalisation of civil society for providing search and rescue at sea and humanitarian assistance to migrants, including on the high seas and in the territory of third countries constitute a key example of preventive criminalisation. States have targeted NGOs via a combination of the over-use of criminal law and sustained stigmatisation of civil society organisations outside the legal process. This dual trend has been highlighted by the Council of Europe Commissioner for Human Rights who noted that:

> A particularly worrying aspect of certain member states' interaction with NGOs engaged in the monitoring in the Mediterranean and, in case of people in distress, operating a rescue operation, is the frequent smear campaigns and media attacks against them, as well as repeated criminal investigations, often on the allegation that NGOs-operated vessels have engaged in smuggling. Whilst states have the authority to investigate and prosecute any criminal acts, this power must be used in good faith and should not simply be deployed as a way to prevent NGOs from doing their work.[35]

The use of criminal law in order to generate a hostile environment towards the involvement of NGOs in search and rescue operations is evident in a number of NGO prosecutions in Italy, with well-reported cases including the ones against *Jugend Rettet, Proactiva Open Arms* and *Sea Watch 3*.[36] From the analysis of these

[33] For a detailed analysis of targeting NGOs on the ground, see S Carrera, V Mitsilegas, J Allsopp and L Vosyliūtė, *Policing Humanitarianism. EU Policies Against Human Smuggling and their Impact on Civil Society* (Oxford, Hart Publishing, 2019).

[34] Council of Europe Commissioner for Human Rights, *Lives Saved. Rights Protected. Bridging the Protection Gap between Refugees and Migrants in the Mediterranean* (Strasbourg, 2019). According to the Report, 'Such measures have been compounded by tougher action against those fulfilling the age-old duty of rescuing persons in distress at sea. Captains of commercial and fishing ships may now face judicial and administrative proceedings for coming to the aid of persons in distress at sea and bringing them to a safe port for disembarkation. The criminalisation and obstruction of such humanitarian acts has especially targeted NGOs. In some cases, governments have closed ports and deliberately kept rescued persons and ships' personnel stuck at sea for prolonged periods of time, amid disagreements among member states over who should be responsible for their disembarkation' (p 8).

[35] ibid, p 38.

[36] Jugend Rettet: Tribunale di Trapani, Ufficio GIP, 2 August 2017 (www.questionegiustizia.it, 18 September 2017); Corte di Cassazione, Prima Sezione Penale, 23 April 2018 (judgment issuing), 13 December 2018 (judgment release), No 56138 (www.italgiure.giustizia.it/sncass). Open Arms: Tribunale di Catania, Ufficio GIP, 27 March 2018 (www.questionegiustizia.it, 31 March 2018); Tribunale di Ragusa, Ufficio GIP, 16 April 2018 (www.questionegiustizia.it, 19 April 2018). Sea Watch 3: Tribunale di Agrigento, Ufficio GIP, 2 July 2019 (www.penalecontemporaneo.it, 3 July 2019); Corte di Cassazione, Terza Sezione Penale, 16 January 2020 (judgment issuing), 20 February 2020 (judgment release), No 6626 (www.sistemapenale.it, 24 February 2020).

cases by Stefano Zirulia in this volume,[37] it is clear that prosecuting NGOs in these cases has a purely preventive purpose, with civil society being targeted in order not to allow the arrival of migrants in Italian territory for the purposes of rescue. In addition to the imposition of smuggling criminal charges, criminalisation occurs via prosecution on different grounds, such as conspiracy or complicity,[38] and by the use of preventive measures such as boat seizures and entry bans, imposed on legally questionable grounds of organised crime and illegal waste disposal. These prosecutions place NGOs on the defensive, and have a direct negative impact on rescue operations by suspending the work of NGOs or putting a stop to it altogether[39] – with the dismantling of humanitarian NGOs constituting the ultimate preventative tool for states. In addition to the negative impact this targeting of NGOs has on the respect of state obligations under EU law and under international human rights, humanitarian and refugee law, the impact on fundamental rights of civil society, and in particular freedom of association as enshrined in Article 12 of the Charter of Fundamental Rights, may be considerable.[40] As demonstrated by Stefano Zirulia in detail in this volume, Italian courts appear to be slowly accepting limits to criminalisation of NGOs and preventive sanctions such as entry bans on grounds of necessity and respect of rescue at sea and refugee law obligations.[41] A key example has been the ruling of the Italian Corte di Cassazione in the well-publicised prosecution of Carola Rackete, the captain of SeaWatch 3.[42] The prosecution did not involve human smuggling (parallel pending proceedings are in place at the time of writing), but prosecution on the grounds of resistance to public officials and resistance and violence against warships. In a significant ruling in favour of humanitarianism, the Cassazione rejected the appeal to uphold the charges by essentially giving precedence to the duty of rescue as enshrined in international law and to obligations under international refugee law, and rejecting the argument that a ship constitutes a safe place for the purposes of rescue at sea. The Court has thus accepted that bringing migrants recovered in the context of rescue activities in international waters, also in the face of an express ban on entry into territorial waters and / or in the absence of authorization to dock, constitutes

[37] S Zirulia, 'Is that a Smuggler? The Blurring Line between Facilitating Illegal Immigration and Providing Humanitarian Assistance at the European Borders', ch 11 in this volume.

[38] See also in the context of the Jugend Rettet case that the crew was *charged not with being part of a criminal organisation but with complicity to facilitation* – Spena, above n 21, 40.

[39] The Commissioner for Human Rights has also noted that the mere initiation of an investigation is sufficient to disrupt their activities for a long time, or even permanently (see n 34 above, p 44). For an example of discontinuation see section II.B below.

[40] On the question of the adverse impact of funding restrictions by states to NGOs in the context of the right to freedom of assembly as enshrined in Article 12 of the Charter see the Opinion of Advocate General Campos Sánchez-Bordona in case C-78/18, *Commission v Hungary (Transparency of associations)*, delivered on 14 January 2020.

[41] S Zirulia, 'Is that a Smuggler?', ch 11 in this volume, section IV.

[42] Corte di Cassazione, Terza Sezione Penale, 16 January 2020 (judgment issuing), 20 February 2020 (judgment release), No. 6626 (www.sistemapenale.it, 24 February 2020).

fulfilment of the duty of rescue at sea.[43] It has been said that the ruling by the Cassazione can be read as enshrining a 'right of resistance' against state action in breach of hierarchically higher legal principles.[44] The ruling is indeed a welcome development, in sending a clear signal to the executive and to the prosecutors that the end does not justify the means in the name of controlling borders and immigration and that well-established principles of international law, including international humanitarian law, law of the sea and refugee law, must be complied with in the management of migration flows at sea. By recourse to international law, the *Cassazione* built a line of defence for humanitarian action against a sustained attack of civil society by state institutions.

While the legal battles regarding limits to the criminalisation of facilitation of entry in Italy have focused on the activities of NGOs, it is important to examine the impact that criminalisation may have on the actions of individuals. A test case in this context has arisen in France, concerning the prosecution of two individuals (an academic and the activist farmer Cédric Herrou) relating to facilitation offences in the context of the crossing of the land border between Italy and France in Val Roya. This litigation has led to the examination of the extent of the humanitarian exception to the criminalisation of human smuggling by the French Conseil Constitutionnel in its so-called 'Fraternité' ruling.[45] The ruling is significant in that the Conseil Constitutionnel has used the constitutional principle of *fraternité* as the basis of the freedom to provide humanitarian assistance, without consideration of the regular character of the assisted person's stay in the national territory.[46] However, the Conseil Constitutionnel went on to balance (or, in its own words, to reconcile) the principle of *fraternité* with the safeguarding of public order, in whose framework the fight against irregular migration falls.[47] The outcome of this exercise in the particular case was for the Conseil Constitutionnel to accept the limitation of criminalisation in cases of facilitating irregular movement (*circulation*) on humanitarian grounds, without this limitation being extended to cases of irregular entry.[48] The Court's ruling leaves the preventive aim of the criminalisation of the facilitation of irregular entry intact. Yet, the ruling is of significance in engaging a fundamental – albeit ambivalent – constitutional principle in French law with the need to take into account humanitarian conduct in the context of immigration control, and in the developing (admittedly in the limited sphere of humanitarian conduct after entry) of what has been accurately described as a 'humanistic, universal, and liberal ideal', applicable to citizens and foreigners alike,

[43] S Zirulia, 'La Cassazione sul caso Sea Watch: le motivazioni sull'illegittimità dell'arresto di Carola Rackete' (www.sistemapenale.it, 24 February 2020).

[44] ibid, n 7.

[45] Conseil Constitutionnel, Décision No. 2018/717-718 QPC, 6 July 2018.

[46] Para 8.

[47] Paras 9–10.

[48] Para 12.

closer to the principle of human dignity than to an idea of national kinship.[49] The principle and right of human dignity may form one of the key foundations in rethinking the uncritical over-criminalisation of human smuggling as promoted by EU and national law. Evoking the principle of *fraternité* in the context of humanitarian assistance may work in developing constitutional protective principles both at the level of humanitarian actors and at the level of those receiving humanitarian assistance.

C. Limiting Criminalisation – Framing Smuggling as Organised Crime

Re-thinking the uncritical preventive over-criminalisation of human smuggling in EU law can occur not only by placing such criminalisation in the framework of international and EU human rights, refugee and humanitarian law, but also by comparing the EU legal framework with the criminalisation of smuggling in international law. The primary international law framework for the criminalisation of human smuggling is the 2000 United Nations Convention on Transnational Organised Crime (the Palermo Convention).[50] A separate Protocol addresses human smuggling, and its opening provision confirms that the Protocol supplements the Palermo Convention and must be interpreted together with it.[51] The European Union (or European Community and European Union as it was then) has negotiated and ratified the Palermo Convention and the smuggling Protocol.[52] Key in the comparison between EU secondary law and the UN smuggling Protocol is the fact that, in international law, human smuggling offences are framed as organised crime offences. The framing of human smuggling within an organised crime context is further confirmed by its very definition: according to the Protocol, smuggling of migrants means 'the procurement, in order to obtain, directly or indirectly, *a financial or other material benefit*, of the illegal entry of a person into a State Party of which the person is not a national or a permanent resident'.[53] Criminalisation of smuggling must be based on intentional conduct with the aim of obtaining a financial or other material benefit.[54] The express inclusion of the requirement to obtain such a benefit is a clear indication that the drafters of the Protocol on the one hand viewed smuggling within the framework of organised

[49] 'Editorial' (2019) 15 *European Constitutional Law Review* 183, 189.

[50] The United Nations Convention against Transnational Organized Crime and the Protocols thereto adopted by the UN General Assembly on 15 November 2000.

[51] Article 1(1) of the Protocol Against the Smuggling of Migrants by Land, Sea and Air, supplementing the United Nations Convention Against Transnational Organized Crime (Smuggling Protocol).

[52] V Mitsilegas, 'The European Union and the Globalisation of Criminal Law' (2010) 12 *Cambridge Yearbook of European Legal Studies* 337–407.

[53] Article 3(3) of the Smuggling Protocol. Emphasis added.

[54] Article 6(1) of the Smuggling Protocol.

crime, and on the other that they wished to exclude from the definition and criminalisation of smuggling acts which did not have a material/financial motive such as humanitarian assistance. According to an Interpretative Note to the Protocol,

> the reference to 'a financial or other material benefit' was included in order to emphasize that the intention was to include the activities of organized criminal groups acting for profit, but to exclude the activities of those who provided support to migrants for humanitarian reasons or on the basis of close family ties. It was not the intention of the Protocol to criminalise the activities of family members or support groups such as religious or non-governmental organisations.[55]

The above analysis helps to clarify what human smuggling is about (organised crime) and what it is not about (humanitarian or family assistance) in the eyes of the United Nations legislator.[56] A further question which arises is whether criminalisation under the Protocol includes criminalisation of irregular entry. The smuggling Protocol contains two different provisions which are relevant in this context. On the one hand, Article 5 states that migrants must not become liable to criminal prosecution under the Protocol for the fact of having been the object of the smuggling offences set out therein. On the other hand, Article 6(4) of the Protocol appears to leave a degree of discretion to Member States regarding the criminalisation of non-smuggling related immigration offences, by stating that nothing in the Protocol prevents State Parties from taking measures against a person whose conduct constitutes an offence under its domestic law. The combination of the two provisions does not provide with optimal legal certainty. Gallagher and David are of the view that the Protocol takes a neutral position on whether those who migrate irregularly should be the subject of any criminal offences.[57] McClean notes that the final position reflects disagreement among States, with certain states being apprehensive regarding granting immunity to illegal migrants

[55] UN General Assembly, 'Report of the Ad Hoc Committee on the elaboration of a Convention against Transnational Organized Crime on the work of its first to eleventh sessions, Addendum: Interpretative notes for the official record (travaux préparatoires) of the negotiations for the United Nations Convention against Transnational Organized Crime and the Protocols thereto', UN Doc. A/55/383/Add.1, 3 November 2000, p xxv. See also UNODC, 'Legislative Guide for the United Nations Convention against Transnational Organized Crime and the Protocols thereto' (New York, 2004) p 24, according to which the intention of the drafters was to require legislatures to create criminal offences that would apply to those who smuggle others for gain, but not those who procure only their own illegal entry or who procure the illegal entry of others for reasons other than gain, such as individuals smuggling family members or charitable organizations assisting in the movement of refugees or asylum-seekers (para 32).

[56] See UNODC, 'The Concept of "Financial or Other Material Benefit" in the Smuggling of Migrants Protocol' (Vienna, 2017) p 14, according to which the Protocol does not seek, and cannot be used as the legal basis for, the prosecution of those acting with humanitarian intent or on the basis of close family ties where there is no purpose to obtain a financial or other material benefit.

[57] AT Gallagher and F David, *The International Law of Migrant Smuggling* (Cambridge, Cambridge University Press, 2014) 47.

especially if they had committed a crime, including the smuggling of other illegal migrants.[58] On the other hand, di Martino points out that the Protocol does not apply to those immigrants who, according to international law, should not be criminally liable for the mere fact of their irregular immigration.[59] There are two arguments which militate in favour of the exclusion of criminalisation of irregular entry from the scope of the smuggling Protocol. The first argument relates to the protection of the rights of the smuggled migrants, which forms – together with combatting smuggling and promoting inter-state cooperation – the key purpose of the Protocol.[60] The second argument relates to the Protocol's explicit treatment of human smuggling as a form of organised crime. According to the Legislative Guide for the Implementation of the Protocol,

> [t]wo basic factors are essential to understanding and applying the Migrants Protocol. The first is the intention of the drafters that the sanctions established in accordance with the Protocol should apply to the smuggling of migrants by organized criminal groups and not to mere migration or migrants, even in cases where it involves entry or residence that is illegal under the laws of the State concerned (see articles 5 and 6, paragraph 4, of the Protocol). Mere illegal entry may be a crime in some countries, but it is not recognized as a form of organized crime and is hence beyond the scope of the Convention and its Protocols. Procuring the illegal entry or illegal residence of migrants by an organized criminal group (a term that includes an element of financial or other material benefit), on the other hand, has been recognised as a serious form of transnational organized crime and is therefore the primary focus of the Protocol.[61]

This teleological approach, emphasising the dual primary purposes of the smuggling Protocol to counter transnational organised crime, while at the same time protecting the rights of migrants, has been influential in a major interpretation of the scope of criminalisation of human smuggling by the Canadian Supreme Court. In the case of *Appulonappa*,[62] the Canadian Supreme Court rejected the broad criminalisation advocated by the Canadian Government by interpreting domestic law in conformity with international law, in particular with the Smuggling Protocol. The Court stressed the requirement of the Protocol to criminalise smuggling for financial or other material benefit and noted that it would depart from the balance struck in the Protocol to allow prosecution for mutual assistance among refugees,

[58] D McClean, *Transnational Organized Crime: A Commentary on the United Nations Convention and its Protocols* (Oxford, Oxford University Press, 2007) 388–89.

[59] A di Martino, F Biondi Dal Monte, I Boiano and R Raffaelli, *The Criminalzation of Irregular Immigration: Law and Practice in Italy* (Pisa, Pisa University Press, 2013) 83.

[60] Article 2 of the Smuggling Protocol. On the drafting history and importance of adding human rights protection expressly as a Protocol objective see McClean, above n 58, 379. Also see Gallagher and David, above n 57, 47–48. See also the savings clause in Article 19(1) of the Smuggling Protocol according to which nothing in the Protocol must affect the other rights, obligations and responsibilities of States and individuals under international law, including international humanitarian law and international human rights law.

[61] UNODC, 'Legislative Guide' (2004), n 55 above, para 28.

[62] *R v Appulonappa* [2015] 3 RCS 754.

family support and reunification, and humanitarian aid.[63] According to the Court, Canada's international commitments support the view that the purpose of domestic criminal law is to permit the robust fight against people smuggling in the context of organised crime, which excludes criminalising conduct that amounts solely to humanitarian, mutual or family aid.[64] While the security goals of domestic law are important, they do not supplant Canada's commitment to humanitarian aid and family unity.[65] In a powerful statement, Judge Beverley McLachlin noted that under the Crown's interpretation, 'a father offering a blanket to a shivering child, or friends sharing food aboard a migrant vessel, could be subject to prosecution'.[66] By stressing the need for the existence of the element of the financial gain for the criminal offences of human smuggling to be substantiated, the Canadian Supreme Court has placed important limits to the criminalisation of smuggling and has reminded us of the original purpose of the UN legislator in the field. While one can question the extent to which human smuggling constitutes crime which is highly organised,[67] and whether the traditional concepts of a structured criminal organisation apply in this context regarding the operations of looser smuggling networks,[68] the approach adopted by the Palermo Convention is important in setting out parameters to criminalisation and in putting forward a clear rationale for criminalisation under international law.

For all the conceptual ambiguities of the term 'organised crime', framing the criminalisation of human smuggling within its context and requiring expressly financial gain as an element of the offence will serve to address to some extent the current prevention-led over-criminalisation of smuggling in EU law. Such a move would not negate the requirement for direct exemption from criminalisation of acts consisting of humanitarian assistance and acts conducted in order to comply with international and EU law obligations in the field of humanitarian and refugee law and human rights. In addition to the need to decriminalise to some extent human smuggling in EU law 'in the books', enhanced vigilance is required in scrutinising the uses and abuses of criminal law at national level. A current case in Greece demonstrates the risks of wide-reaching prosecutions targeting civil society. The NGO Emergency Response Centre International (ERCI) has been described

[63] Para 44.

[64] Para 45.

[65] Para 57.

[66] Para 57.

[67] For a contribution highlighting the operation of human smuggling in North Africa in terms of networks and not necessarily highly organised ground see P Campana, 'Out of Africa: The Organisation of Migrant Smuggling across the Mediterranean' (2018) 15 *European Journal of Criminology* 481–502.

[68] On the challenges for the legal definitions of a criminal organisation in international and EU law to address the less structured character of criminality in this context see V Mitsilegas, 'From National to Global, from Empirical to Legal: The Ambivalent Concept of Transnational Organised Crime' in M Beare (ed), *Critical Reflections on Transnational Organized Crime, Money Laundering and Corruption* (Toronto, University of Toronto Press, 2003) 55–87.

as a criminal organisation with a perpetual action group of more than three persons, with internal and hierarchical structure, acting with intent of facilitation. A money laundering charge has been added because, despite its non-profit status, it accepted donations of physical objects and payments by private individuals or other collective bodies, and subsequently sabotage and fraud charges have been added.[69] The case is pending at the time of writing, but one cannot help but notice the targeting of an NGO under organised crime and money laundering charges, in spite of its non-profit status and the addition and accumulation of parallel charges in the criminal justice process. In addition to its impact on humanitarian assistance, the case raises questions on freedom of association related to the funding of NGOs and the ultimate aim of criminal prosecutions on these grounds. It appears that the NGO in question has ceased its operations – with once again an actual prosecution acting as the ultimate preventive tool.[70]

III. The Criminalisation of Irregular Entry, Transit and Re-Entry

In addition to the criminalisation of smuggling, a key component of the criminalisation of migration has been the introduction of criminal offences and sanctions for irregular entry, transit and stay. Criminalisation has not occurred at EU level, but at national level. This section will cast light on the shaky normative foundations of such criminalisation, with over-criminalisation being resorted to in order to defend vague legal interests such as public order and the ability and authority of the state to control its borders. The challenges to this catch-all approach from a criminal law perspective will be highlighted. The section will then analyse the limits EU law itself places on the broad criminalisation of irregular entry, transit and stay – limits which stem from the requirement to ensure effectiveness of EU law (including 'enforcement' EU law such as the Return Directive), as well as from the structural underpinnings of an Area of Freedom, Security and Justice (AFSJ) without internal borders.

A. The Shaky Normative Foundations of Criminalisation

The above analysis on the criminalisation of human smuggling, especially as regards efforts by states to broaden the scope of criminal offences, demonstrates that the main purpose behind the criminalisation of human smuggling by certain

[69] L Vosyliūtė and C Conte, *Crackdown on NGOs and volunteers helping refugees and other migrants* (ReSOMA Report, June 2019) 27.

[70] On cessation of activity, see the ReSOMA Report, ibid.

legislators is really the prevention of migration flows towards their territory. It is hoped that the threat of criminalisation and prosecution of smugglers will ultimately target migrants and lead to a reduction of migrant flows. A key question to be addressed in this context is whether the criminalisation of human smuggling leads to the direct or indirect criminalisation of migrant mobility per se. As mentioned above, the Smuggling Protocol does not provide expressly for the criminalisation of migrants themselves in the form of irregular entry or stay. Indeed, such criminalisation would not be consistent with the framing of human smuggling as a manifestation of organised crime committed for financial gain. Irregular entry and stay are not criminalised as such in EU law either.[71] Yet they are treated as criminal offences in the legal systems of a number of EU Member States.[72] The criminalisation of irregular migration along these lines has been characterised as 'precautionary criminalisation', with irregular entry viewed as a wrong of a public kind (*malum in se*).[73] The use of criminal law in this manner is however problematic. It is unclear what criminal law is designed to achieve, where the harm in the criminalised conduct lies and what the legal interest to be protected consists of. Prevention is key in the criminalisation of irregular entry and stay, with criminal offences being designed in order to prevent the presence of undesirable individuals within the territory of the state. Criminal law is used here in addition to administrative immigration law, although the arrangements of the latter would suffice to legally regulate migration flows. Spena highlights in this context the stigmatisation of migrants by criminal law, which moves from targeting unlawful conduct to targeting undesirable individuals in a logic of pre-emption, where 'crimes should be averted by directly selecting and picking out those persons who, because of their matching a given actor stereotype (*Tätertyp*), can be assumed/presumed to be dangerous, deviant, disloyal, and so on'.[74] Instead of addressing a concrete harm which has been committed, criminal law is used here to prevent, and to send a strong symbolic message against specific categories of individuals and their undesirable conduct. In this manner, the concept of harm is stretched beyond its limits: criminal law is being used to punish conduct which can be regulated by administrative law, and thus becomes symbolic criminal law in sending a signal on the undesirability and dangerousness of the migrant. As Aliverti has eloquently noted,

> We should resist that expansive conception of harm, which runs the risk of turning it in a meaningless principle because the conducts that can be criminalised under it are too far removed from the causation of actual harm … that diluted version of the harm

[71] V Mitsilegas, *The Criminalisation of Migration in Europe. Challenges for Human Rights and the Rule of Law* (Cham, Springer, 2015).

[72] See European Union Agency for Fundamental Rights (FRA), *Criminalisation of migrants in an irregular situation and of persons engaging with them* (2014).

[73] A Spena, '*Iniuria Migrandi*: Criminalization of Immigrants and the Basic Principles of the Criminal Law' (2014) 8 *Criminal Law and Philosophy* 635–57.

[74] ibid, 646.

> principle can espouse, buttress and legitimise bigoted and prejudiced interests and demands for criminalisation that are motivated by genuine or fabricated social anxieties and fears about suspicious other … embracing of subjective security.[75]

B. Limits to National Criminalisation by EU Law – The Return Directive and its Effectiveness

The criminalisation of migration along these lines not only does not sit well within fundamental principles of criminal law, but is also at odds with one of the key aims of immigration enforcement policy, which is the return of irregular migrants. This contradiction has been highlighted in cases where the CJEU was called upon to rule on the compatibility of national law criminalising irregular entry and stay with the EU Return Directive,[76] which has introduced a considerable level of harmonisation of national legal systems in terms of return procedures, conditions and deadlines.[77] In a series of rulings, the Court of Justice of the European Union has set limits to national powers to criminalise irregular entry and stay on the basis of the need to achieve the effectiveness of EU law, and in this case the Return Directive. The first of these cases is *El Dridi*,[78] who was sentenced to one year's imprisonment for the offence of having stayed illegally on Italian territory without valid grounds. The Court found that Member States may not, in order to remedy the failure of coercive measures adopted to carry out removals under Article 8(4) of the Returns Directive, provide for a custodial sentence on the sole ground that a third-country national continues to stay illegally on the territory of a Member State after an order to leave the national territory was notified to him and the period granted in that order has expired; rather, they must pursue their efforts to enforce the return decision, which continues to produce its effects.[79]

[75] A Aliverti, 'The Wrongs of Unlawful Immigration' (2017) 11 *Criminal Law and Philosophy* 375, 386.

[76] Directive 2008/115/EC of the European Parliament and of the Council of 16 December 2008 on common standards and procedures in Member States for returning illegally staying third-country nationals [2008] OJ L348/98 (Return Directive). For an overview of the Return Directive see among others D Acosta Arcarazo, 'The Returns Directive: Possible Limits and Interpretation' in K Zwaan (ed), *The Returns Directive: Central Themes, Problem Issues, and Implementation in Selected Member States* (Nijmegen, Wolf Legal Publishers, 2011) 7; D Acosta Arcarazo, 'The Good, the Bad and the Ugly in EU Migration Law: Is the European Parliament Becoming Bad and Ugly? (The Adoption of Directive 2008/115: The Returns Directive)' (2009) 19 *European Journal of Migration & Law* 19–39; A Baldaccini, 'The Return and Removal of Irregular Migrants under EU Law: An Analysis of the Returns Directive' (2009) 11 *European Journal of Migration & Law* 1–17.

[77] For an overview of the case law of the EU Court of Justice on criminalisation see N Vavoula, 'The Interplay between EU Immigration Law and National Criminal Law – The Case of the Return Directive' in V Mitsilegas, M Bergström and T Konstantinides (eds), *Research Handbook on EU Criminal Law* (Cheltenham, Edward Elgar, 2016) 294–314.

[78] Case C-61/11 PPU *Hassen El Dridi, alias Karim Soufi* [2011] ECR I-3031.

[79] ibid, paras 57–58.

The Court added that such a custodial sentence risks jeopardising the attainment of the objective pursued by that directive, namely, the establishment of an effective policy of removal and repatriation of illegally staying third-country nationals as it is liable to frustrate the application of the measures referred to in Article 8(1) of Directive 2008/115 and delay the enforcement of the return decision.[80] The Directive must thus be interpreted as precluding a Member State's legislation, such as that at issue in the main proceedings, which provides for a sentence of imprisonment to be imposed on an illegally staying third-country national on the sole ground that he remains, without valid grounds, on the territory of that State, contrary to an order to leave that territory within a given period.[81]

The second important ruling was *Achughbabian*,[82] which concerned the compatibility of French law criminalising irregular entry and residence with the Return Directive. The Court noted that in the particular case there was nothing in the evidence before the Court to suggest that Mr Achughbabian has committed any offence other than that consisting in staying illegally on French territory. National legislation such as that at issue in the main proceedings was likely to thwart the application of the common standards and procedures established by the Return Directive and delay the return, thereby, like the legislation at issue in *El Dridi*, undermining the effectiveness of the Directive.[83] The Court applied the *El Dridi* reasoning and emphasised that the principles of effectiveness and loyal cooperation must be respected in order to ensure the objectives of the Return Directive, in particular that return must take place as soon as possible.[84] That would clearly not be the case if, after establishing that a third-country national is staying illegally, the Member State were to preface the implementation of the return decision, or even the adoption of that decision, with a criminal prosecution followed, in appropriate cases, by a term of imprisonment. According to the Court, such a step would delay the removal and does not appear amongst the justifications for a postponement of removal referred to in Article 9 of the returns Directive.[85] Criminalisation was thus incompatible with EU law.

In setting limits to the blanket criminalisation of irregular entry and stay by EU Member States, the CJEU highlighted the protective function of EU law, all the more remarkable because protection against criminalisation has emerged from an EU Directive focusing primarily on enforcement.[86] Such protective function

[80] ibid, para 59.
[81] ibid, para 62.
[82] Case C-329/11 *Alexandre Achughbabian v Préfet du Val-de-Marne* [2011] ECR I-12709.
[83] ibid, para 39.
[84] ibid, paras 43–45.
[85] ibid, para 45.
[86] V Mitsilegas, 'The Changing Landscape of the Criminalisation of Migration in Europe: The Protective Function of European Union Law' in M Guia, M Van der Woude and J Van der Leun (eds), *Social Control and Justice: Crimmigration in an Age of Fear* (The Hague, Eleven International Publishing, 2012) 87–114.

and its facilitation is justified under EU law only as regards the crossings of the EU *external* border, and does not apply to the crossings of *internal* borders. This conclusion is strengthened by the legislative history of the EU 'facilitation package', which has been clearly framed as Schengen-building, repealing the relevant provisions introduced in the 1990 Schengen Implementing Convention. In both cases – and in particular in the case of the criminalisation of irregular entry – the de-nationalisation of the border under the Schengen logic of the AFSJ clashes with the principle of territoriality in criminal law. However, the principle of territoriality will still apply but limit state power to criminalise entry only in cases consistent with the borderless nature of the AFSJ. In this manner, EU law – and in this case taking full account of structural AFSJ considerations – would place additional limits to the criminalisation of irregular entry and its facilitation. This logic further militates against the criminalisation of irregular exit by Member States, criminalisation which in any case is not called for by EU law in terms of its facilitation legislation.

IV. Conclusion

This chapter has demonstrated that the criminalisation of migration in the European Union reflects a security agenda whose primary aim is to prevent the entry of 'undesirable' migrants in the territory of the European Union and its Member States. This approach has led to the over-criminalisation of migration and to the development of symbolic criminal law with shaky normative foundations. The criminalisation of facilitation offences has been sanctioned by EU secondary law. The chapter has demonstrated how this quite 'old', pre-Lisbon part of the EU substantive criminal law *acquis*, which has been adopted with limited scrutiny and justification, on the basis of a Member State initiative, remains valid law today, almost 20 years later, notwithstanding sustained calls for reform and de-criminalisation in order to take into account the adverse impact that the current legal framework has on the functioning of civil society and on compliance with fundamental obligations under international and EU human rights, humanitarian and refugee law. The chapter has put forward a further proposal for de-criminalisation by calling for the criminalisation of facilitation to be viewed within the organised crime framework of the criminalisation of human smuggling in the relevant Protocol to the Palermo Convention on transnational organised crime. Such framing would provide a double limit to criminalisation, which can arise only if financial gain is involved and only if conduct occurs within an organised crime framework. This approach would not negate the requirement to limit criminalisation by expressly exempting humanitarian assistance from its very scope, but would provide a clearer normative framework for criminalisation consistent with international law. New EU legislation, de-criminalising facilitation in those terms, is required. The legal basis for this new instrument can arguably be the 'securitised criminalisation' legal basis in Article 83(1) TFEU (which confers to the Union competence to define criminal offences and adopt criminal sanctions in areas of particularly serious crime with a cross-border dimension, including organised crime), rather than the 'functional criminalisation' legal basis of Article 83(2) TFEU (which confers to the Union competence to criminalise if this is essential to ensure implementation of a Union policy in an area which has been subject to harmonisation measures).[101] This approach will depart from an uncritical securitisation of migration, and from treating a draconian criminal law approach as key in order to manage migration flows, and focus on the requirement of a link between facilitation and organised crime in order to frame criminalisation at EU level.

Another example of over-criminalisation based on shaky normative foundations centring around vague concepts of protection of public order and state authority involves the criminalisation of irregular entry, transit and stay. Criminalisation here does not stem from EU law, but is a model which has been adopted at national level, at times under very expansive and broad criminal provisions – with states choosing to use criminal law to address phenomena which can be managed largely by administrative law. We see thus the emergence of symbolic criminal law aimed at sending tough signals to undesirable migrants wishing to access the territory of EU Member States. The analysis has demonstrated how EU law here – including enforcement EU law such as the Return Directive – can assume a 'protective' function against uncritical and disproportionate criminalisation at national level. In its case-law in and following *El-Dridi*, the Court of Justice has placed national criminalisation of migration within the broader systemic context of EU law. National criminalisation is limited if this undermines the effectiveness of EU law – placing a migrant in criminal custody is not compatible with the aim of facilitating their speedy return. In subsequent case-law in *Affum* and *Arib*, the Court affirmed the applicability of the Return Directive and its safeguards by focusing on the distinction between internal and external borders in the Area of Freedom, Security and Justice. It is this distinction which forms the basis of a further argument limiting criminalisation at both EU and national level, namely that the criminalisation of irregular entry (if an appropriate justification is found) and its facilitation can be justified only in terms of crossing of the external EU border, not being applicable in crossings of the internal intra-Schengen AFSJ borders. While this view may appear to be radical and challenging the principle of territoriality of national criminal law, it is more attuned with the very logic and structure of a borderless Area of Freedom, Security and Justice.

[101] On this distinction see V Mitsilegas, 'EU Criminal Law Competence After Lisbon: From Securitised to Functional Criminalisation' in D Acosta and C Murphy (eds), *EU Security and Justice Law* (Oxford, Hart Publishing, 2014) 110–29.

3

Global Trends in 'Crimmigration' Policies

From the EU to the USA

GIAN LUIGI GATTA

I. 'Crimmigration', i.e. the Merging of Criminal and Immigration Laws: Three Strategies

'Crimmigration', a term introduced in legal literature by an American scholar[1] in 2006 and currently adopted internationally, refers to the overlapping or merging of criminal and immigration laws. Scholars from different countries have in fact identified, particularly in the past 20 years, a political trend directed towards the 'criminalisation of immigration law'.[2] In American literature, which has extensively

[1] J Stumpf, 'The Crimmigration Crisis: Immigrants, Crime, and Sovereign Power' (2006) 56 *American University Law Review* 367.

[2] There is extensive literature on the subject. For a general overview on the United States, in addition to the aforementioned contribution of Stumpf, the following references may be useful: KR Johnson, R Aldana, BO Hing, LM Saucedo and E Trucios-Haynes, *Understanding Immigration Law* 2nd edn (New Providence, LexisNexis, 2017) 547; JM Chacon, 'Managing Migration through Crime' (2019) 109 *Columbia Law Review Sidebar* 135; AM McLeod, 'The U.S. Criminal-Immigration Convergence and its Possible Undoing' (2012) 49 *American Criminal Law Review* 105; CC García Hernández, 'Creating Crimmigration' (2013) *Brigham Young University Law Review* 1457; Y Vázquez, 'Crimmigration: the Missing Piece of Criminal Justice Reform' (2017) 51 *University of Richmond Law Review* 1093; JA Dowling and JX Inda, *Governing Immigration Through Crime. A reader* (Stanford, Stanford Social Sciences, 2013). Regarding the European Union, as further references, see V Mitsilegas, *The Criminalisation of Migration in Europe. Challenges for Human Rights and the Rule of Law* (Cham, Springer, 2015); MAH Van der Woude, JP Van der Leun and JA Nijland, 'Crimmigration in the Netherlands' (2014) *Law & Social Inquiry* 560. At international level, see the work covering different angles published in K Franko Aas and M Bosworth (eds), *The Borders of Punishment: Migration, Citizenship, and Social Exclusion* (New York, Oxford University Press, 2013). In Italy, criminal law scholars have focused on this subject after the reforms which, some ten years ago, introduced the provisions whereby the status of illegal immigrant amounts to an aggravating circumstance (Article 61 no. 11 *bis* of the Italian Criminal Code), which were considered unconstitutional by the Italian *Corte Costituzionale* (Decision No 249 of 2010), and the crime of illegal immigration (Article 10 *bis* of Legislative Decree No 286 of 1998, the Italian Consolidated Law on Immigration). See, among the many, GL Gatta, 'Aggravante della "clandestinità" (art 61 n 11-bis cp): uguaglianza calpestata' (2009) *Rivista Italiana di Diritto e Procedura Penale*

investigated the subject, some legal scholars even provided three application scenarios by identifying *three different but overlapping criminal policy strategies*:[3]

a) the introduction of criminal law consequences for immigration law violations;
b) the introduction of (administrative) immigration law consequences to criminal convictions; and
c) the introduction of criminal-type tools, such as custodial measures, and related procedures for immigration law violations.

Despite occurring in the framework of different legal systems – and likewise different immigration developments and related political, economic and social issues – crimmigration results in the establishment of *a parallel legal system*: a hybrid one blending criminal and administrative/immigration law, the underlying logic and practices of which resemble the criminal justice system, despite being foreign to it.[4] As Juliet Stumpf pointed out,[5] such a system, like the criminal one, represents the highlight of the government's sovereign power exerted over individuals; a system aimed at *social control and exclusion* of those who are not welcome based on political choices. The social exclusion aim allows to better grasp the intrinsic similarity between criminal and immigration laws: they both affect and focus on individuals' personal freedom; specifically, whereas one pursues the social exclusion aim through *imprisonment*, the other pursues a similar, perhaps even more radical objective, by *removing* the individual from society, in which case detention is often a preparatory step.

In this work, I am going to show how the crimmigration process has developed along similar lines – i.e., the three paths described above – in Europe and in the United States, essentially giving rise to a universal *issue of insufficient guarantees of the foreigner's fundamental rights*: immigration law tends to borrow practices and procedures from criminal law to protect the public interests at stake but, at the same time, purposefully fails to implement the guarantees provided under the criminal justice system.[6]

713; GL Gatta, 'Il "reato di clandestinità" e la riformata disciplina penale dell'immigrazione' (2009) *Diritto penale e processo* 1323; GL Gatta, 'La criminalizzazione della clandestinità tra scelte nazionali e contesto europeo' (2015) *Rivista Italiana di Diritto e Procedura Penale* 188; L Masera, '"Terra bruciata" attorno al clandestino: tra misure penali simboliche e negazione reale dei diritti', in O Mazza, F Viganò (eds), *Il "Pacchetto sicurezza" 2009* (Torino, Giappichelli, 2009) 27; F Viganò, 'Diritto penale e immigrazione: qualche riflessione sui limiti alla discrezionalità del legislatore' (2010) *Diritto, immigrazione e Cittadinanza* 13.

[3] Among leading works, see, in particular, Stumpf, above n 1, 381 and ff.; SH Legomsky, 'The New Path of Immigration Law: Asymmetric Incorporation of Criminal Justice Norms' (2007) 64 *Washington and Lee Law Review* 469, 481; DA Sklansky, 'Crime, Immigration, and Ad Hoc Instrumentalism' (2012) 15 *New Criminal Law Review*, 157, 164.

[4] See T Miller, 'Citizenship & Severity: Recent Immigration Reforms and the New Penology' (2003) 10 *Georgetown Immigration Law Journal* 611. See, also, IV Eagly, 'Prosecuting Immigration' (2010) 104 *North-western University Law Review* 1281.

[5] Stumpf, above n 1, 377 and ff.

[6] See Legomsky, above n 3, 472 and ff.

II. First Strategy: Criminal Law Consequences for Immigration Law Breaches

A first line of development in the process of criminalising immigration law is represented by the *use of criminal law to punish immigration law breaches.* In this respect, the choice to punish as a criminal offence the baseline unlawful acts contemplated thereunder, such as entering or staying in the territory of a country without a permit or re-entering the same after an order of removal has been issued, and in breach of the same, is a classic example. Such a choice entails an *overlapping between criminal and immigration laws*: criminal law carries out an ancillary function with respect to immigration law, which, however, does not simply identify the criminally relevant behaviour, but also punishes the same by applying the sanctions generally provided for under its body of rules, without any adjustment whatsoever, unlike what normally happens when criminal laws complement other branches of the legal system. Removal of an undocumented immigrant (after a period of administrative detention) is ordered even when a penalty (imprisonment and/or a fine) is imposed in connection with an immigration-related offence. The administrative breach occurs merely as a result of entering or staying illegally, and any ensuing consequence – removal/ administrative detention (i.e., refusal of entry at the border) – remains unaffected even when a criminal penalty may be imposed; likewise, the related proceedings take place regardless of any ongoing criminal proceedings, which run parallel tracks and are connected in various ways.

This is the case in Italy, for example, where – like in other European countries[7] – the offences of illegal entry or stay on national territory (as well as the failure to comply with an order of removal and re-entry after removal) coexist with as many related administrative offences involving removal; this is also the case in the United States of America, where the same facts constitute federal offences and breaches of federal immigration law at the same time, entailing deportation or removal.[8]

However, the fact that the same conduct is relevant under both criminal and immigration laws, without criminal law ensuring a more effective protection of the interests at stake, is in breach of the principle of subsidiarity: removal (and refusal of entry at the border) is the ultimate goal of the administrative regulation on entering and staying on a national territory, which aims to satisfy various

[7] For a broader and more detailed analysis, see FRA (European Union Agency for Fundamental Rights), *Criminalisation of Migrants in an Irregular Situation and of Persons Engaging with Them* (2014).

[8] See D Weissbrodt, L Danielson and HS Myers III, *Immigration Law and Procedure in a Nutshell* 7th edn (USA, West Academic, 2017) 645 and ff. It is worth pointing out that, in the USA, immigration and criminal law is primarily dealt with at the federal level (see ibid, 103 and ff.).

public interests (economy, health, order and safety).[9] Administrative law indeed directly pursues that objective, without criminal law representing a more effective alternative, or even a complementary instrument, with a view to protecting those interests, thus justifying its application.

A. In Europe

In Europe, this is certainly true in Italy, where it is safe to assume that criminalising unlawful immigration serves no purpose: it neither involves removal (which is still governed by administrative law, under the conditions and procedures set forth thereunder), nor serves a preventive purpose, considering that the crimes of unlawful entry and stay (with the only exception of re-entry following removal), as well as failure to comply with an order of voluntary removal, are punished with a fine. This choice of penalty was influenced by the EU Court of Justice, which – in 2011 – established, under its landmark *El Dridi* ruling, that a national provision, such as the one established, at that time, under Article 14, paragraph 5 *ter* of the Italian Consolidated Act on Immigration (Legislative Decree No. 286/1998) on the failure to comply with an order of removal, whereby a breach committed in relation to removal proceedings and governed by administrative law is punished by detention, breaches the Return Directive (No. 115/2008).[10] As a matter of fact, nowadays EU law prevents Member States from imposing a custodial sentence during removal proceedings, to fight and control unlawful immigration. This is so because the objective pursued by the Directive – i.e., ensuring the repatriation of non-EU citizens – is thwarted when an individual is detained on EU territory instead of being removed. Nonetheless, in Italy, as in most EU member states, the aforementioned conduct is still punished under law as a criminal offence. The reason, at least in the Italian legal system, can be found in the highly symbolic significance carried by criminal law, which:

a) does not result in the illegal immigrant being detained and removed, insofar as this [process] is regulated under immigration law (where applicable);
b) does not discourage the illegal immigrant from entering or staying illegally in the country, since the weapon in question is blunt (in Italy, this is so, among other things, because fines are virtually never enforced); and
c) on the other hand, only serves the purpose of *placing on the individual the stigma of social disapproval usually associated with the criminal offence*, with a view to addressing xenophobic safety concerns, which are unfortunately reinforced by Islamic terrorism.

[9] See Corte Costituzionale, Decision No 250 of 2010.

[10] Case C-61/11 PPU *Hassen El Dridi, alias Karim Soufi* [2011] ECR I-3031. On this judgment, see F Viganò and L Masera, 'Addio Articolo 14' (2011) *Diritto penale contemporaneo*, 29 April.

B. In the United States

In the United States, criminal law plays a different role in criminalising unlawful immigration. In that system, illegal entry became a criminal offence a long time ago. The offence of unlawful entry was introduced as early as 1929.[11] Today, the offence is governed by US Code § 1325 (a), where this is a misdemeanour and imprisonment for up to six months and/or a fine may be imposed.[12] On the other hand, illegal re-entry of removed illegal immigrants (US Code § 1326) is a more serious offence (felony), punishable with a fine and/or imprisonment for up to two years, which may be increased, however, up to 10 or even 20 years in the event that removal was subsequent to a conviction for having committed more serious criminal offences.

Unlike in Italy, in the United States the punishment for the aforementioned offences is actually issued and enforced. In that system, criminal prosecution is not mandatory, and prosecutors may decide whether to apply immigration law and remove the individual immediately, after having served an administrative detention order, or prosecute the illegal immigrant for the offence. In the latter case, removal occurs once the detention order has been served; the latter represents a preliminary step. In other words, criminal prosecution represents an additional measure and is not a substitute for removal.[13] More often than not, criminal proceedings are initiated to streamline the removal process by providing for a voluntary departure agreement as part of a plea bargain, in exchange for a less severe punishment and pleading no contest.[14] This is all the more significant considering that the percentage of plea bargains is around 99.5 per cent and that in the districts along the border with Mexico, 'mass' deals are entered into: 25000 a year, for example, before the Arizona District Court, in many cases with simultaneous deals made with 40/50 individuals.[15]

Unlike in Italy and other European Countries, in the United States, the penalties imposed and enforced for immigration law breaches are a complement to immigration law and do not play just a nominal role in practice; rather, they are instrumental to achieving the ultimate goal pursued thereunder: arresting, detaining and removing undocumented immigrants.[16] Criminal law enforcement statistical data speaks for itself.

[11] See Johnson et al, above n 2, 548–49. For a broader historical and critical analysis, see D Keller, 'Re-thinking Illegal Entry and Reentry' (2012) 44 *Loyola University Chicago Law Journal* 65.

[12] Imprisonment for up to two years is envisioned for repeated offenders (in case of a felony).

[13] See Legomsky, above n 3, 482.

[14] ibid. See, also, Keller, above n 11, 69.

[15] See Weissbrodt, Danielson and Myers III, above n 8, 647.

[16] This does not mean that no criticism is raised, even in the US, regarding the indictments under consideration, which allegedly entail massive expenditure and human resources, nonetheless failing to curtail migration flows. See Keller, above n 11, 65 and ff. As is the case, in Italy, with respect to the offence provided for by Article 10 bis of the Italian Consolidated Act on Immigration, another line of criticism focuses on the fact that the offences in question tie criminal liability to a status, not without racial implications. See GJ Chin, 'Illegal Entry as a Crime, Deportation as Punishment: Immigration

In 2018, approximately 61 per cent of criminal prosecutions brought by federal prosecutors concerned immigration-related offences.[17] In the same year, 55 per cent of federal arrest warrants concerned immigration offences; 95 per cent of the increase in the number of federal arrests occurred as a result of those offences.[18] It is a tangible sign of the extent to which the federal government relies on criminal law in the fight against illegal immigration: even more so during the Trump administration. In 2018, federal convictions (including plea bargains) for immigration offences represented more than a third of the overall percentage (34.4 per cent): this is the most common federal offence (even more so than drug-related offences).[19] The percentage of plea bargains for federal offences in general (97.8 per cent) is staggering in the eyes of a European legal scholar. In 93.7 per cent of cases, (only) a prison sentence was issued for immigration-related offences, with an average 10 months to be served. Probation was granted, for those offences, only in 5.3 per cent of the cases, whereas a sentence issuing a fine was handed down in one case alone (!) Regarding gender and race, 92.7 per cent of defendants convicted of immigration-related crimes were men and 96.3 per cent were Latinos.

Finally, an insight into prison population. In September 2017 (latest available data), the inmates for immigration-related offences in the United States were 11,100, or 7 per cent of the prison population in federal prisons. This figure is very different in Italy, where, as a result of the *El Dridi* ruling, the number of immigrants detained in prison for immigration offences has become irrelevant. On 30 June 2019, only 1395 immigrants were detained for immigration-related offences in Italian prisons, i.e., 2.3 per cent of the total number of inmates.[20]

III. Second Strategy: Immigration Law Consequences Ensuing from Criminal Convictions

A second and distinct aspect of the crimmigration process concerns the provision of immigration law consequences ensuing from criminal convictions for offences that are not specific to a certain class of offenders (*reato comune*). A criminal record *may constitute grounds for denied entry* into the territory of the immigrant's country of destination or may result in his or her *removal*. This is the case both in Europe and in Italy – where immigrants have represented approximately one third of the prison population for years – and the United States.

Status and the Criminal Process' (2011) 58 *UCLA Law Review* 1417; VC Romero, 'Decriminalizing Border Crossings' (2010) 38 *Fordham Urban Law Journal* 273.

[17] Source: www.trac.syr.edu.

[18] Source: www.bjs.gov.

[19] Source: US Sentencing Commission, *Overview of federal criminal cases – Fiscal year 2018*, www.ussc.gov.

[20] Source: www.giustizia.it.

A. In Europe

As for Europe, Italy is an example of the above: a conviction or a plea bargain, including a non-final one, for some offences committed on national territory, which are, for the most part, serious offences (e.g., drug-related offences, sexual offences, offences for which mandatory arrest is provided in case of *flagrante delicto*), constitute *grounds for denied entry* to an immigrant who is not already residing on the territory (Article 4, paragraph 3 of the Italian Consolidated Act on Immigration), or *for revoking or not renewing a residence permit* (Article 5, paragraph 5 and 5 bis), in which case administrative removal will ensue (Article 13).[21]

According to a similar line of reasoning, a criminal conviction may also affect a refugee or *subsidiary protection* status granted to those who do not qualify as refugees. The applicable provisions are set out in Legislative Decree No. 251 of 19 November 2007, as amended in 2018, whereby:

a) a final conviction for some criminal offences involves, subject to a case-by-case assessment, denial of the refugee status (Article 12);
b) such a conviction also entails denial of subsidiary protection, where reasonable grounds exist to believe that the judgment provides a relevant indication as to the danger posed to public policy regulations and safety. Subsidiary protection is also denied when the requesting immigrant has committed a crime against peace, a war crime or a crime against humanity, as defined in the international instruments concerning these offences, or has committed a serious criminal offence, *outside the country of refuge prior to his or her admission as a refugee* (Article 16); and
c) a final conviction for an offence punished by a minimum term of imprisonment of four years or a maximum of 10 years, provides a relevant indication to assess the danger posed to public policy regulations and safety and entails removal of the refugee or immigrant to whom subsidiary protection has been granted, unless a prohibition on removal applies in accordance with Article 19 of Legislative Decree No. 286/1998 (or a prohibition established under an international convention), due to the danger of being subjected to torture or to persecution for racial, religious, political-social or personal reasons (Article 20).

On the other hand, the fact that removal – which thus far we have considered as an administrative consequence of a criminal conviction – is multifaceted further demonstrates the interconnecting and overlapping of immigration and criminal

[21] In accordance with Article 18 bis, para 4 bis, revocation of the residence permit and removal may also be ordered against an immigrant when convicted of certain crimes involving gender-based violence or convicted for copyright and industrial trademark violations, pursuant to Article 26, para 7 bis.

law in the Italian system. Under Italian law, multiple cases of removal of an immigrant are provided for as a result of criminal convictions, falling within the criminal system instead.

Removal may be ordered:

a) as a *security measure* for an immigrant who poses a danger to society and has been sentenced to imprisonment exceeding two years (Article 235 of the Italian Criminal Code), or, irrespective of the term to be served, convicted for a criminal offence committed against the State (Article 312 of the Italian Criminal Code)[22] or a drug-related offence (Article 86 of Presidential Decree No. 309/1990);
b) as an alternative penalty to *imprisonment* imposed for an offence committed with criminal intent, on individuals who may be subjected to administrative removal because of their unlawful presence in the country (Article 16 of Legislative Decree No. 286/1998), or as an alternative penalty to a fine imposed for the offences of illegal entry and stay on national territory (Article 10 bis of Legislative Decree No. 286/1998) and failure to comply with an order of voluntary departure (Article 14, paragraph 5 ter and paragraph 5 quater of Legislative Decree No. 286/1998);
c) as an *alternative measure to imprisonment* (Article 16, paragraph 5 of Legislative Decree No. 286/1998) that may be issued against an immigrant who has been identified and detained, and may be subjected to administrative removal because of his or her unlawful presence in the country, and who must serve a prison sentence, including time yet to be served, not exceeding two years.[23]

Even when regulated under criminal law, removal is instrumental to achieving *immigration law objectives* (removal of an illegal immigrant).

Unfortunately, we do not have any empirical data concerning the number of *administrative* removals ordered and carried out against foreign citizens as a result of a criminal conviction, nor the number of removals ordered and carried out as a custodial measure or as a penalty alternative to imprisonment.

B. In the United States

Even in the United States, as is generally the case in Italy and in Europe, the fight against illegal immigration has long been one of the main debates in the public spotlight, and is included on political agendas: it has been at least since the second

[22] The provisions of the Italian Criminal Code (Articles 235 and 312) also apply to those immigrants who are EU citizens. In this case, the measure is referred to by using a more politically correct name: 'an order to leave the national territory'.

[23] The measure may not be ordered if the conviction relates to certain serious criminal offences, including those referred to in Article 407, para 2, letter a), of the Italian Code of Criminal Procedure. Similar considerations apply to a removal order when this is imposed as an alternative penalty.

half of the 1980s and it is even more so today, under Donald Trump's presidency. Like in Europe, illegal immigration has become a national security issue more than ever, especially in the aftermath of 9/11 and the increased threat represented by international terrorism.[24] Nowadays, the fight against terrorism is conducted, in the United States as well as in Europe, not only through criminal law and justice, but also and especially through immigration law and its related enforcement.[25] The 'national security' rhetoric offers fertile ground everywhere to justify restricting the fundamental guarantees of civilised legal systems and gives rise to zealous strategies aimed at controlling 'unwanted' immigration, including – first and foremost – 'criminal aliens'. These are immigrants *suspected* of being involved in criminal activities – deported on a preventive basis (it is the fate of thousands of Arabs and Muslims after 11 September, in the United States and Europe, including Italy) – and immigrants *convicted* of various crimes.

In the United States, this latter group has explicitly represented, for years, one of the core missions of the Department of Homeland Security (DHS), established in 2002, in the aftermath of 11 September. It is the third largest department of the American government, to which the two main agencies engaged in the fight against illegal immigration report: the Customs and Border Protection Agency (CBP), responsible for monitoring land (approximately 2000 miles along the border with Mexico and approximately 5500 with Canada), air and maritime borders, and the Immigration and Customs Enforcement (ICE), responsible for carrying out deportations and mainly engaged in promoting homeland security through 20,000 employees, over 400 offices and an annual budget of about six billion dollars, which is allocated by Congress pursuant to a request by the President of the United States.[26] The 2018 report on ICE activities shows that the agency's enforcement focus included those who: a) have been convicted of any criminal offence; b) have been charged with any criminal offence that has not been resolved; c) have committed acts constituting a chargeable criminal offence.[27] This constitutes further evidence of the fact that immigration law and enforcement are used to pursue criminal justice policies.

Essentially, in the US, when an immigrant gets caught in the web of the criminal justice system – for example, 'just' for driving under the influence of drugs or

[24] See, for instance, J Margulies, *What Changed When Everything Changed: 9/11 and the Making of National Identity* (New Haven, Yale University Press, 2013); AL Rizer III, *The National Security Implications of Immigration Law* (ABA, 2012); JM Chacon, 'Unsecured Borders: Immigration Restrictions, Crime Control and National Security' (2007) 39 *Connecticut Law Review* 1827; T Miller, 'Blurring the Boundaries between Immigration and Crime Control after September 11th' (2005) 25 *Boston College Third World Law Journal* 81; JAE Vervaele, 'The Anti-Terrorist Legislation in the US: Inter Arma Silent Leges?' (2005) 13 *European Journal of Crime, Criminal Law and Criminal Justice* 201; NV Demleitner, 'Immigration Threats and Rewards: Effective Law Enforcement Tools in the "War" on Terrorism' (2002) 51 *Emory Law Journal* 1059.

[25] See, for instance, Miller, above n 4, 659.

[26] See the overview on 'administrative structure of immigration law' in Johnson et al, above n 2, 224 and ff.

[27] *Fiscal Year 2018 ICE Enforcement and Removal Operations Report*, www.ice.gov.

alcohol – he or she has a good chance of being removed, in addition to being punished. This was true even during the administration of the former Democratic President, Barack Obama – during his eight-year presidency, over two million immigrants were removed on various grounds and about 400,000 were detained every year[28] – and this is all the more so today, after the election of Republican President Donald Trump, who verbally declared war on 'criminal aliens' during the election campaign, and then followed through right away by signing one of his first executive orders in January 2017. Statistical data shows that, in the US, words are followed up with action.[29] In 2018, 56 per cent of individuals expelled from ICE were 'criminal aliens', that is, individuals with a criminal record; 9 per cent were individuals undergoing criminal proceedings.

The data concerning ICE and CBP's activities is indicative of a multi-level strategy to tackle unlawful immigration, carried out in the United States through the overlapping of immigration and criminal law: a strategy which Donald Trump endorsed and even boosted shortly after he was elected President of the United States.[30] The main enforcement agencies are responsible for monitoring two flows.

a) On the one hand, *they contrast illegal entries*, mostly along the border with Mexico, by deporting and denying entry to undocumented immigrants with or without a criminal record, engaging in synergistic coordination with CBP (especially the US Border Patrol, which reports to it) and ICE. In 2018, as many as 4,041,426 non-citizens were arrested by Border Patrol agents (of which 279,009 were identified at the border, that is, at the ports of entry). In the same year, ICE removed 174,923 undocumented immigrants arrested at the border;
b) On the other hand, the agencies *assist in the process of removing* unwanted immigrants. For the most part, ICE deals with this task by deporting not only those who are illegally found on US soil, but also those who, despite being legal residents, have been convicted of certain criminal offences. In 2018, 56 per cent of the cases processed showed a criminal record as grounds for removal enforced by ICE.

[28] See JM Chacon, 'Immigration and the Bully Pulpit' (2017) 130 *Harvard Law Review Forum* 243, 247 and ff.

[29] All the data shown below, concerning ICE, are drawn from the aforementioned 2018 Fiscal Year Report, to which the tables referenced in the following notes also refer. The data reported in the text, concerning CBP, are drawn from the CBP Border Security Report for Fiscal Year 2018, which can be found at www.cbp.gov.

[30] As one of his first actions (Executive Order: Enhancing Public Safety in the Interior of the United States), dated 25 January 2017 and available at www.whitehouse.gov, Trump reiterated that the removal of the 'criminal aliens' is a priority and has also increased the number of immigration officers available to enforcement agencies. For an introductory and interesting analysis of immigration policies in the aftermath of Trump's election, with a particular focus on the correlations with the ambiguous policies that characterised the Obama presidency, see Chacon, above n 28, 247 and ff.

The first flow is managed close to the border; the second across the vast US territory. Federal law interconnects immigration and criminal law; such body of law, which has been reformed several times, especially in the last 20 years, in constant pursuit of stricter penalties for 'criminal aliens', and established through the gradual expansion of the list of criminal convictions which, pursuant to Immigration and Nationality Act (INA), result in denied entry to the US or removal.

Paragraph 212 INA lists various grounds of inadmissibility, such as health, security, immigration or public charge-related, and – among the most significant – criminal-related grounds (§ 212 (a) 2). In all these cases, *entry may be denied* and, where occurring after a visa has been granted, may result in removal. In principle, the logic underlying this body of rules is the same adopted under Italian law in regulating the issuance of a residence permit, which may be denied pursuant to Legislative Decree No. 286/1998 to those who have a record of conviction for certain crimes, thus causing damage to society and proving to be *dangerous* or, in any case, *unwanted*. US regulation appears stricter than the Italian one in at least two respects: a) the larger number of convictions constituting grounds for inadmissibility, which are relevant even when disclosed by the concerned party; b) the fact that even foreign convictions are relevant for those purposes.[31]

In the United States anyone convicted (or disclosing to have been convicted) of one of the following offences[32] is inadmissible.

a) First, the 'crime of moral turpitude'. This concept, which has been adopted in the United States since 1891, is hard to define due to its inherent vagueness. The courts generally agree on interpreting this concept as a reference to a criminal offence – be it a felony or a misdemeanour – characterised by violence or involving 'depravity', 'baseness' or 'vileness', according to common perception.[33] In case law, the list of offences involving moral turpitude is long and varied: it includes, among other things, such offences as bigamy, theft, those committed for damaging purposes and false statements issued to obtain a driving licence, in addition to offences against individuals. It also includes offences associated with fraud. The Supreme Court established such principle in 1951 in *Jordan v. De George*: this case involved an Italian citizen who had legally entered the United States and then engaged in the sale of alcohol and concocted a tax fraud, facing deportation.[34] On that occasion, the Supreme

[31] As mentioned, in our legal system, foreign convictions are far less relevant, since they may result in international protection not being applicable, pursuant to Article 16 Legislative Decree No 251 of 2007.

[32] See Johnson et al, above n 2, 337 and ff.

[33] The law provides for some exceptions to these cases of inadmissibility as a result of convictions for a criminal offence involving moral turpitude; those exceptions concern individuals who were younger than 18 years of age when they committed the offence, where committed at least five years before the visa application, or individuals convicted of offences punishable by imprisonment for a maximum term of one year, or when the term of the prison sentence handed down does not exceed six months. Other exceptions, which are subject to the judge's discretionary power, are envisioned where the offence was committed over 15 years ago or the perpetrator is married to an American citizen or is his/her parent or child.

[34] U.S. Supreme Court, *Jordan v De George*, 341 US 223 (1951).

Court ruled that the wording in question was not flawed by vagueness, establishing that its essence was sufficiently precise, having regard to case law and common understanding. American lawyers are well aware that in proceedings against foreign residents in the United States, the legal classification of the alleged crime – including for purposes of a plea bargain – is ultimately crucial in deciding the fate of the defendant, with risks arising from applying such a vague concept as 'moral turpitude'.

b) Any immigrant who has breached any state or federal law, including of a foreign country, concerning narcotics is also inadmissible: even petty offences, such as possession of small quantities of marijuana, may result in a denied visa.[35]

c) Moreover, entry into the US may be denied to an immigrant convicted of two or more offences, when sentenced to imprisonment exceeding five years overall.

d) Lastly, admission to the United States may be denied in the event of a conviction for certain serious criminal offences for which the offender was not punished due to immunity from prosecution, as well as in case of participation in criminal activities involving prostitution, human trafficking and money laundering, where no conviction has been entered.

Some criminal convictions may constitute grounds for denial of asylum seeker or refugee status in the US as well.[36]

Finally, as mentioned, an increasing number of convictions or plea bargains for different offences may result in removal of the illegal immigrant previously admitted to the United States. The number of criminal grounds for removal has been rising since the mid-1980s, so much so that – according to an immigration law manual – 'virtually any criminal activity other than most petty offenses and misdemeanors can have serious adverse consequences to non-citizens and their family members'.[37]

Paragraph 237(a)(2) INA contains the following criminal grounds of removal.[38]

a) An immigrant may be removed where convicted of a crime involving moral turpitude committed within five years of the date of admission (or 10 years in the case of an immigrant with lawful permanent resident status), where a

[35] See Johnson et al, above n 2, 339. The law provides that that anyone suspected of being involved in drug trafficking may not be admitted, even where no conviction is entered. In this case, his or her wife and children are also inadmissible, where they have benefited from the criminal offence in the previous five years. There is more: the law includes mere (current) drug use, even without developing a drug addiction, among the health-related grounds of inadmissibility (see ibid, 346).

[36] See Johnson et al, above n 2, 346 and ff.

[37] See Weissbrodt, Danielson and Myers III, above n 8, 292.

[38] See Johnson et al, above n 2, 401 and ff.

sentence of one year or longer may be imposed.[39] Any undocumented immigrant who at any time after having been admitted is convicted of two or more of the aforementioned criminal offences may be removed, as long as these are not committed for purely political reasons and do not arise out of a single scheme of criminal misconduct (*disegno criminoso*). The considerations made above in relation to the concept of 'moral turpitude' apply here: this is a flexible construct which in many cases constitutes grounds for removing unwanted criminal aliens, since the list of crimes involving moral turpitude in case law is long: 'volumes have been written cataloguing the crimes that courts have held involving moral turpitude'.[40]

b) Removal may also be ordered as a result of any 'aggravated felony' committed at any time after admission. This legal construct is defined for immigration law purposes (§ 101(a)(43)), and amounts to a long list of criminal offences, including, among others murder, rape, sexual abuse of a minor, drug trafficking, violent crimes, theft, bribery, perjury.[41]

c) Over the years, Congress has incorporated into the general provisions on criminal offences involving turpitude and aggravated felonies convictions for specific offences as additional grounds for removal.[42] These include convictions entered by state, federal or even of foreign courts for drug-related offences, except for the crime of possession 30 grams or less of marijuana for personal use, as is the case with the grounds of inadmissibility.

IV. Third Strategy: Implementation of Criminal Penalties and Proceedings for Immigration Law Purposes

The most blatant and disturbing aspect of the criminalisation of immigration law process, in Europe and the United States, is certainly represented by a third political strategy: the implementation of custodial measures (and related enforcement procedures), typically envisaged by criminal law, for immigration law purposes. Through criminal-type tools, under immigration laws, millions of individuals are currently arrested, detained and removed on both sides of the Atlantic Ocean: as mentioned, in some cases, this is the result of criminal convictions; in other cases, this is due to not having a residence permit or valid visa to enter the country.

[39] Conviction entails removal when the criminal offence is punished by imprisonment of less than one year; on the contrary, no grounds of inadmissibility exist when an offence involving moral turpitude is punished with imprisonment not exceeding six months. The rules governing removal are therefore more stringent.

[40] To this effect, Johnson et al, above n 2, 402.

[41] Although a legal definition exists, in practice, the classification of a criminal offence as an aggravated felony, including and especially in the event of concurrent offences, may be controversial. For an overview of the criteria adopted in case law, see Johnson et al, above n 2, 403 s.

[42] ibid, 405.

This process is implemented through police officers who, at the borders or across the country, limit the freedom of individuals who are: a) apprehended; b) turned back at the border; c) detained in prison-like facilities while the removal process is underway; d) removed, often using coercive measures.

The extent of human suffering of the illegal immigrants who get caught in the web of deportation or removal proceedings is such that a serious reflection on the actual legal classification (criminal/administrative) of the tools employed by governments to manage immigration-related issues appears necessary. This is not a theoretical exercise: as mentioned, and as we will see in more detail below, the level of constitutional guarantees, including those arising from international conventions, varies depending on such legal classification.

Criminal lawyers must go through this process for at least two reasons. The first is the noblest of reasons, i.e., the commitment to principles and the need to protect fundamental human rights and guarantees, must be strongly defended, irrespective of whether citizens or non-citizens are involved, teaching these values to the new generations, especially given that security concerns set the tone for the times we live in, characterised by the emergence of terrorism and, ultimately, xenophobia, especially against Arabs or Muslims. The second reason is an empirical one, i.e., that criminal science cannot disregard the disconcerting number of individuals whose personal freedom has been restricted, with ramifications on family life, work, health, life prospects, etc. Those numbers prove it is no longer safe to assume that measures restricting personal freedom, including detention, are solely governed by criminal law.

A. In Europe

In the European Union, the immigration law enforcement agencies of the Member States are responsible for fighting illegal immigration, in cooperation with Frontex (European Border and Coast Guard Agency) since 2004. Some interesting data, which highlights the adoption of different policies to tackle unlawful immigration and various degrees of relevance of immigration-related issues, including as a result of the countries' specific geographic structure, are provided by the EU Statistical Office. According to Eurostat,[43] in 2018 471,200 individuals were denied entry into the EU-28 territory ('entry refusal'): mostly in Spain (49 per cent), France (15 per cent) and Poland (11 per cent). In Italy, the percentage was only 1.7 per cent. In 84.4 per cent of cases, immigrants were turned back at the borders. Italy, the United Kingdom and Spain are the countries relying the most heavily on intercepting vessels.

[43] The data provided here and below is drawn from the document entitled 'Enforcement of immigration legislation statistics', available at www.ec.europa.eu/eurostat.

Even more significant, however, is the number of apprehensions: in 2018 over 600,000 non-EU citizens were 'arrested' within EU territory, because they were undocumented. In the same year, almost half a million orders of removal were issued against non-EU citizens (478,200) on EU-28 territory. The Member States with the highest number of removal orders were France (22 per cent), Spain (12.4 per cent) and Greece (12.2 per cent). Italy (5.7 per cent) and the UK (4.5 per cent) trail behind.

In the same year, 157,900 individuals were deported (the figure is down compared to 2017 but has been relatively steady in the last 10 years). Further data is available, but only with respect to 22 Member States (noticeably lacking any data for Germany and the UK) concerning removal proceedings. In 50.6 per cent of cases, the same entailed voluntary departure, whereas in 45.7 per cent of cases they entailed forcible return proceedings. For instance, voluntary departure represents, by far, the most common instance of removal proceedings in Poland, Sweden and Romania; on the other hand, forcible returns are, by far, the most common form of removal in Hungary, Portugal, Spain and Italy.

Under EU legislation, removal is referred to as 'repatriation', as regulated under Directive No. 115 of 2008. Repatriation is intended as an administrative measure,[44] subject to appeal before the administrative or judicial authorities (Article 13), to be preferably carried out as voluntary departure, within a reasonable period ranging from seven to 30 days (Article 7). It might entail a re-entry ban usually not exceeding five years – although in some cases this is mandatory (Article 11). Unless other sufficient but less coercive measures are not available in a specific case,

> Member States may only keep in detention a third-country national who is the subject of return procedures in order to prepare the return and/or carry out the removal process, in particular when: a) there is a risk of absconding or b) the third-country national concerned avoids or hampers the preparation of return or the removal process.[45]

Detention may be ordered by administrative or judicial authorities (in the first case, subject to a review by the judicial authority); it may not be maintained for longer than six months, extendable for a limited period not exceeding a further 12 months in case of a lack of cooperation by the individual concerned (for instance, in case of identification issues) or delays in obtaining the necessary documentation from third countries. When it appears that 'a reasonable prospect of removal no longer exists for legal or other considerations' or the aforementioned conditions no longer exist, 'detention ceases to be justified and the person concerned shall be released immediately' (Article 15, paragraphs 4 and 6). Regarding the

[44] Pursuant to Article 2, para 2, letter b) of the Directive, Member States may decide not to apply these provisions 'to third-country nationals who are subject to return as a criminal law penalty or as a consequence of a criminal law penalty, according to national law, or who are the subject of extradition procedures'.

[45] Article 15, paragraph 1.

conditions of detention (Article 16), the Return Directive states that this must take place 'as a rule in specialized detention facilities' and that if a Member State 'cannot provide accommodation in a specialized detention facility and is obliged to resort to prison accommodation, the third-country nationals in detention shall be kept separated from ordinary prisoners'. 'Detainees' must be allowed 'on request, to establish in due time contact with legal representatives, family members and competent consular authorities'. Furthermore, the Directive states that: 'Particular attention shall be paid to the situation of vulnerable person. Emergency health care and essential treatment of illness shall be provided'; 'Relevant and competent national, international and nongovernmental organizations and bodies shall have the possibility to visit detention facilities … Such visits may be subject to authorization'; 'Third-country nationals kept in detention shall be systematically provided with information which explains the rules applied in the facility and sets out their rights and obligations. Such information shall include information on their entitlement under national law to contact the organizations and bodies' referred to above.[46]

Article 1 of the Return Directive sets out a principle which represents – as it should – a cornerstone of immigration law in Europe: returns must take place 'in accordance with fundamental rights as general principles of Community law as well as international law, including refugee protection and human rights obligation'. Unfortunately, in practice, this aim, which is synonymous with a civilised society, is far from being accomplished: administrative detention often violates this principle, taking place in facilities in which conditions are worse than in prisons and which are cleverly and provokingly referred to, by some, as 'administrative detention centres'.[47]

Unfortunately, comprehensive statistical data on the scope of administrative detention is not available for the EU. Some domestic figures are, however, significant, including those relating to Italy and drawn from the 2019 Report to the Parliament presented by the Italian Ombudsman for the Protection of the Rights of Persons Detained or Deprived of Personal Liberty (*Garante Nazionale dei diritti delle persone detenute o private della libertà personale*). In 2018 about 4092 foreigners (43 per cent of whom have been repatriated) were detained in Italian immigration detention centres (under Law Decree n. 13 of 2017, these centres are named '*centri di permanenza per i rimpatri*' or CPR).[48] Illegal immigrants detained

[46] Further provisions are envisaged for the detention of minors and families (Article 17), as well as for dealing with emergency situations, due to the considerably high number of illegal immigrants to be repatriated.

[47] See, among the many, M Bosworth, *La "galera amministrativa" degli stranieri in Gran Bretagna. Un'indagine sul campo* (Napoli, Editoriale Scientifica, 2016); A Pugiotto, 'La "galera amministrativa" degli stranieri e le sue incostituzionali metamorfosi' (2014) 3 *Quaderni Costituzionali* 573.

[48] *Garante Nazionale dei diritti delle persone detenute o private della libertà personale, Relazione al Parlamento* (Rome, 2019) 134, table 2.5. The Report is available at www.garantenazionaleprivatiliberta.it.

therein were third-country nationals who had received an administrative removal order entailing forcible return or a deferred forcible departure order, when these measures cannot be enforced without delays and the conditions for a less coercive measure are not met. The detention may not exceed 180 days and is subject to review by a judge within 48 hours. Legal assistance must be guaranteed, including through the appointment of an attorney at the government's expense.

Alongside CPRs, reception centres are available (first aid centres, first-hospitality centres and centres for asylum seekers), which are not detention facilities, to cope with the ever-increasing emergency of arrivals on the Italian coasts. On the other hand, the situation inside some centres is more problematic due to the restrictions on personal freedom, resulting in de facto detention, occurring quite frequently. The reference is to the five 'hotspots' located in Sicily and Puglia.[49] These 'hotspots', established in 2015, are intended to accommodate undocumented immigrants identified mostly as a result of rescue operations at sea. Here, migrants are identified and then face one of the following decisions: relocation to another facility in Italy or in another EU country, asylum, removal/deportation. In 2018, 13,777 individuals entered these 'hotspots', with their average stay ranging between five and six days. These facilities are surrounded by gates and barbed wire and are guarded by military personnel. Immigrants cannot freely move around in these facilities and usually cannot leave the premises. Detention in these centres is not subject to any judicial review (this is the general rule, according to a certain interpretation, except in case of asylum seekers): on the one hand, this choice can be explained in light of the aim pursued by the law to provide immediate assistance, presumably within 48 hours, after entering the country; on the other hand, we must, however, underline the fact that, in practice, immigrants are held in the centres for longer periods.

Immigration detention centres represent a very problematic issue also in other European countries, where numbers are much higher than in Italy. In the UK,[50] for instance, in 2018, 24,700 people were detained in these centres. There is no maximum detention period and about one third of individuals were detained for more than 28 days.

In France,[51] the *centres et locaux de rétention administrative* hosted, in 2018, more than 45,000 people (42 per cent of which in overseas territories). The average detention period is 14 days (four in overseas territories).

Numbers are smaller in Spain:[52] in 2018, migrants detained in the *Centros de Internamiento de extranjeros* were 7855.

[49] See the *Relazione al Parlamento* (2019) 87.

[50] Source: migrationobservatory.ox.ac.uk.

[51] Source: *Centres et locaux de rétention administrative – Rapport 2018*, at www.lacimade.org.

[52] Data is drawn from *Informe anual 2018 – Mecanismo Nacional de Prevención de la Tortura*, at www.defensordelpueblo.es.

B. In the United States

The fight against illegal immigration in the USA is conducted through large-scale enforcement operations carried out under three policies: apprehend, detain and remove.

The identification of undocumented immigrants on national soil is ICE's main responsibility, whereas CBP is essentially engaged in stopping illegal entries. The number of apprehensions, which are mostly carried out along the border with Mexico, and in the surrounding areas, has been remarkable for quite some time now. Depending on the specific circumstances, apprehended individuals were removed, i.e., forced to go back voluntarily, crossing the border, and/or to waive their application for admission to the United States.[53] Together, ICE and CBP arrested over half a million of undocumented immigrants in 2018: as mentioned, at least the same number of individuals were arrested throughout the EU within the same year.

Paragraph 287 (a) INA authorises immigration officers to arrest without a warrant any undocumented immigrant entering or attempting to enter the United States illegally, or when it is believed that an undocumented immigrant is in the US illegally and is likely to escape where not arrested. Also, officers have the power, without a warrant, to search any vehicle within one hundred air miles from any US border for undocumented immigrants, and to interrogate any individual arrested, detaining the same for a short period.[54] Once arrested, the undocumented immigrant must be taken 'without unnecessary delay' before another officer for further examination, to make any relevant determinations, which are largely subject to discretionary powers.

a) A *first possible outcome* is the undocumented immigrant's release: unless he or she is a suspected terrorist, an individual to be removed as a result of criminal convictions or for whom administrative detention is mandatory (when convicted of aggravated felonies), an undocumented immigrant may be released on conditional parole, pending a removal hearing, or on an immigration bond, which entails payment of no less than USD 1500.[55] For all intents and purposes, these are alternative measures to detention, which ICE has recently combined with Electronic Monitoring Programs involving the use of an electronic bracelet or a voice recognition system through a telephone line (in February 2014, the individuals involved in similar programs were over 20,000).[56]
b) A *second possible outcome* is the placement in expedited removal proceedings, whereby undocumented immigrants are removed *without a hearing before*

[53] See CBP Report (FY 2018), see above n 29.
[54] See Weissbrodt, Danielson and Myers III, above n 8, 308 and ff.
[55] ibid, 327 and ff.
[56] See ICE Report '*Alternative to detention*' of 4 February 2015, at www.oig.dhs.org.

a judge and without any judicial review (unless they are asylum seekers and grounds exist for such review).[57] Therefore, immigration officers are unquestionably vested with 'a broad discretionary power'[58] to remove undocumented immigrants and ban them from re-entering the country for five years. This procedure, despite not being ordinary, has a significant scope of application, so much so that it is followed in 40 per cent of removal cases.[59] These provisions apply to anybody: 1) attempting to enter the USA as an undocumented immigrant or having committed fraud or presented false documentation; 2) who has illegally been in the United States for less than two years, having circumvented border immigration checkpoints;[60] 3) who has been arrested within 100 miles of the border and cannot demonstrate that they have been in the US for more than 14 days.[61]

c) Finally, a *third outcome* is to bring the undocumented immigrant (or summon him or her to appear in court) before an immigration judge for a removal hearing, in the case of individuals who were previously staying in the United States, either because he or she entered the country illegally or because he or she lost his or her legal status (known as 'overstayers'). Usually, undocumented immigrants who are denied entry to the US are not brought before a judge. The immigration judges report to the Department of Justice: they are attorneys appointed by the Attorney General (the United States Minister of Justice),[62] called upon to decide on the removability of the undocumented immigrant, acquiring evidence and cross-examining the concerned party and witnesses. ICE officials act as 'prosecutors'. The hearing is usually public and a notice to appear is served beforehand[63] which includes the charge(s) (in terms of removability) and legal warnings, including the right to appoint a lawyer, who may be chosen from a list of pro-bono lawyers and whose services must be made available to the undocumented immigrant.[64] No legal aid is provided. As is the case with criminal proceedings,[65] the

[57] The expedited removal orders are only subjected to habeas corpus proceedings, which essentially formally establish the immigrant's lawful immigration status in the U.S. based on any related evidence provided by the same. See Weissbrodt, Danielson and Myers III, above n 8, 345.

[58] To this tune, see Weissbrodt, Danielson and Myers III, above n 8, 346.

[59] ibid, 345.

[60] In 2002, this procedure was established to remove a considerable number of Haitians who had arrived by sea (ibid, 344).

[61] Undocumented immigrants convicted of aggravated felonies are subject to partially different expedited removal proceedings (in terms of the administrative or judicial appeals available). See Weissbrodt, Danielson and Myers III, above n 8, 346 and ff.

[62] Up to 1983, immigration judges were part of INS (in other words, they were INS officers). See, ibid, 113.

[63] Where the undocumented immigrant does not appear in court, a default judgment is handed down.

[64] By law, not only lawyers, but also representatives of recognised organisations, as well as law school students or graduates may provide legal assistance, even if not yet licensed to practice law. See, ibid, 335.

[65] For an analysis of such analogy, see, ibid, 339.

immigrant in question is asked to concede or deny the charges. Where the immigrant concedes the charges, as is often the case, the judge accepts the 'plea bargain' and decides whether he or she is eligible for discretionary relief or not, i.e., the granting of various benefits which, under certain conditions, results in removal proceedings being delayed or sometimes simply prevented: voluntary departure (which, in practice, is the most common outcome), cancellation (or suspension) of removal (only for undocumented immigrants who have legally resided in the United States for a certain number of years); status adjustment (for those who satisfy the requirements to obtain a visa immediately); an asylum application.[66] On the contrary, where the undocumented immigrant denies the charges, the proceedings will move forward, and a subsequent hearing will be scheduled (which often entails an extended detention period). Like in a criminal trial, both the prosecutor and the undocumented immigrant may present evidence, although the evidence-gathering rules are different in the two proceedings, and the burden of proof on the public and private parties is also different.[67] ICE has the burden of proving 'by clear and convincing evidence' that the undocumented immigrant previously admitted to the United States is 'deportable'; on the other hand, the alien must demonstrate, once again 'by clear and convincing evidence', his or her lawful immigration status in the US, including after his or her initial admission (§ 240(c)(2) INA).[68]

The decisions of the immigration judge – including those relating to detention and denial of discretionary relief – are for the most part subject to administrative appeal before a Board of Immigration Appeals (BIA), whose members (currently only 15) are appointed by the Department of Justice (by the Attorney General). The appeal proceedings are usually presided over by individual members of the board (who adjudicate cases in panels of three members only where complex matters are involved, suitable to establish a precedent). When initiated, these proceedings stay the enforcement of any removal decision and essentially amount to scrutiny in terms of legality. The immigration judges and the BIA decisions, as well as – in some cases – ICE's administrative orders are subject to judicial review before the district federal courts. However, judicial review – which is admissible, among other things, for detention-related matters, and which entails a constitutional scrutiny and the referral of the related questions to the Supreme Court[69] – was

[66] See, ibid, 347 and ff.

[67] ibid, 340.

[68] A more stringent burden of proof is placed on the undocumented immigrant who has been arrested at the border as a result of being inadmissible, when expedited removal proceedings are not instituted because he or she applied for judicial review: he or she must in fact demonstrate 'clearly and beyond doubt' that they are admissible.

[69] Immigration judges do not have the authority to raise constitutional questions. See Weissbrodt, Danielson and Myers III, above n 8, 338.

significantly restricted as a result of two reforms in 1996 and 2005.[70] The role of immigration judges is actually controversial in the American public debate, where the expression 'ideological minefield' has been used to describe the different positions on this issue, entailing a conflict of visions: on the one hand, there are those 'who perceive the judiciary as an obstructive, anti-democratic institution that delays the removal of deportable non-citizens and displays undue sympathy toward undeserving violators of our laws' (the tone echoes certain conservative rhetorical propaganda used in Italy); on the other hand, there are those 'who perceive the judiciary as a principled and dispassionate dispenser of justice and a bulwark against unlawful government action, particularly important when the litigants (noncitizens) are distinctively exposed to volatile and often hostile political sentiments'.[71]

This clear ideological conflict is even more disturbing considering that, throughout the entire removal proceedings – from arrest to enforcement of the removal order, pending the removal hearing and, in some cases, after unsuccessfully filing administrative or, where admissible, judicial appeals – an undocumented immigrant is often detained in special centres managed by ICE. INA authorises immigration officers to detain undocumented immigrants arrested at the border and not immediately removed (when grounds exist to challenge denied entry into the US before an immigration judge), as well as undocumented immigrants arrested on US soil after having entered the US illegally.[72] Usually, ICE detention centre doors open when ICE officers, following an arrest, do not release an undocumented immigrant on bail or parole and the immigration judge, who must rule within 48 hours of arrest,[73] validates the measure (§§ 236(a), 212(d)(5) INA). The same fate befalls undocumented immigrants in a number of cases in which detention is even mandatory.[74] Mandatory detention also applies to undocumented immigrants who are not authorised to enter and reside in the US as a result of a criminal conviction within a long list of criminal offences (§§ 237 (a) (2), 212 (a) (2)) – including offences involving moral turpitude, aggravated felonies, drug-related crimes, firearms offences and many more – or who are suspected terrorists (§ 1226 (a) INA), as well as those who are not eligible for parole or release on an immigration bail, suffer the same fate. Mandatory detention is also envisaged for asylum seekers when expedited removal proceedings are initiated as a result of failing to provide credible evidence of fears of persecution.[75]

[70] See Johnson et al, above n 2, 434.

[71] SH Legomsky and CM Rodriguez, *Immigration and Refugee Law and Policy* 6th edn (New York, Foundation Press, 2015) ch 9.

[72] See Johnson et al, above n 2, 420 s.

[73] See § 287.3(d) of the Code of Federal Regulations (CFR). Such term does not apply in case of terrorists: ibid, 422.

[74] See Johnson et al, above n 2, 421.

[75] ibid.

Immigration judge decisions are subject to administrative appeal before BIA but are not subject to judicial review when the release on parole or immigration bail is denied, since these decisions are subject to administrative discretion and may not be challenged. However, since the personal freedom of an individual is at stake, habeas corpus proceedings may be instituted before the federal courts of appeal on grounds of a legal error or constitutionality issues (§ 242 (a) INA).[76]

In practice, even in the United States, detention centres for illegal immigrants are 'prison surrogates' and a cause for concerns for activists, lawyers, scholars and, in general, human rights organisations, like in Europe. The author of a recent essay, who did not mince words and titled his paper 'Abolishing immigration prisons', reports a strong statement from a woman who experienced what is referred to as 'civil detention': 'they call immigration detention civil confinement, but prison is prison no matter what label you use, and prison breaks people's souls, hearts, and even minds'.[77] Detention figures – concerning a country that has implemented mass incarceration policies for decades, with about 2,300,000 individuals being detained,[78] a colossal number, are astonishing: in 2012 (record year) 477,523 individuals came within ICE custody[79] and 396,448 in 2018; however, in 2001, i.e., before everything changed after 9/11, this number was down to 95,214.[80] Before the 1980s, no more than 30 immigrants were detained every day.[81]

The percentage of removal orders is around 50 per cent; most individuals are detained in centres located in one state along the Mexican border: Texas.[82] In April 2019, detainees were over 60,000.[83] According to 2016 data, 10 per cent of detainees in immigration centres are held in federally owned and operated facilities; 25 per cent in facilities operated at state level, including prisons scattered in various counties; lastly, 65 per cent are held in facilities run by private entities, obviously for profit.[84] This last figure is very significant: when running detention centres turns into a business, the interest of those who manage it is that centres are crowded, so as to increase their profits. Therefore, in the United States the immigration detention debate does not only focus on human rights issues arising from the restrictions on personal freedom and detention conditions, with individuals being held in centres located outside cities that are hard to reach for family members and

[76] See Weissbrodt, Danielson and Myers III, above n 8, 375 and ff.

[77] See CC García Hernández, 'Abolishing Immigration Prisons' (2017) 97 *Boston University Law Review* 245.

[78] See *Mass incarceration: the whole pie 2019*, at www.prisonpolicy.org. As part of the extensive US literature on mass incarceration, see JF Pfaff, *Locked in. The true causes of mass incarceration and how to achieve real reform* (New York, Basic Books, 2017).

[79] See García Hernández, above n 77, 253.

[80] See Weissbrodt, Danielson and Myers III, above n 8, 45.

[81] See *Immigration Detention Map & Statistics*, at www.endisolation.org.

[82] Source: www.trac.syracuse.edu.

[83] Source: www.trac.syracuse.edu.

[84] DHS-Homeland Security Advisory Council, *Report of the Subcommittee on Privatized Immigration Detention Facilities* (1 December 2016, 7 and ff).

lawyers, but also extends to the related public expenditure, as a result of the pressure exerted on politicians by industry lobbies (which, among other things, are the same lobbies that have operated, since the 1990s, some private prisons which were also 'coincidentally' reserved for immigrants):[85] in the 2018 fiscal year alone, the President of the United States requested that Congress approve, under the DHS budget, a USD 2.7 billion budget to cover the cost for 51,379 beds in immigration detention centres, which have been growing both in number and capacity: in the 2017 fiscal year, approval of a USD 2.2 billion dollar budget was requested to cover the cost for managing 'as little as' 31,000 beds.[86]

Even though a deadline to enforce a removal order, which is 90 days after the order has become final, is provided, a maximum detention period is not provided for by law. However, the Supreme Court introduced a six-month maximum period in 2001 after stressing the fact that an indefinite detention – as is the case when the country of origin refuses to repatriate their citizens – violates the due process of law guaranteed by the Fifth Amendment to individuals deprived of their personal freedom.[87] Moreover, the Supreme Court has stated, on that occasion, that the six-month detention period may be extended, following expiry, in case the undocumented immigrant does not provide sufficient reasons to believe that his or her repatriation is unlikely to take place in the near future and the Government, on its part, provides sufficient evidence to the contrary. In 2019, the Trump administration allowed for the indefinite detention of families with minors.[88] Statistics show that the detention period varies significantly, as reported by the media.

Finally, as regards detention conditions, a very detailed regulation is contained in ICE's Performance-Based National Detention Standards (PBNDS), which dates back to 2011.[89] Such body of rules aims to establish uniform standards in the various centres with respect to several aspects. However, in actual fact, regulatory standards are far from being complied with: civil rights organisations have reported serious issues for some time:

> People in immigration detention are vulnerable to abuse. Immigrants in detention facilities around the United States are often subjected to punitive and long-term solitary confinement. They are subject to inadequate medical care, vulnerable to rape and assault, and often isolated from access to legal assistance and community support.[90]

[85] See JM Chacon, 'Privatized Immigration Enforcement' (2017) 52 *Harvard Civil Rights-Civil Liberties Law Review* 1. See, also, *A toxic relationship: private prisons and U.S. immigration detention* (Detention Watch Network, 2016), www.detentionwatchnetwork.org.

[86] See DHS, Fiscal Year 2018 Budget in brief, at www.dhs.gov.

[87] US Supreme Court, *Zadvydas v Davis*, 533 US 678 (2001).

[88] See B Naylor, *New Trump Policy Would Permit Indefinite Detention Of Migrant Families, Children*, 2019, August 21, knpr.org.

[89] For a detailed analysis covering different scenarios and analyzing the case law, see IJ Kurzban, *Immigration Law Sourcebook* 15th edn (American Immigration Council, 2016) 217 and ff.

[90] See *Immigration Detention Map & Statistics*, at www.endisolation.org. On solitary confinement, see Kurzban, above n 89, 219, as well as ICE Policy No. 11065.1, 'Review of the Use of Segregation for ICE Detainees' (4 September 2013).

In September 2017, a renowned magazine – *The New Yorker* – published an article notably titled, 'A Medical Emergency, and the Growing Crisis at Immigration Detention Centers', in which, among other things, suicides and deaths were reported in the centres: around 170 since 2003.[91] Largely privately run, and widely financed, detention centres clearly do not ensure high detention standards; moreover, it is reasonable to assume – as pointed out by some human rights organisations[92] – that this is a disastrous result of merciless profit-maximising policies implemented with respect to the business of running detention centres.[93]

V. Concluding Remarks: A Problem Concerning Fundamental Human Guarantees and Rights Overlapping with Criminal Law, i.e. the Prohibition against Borrowing Protection Measures and Tools from the Criminal Justice System without Implementing Equivalent Substantive and Procedural Guarantees

In different countries and social backgrounds, on both sides of the Atlantic Ocean, the policies implemented in response to mass immigration have led to the establishment, under public law, of sub-systems governed by administrative law, which, however, have certain features that are specific to criminal law and criminal proceedings. Faced with the need to fight illegal immigration, and by way of enforcement of the administrative rules on entering and residing on State territory, a hybrid, substantially criminal-type system has been established in various countries due to the enforcement agencies deployed and, above all, the *custodial measures being implemented* (arrest, detention and removal) *and related proceedings*. In the fight against illegal immigration, managed by administrative bodies, the use of law enforcement authorities – including police forces – is still a priority to this day. This is corroborated by the public funds that politicians pledge to invest, in all countries, to fight illegal immigration by taking the following steps: improving border immigration enforcement and increasing the number of law enforcement officers on national soil, building walls and fences, increasing the number of beds in detention centres, and so on. This struggle is tightly

[91] The article, written by C Bethea, was published on 13 September 2017 and can be found at www.newyorker.com. See also a recent and interesting report on the conditions of detention centres in Georgia, titled '*Imprisoned justice*', available at www.progectsouth.org.

[92] See *A toxic relationship*, above n 85.

[93] GAO (Government Accountability Office) regularly publishes reports in which it highlights any unmet standards and indicates the actions to be implemented. See, for instance, at in www.gao.gov, the document published on 29 February 2016 entitled 'Additional Actions Needed to Strengthen Management and Oversight of Detainee Medical Care'.

connected – due to criminological issues – to the fight the same entities carry on against some of the criminal activities largely carried out, virtually everywhere, in the framework of illegal immigration, and which cause social alarm: illicit drug trade, trafficking and exploitation of human beings, terrorism. Fighting illegal immigration entails fighting drug trafficking, the smuggling of human beings involving various forms of exploitation (labour and sexual exploitation, such as prostitution), by members of criminal organisations and Islamic terrorists, including potential ones. Nowadays, illegal immigration is a national security issue and entails fighting some of the most serious criminal activities: an issue socially perceived as serious, such as to justify government action to remove, arrest, detain and deport undocumented immigrants who are unwanted as a result of political choices on open borders and on the actual socio-economic benefits and feasibility of reception.

Against this backdrop, one can easily understand the reason behind the broad overlapping of criminal and administrative penalties in different legal systems and the fact that this latter body of legal tools has borrowed, at least in part, from the former, giving rise to crimmigration. This process is based, everywhere, on *conscious political choices*: the use of criminal law tools and techniques *outside the scope of the criminal justice system* to *maximise their efficiency*, leaving out those guarantees which, in such other parallel system, limit the former's scope of application. In US literature, Legomsky pointed this out, speaking of an 'asymmetric incorporation of criminal justice norms' into immigration law: asymmetric because the criminal justice model was essentially introduced without the guarantees set out therein.[94] This happened, to a different extent but in similar ways, both in the United States and in Europe. The legally – and politically – relevant process in question is an expression of what Sklansky effectively described as 'ad hoc instrumentalism': the criminalisation of immigration law essentially entails rules and procedures conceived by politicians as a usable 'set of interchangeable tools' to achieve its ultimate goal, that is, removing undocumented immigrants.[95]

However, both in the United States and in Europe, the issue is that constitutional and supranational principles are incompatible with the idea of stripping 'criminal tools' of their underlying guarantees. Also, 'criminal tool' is a concept formally and substantively falling within the notion of 'criminal matters'. European criminal lawyers and constitutional judges are slowly but surely becoming aware of this on the strength of the case law of the European Court of Human Rights, whereas in the United States such process has just begun. In short, the risk of using misleading terms under immigration law exists with regard to different aspects. Theoretically, such risk is similar to that which Italian criminal lawyers have long

[94] Legomsky, above n 3, 469 and ff.
[95] See Sklansky, above n 3, 161.

identified in other grey areas overlapping, once again, with criminal law: custodial and preventive measures – including confiscation, symbolising, in this context, a Trojan horse – tax and financial offences entailing both criminal and administrative penalties, and others. Indeed, history shows us that legal civilisation requires, everywhere, acknowledging and affirming principles, which must be then faithfully applied, *without looking away*. Fundamental principles – i.e., the guarantees associated with punishment – must apply to everyone, including undocumented immigrants, who, despite being non-citizens, are nonetheless human beings entitled to certain rights that cannot be trampled upon. The scope of fundamental guarantees, which apply with respect to criminal law and even beyond its scope, is imposed by cardinal legal principles, including the principle of equality, which should not come into play only when major economic interests are involved, as is the case with confiscation and tax and market abuse offences,[96] but also – and above all – when the fate of human beings, such as immigrants and their families, are at stake. Such awareness is certainly the result of legal civilisation and must be preserved and handed down to future generations, so as to influence the public opinion and create the conditions for changing the current legal framework, which – as a result of the crimmigration process – often does away with fundamental guarantees. It is a question of enhancing a cultural process, one involving legal civilisation, in which civil rights movements have been playing a major role for some time, often pro-bono, in Europe and in the United States, including many lawyers and college professors, in the context of legal clinics.[97]

Experience shows that such process can produce its greatest and tangible results when what should be institutionally and naturally regarded as the main path is followed, a path that entails enforcing rights *in court*, and in particular, in the higher courts responsible for enforcing fundamental guarantees. This is the course taken in Europe, mainly on the strength of the case law of the European Court of Human Rights,[98] whereas in the United States such process appears to have only recently begun. In this regard, two decisions of the Grand Chamber of the ECtHR are especially significant, both of which concern Italy, whereby breaches of fundamental rights have been ascertained in relation to collective forcible returns at sea, specifically towards Libya[99] and the detention of immigrants in the 'early reception and aid centre' ('*centro di soccorso e prima accoglienza*' or CSPA) of Lampedusa.[100]

[96] Reference is made to certain notorious Italian (and other) cases brought to the attention of the ECtHR.

[97] Legal clinics, which often focus on immigration law, appeared at least forty years ago in the United States. In Italy, the commitment of two academics, Luca Masera (University of Brescia) and Stefano Zirulia (University of Milan), who provided pro-bono legal assistance in notorious proceedings before the European Court on Human Rights (*Khlaifia and others v Italy*, 2016) resulting in Italy being found responsible for the violation of the right to personal liberty (article 5 ECHR) of migrants detained in the first reception centre of Lampedusa.

[98] See the interesting case law, updated to 2019, referenced in *Migrants in detention*, at www.echr.coe.int.

[99] *Hirsi Jamaa v Italy* [GC], Application No 27765/09 (23 February 2012).

[100] *Khlaifia and Others v Italy* [GC], Application No 16483/12 (15 December 2016).

In *Hirsi*, on the one hand, the breach of Article 4 of Protocol 4 ECHR is established, which prohibits collective forced returns, on the grounds that the right of defence is breached; on the other hand, the breach of Article 3 of the ECHR is ascertained due to the risk of migrants being subjected to inhuman or degrading treatment after returning to Libya. In *Khlaifia*, the ECtHR found that immigrants were essentially 'imprisoned without access to a judge', and as a result established that Article 5 of the ECHR had been breached on two grounds, i.e., the lack of a legal basis for restricting an individual's personal freedom and the lack of the conditions for effectively exercising the right of defence. This latter issue was also considered relevant in another decision of the ECtHR,[101] which in 2016 fined Italy for having breached Article 5 ECHR in a case concerning the prolonged detention of non-EU citizens in an immigration detention centre (at that time, 'centres for identification and expulsion' or CIE) summarily ordered by a small claims court (*giudice di pace*), without hearing the concerned parties and their lawyer.

The EU Court of Justice also contributed to affirming the rights of immigrants who get caught in the web of the European 'version' of the crimmigration system.[102] For instance, in interpreting the provisions of the Return Directive in two cases concerning Germany, it established a ban on detaining undocumented immigrants in prison, pending repatriation, together with other ordinary prisoners,[103] stating that the former must be kept in specialised detention centres.[104] Other rulings of the EU Court of Justice concerning 'administrative detention' underlined, based on the principle of proportionality, that this is a last resort measure, and stressed the fact that the right to a defence must be guaranteed, including, first and foremost, in case of prolonged detention (and of its extension), which is not to be granted where it appears unlikely that the person concerned will be admitted to a third country.[105]

It is worth mentioning that the European case law referenced above establishes rights and guarantees *irrespective of whether* the removal proceedings, and detention in immigration centres pending such proceedings, *are subject to criminal law* or otherwise, such issue being utterly irrelevant for the purposes of the ECHR and the Return Directive. On the other hand, should the ECtHR expressly state that administrative detention and/or removal proceedings (especially in case of removal of an immigrant with a residence permit, as a result of his or

[101] *Richmond Yaw and Others v Italy*, Applications No 3342/11, 3391/11, 3408/11 et 3447/11 (6 October 2016).

[102] See Mitsilegas, above n 2, 93–94.

[103] Case C-474/13 *Thi Ly Pham v Stadt Schweinfurt, Amt für Meldewesen und Statistik* [2014] ECLI:EU:C:2014:2096.

[104] Joined Cases C-473/13 and C-514/13 *Adala Bero v Regierungspräsidium Kassel and Ettayebi Bouzalmate v Kreisverwaltung Kleve* [2014] ECLI:EU:C:2014:2095.

[105] Case C-357/09 PPU *Said Shamilovich Kadzoev (Huchbarov)* [2009] ECR I-11219; Case C-383/13 PPU *M G and N R v Staatssecretaris van Veiligheid en Justitie* [2013] ECLI:EU:C:2013:533; Case C-146/14 *Bashir Mohamed Ali Mahdi* [2014] ECLI:EU:C:2014:1320.

her criminal conviction) constitute a criminal matter – based on Engel criteria – the level of guarantees to be granted would be considerably higher (for instance, the *ne bis in idem* principle would apply and, as a result, punishing immigration law breaches as criminal and administrative offences would be problematic). A decision concerning removal proceedings handed down in 2009 on the grounds of Article 7 ECHR seems to provide an indication to that effect. This decision found that a 2003 Spanish law providing that removing an undocumented immigrant convicted of certain offences was mandatory and prolonging the duration of the ensuing re-entry ban was in breach of the prohibition on retroactive application.[106] On the other hand, on the strength of the case law of the ECtHR on the extension of ordinary guarantees to 'criminal matters', in 2010 the Inter-American Court of Human Rights found that the administrative detention of an undocumented immigrant is essentially a criminal penalty and that the principles of due process and legality in criminal proceedings must apply in relation thereto.[107]

As mentioned, the situation in the USA is different: the assessment in terms of constitutionality of the crimmigration system is subject to the legal constraints preventing, or at least limiting, a judicial review by the federal courts, which, unlike immigration judges, have the authority to refer a matter to the Supreme Court. There is more: the Supreme Court traditionally refuses to hear cases concerning such matters, due to the fragile political relations with the Federal Government. The fight against illegal immigration was essentially construed – following a well-known decision handed down in 1889[108] – as a matter implicating foreign affairs, which are traditionally dealt with by the Federal government (known as the 'Plenary Power Doctrine').[109] This constitutional law doctrine represented the strongest argument to justify immigration exceptionalism, as summarised in a 1976 Supreme Court decision: 'in the exercise of its broad power over naturalization and immigration, Congress regularly makes rules that would be unacceptable if applied to citizens'.[110] A further fundamental argument exists that has characterised, for over a hundred years, the case law of the Supreme Court and other federal courts, representing a real 'leitmotif'. Such argument, which has a 'snowballing effect', is that removal orders and related immigration detention must be regarded 'as civil remedies, not as punishment comparable to criminal sanctions'.[111]

[106] *Gurguchiani v Spain*, Application No no 16012/06 (15 December 2009).

[107] Inter-American Court of Human Rights, *Vélez Loor v Panama* (23 November 2010). In this regard, see F Viganò, 'Commento all'art. 9 (Principio di legalità e di retroattività)' in L Cappuccio, M Tanzarella (eds), *Commentario alla prima parte della Convenzione Americana dei Diritti dell'Uomo* (Napoli, ESI, 2017) 303.

[108] US Supreme Court, *Chae Chan Ping v. United States*, 130 U.S. 581 (1889). See, also, a later similar case, US Supreme Court, *Fong Yue Ting v US*, 149 US 698 (1893): 'the right to exclude or to expel all aliens, or any class of aliens … [is] an inherent and inalienable right of every sovereign and independent nation'.

[109] See Johnson et al, above n 2, 123.

[110] US Supreme Court, *Mathews v. Diaz*, 426 U.S. 67 (1976), para II.

[111] To this effect, Stumpf, above n 1, 392.

Following a 1893 landmark ruling,[112] the Supreme Court has consistently maintained that 'the order of deportation is not a punishment for crime':[113] this statement constitutes the grounds for denying the application of the guarantees granted under the criminal justice system to immigration law breaches, which in turn results in situations which, to quote Legomsky, would be 'unthinkable in criminal cases'.[114] The list of guarantees that case law does not extend to immigration law is long and includes principles enshrined in the American Constitution,[115] such as the ban of cruel and unusual punishment,[116] double jeopardy clause (*ne bis in idem* principle),[117] the prohibition of ex post facto laws,[118] the Miranda warnings,[119] the presumption of innocence,[120] the privilege against self-incrimination,[121] the exclusionary rule (prohibition against using illegally obtained evidence, for instance as a result of an (illegal) search),[122] the right to counsel[123] and the right of trial by jury.[124] The situation in which the undocumented immigrant finds himself in the US system is clearly described by Kanstrom:

> Imagine a non-citizen about whom the government has some suspicion. He might be arrested … as a suspected undocumented alien, an overstay, for failure to report an address change, etc. This might occur pursuant to a tip, during a workplace raid, or even on the street simply because he 'looks' undocumented to an agent. What rights will

[112] Above n 108.

[113] 'It is not a banishment, in the sense in which that word is often applied to the expulsion of a citizen from his country by way of punishment. It is but a method of enforcing the return to his own country of an alien who has not complied with the conditions upon the performance of which the Government of the nation, acting within its constitutional authority, and through the proper departments, has determined that his continuing to reside here shall depend'.

[114] Legomsky, above n 3, 518.

[115] ibid, 511–12.

[116] Above n 108.

[117] See US Court of Appeals, Second Circuit, *Oliver v INS*, 1975.

[118] See US Supreme Court, *Mahler v Eby*, 264 US 32 (1924): deportation as a result of convictions for which they were not deportable at the time when the crime was committed does not violate the inhibition of ex post facto laws, which applies only to criminal laws ('deportation is not punishment').

[119] US Court of Appeals, Second Circuit, *US v Silva*, 1983.

[120] US Court of Appeals, Seven Circuit, *Chavez-Raya v INS*, 1975.

[121] US Court of Appeals, Seven Circuit, *Laqui v INS*, 1970: in removal hearings, non-citizens may claim the privilege against self-incrimination only if their alleged actions constitute a crime. On the other hand, the Supreme Court (*Hyun v Landon*, 350 US 590 1956) affirmed the right of the immigration judge to draw unfavourable inferences from the non-citizen's silence.

[122] See US Supreme Court, *INS v Lopez-Mendoza*, 468 US 1032 (1984): 'The exclusionary rule does not apply in a deportation proceeding'; 'A deportation proceeding is a purely civil action to determine a person's eligibility to remain in this country. The purpose of deportation is not to punish past transgressions, but rather to put an end to a continuing violation of the immigration laws. Consistent with the civil nature of a deportation proceeding, various protections that apply in the context of a criminal trial do not apply in a deportation hearing'.

[123] Reference is made to the fact that no pro-bono legal representation is available (as is the case, on the contrary, in criminal proceedings), but also to other scenarios. For instance, an applicant for admission at the border is not provided with the right to representation, unless he or she has become the focus of a criminal investigation and has been taken into custody (§ 292.5(b) Code of Federal Regulation).

[124] See US Supreme Court, *Fong Yue Ting v US*, 149 US 698 (1893).

> such a person have? As to the arrest, his rights will be minimal. He will be very unlikely to argue for suppression of evidence that may have been seized in violation the Fourth Amendment. He will not be read Miranda rights. Indeed, he may not even be advised that he has the right to obtain a lawyer until after a government agent has interrogated him. He will never have the right to appointed counsel. He will, of course, never have a right to a jury trial. At his hearing before the immigration judge, he may even find that the burden of proof will be shifted to him, once the government has made a showing of 'alienage.' And that showing may be as minimal as a birth certificate from a foreign country with a name on it that is similar to his. If he seeks an appeal of the Immigration Judge's decision he may well face incarceration during the length of that appeal – which could easily be years. He may then receive a summary decision by a single member of the Board of Immigration Appeals that is the product of ten minutes of review of his case. If he seeks a further appeal to a federal court he may well find that court declining review of 'discretionary' questions such as his potential eligibility for 'relief' from removal.[125]

Against this disheartening scenario, driven by centuries-old case law, a possible reversal of this trend may be signalled by a 2010 decision by the Supreme Court, upheld by legal scholars, which envisioned a 'reason to hope'.[126] In *Padilla v Kentucky*,[127] the Court was called upon to determine whether the right to effective defence guaranteed by the Constitution 'in criminal proceedings' applies only to criminal penalties or extends to non-criminal ones, including removal; in other words, the Court was called upon to establish whether such guarantee, enshrined in the VI Amendment, entails an obligation for the defendant's lawyer to inform him or her as to the risk of being removed where a plea bargain is entered for a criminal offence involving removal. The facts of the case submitted before the Court are as follow: Jose Padilla, born in Honduras, had been a lawful permanent resident of the United States for over 40 years, and – among other things – had served the United States as a member of the military during the Vietnam war. His run-ins with justice began when he was pulled over while driving a truck transporting a large quantity of marijuana. The charge was among those entailing compulsory removal in case of conviction or plea bargain. Padilla's lawyer failed to advise him that deportation would follow from the proposed plea when proposing it, reassuring him that he had no reason to worry about his immigration status, having been a permanent resident for a long time. As a result of his lawyer's incompetence, Padilla accepted the plea bargain and a removal order was issued. The Kentucky Court denied the related appeal, claiming that the VI Amendment did not apply to that case, on the grounds that such order was a mere 'collateral effect'

[125] D Kanstrom, 'Criminalizing the Undocumented: Ironic Boundaries of the Post-September 11th "Pale of Law"' (2004) 29 *North Carolina Journal of International Law and Commercial Regulation* 639, 650.

[126] See, for instance, PL Markowitz, 'Deportation is Different' (2011) 13 *University of Pennsylvania Journal of Constitutional Law* 1299.

[127] US Supreme Court, *Padilla v Kentucky*, 559 US 356 (2010).

of the decision. On the contrary, the Supreme Court endorsed the opposing view by a majority vote:

> The counsel must inform her client whether his plea carries a risk of deportation. Our longstanding Sixth Amendment precedents, the seriousness of deportation as a consequence of a criminal plea, and the concomitant impact of deportation on families living lawfully in this country demand no less.[128]

In his dissenting opinion, Justice Scalia, a traditionally conservative member, denied that the grounds for applying the guarantee, which was instead granted by the Court, was based on a well-established principle, arguing that the right to an effective defence should be limited to criminal consequences. Whereas the opinion of the Court delivered by Justice Stevens did not expressly spell out the principle that removal as a result of a plea bargain is a criminal penalty, it came very close to doing so by rejecting the distinction between direct and collateral consequences of a plea bargain, stressing the fact that removal 'as a consequence of a criminal conviction is, because of its close connection to the criminal process, uniquely difficult to classify as either a direct or a collateral consequence'. The Supreme Court went so far to state that it 'is an integral part – indeed, sometimes the most important part – of the penalty that may be imposed on noncitizen defendants who plead guilty to specified crimes'. This does not mean that it constitutes a criminal penalty:

> We have long recognized that deportation is a particularly severe 'penalty', Fong Yue Ting v United States, 149 US 698, 740 (1893); but it is not, in a strict sense, a criminal penalty. Although removal proceedings are civil in nature, see INS v Lopez-Mendoza, 468 US 1032, 1038 (1984), deportation is nevertheless intimately related to the criminal process. Our law has enmeshed criminal convictions and the penalty of deportation for nearly a century. And, importantly, recent changes in our immigration law have made removal nearly an automatic result for a broad class of noncitizen offenders. Thus, we find it 'most difficult' to divorce the penalty from the conviction in the deportation context. United States v Russell, 686 F. 2d 35, 38 (CADC 1982). Moreover, we are quite confident that noncitizen defendants facing a risk of deportation for a particular offense find it even more difficult. See St. Cyr, 533 US, at 322 ('There can be little doubt that, as a general matter, alien defendants considering whether to enter into a plea agreement are acutely aware of the immigration consequences of their convictions').[129]

Perhaps due to the specific circumstances of the case – removal of a Vietnam War veteran who had resided in the US for over 40 years – and the political background (the decision was handed down in the early days of Obama's presidency), the Supreme Court seemed open to extending criminal guarantees to immigration law. It is a landmark decision because there was no precedent along those lines, except for the aforementioned decision which, in 2001, stated that the maximum

[128] ibid, para V.
[129] ibid, para II.

term for 'civil detention' was six months[130] and the aforementioned decision issued in 1951,[131] in which the concept of 'crime of moral turpitude' is subject to a sufficient definiteness scrutiny, i.e., the same standard of review applicable to criminal statutes. More specifically, the Court pointed out that, despite not being contained in a criminal statute, such concept applies (as a precondition) to a measure – removal – essentially amounting to a criminal penalty: 'deportation is a drastic measure and at times the equivalent of banishment or exile. It is the forfeiture for misconduct of a residence in this country. Such a forfeiture is a penalty'.[132] Another recent landmark decision of the Supreme Court later endorsed this principle. In 2018, in *Sessions v Dimaya*,[133] for the first time in its history (as pointed out by Justice Thomas in his dissenting opinion), the US Supreme Court found that a provision of the Immigration and Nationality Act (INA) on removal of an undocumented immigrant as an administrative consequence of a criminal conviction was 'unconstitutionally vague'. It did so after emphasising the fact that a removal order constitutes punishment: 'a particularly severe penalty which may be of greater concern to a convicted alien than any potential jail sentence', a penalty that, when it is the result of a criminal conviction, it is 'intimately related to the criminal process', and therefore must be subjected to the same standard of review with respect to the principles of legality and definiteness of criminal statutes.

The path towards rooting fundamental rights within legal systems fighting illegal immigration is long and challenging in all countries. The decisions in *Padilla v Kentucky*, first, and then in *Sessions v Dimaya*, show that such path entails acknowledging that removal of a lawful resident as a result of a criminal conviction is essentially a criminal penalty, amounting to a modern 'version' of a banishment or exile,[134] whereas it is not a restorative measure, as one could reasonably argue in relation to a removal order resulting from an immigration law breach with regard to entering and residing in a host country.[135] At the same time, the views that unfolded in Europe – with reference to the case law of the ECtHR – on the one hand, reinforce the idea that such path is a viable option, on

[130] *Zadvydas v Davis*, n 87 above.

[131] *Jordan v De George*, n 34 above.

[132] On this subject, including later development in the Supreme Court case law, see JL Koh, 'Crimmigration and the Void for Vagueness Doctrine' (2016) 6 *Wisconsin Law Review* 1127.

[133] US Supreme Court, *Sessions v. Dimaya*, 584 U.S. (2018). Observations on this aspect are provided in GL Gatta, 'La 'materia penale' oltre Oceano: una storica sentenza della Corte Suprema U.S.A. innalza lo standard di tutela delle garanzie fondamentali correlate all'espulsione dello straniero' (2018) *Diritto penale contemporaneo*, 7 May.

[134] See D Kanstrom, 'Deportation, Social Control, and Punishment: Some Thoughts about Why Hard Laws Make Bad Cases' (2000) 113 *Harvard Law Review* 1890. See, also, J Bleichmar, 'Deportation as Punishment: a Historical Analysis of the British Practice of Banishment and its Impact on Constitutional Law' (1999) 14 *Georgetown Immigration Law Journal* 114.

[135] On the distinction between restorative justice and penalties, see CE Paliero and A Travi, *La sanzione amministrativa. Profili sistematici* (Milano, Giuffrè, 1988) 43 and ff.

the strength of Engel criteria, upon recognition that removal orders and administrative detention are 'criminal matters'; on the other hand, it shows another, perhaps even more straightforward, option involving the acknowledgement of fundamental rights, as the ECHR provisions do, to some extent, focus on the protected value (i.e., individual and personal freedom) rather than the measures restricting the same (i.e., the criminal penalty). This is the case with Article 3 of the ECHR which, in establishing the prohibition against 'inhuman or degrading treatment or punishment', does not limit the scope of action to criminal penalties alone, thus covering the administrative detention of immigrants and the entire removal or forced return proceedings. This is also the case with Article 5 ECHR, which, in establishing the rights and guarantees concerning personal freedom in case of arrest or detention, does not exclude from its scope of action measures adopted outside the criminal justice system that are instrumental to identifying and removing undocumented immigrants (the decisions in *Khlaifia v Italy* and *Richmond Yaw v Italy* endorse such view).

The path allowing for the bar to be raised in relation to guarantees under immigration law, in line with the severity of criminal law instruments, appears to have been outlined, at least in principle. There is no need to incorporate immigration law into the criminal system to achieve this goal. The two systems can and must remain separate. However, in those cases in which immigration law veers dangerously close to criminal law, the guarantees established therein must also apply, due to the severity of the penalties or the fact that, in any case, fundamental human rights are affected. If the price to pay is a less effective or less simplified action to contrast phenomena giving rise to social alarm, that price must be paid: the commitment to principles requires just that, to protect fundamental human rights and the rule of law, under which we all wish to continue living, rather than in a police state.

4

The Connections between Migration, Crime and Punishment

Historical and Sociological Questions

DARIO MELOSSI*

I. Introduction

The issue of migration and, together with it, of migrants' criminal behaviour, has been central to the socio-criminological enterprise from its very beginning.[1] The issue of migrants' crime has accompanied migration processes, no matter what kind of migration was involved. No matter, for instance, whether the migrants were national or international migrants. Even if the 'foreign' label of migrants may certainly increase the possibility of 'othering' (that is the fixation, in social interaction, of a negative label based on some supposedly essential negative features of the 'other') such othering is connected to the very fact of masses of population moving from one area to another, also inside the borders of a national territory. Indeed, some of the most obvious examples of othering in the twentieth century have been connected to migratory movements *inside* a nation, such as in the case of African-Americans moving from the Southern States in

* This is the written and deeply revised version of a talk that I gave at the Conference 'Managing Migration through Criminal Law Tools', 3–4 December 2018, University of Milan. I would like to thank the organisers of the Conference, Gian Luigi Gatta, Valsamis Mitsilegas and Stefano Zirulia for having invited me and for their feedback on previous versions of this chapter. This is largely based on a Seminar I have been teaching for many years at the School of Law of the University of Bologna on 'Migration, Deviance, and Social Control'. I would like to thank the many participants to those seminars, colleagues, young researchers and students, for having helped me to try and think through many of the issues that are here to follow.

[1] D Melossi, *Crime Punishment and Migration* (London, SAGE, 2015).

Northern and Western direction between the 1920s and 1960s,[2] Southern Italians moving North – toward Central and Northern Europe but also toward Northern Italy – in the 1950s and 1960s[3] or finally, more recently, Chinese people moving from the countryside toward the seaboard of China in the last few decades.[4] In other words, the othering can be constructed in a way that is not necessarily marked by a different nationality.

II. Savage Others

It is rather the basic 'savagery' of the others, the reason for the horror of the self-righteous conformists who help construct their image. Such savagery may be applied to any subject: Lombroso's 'criminals resemble savages and the colored races. These three groups have many characteristics in common ….'[5] Savagery however applies also to class or gender inferiors, as in the description of those who were massacred in the aftermath of the Paris Commune,[6] or to the women 'witches' of Silvia Federici.[7] One of the essential characteristics of the savage, besides a number of supposedly annoying features (like being dirty, smelly, lazy, oversexed, promiscuous, etc) is that of being violence- and crime-prone. That such threatening features may apply to the most disparate human subjects is a good indication of the fact that, very probably, the source for such label of dangerousness is to be looked for in the very definitions of these outsiders as, in fact, outsiders, others, savages, etc. As Marx was writing at the very eve of modernity, commenting on the peasants expelled from their lands by those 'enclosures' that signaled the entry of capitalism into their lands and society:

> The proletariat created by the breaking up of the bands of feudal retainers and by the forcible expropriation of the people from the soil, this 'free' proletariat could not

[2] I Wilkerson, *The Warmth of Other Suns: The Epic Story of America's Great Migration* (New York, Random House, 2010); C Muller, 'Northward Migration and the Rise of Racial Disparity in American Incarceration, 1880–1950' (2012) 118 *American Journal of Sociology* 281–326.

[3] D Montaldi and F Alasia, *Milano, Corea. Inchiesta sugli immigrati negli anni del 'miracolo'* (Milano, Feltrinelli, 1960).

[4] LY Zhong, *Communities, Crime and Social Capital in Contemporary China* (Cullompton, Willan, 2009), A Shen, *Internal Migration, Crime, and Punishment in Contemporary China* (Cham, Springer, 2018).

[5] C Lombroso, *Criminal Man*, translated with a new Introduction by M Gibson and NH Rafter (Durham, Duke University Press, 2006) 91.

[6] J Merriman, *Massacre. The Life and Death of the Paris Commune of 1871* (New Haven, Yale University Press, 2014) 207.

[7] S Federici, *Caliban and the Witch. Women, the Body and Primitive Accumulation* (Brooklyn, Autonomedia, 2004).

> possibly be absorbed by the nascent manufacturers as fast as it was thrown upon the world. On the other hand, these men, suddenly dragged from their wonted mode of life, could not as suddenly adapt themselves to the discipline of their new condition. They were turned *en masse* into beggars, robbers, vagabonds, partly from inclination, in most cases from stress of circumstances. Hence at the end of the 15th century and during the whole of the 16th century, throughout Western Europe a bloody legislation against vagabondage. The fathers of the present working class were chastised for their enforced transformation into vagabonds and paupers. Legislation treated them as 'voluntary' criminals and assumed that it depended on their own good will to go on working under the old conditions that no longer existed.[8]

This very phenomenon, of a legislation and a society that punishes people for having become what that society has helped them to become, has been going on continuously till our very days. Together with that phenomenon, we have also had apologists of capitalism and moralists who have been proclaiming that indeed such 'criminals' are criminals and they should therefore be recognised as such and punished.[9] That under the image of criminals may dwell the most diverse human beings in terms of sex, age, origins, social class, etc, all made similar by their label of foreigners or anyway outsiders, has never being an obstacle to the activities of moral entrepreneurs, questionable social scientists perhaps but such pious individuals!

III. Sociology, Migration and Crime

So, we found migration and crime to be a focus of debate within the Positive School, with Cesare Lombroso, the mercurial founder of the new School of Criminal Anthropology, lambasting migrants for being crime-prone[10] and his junior colleague Enrico Ferri[11] upholding emigration as one of the best 'penal substitutes', at least for the country that migrants leave. This seems to be borne out in Figure 1, where the data of Italian imprisonment admissions appear inversely related to data on emigration from Italy, especially during the main emigration periods, at the beginning of the twentieth-century and after World War Two.

[8] K Marx, *Capital. Volume I, 1867* (New York, International Publishers, 1967) 734.

[9] For the Italian case see M Barbagli, *Immigrazione e sicurezza in Italia* (Bologna, il Mulino, 2008).

[10] Lombroso, above n 5, 316–17.

[11] E Ferri, *Sociologia criminale, 1884* (Milano, Feltrinelli, 1979) 93; E Ferri, *Dei sostitutivi penali* (Torino, Roux and Favale, 1880).

Figure 1 Prison Admission Rates and Emigration Rates in Italy (1881–1965) per 100,000

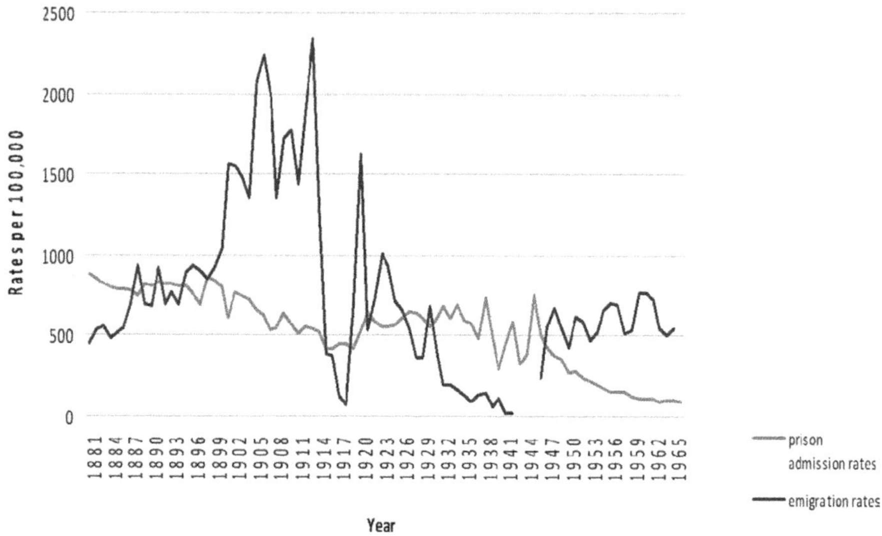

Source: My elaboration of ISTAT data.

It will only be with the rise of American social sciences in the twentieth century, however, that the issue of migration would become central to sociological debate, starting with the American school of sociology par excellence, the Chicago School of sociology. It could not be otherwise. Chicago, in the first few decades of the twentieth century, was the quintessential city of the American dream built on migrants: a magnet for industry, jobs and urbanisation, the sociology of migration in these very years became one and the same with sociology in general. The story of American migration was the story of America itself. The Chicago sociologists were unabashedly pro-migration and certainly not only for reasons having to do with human rights. Paradoxically, their being pro-migration was steeped in their Social Darwinist vision, a Social Darwinism that only the contact with Pragmatism will later make more sophisticated, both politically and sociologically. In a landmark essay on 'Human Migration and the Marginal Man' the doyen of the Chicago School, Robert E Park, countered theories basing cultural differences on 'physical environment' or 'race' and favoured instead what he called a 'catastrophic theory of progress', according to which 'the forces which have been decisive in the history of mankind are those which have brought men together in fruitful competition, conflict, and co-operation'. And, he goes on, 'among the most important of these influences have been migration and the incidental collisions, conflicts, and fusions of people and cultures which they have occasioned'.[12]

[12] RE Park, 'Human Migration and the Marginal Man' (orig publ 1928) in RE Park, *On Social Control and Collective Behaviour* (Chicago, The University of Chicago Press, 1967) 194, 195.

The debate about migration, and more specifically about migration and crime, has often been fraught with charged political and cultural meaning. Indeed, migrants are part of that section of the population which has been more likely to become the focus of social pressure and criminal justice interest. And always the debate among sociologists and criminologists has been about whether the reason of such interest was the higher crime propensity of migrants or their higher exposure to processes of criminalisation. At the beginning of his career, a young Edwin Sutherland would write:

> Poverty in the modern city generally means segregation in low-rent sections, where people are isolated from many of the cultural influences and forced into contact with many of the degrading influences. Poverty generally means a low status, with little to lose, little to respect, little to be proud of, little to sustain efforts to improve. It generally means bad housing conditions, lack of sanitation in the vicinity, and lack of attractive community institutions. It generally means both parents being away from home for long hours, with the fatigue, lack of control of children, and irritation that go with these. It generally means withdrawal of the child from school at an early age and the beginning of mechanical labour, with weakening of the home control, the development of anti-social grudges, and lack of cultural contacts. Poverty, together with the display of wealth in shop-windows, streets, and picture shows, generally means envy and hatred of the rich and the feeling of missing much in life, because of the lack of satisfaction of the fundamental wishes. Poverty seldom forces people to steal or become prostitutes in order to escape starvation. It produces its effects most frequently on the attitudes, rather than on the organism. But it is surprising how many poor people are not made delinquents, rather than how many are made delinquents.[13]

Today, we could write, 'it is surprising how many migrants are not made delinquents, rather than how many are made delinquents'!

IV. The Double Dark Figure of Migrants' Crime

The poor, the (poor) ethnic and national minorities, the migrants, have always been the focus of more intense scrutiny by apparatuses of control, and this essentially for two reasons.

Basing ourselves on official Italian statistics, we have some information about the types of crime for which foreigners have especially been reported (in Italy).[14] Thefts are certainly important, and make up about 15 per cent of reports against foreigners. The other crimes for which foreigners are usually reported, in measure

[13] EH Sutherland, *Criminology* (Philadelphia, Lippincott, 1924) 169–70.

[14] In what follows I base myself on my critique of Barbagli's work in D Melossi, 'Soliti noti' (2010) III(3) *Etnografia e ricerca qualitativa* 449–58. I refer to this work for all information and details.

substantially higher than their proportion in the population, are those connected to migration laws ('status crimes', that only the migrants can commit!), falsity in statements and acts, drug peddling, resistance to public officer, organising prostitution rings, all crimes for which intervention or investigation by law enforcement are essential, therefore crimes that, for the most part, are initiated by the public authority, usually the police.

Furthermore, in order for us to know that such crimes have been committed by migrants (or at least foreigners), we must (obviously) have that kind of information. We are dealing, that is, with actual crime reports against suspected individuals. In these cases, there has usually been therefore a minimum of investigation which led to the conclusion that Mr (or more rarely Mrs) so and so is suspected of having committed a certain crime. The crime reports against known suspects are much fewer than the reports against unknown, usually, in Italy, about one fourth of the total reported crimes. If we want to compare, therefore, the number of crimes for which a foreigner was incriminated to the universe of crimes reported (for which somebody was incriminated) we have, first of all, to trust the total number of reports as an unbiased representation of the real number of crimes committed. Victimisation surveys, however, tell us that generally, at least in Italy, approximately 35 per cent of crimes committed are reported (with very large differences from crime to crime). Among the reported ones, only one fourth, as we have seen, have a known authors who has been incriminated. If we multiply 0.35 by 0.25 we obtain a number that is a bit less than one in 10 cases. Therefore, when somebody comes to the conclusion that 'data available leave us no doubt that foreigners present in our country commit a quantity of crimes out of proportion to their number in the population',[15] this statement is based on consideration of what goes on in a sample of about 10 per cent of all committed crimes. That statement would still be correct, however, if we could consider this (less than) 10 per cent as an *unbiased* sample taken from the universe of all those who have committed a crime. Unfortunately, this is very unlikely. The data on which analyses of migrants' over-representation in crime statistics are based (such as Barbagli's) are data essentially produced by police activity and they cannot be considered unbiased representations of the universe of crimes (even if we were to abstract from economic and financial crimes!). Comparing the percentage of crime reports lodged against foreigners to the percentage of foreigners in the population means ignoring the enormous filtering function that control agencies carry out to somehow "select", out of 10 potential crimes, the one that will ultimately produce a crime report against a foreigner! This is what I call the 'double dark figure' of migrants' crime.

Why, however, would law enforcement agencies have a greater chance to report foreigners? There is, first of all, ethnic, or national, or racial, profiling.

[15] Barbagli, above n 9, 104.

Discrimination by the police is not so much an openly ideological or voluntary matter – even if that also may be present! – it is a much more complicated question, of course, because, as the whole debate on 'institutional' or 'structural' discrimination in English speaking countries taught us, it concerns the type of crime the police are concerned with, the interaction between the police and the migrants, the type of guidance that is given to the police by its political overseers, the pressure of the media, and many other questions that in a certain sense end up predetermining the result.[16] As it was observed by an Italian police unionist, Rita Parisi,

> cops are [not] more racist than others, it just is that, like many, they struggle to recognize a racist act. … When you read newspapers immigrants are all criminals. Add to this the fact that the police officer divides the world between suspects and non-suspects; and that for him to find a foreign drug dealer is the easiest thing in the world. Then you will understand why courts are full of foreigners.[17]

If there is more 'attention' paid towards one group than another, it is clear that this will then have repercussions at all levels of the process, from the reports against known suspects to convictions, from detentions to punishments. This overall situation therefore sets in motion what Bernard Harcourt called 'ratchet effect':[18] if we fish more intensely in a certain stretch of sea, it is clear that we will catch more fish there, catching more fish will then be interpreted as 'hard evidence' of the appropriateness of the decision to fish more intensely in that stretch of sea, so that it will be decided to invest even more resources in that specific area, and so on, and so on, until a situation is reached when a disproportionate amount of resources is wasted in trying to pursue results which are characterised by an increasingly lesser marginal utility.

V. Lack of Documentation and Overrepresentation of Migrants in the Criminal Justice System

After all that has been said, it should be noted that the migrants who are reported are, however, largely 'undocumented', between 60 and 80 per cent of all those

[16] D Melossi (ed), *Multiculturalismo e sicurezza in Emilia-Romagna: prima parte*, Quaderno n. 15, Città Sicure Project (Bologna, Regione Emilia-Romagna, 1999); G Fabini, 'Internal Bordering in the Context of Undeportability. Border Performances in Italy' (2019) 23 *Theoretical Criminology* 175–93; G Fabini, 'Managing Illegality at the Internal Border. Governing through "Differential Inclusion" in Italy' (2017) 14 *European Journal of Criminology* 46–62; F Jobard and R Lévy, *Profiling Minorities: A Study of Stop-and-Search Practices in Paris* (New York, Open Society Institute, 2009); N Jones, 'Color-Blind Cops: How Racism Makes Its Way into Everyday Policing', Invited Talk at the Center for the Study of Law and Society, School of Law, University of California, Berkeley, 21 October 2019.

[17] Melossi, above n 14, 455.

[18] BE Harcourt, *Against Prediction: Profiling, Policing, and Punishing in an Actuarial Age* (Chicago, The University of Chicago Press, 2007).

reported, according to the type of crime.[19] For these, there are very good reasons to assume that the reporting mechanism just described, simply *amplifies* a situation of possible greater contribution to criminal activities (to which one should always add: those criminal activities which are more likely to fall under the purview of the police), both those relating to crimes of subsistence and those concerning the attempt to pass themselves off as regulars.[20] In such connection, it is very interesting to consider an elaboration of ISTAT and Caritas data done by Zelia Gallo[21] on the number of inmates and foreign inmates in Italy between 1990 and 2016 (see Figure 2), which also reports the rate of overrepresentation of foreigners.

Figure 2 Italy – Total inmates and foreign inmates 1990–2016 with rate of over-representation

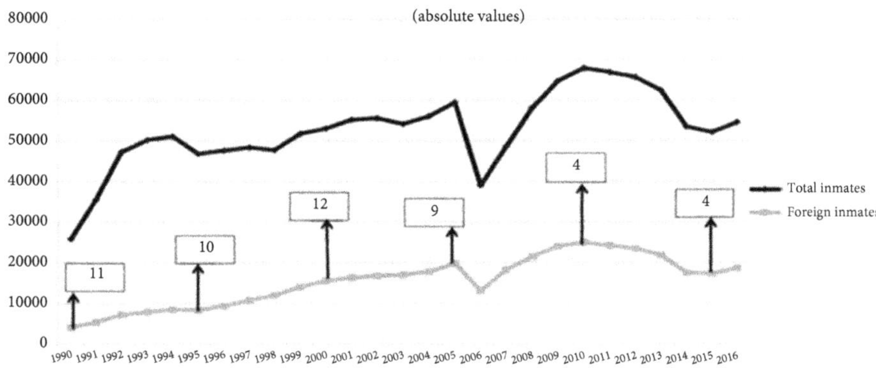

Source: Gallo, above n 21.

The rate of overrepresentation is calculated simply by dividing the percentage of foreigners among the prison population by the percentage of foreigners in the general population (numbers in the squares). In this manner one has an estimate of the higher likelihood to meet a foreigner in prison vis à vis to meet one in the general population. As one can see, in the 1990s, in Italy, notwithstanding the low total numbers of foreigners in the population, the rate of overrepresentation was quite high, hovering around 10 times and higher until the onset of the economic crisis and of the so-called 'Arab Spring', about 2010. As one can see in Figure 2, the rise of detentions after the amnesty provision of 2006 is steeper for the total number of prisoners than for the number of foreign prisoners, to the point that the rate of overrepresentation goes down to 'only' four times, a number that stays stable until 2016. The two processes that start in conjunction with the economic

[19] S Crocitti, 'Immigration, Crime, and Criminalization in Italy' in S Bucerius and M Tonry (eds), *Ethnicity, Crime, and Immigration* (New York, Oxford University Press, 2014) 791, 816–18.

[20] V Ferraris, *Immigrazione e criminalità* (Roma, Carrocci, 2012).

[21] Z Gallo, 'I migranti nella penalità contemporanea: penalità, politica, economia e migrazione' Invited Lecture at the Course of Criminology, School of Law, University of Bologna, 28 April 2017.

crisis and the Arab Springs and that are relevant to what we are discussing here are, on the one hand, the relative slowdown in the in-flow of 'economic migrants' due to the economic crisis (an inflow that until then had been characterised by a steady number of undocumented people whose positions would be later somehow 'remedied' (*sanata*) by governmental decrees or parliamentary acts). On the other hand, there was a rather sudden increase in the flow of 'refugees' from war-torn areas of Africa and the Middle East, refugees whose status as such started to be recognised by Italian authorities around the same time. Such status would still be very 'precarious', especially because very rarely would the refugee be recognised with the full rights of an asylum seeker but much more often he or she would be granted the limited and temporary position of 'humanitarian protection' (a possibility that the Conte-Salvini government of 2018–19 has cancelled and that, at time of writing, the current Italian government has not yet reinstated). Such limited status however would still be preferable to that of an undocumented migrant because it would confer limited rights among which the right to employment. And indeed, what followed in the years of the crisis and immediately afterwards was a true 'refugeeization of the workforce' as Dines and Rigo called it,[22] particularly in agriculture, where migrants, especially from Africa, were recruited as daily labourers in precarious occupations. A possible hypothesis we could then make in order to explain the decline in prison overrepresentation after 2010 is that such limited possibility of lawful employment (even if lawful according to migration laws, certainly not according to labour and fiscal laws) may have however in part protected the migrants from entering in the vicious circle of illegality where the only possibility of making an income are illegal or downright criminal, which in turn brings to processes of criminalisation that are self-perpetuating, as thoroughly explained by the 1960s sociology of deviance.[23] In this sense, the Conte-Salvini government of 2018–19 has set up a true socio-criminological experiment by abolishing the possibility of claiming humanitarian protection. In the years after October 2018, the year of the promulgation of Salvini's so-called 'security decree', the processes of criminalisation of migrants who cannot any longer claim a right to humanitarian protection, should increase, and the rate of overrepresentation of foreigners in jail should therefore start again to increase.

Such situation of overrepresentation, however, is not only Italian. As one can see from Table 1 – a table that I have elaborated a long time ago from Eurostat and the King's Centre for Prison Studies data and that I have been regularly updating until the latest version here presented – almost all the countries of the European Union have an estimate of overrepresentation of foreigners in correctional institutions that goes from the one to three times of the UK and Ireland to the seven to 10

[22] N Dines and E Rigo, 'Postcolonial Citizenships and the "Refugeeization" of the Workforce: Migrant Agricultural Labor in the Italian Mezzogiorno' in S Ponzanesi and G Colpani (eds), *Postcolonial Transitions in Europe: Contexts, Practices and Politics* (Lanham, Rowman & Littlefield Publishers, 2015) 151–72.

[23] H Becker, *Outsiders* (New York, The Free Press, 1963).

of Greece[24] (for comparison purposes, one should think that the same number for African Americans in the US – usually mentioned as a paragon of prison population disparity! – is slightly higher than three).

Table 1 Over-representation of foreigners in prison systems

Country	Percent of foreign prisoners	Percent foreign. in gen. pop./Extra UE (2016)	Estimate of overrepresentation
Austria	54.7 (2018)	14.4/7.25	3.79–7.54
Belgium	44.3 (2016)	11.7/3.97	3.78–11.15
Denmark	28.6 (2018)	8.1/4.67	3.53–6.12
Finland	16.7 (2018)	4.2/2.44	3.97–6.84
France	21.7 (2014)	6.6/4.31	3.28–5.03
Germany	31.3 (2015)	10.5/5.88	2.98–5.32
Greece	52.9 (2018)	7.4/5.48	7.14–9.65
Ireland	13 (2017)	12.4/4.24	1.04–3.06
Italy	33.8 (2018)	8.3/5.73	4.07–5.89
Netherlands	19.1 (2015)	4.9/2.15	3.89–8.88
Portugal	15.2 (2018)	3.8/2.77	4–5.48
Slovenia	17.5 (2018)	5.2/4.35	3.36–4.22
Spain	28 (2018)	9.5/5.33	2.94–5.25
Sweden	22.1 (2016)	7.8/4.51	2.83–4.9
UK	11 (2018)	8.6/3.71	1.2–2.96
USA	5.2 (2014)	7.23 (2010)	0.71

Source: International Centre for Prison Studies, King's College, London and EUROSTAT.

In Table 1 I also included, for comparison purposes, the same estimate for the US, which is surprisingly low. Actually, in the US, according to official data,[25] it would seem to be more likely to meet a foreigner free in the streets than in prison. As mentioned in footnote 25, we may have to take that with a grain of salt, but there is indeed

[24] The column in the middle of the Table, about percentage of foreigners in the general population, carries two numbers, the first referring to foreigners in general, the second to foreigners from outside the EU. We do not have the same possibility of distinction for the foreigners in prison therefore the rate of overrepresentation is somewhere between the two numbers. However, given that by far most foreigners in prison are from outside the EU, the higher estimate is probably more accurate.

[25] It is necessary to emphasise 'according to official data' because the ways in which information about prisoners' nationality are collected, in the US, vary from State to State and probably produce underestimation.

a consolidated tradition of studies, from the Chicago School to Ruben Rumbaut[26] to Robert Sampson,[27] which claims a lesser level of first generation migrants' criminalisation vis à vis the general American population and more particularly their offspring, as shown in Table 2, taken from an essay by Rumbaut.[28] Table 2 shows the percentage of males from 18 to 39 years incarcerated, according to place of birth (whether in the US or not) and ethnicity. In Table 1, on the other hand, the closest number to the US one is the estimate for the UK and Ireland. If we think of the specific features of immigration history in these countries, we may now want to turn our attention to the relationship of migration to race, in connection with processes of criminalisation.

Table 2 Percentage of Males 18 to 39 Years Old Incarcerated in the United States, 2000, by Nativity, in Rank Order by Ethnicity

	Males, Ages 18–39		**Nativity**	
Ethnicity (Self-Reported)	**Total in U.S. (N)**	**% Incarcerated**	**Foreign Born**	**U.S. Born**
Total	45,200,417	3.04	0.86	3.51
Latin American Ethnicities				
Saivadoran, Guatemalan	433,828	0.68	0.52	3.01
Colombian, Ecuadorian, Peruvian	283,599	1.07	0.80	2.37
Mexican	5,017,431	2.71	0.70	5.90
Dominican	182,303	2.76	2.51	3.71
Cuban	213,302	3.01	2.22	4.20
Puerto Rican[a]	642,106	5.06	4.55	5.37
Asian Ethnicities				
Indian	393,621	0.22	0.11	0.99
Chinese, Taiwanese	439,086	0.28	0.18	0.65
Korean	184,238	0.38	0.26	0.93
Filipino	297,011	0.64	0.38	1.22

(continued)

[26] R Rumbaut, RG Gonzales, G Komaie, CV Morgan and R Tafoya-Estrada, 'Immigration and Incarceration. Patterns and Predictors of Imprisonment among First- and Second-Generation Young Adults' in R Jr Martinez and A Valenzuela (eds), *Immigration and Crime: Race, Ethnicity and Violence* (New York, New York University Press, 2006) 64–89.

[27] RJ Sampson, 'Rethinking Crime and Immigration' (2008) 7 (1) *Contexts* 28–33.

[28] Rumbaut et al, above n 26, 71.

Table 2 ***(Continued)***

Ethnicity (Self-Reported)	Males, Ages 18–39		Nativity	
	Total in U.S. (N)	% Incarcerated	Foreign Born	U.S. Born
Vietnamese	229,735	0.89	0.46	5.60
Laotian, Cambodian	89,664	1.65	0.92	7.26
Other				
White, nan-Hispanic	29,014,261	1.66	0.57	1.71
Black, non-Hispanic	5,453,546	10.87	2.47	11.61
Two or more race groups, other	1,272,742	3.09	0.72	3.85

Source: 2000 U.S. Census, 5% PUMS. Data are estimates for adult males, ages 18 to 39, in correctional institutions at the time of census.

[a]Island-born Puerto Ricans, who are U.S. citizens by birth and not immigrants, ane classified as 'foreign born' for purposes of this table; mainland-born Puerto Ricans are here classified under 'U.S. born'.

VI. Race and Migration

First of all, the very open citizenship law tradition of the US, centred around the principle of *ius soli*, means that only first-generation migrants born abroad would be counted as foreigners once in prison. That is certainly not the case in Europe, where all countries know some kind of compromise between *ius soli* and *ius sanguinis* and therefore there are persons born in the country who are counted as foreigners. This obviously increases the number of foreigners in prison in a sort of 'artificial' way. Beyond that, however, remember that, as already mentioned, the comparable overrepresentation rate in the US concerns Blacks, not immigrants. Also in the UK, the overrepresentation for Afro-Caribbeans in prison (mostly British nationals) is much higher than for migrants, reaching seven times the likelihood of white or South Asian people to be in prison, an overrepresentation even higher than that of African Americans in the US.[29] And in France too, where we do not have, due to policy, data on ethnicity, there is no doubt that if one enters a large French prison in an urban centre, one will see French citizens who look very much like migrants, as far as their physical features are concerned!

[29] DJ Smith, 'Ethnic Origins, Crime, and Criminal Justice in England and Wales' (1997) 21 *Crime and Justice* 101–82; B Agozino, *Counter-colonial Criminology: a Critique of Imperialist Reason* (London, Pluto Press, 2003).

So, the question that should be asked, I believe, is whether we might be witnessing a process, in many different socio-historical situations, where, slowly and over time, xenophobia gives in to racism, by distinguishing, so to speak, among the various immigrant groups, those who will become invisible, in terms of otherness – especially going from the first to the following generations – from those instead who will stay well visible! A number of American historians and sociologists have given evidence of the crucial transition, between the 1920s and the 1930s, from processes of criminalisation of European 'ethnics' who, according to the famous insight by Daniel Bell,[30] had substantially used organised crime as a form of social ladder to becoming successful and established members of the North American establishment, to criminalisation instead of the recent Afro-American migrants from the South, especially in the Midwest and urban centres. This has happened in the context of a 'great migration' that has marked the fate of the contemporary African American community in a way often unnoticed (but that did not go unnoticed by the most brilliant of African American writers – as in the lasting portrait of Joe Bigger by Richard Wright).[31] Not all the European immigrant groups used the same type of social ladder and to the same degree, of course. Irish Americans 'became white'[32] also thanks to their entry into the ranks of police forces and more generally of public service and politics, as in the so-called 'Tammany Hall' system. Italian Americans, who could not speak the language and were, if possible, even less educated, had to rely more on forms of organised crime outside of the law, so to speak. All ethnic European groups, however, were keen on distinguishing themselves from the great-grandchildren of the slaves who were arriving from the South, and were more than happy to have found somebody who could now rightly occupy the tail end of the line.[33] Christopher Muller has shown that the rise of racial disparity in imprisonment in the urban centres of the North, Midwest and West goes back to the period of the great migration and is amplified in those states where the Irish were recruited in force in police organisations.[34] Such an interpretive change, from an emphasis on the fragmentation and conflict of America in connection with the great European migration, to an emphasis instead on social homogeneity but with 'anomic' social areas due to racial and/or individual maladjustment, was reflected also in the sociology and criminology of the time. As Donald Cressey would point out,

[30] D Bell, 'Crime as an American Way of Life' (1953) 13 *The Antioch Review* 131–54 (included in D Bell, *The End of Ideology: On the Exhaustion of Political Ideas in the Fifties* (Cambridge, Harvard University Press, 2000)).

[31] R Wright, *Native Son* (New York, Harper & Brothers, 1940).

[32] N Ignatiev, *How the Irish Became White* (New York, Routledge, 1995).

[33] This is of course a gross generalisation. The process of 'racialisation' and 'deracialisation' of Italian Americans, for instance, was quite complex and contested: see J Guglielmo and S Salerno (eds), *Are Italians White?* (New York, Routledge, 2003). European American leftist political organisations generally fought racism against African Americans in the name of class solidarity.

[34] Muller, above n 2.

attention was to shift from the first generation of migrants to the issue of the integration of so-called 'second generations',[35] therefore from the centrality of 'culture conflict' with Thorsten Sellin[36] to Sutherland's ideas of 'normative conflict' and 'differential association'[37] and Merton's concept of 'anomie'.[38] In other words, social conflict would not be reconnected any longer to cultural and national differences, but, in a society where the various migrants groups had by and large contributed to a 'melting pot', social class stratification was emerging as a central organising concept, often disguised as 'race'.

VII. Demography, Globalisation, Migration and Neo-Nationalism

As we have seen, already the doyen of the Chicago School, Robert E Park, had stressed the importance of migration flows for causing epochal changes 'in the history of [hu]mankind'.[39] Therefore, what we would need today from politicians and also from scholars would be ways to understand what is happening and probably also help with favouring the unavoidable processes of adaptation to novelties that can be, no doubt about that, quite disconcerting. On the contrary, what we get, at least from certain politicians and self-described social scientists, is what amounts to, literally, reactionary diatribes against social change – camouflaged sometimes under the supposed objectivity of social science – which are setting the clocks of Italian society, and more generally of Europe, quite a bit behind, making much more difficult and painful, for everybody, the inevitable adjustment to what is going on. In Italy, the League's slogan 'Italians First' represents therefore a cruel misnomer, a misnomer addressed not so much against migrants – even if that is also certainly the case – but especially against Italians, because the pain that Italian members of the public, and especially their children and grandchildren will have to suffer because of such silly and short-sighted policies, will be dramatic and will last a long time.

One of the most obvious aspects that such reactionary positions are completely eschewing is what is going on with the birth rate in Italy and in Europe more generally. We present here two figures of what is going on in that respect.

[35] DR Cressey, 'Culture Conflict, Differential Association, and Normative Conflict' in ME Wolfgang (ed), *Crime and Culture: Essays in Honor of Thorsten Sellin* (New York, Wiley, 1968) 43–54.

[36] T Sellin, *Culture Conflict and Crime* (New York, Social Science Research Council, 1938).

[37] EH Sutherland, 'Development of the Theory' in EH Sutherland, *On Analyzing Crime* (Chicago, University of Chicago Press, 1973).

[38] RK Merton, 'Social Structure and Anomie' (1938) 3 *American Sociological Review* 672–82.

[39] Park, above n 12, 195.

Figure 3 Natural population change and net migration in Germany

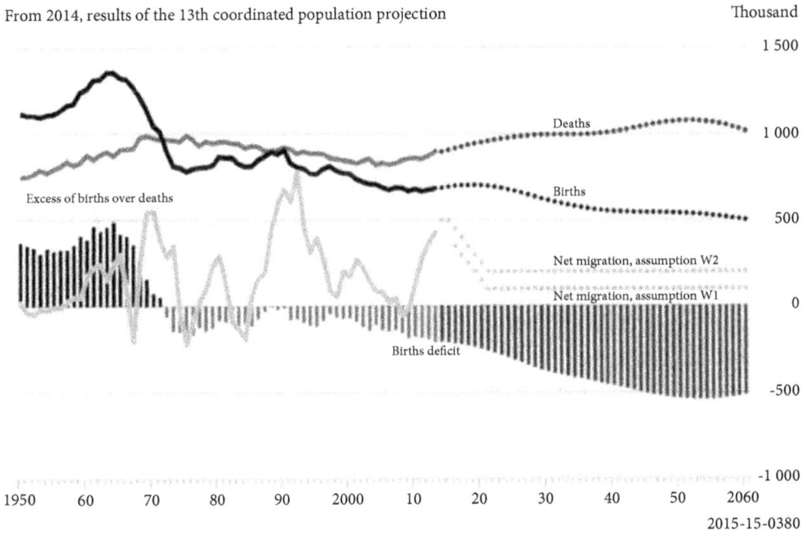

Source: See n 40.

In Figure 3, taken from a German Report[40] we can see that the excess of deaths over births already started in the 1970s in Germany and it is certainly unlikely that even the most open immigration policy may be able to make up for the loss of population deriving from such preponderance of death.

Figure 4 Demographic Transition in Italy

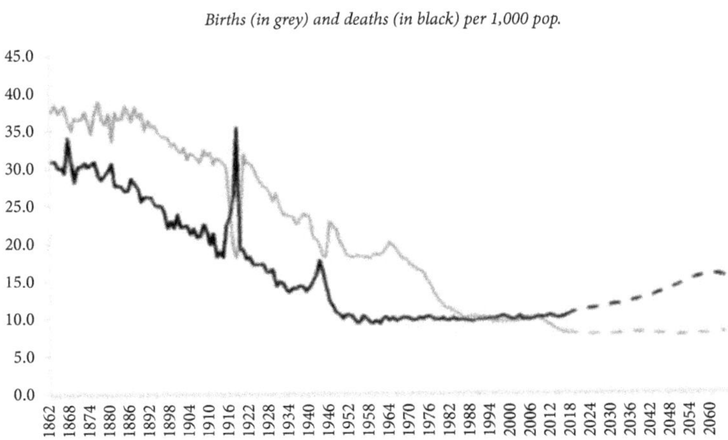

Source: See n 41.

[40] *Germany's Population by 2060. Results of the 13th coordinated population projection* (Wiesbaden, Federal Statistical Office of Germany, 2015).

In Figure 4, representing instead the case of Italy,[41] we can see exactly the same situation, the only difference being that the preponderance of death started much later, around 2010. Indeed, in spite of Italy having today more than five million of regularly sojourning immigrants in its population, the total amount of Italian population has not changed a bit in the last 10 years. Foreigners are simply replacing dying Italians and lately they have had a hard time even doing that. Similar is the situation in the major countries of Europe, with the partial exception of France.

Worldwide migration flows have essentially followed processes of globalisation. Two international waves of globalisation are usually identified, one between the last decades of the nineteenth century and World War One and the other between the Reagan and Thatcher so-called 'neoliberal revolution' in the 1980s and the world crisis of 2008, when the 'Great Recession' started.

Figure 5 Migration, financial integration and trade openness, World, 1880–1996

This chart shows the evolution of three indicators measuring integration in commodity, labor, and capital markets over the long run. All indicators are indexed, so that 1900=100.

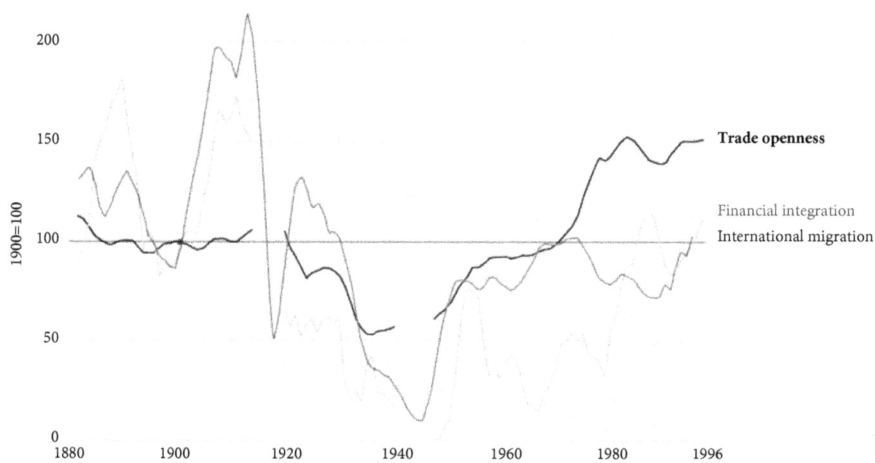

Note: Commodity market integration is measured by computing ratio of goods exports to GDP Labour market integration is measured by dividing the migratory turnover by population. Finanical integration is measured using Feldstein-Horioka estimators of current account disconnectedness.

Source: S Broadberry and K O'Rourke (2010), The Cambridge Economic History of Modern Europe: Volume 2. 1870 to the Present. Cambridge University Press. This is a visualization from OutWorldinData.org. where you find data and research on how the world is changing. Licensed under CC-BY-SA by the authors Esteban Ortiz-Ospina and Diana Beltekian.

[41] M Sgroi, 'Il costo salato della denatalità italiana per Pil e redditi. E sull'immigrazione …' (2018) *Il Sole 24 Ore*, www.econopoly.ilsole24ore.com.

Interestingly, those are also the periods which have seen a growth in worldwide international migrations (see Figure 5) and which are indicated, in Thomas Piketty's famous 'one per cent' graph,[42] as periods of rising inequalities (see Figure 6).

Figure 6 Decomposing the top decile US income share into three groups, 1913–2015

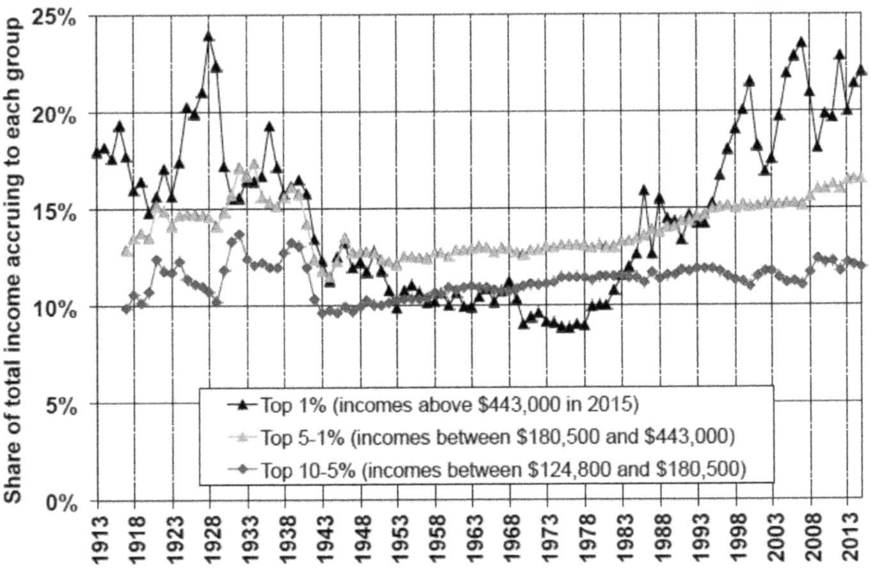

Source: See Saez n 42.

In other words, the openness of markets seems to be related to economic development and economic development in turn to rising inequalities and migrations flows. The mechanism is probably quite simple to describe. A rising capitalist economic development usually increases inequalities, both internationally and domestically, and those inequalities become the reason for (and also the effect of) extensive worldwide migration flows – migration flows which are also a way for the labour market to adjust to the consequences of economic development. Of course, nothing of this is planned or even forecast. Everything happens quite serendipitously, carrying with itself an enormous amount of pain, sorrow and conflict (and crime, and punishment). Once again, as Park described it, a 'catastrophic' theory of progress. But, are the periods without migrations (and with lower inequalities) any better? If we look at the period between the two waves of globalisation, approximately between World War One and 1980, only the second part of this period, the one after World War Two, is the period, usually described as very desirable, of the

[42] T Piketty, *Capital in the Twenty-First Century* (Cambridge, Harvard University Press, 2014); E Saez, *Striking it Richer: The Evolution of Top Incomes in the United States (Updated with 2015 preliminary estimates)* (https://eml.berkeley.edu/~saez/saez-UStopincomes-2015.pdf).

so-called economic miracle and the welfare state. The first part instead is a period marked by two world wars, the worst economic crisis in the history of capitalism (until the current one!) and the rise of totalitarian regimes in almost all the most developed countries. And indeed, those are conditions which are mightily inimical to migrations. There is nothing like war to prevent both migrations and rising inequalities, because in times of war States become exacting power monopolists within tight borders.

At the same time, such periods characterised by authoritarianism and nationalism can be understood perhaps as a reaction against the previous, unplanned, conflictual, indeed 'catastrophic' rise in mobility and inequality, an excess of social change, both in social and geographic terms, that seems to call for the closeness, stationarity and predictability of authoritarianism. One wonders whether we may not have been living one of those moments lately, after the Great Recession. A purely 'reactionary' movement, trying to go back to a 'status quo' no longer existing. As Marx reminded us of – we saw it at the beginning – writing about the origins of the working-class in England, 'legislation treated [the migrants] as "voluntary" criminals, and assumed that it depended on their own good will to go on working under the old conditions that no longer existed'. Therefore when they became bandits, brigands, criminals, beggars, prostitutes or simply wanderers, the reaction was one of stopping them, detaining them, punishing them, controlling a movement that had been set in motion by circumstances much more than 'personal inclinations', an effort at pushing back social change in the very persons who had been left to deal individually and personally with such social change.[43] As Angela Davis noted recently in an interview commenting on the building of new prisons in Latin America,

> More prisons are being built to catch the lives disrupted by this movement of capital. People who cannot find a place for themselves in this new society governed by capital end up going to prison. In many countries, such as South Africa and Colombia … deterritorialization is underway to allow agribusiness to expand, thus producing surplus populations. In Colombia, people have been removed from their land to make way for sugarcane production for the biofuel consumed by us in the West who wish to minimize our carbon footprint. All the people ejected from that land, who had protected its biodiversity, are being pushed into slums. It is most intense near Cali, in the western part of Colombia, where they are building the largest prison in South America – in part to catch those people who have been deprived of their land and have no source of cash …[44]

Literally, 'to catch those people who have been deprived of their land and have no source of cash …'. 'Catch' them indeed! Catch them and detain them! The introduction of a regime of modern private property and the substitution of a cash

[43] D Melossi, '"In A Peaceful Life": Migration and The Crime of Modernity in Europe/Italy' (2003) 5 *Punishment and Society* 371–97.

[44] T Platt, 'Interview with Angela Davis' (2014) 40 (1–2) *Social Justice* 37, 51.

economy for a cashless one goes together with the resulting necessary prisonisation (and, therefore, criminalisation) of those who remain outside of the cash economy nexus.[45] Indeed the 'crimes' punished in the early European workhouses were begging and vagabondage, the refusal to work in given conditions, petty theft.[46] What are the 'crimes' for which migrants are punished today in our so 'modern' European societies? As we have seen, they are theft, crimes related to the migrants' migration status (including falsity in statements and acts), and crimes related to the two activities that their 'illegal' personal status has 'reserved' to them, drugs and prostitution, not to mention of course the possible crimes of violence and resistance to public officer which may be triggered by that involvement.

What follows from all of this is a possible way to deal with an issue which is undoubtedly of very vast proportions. Setting up ways to migrate to the European Union in a certain and predictable way would not solve all problems but would at least diminish the likelihood of undocumented migrants to become the cannon fodder of organised (and also, un-organised) crime. We have seen for instance that the 'refugeeisation of workforce' in Italy – even if it may be questioned on many counts – corresponded however to a decrease in the overrepresentation of foreigners in Italian prisons for the very simple reason that this at least gave them a 'document' with which to work (more or less) legally. Paradoxically, one of the reasons why, as we have seen, the criminalisation of migrants has traditionally been quite low in the US may also be because of the facility with which, until a few years ago, an undocumented migrant could secure some kind of (usually fake) documentation, with which he or she could work and therefore be protected from getting involved in criminal behaviour (except criminal behaviour having to do with migration laws!). And, correspondingly, measures supposedly intended to fight the ills of irregular migration – such as the 'security decrees' of the Conte-Salvini government in Italy recently – will probably end up contributing to higher migrants' crime rates because they will make it much harder for migrants to work in non-criminal enterprises. In countries where (unregulated) migration flows are not even enough to offset the birth deficits due to increasingly lower natality rates, migration policies should respond to the needs of labour markets – besides to the requirements of human rights and international law. As Durkheim wisely noted a long time ago, however, the boundaries of deviance and social control respond to the attempts to create a moral (and political) consensus rather than to any abstract governmental rationality.[47] Nowhere is this clearer than in Europe today about the connections between crime, punishment and migration.

[45] Marx had described this process, writing on the theft of wood in Germany in the mid-nineteenth century: K Marx, 'Proceedings of the Sixth Rhine Province Assembly. Third Article: Debates on the Law of the Theft of Wood' in *Marx/Engels Collected Works*, Volume 1 (New York, International Publishers, 1975); P Linebaugh, 'Karl Marx, the Theft of Wood, and Working Class Composition: A Contribution to the Current Debate' (1976) 6 *Crime and Social Justice* 5–16.

[46] D Melossi and M Pavarini, *The Prison and the Factory (40th Anniversary Edition)* (London, Palgrave Macmillan, 2018).

[47] E Durkheim, *The Division of Labor in Society* (orig publ 1893) (New York, Free Press, 1997).

5

Current Trends, Numbers and Routes in EU Migrations

Is Existing Legislation Creating More Irregularity?

MARIA GIOVANNA MANIERI

I. Introduction

The prominence of migration as a newsworthy and high-priority policy issue has perhaps never been more pronounced. Yet, despite a growing politicisation around the issue of migration, which in the European Union has translated into a political debate often characterised by a negative rhetoric of criminalisation of migration and of actors providing humanitarian assistance to migrants, making migration safer and better regulated has become a key global priority with the adoption in December 2018 of the Global Compact on Safe, Orderly and Regular Migration.

In this context, it is timely for the European Union to reflect on whether the existing policies addressing irregular migration on the one hand, including the return acquis, and policies addressing regular migration and asylum on the other hand, including the ongoing reform of the Common European Asylum System, may have the unintended consequence of increasing precariousness of status by further pushing migrants into irregularity.

This chapter analyses said risks and investigates possibilities for EU policy-makers to develop a coherent migration acquis and achieve an overall reduction of irregular migration as one of the aims of the Union's common migration policy, in line with article 79 of the Treaty on the Functioning of the European Union (TFEU), by promoting measures preventing the loss or precariousness of status and encouraging cooperation with national authorities, instead of privileging a punitive approach against irregular migration.

II. Setting the Scene: Current Trends, Numbers and Routes in EU Migrations

Migration is a complex and rapidly evolving human phenomenon that intersects a multiplicity of economic, social and legal factors affecting its regulation. In the European Union context, the diverse and fast-changing nature of migration has become particularly evident in recent years: while Europe has faced the highest number of spontaneous arrivals since the Second World War in 2015, numbers have steadily and significantly dropped since, with the lowest numbers of arrivals recorded today since 2010.[1]

Yet, asylum seekers and migrants attempting to reach Europe keep losing their lives at an alarming rate in 2018 and 2019 and routes to Europe are five times deadlier as compared to 2015. While arrivals keep falling – they have dropped by almost 88 per cent in 2019 as compared to 2015 – migration routes to Europe have never been so deadly: in 2019, an estimated 1291 persons died or went missing crossing the Mediterranean. Cuts in search and rescue operations have reinforced the position of the Mediterranean as the world's deadliest sea crossing.[2]

It is worthy to note that the majority of migrants coming to Europe do so in a legal way, mainly for work, family reunification, study or resettlement and refugee protection: in 2018, the 28 Member States issued about 3,200,000 first residence permits to non-EU citizens, an increase by 0.4 per cent (or 13,000) as compared with 2017 and equating to the highest number of first residence permits issued by EU Member States since 2008.[3] On the other hand, the number of irregular border-crossings in 2018 was the lowest in the EU since 2013, dropping by a 27 per cent to a total of 150,114 as compared with the previous year.[4]

Against this backdrop, the EU legislators have recently failed to recognise three essential elements characterising today's EU migrations as the key starting points for much needed evidence-based policies regulating human mobility: first, the differences characterising the notions of migrant stocks and migrant flows; second, the fact that artificially created migration categories are very fluid concepts and; third, the fact that, despite a large focus on irregular migration, the majority of migrants come to Europe legally.

A. Distinguishing Migration Flows and Migration Stocks

The two most common notions for measuring migration are migrant flows and migrant stocks. Migrant flows refer to the number of migrants entering and

[1] UNHCR Operational Portal, available at: www.data2.unhcr.org/en/situations/mediterranean.
[2] ibid.
[3] Eurostat, First permits by reason, length of validity and citizenship, last update: 28 October 2019. See also: Eurostat, Newsrelease 164/2019, 25 October 2019.
[4] Frontex, Risk Analysis for 2019, February 2019.

leaving a country over the course of a specific period, while migrant stocks are the estimates of the total number of migrants present in a given country at a particular point in time.[5] In other words, while migrant flows offer a moving picture of the situation at the external borders of the European Union in terms of entries and exits, we can only obtain a static picture of the number of migrants actually present in the territory of the European Union at a given time by referring to migrant stocks.

While data on migration flows are essential for understanding migration patterns and routes and for deriving the potential impact of different factors, including migration policies in countries of origin, transit and destination on such flows (i.e., has the EU-Turkey Statement had an impact in terms of reducing the number of irregular arrivals – i.e. flows – to the European Union?), only a reference to migrant stocks can offer policy-makers the actual magnitude of the phenomenon to be regulated and be instrumental to reflect on the potential impact of existing and future policies on such stocks (i.e., is existing EU legislation on migration and asylum creating more irregularity?).

Proposals for legislation reform and policy guidance in the European Union in recent years however, seem to stem mainly from analysis of migrant flows, while little or no attention is devoted to the impact of such proposed policies on future migrant stocks.[6] This approach is contributing to the development of an overall EU policy response largely looking into short-term and immediate solutions, aimed at reducing the numbers of irregular migration flows, rather than contributing to a long-term and sustainable response to migration management needs that would aim at reducing the irregular migration stocks and preventing migrants from falling into situations of irregularity, and thus prove more effective in the long run. Moreover, a continued focus on migrant flows rather than migrant stocks contributes to fuel the misperception of migration as a temporary and unregulated phenomenon which in turn leads to negative narratives surrounding migration prevailing.

B. Understanding Migration Categories as Fluid Concepts

Another issue often disregarded by EU policy-makers is the fact that the existing conceptualisation of migrant categories, distinguishing, among others, between

[5] United Nations Department of Economic and Social Affairs, Handbook on Measuring International Migration through Population Censuses, 1 March 2017, 9–11.

[6] See, eg: European Commission and High Representative of the Union for Foreign Affairs and Security Policy, Joint Communication on Migration on the Central Mediterranean route Managing flows, saving lives, 25 January 2017 or European Commission Communication on establishing a new Partnership Framework with third countries under the European Agenda on Migration, 7 June 2016.

'migrants', 'refugees', 'asylum seekers' and 'irregular migrants', does not take into account the evolving dynamics of migration which often do not allow for a straightforward differentiation between one or the other category, contrary to what some of the most recent proposals for accelerated and border asylum and return procedures seem to imply, namely that a swift and prima facie distinction could be easily drawn between asylum seekers whose claims should be assessed and other migrants who would have to be swiftly returned, including through the use of specific 'lists of safe countries of origin' or 'safe third countries'.[7]

On the contrary, migrant categories are fluid concepts and it would be unrealistic to ignore the fact that migrants can and often do shift between and across categories during their journeys through space and time: irregular migrants become asylum seekers the moment they claim asylum and fall back into irregularity as their asylum claim is denied and similarly, third-country nationals having entered the European Union with a valid visa may lose their status as a consequence of multiple reasons, often intersected, such as loss of employment or the end of a relationship.[8]

Current EU legislation does not sufficiently take into account the dynamic nature of migrant categories and often does not allow for sufficient flexibility, for instance by legally allowing the shifting across categories or regularisation of status from within the European Union.[9]

C. Acknowledging the Magnitudes of Regular and Irregular Migration

Despite a very mediatic and continued focus on irregular arrivals in the European Union, the majority of migrants coming to Europe do so in a legal way: as highlighted above, in 2018, the 28 Member States issued about 3,200,000 first residence permits to non-EU citizens, the highest number since 2008.[10]

The number of irregular border-crossings in 2018 was the lowest in the EU since 2013, dropping by a 27 per cent to a total of 150,114 as compared with the previous year.[11]

[7] See, eg: European Commission draft proposals on the Asylum Procedures Regulation, Proposal for a Regulation establishing a common procedure for international protection in the Union and repealing Directive 2013/32/EU, 2016/0224 (COD), 13 July 2016 and recast Return Directive, Proposal for a Directive on common standards and procedures in Member States for returning illegally staying third-country nationals (recast), 2018/0329 (COD), 12 September 2018.

[8] H Crawley and D Skleparis, 'Refugees, Migrants, Neither, Both: Categorical Fetishism and the Politics of Bounding in Europe's "Migration Crisis"' (2017) 44 *Journal of Ethnic and Migration Studies* 48–64.

[9] See, eg: B Speciale, 'Immigration Policies in the EU: Challenges and Priorities' (2010) 2 *Reflets et perspectives de la vie économique* 121–35.

[10] Eurostat, First permits by reason, length of validity and citizenship, last update: 28 October 2019. See also: Eurostat, Newsrelease 164/2019, 25 October 2019.

[11] Frontex, Risk Analysis for 2019, February 2019.

As highlighted by Guild and Acosta (2019), there are some important lessons to learn from this data. First, 'irregular migration is the small exception to the rule of regular migration', with a very low proportion of the total number of migrants residing in the European Union being in an irregular situation.[12] Second, as data collected by Frontex, as well as research conducted in 12 EU countries under the CLANDESTINO project indicates, irregular entry is the least frequent pathway into irregularity, with the majority of undocumented migrants falling into a situation of irregularity as a consequence of overstaying a visa or residence permit or losing their status due to a variety of reasons, including for example loss of employment.[13] Yet, the policy response to irregular migration is mainly centred on preventing irregular migration intended as irregular entry rather than irregular migration intended as loss of status as a consequence of a multiplicity of factors.

The disproportionate focus on migrant flows and irregular migration, coupled with the lack of recognition of the dynamic nature of migrant categories, is further fuelling policy-makers' efforts on short-term, immediate measures mostly aiming at contrasting irregular migration and deviating the EU legislators from the development of much needed long-term measures for comprehensive migration management and prevention of loss of status.

III. Managing Irregular Migration and the Impact of EU Migration and Asylum Policies: A Warning against Unwarranted Effects

A. Is Existing Legislation Creating More Irregularity?

Throughout the last 15 years, the role and legal competence of the European Union in the development of EU legislation and instruments providing for common European standards, procedures and conditions for the treatment of third-country nationals irregularly entering or staying in the territory of the European Union, has significantly increased.

[12] Guild and Acosta (E Guild and D Acosta, *Challenges Presented by Migration and Refugees from a Euro-Mediterranean Perspective* (European Parliament, Policy Department for External Relations, 2019)) estimate that, concerning the EU, it can be said that the proportion of migrants in an irregular situation is only 2.5 per cent of the migrant population. Data compiled by Eurostat on the number of migrants in an irregular situation subject to an expulsion order supports this claim. See: Eurostat, Migration and Migrant Population Statistics, October 2019.

[13] Frontex Risk Analysis 2019, which points out to a total number of 150,114 detections of irregular border crossings as compared to a total of 361,636 detections of persons staying in EU Member States irregularly. See also: CLANDESTINO Project, Final Report, November 2009; See also F Düvell, 'Paths into Irregularity: The Legal and Political Construction of Irregular Migration' (2011) *European Journal of Migration and Law* 275–95.

Since the Tampere European Council of 1999, one of the key elements of the EU's common policy on migration and asylum has been the prevention of irregular migration, with a strong focus on the one hand on the 'fight against human smuggling' as one of the key objectives for the EU Area of Freedom, Security and Justice, and, on the other hand, on the creation of a Common European Asylum and Migration policy.[14]

This reflects the logic later on introduced in article 79 of the TFEU, which includes both preventing irregular migration and the efficient management of migration flows and fair treatment of third-country nationals residing legally in Member States, among others, as aims of an EU 'common immigration policy'. In line with article 67 TFEU, such common immigration policy must respect the rights, freedoms and principles reaffirmed in the Charter of Fundamental Rights of the European Union.

Since the Tampere European Council, EU tools relating to irregular migration have been approaching the issue from a perspective centred on preventing the phenomenon, detecting and punishing those who facilitate it[15] and establishing common standards for the return of irregular migrants.[16] However, little or no attention has been given since to the need of reducing irregular migration by preventing precariousness and loss of status and, through a careful look, it could be argued that a number of provisions in the proposed reform of the Common European Asylum System and recast Return Directive point to a risk of creating more irregularity, including precariousness and loss of status in a number of ways as outlined below.

B. The Return Directive and its Recast Proposal: A Warning against Unwarranted Effects

Making returns more effective and stepping up Member States' return rates has been a priority for the European Union in recent years, as stated in the 2015 European Agenda on Migration, the 2015 EU Action Plan on return, and in the 2017 Renewed Action Plan on return.

[14] European Council, Presidency Conclusions, Tampere European Council, 15–16 October 1999.

[15] Regulated at EU level through the so-called EU Facilitators' Package comprising the EU's Facilitation Directive: Council Directive 2002/90/EC of 28 November 2002 defining the facilitation of unauthorised entry, transit and residence, [2002] OJ L328/17 and by Council framework Decision of 28 November 2002 on the strengthening of the penal framework to prevent the facilitation of unauthorised entry, transit and residence, 2002/946/JHA, [2002] OJ L328/1. On this issue, see also: S Carrera and L Vosyliute, *Fit for purpose? The Facilitation Directive and the criminalisation of humanitarian assistance to irregular migrants: 2018 update* (European Union, European Parliament, 2018) and S Carrera and E Guild, *Fit for purpose? The Facilitation Directive and the criminalisation of humanitarian assistance to irregular migrants* (European Union, European Parliament, 2016).

[16] S Carrera and J Parkin, *Protecting and Delivering Fundamental Rights of Irregular Migrants at Local and Regional Levels in the European Union* (European Union, Committee of the Regions, 2011) 5. See also: RI Cholewinski, *Irregular Migrants: access to minimum social rights* (Strasbourg, Council of Europe Publishing, 2005) 20.

The 2008 Directive on common standards and procedures in Member States for returning illegally staying third-country nationals (Return Directive) sets out common standards and procedures for returning irregularly staying third-country nationals from the European Union. The European Commission published a first evaluation of the Return Directive in March 2014, where it was noted that the transposition and implementation of the Return Directive had 'positively influenced the situation regarding voluntary departure and forced return monitoring, and had contributed to achieving more convergence on detention, for example'.[17] The report also highlights that the implementation of the Return Directive had increased legal security for returnees and that the main reasons for failure in return procedures dealt with practical problems in the identification of returnees and in obtaining documentation from non-EU authorities.[18] However, following increased spontaneous arrivals at the external borders of the European Union in 2015, and noting continued low return rates from EU Member States to third countries, the European Commission published a series of guidelines to Member States, including an EU Action Plan on Return,[19] a Return Handbook[20] and, in 2017, a Recommendation on making returns more effective when implementing the Return Directive.[21] The 2015 EU Action Plan on Return outlined an ambitious set of measures to increase the absolute numbers of returns, including: promoting more convergence in voluntary returns throughout the EU; the introduction of a uniform EU Travel Document to facilitate returns;[22] reforming Eurodac and the Schengen Information System (SIS) for databases to cover aspects concerning irregular migration, including alerts as in the case of SIS;[23] an EU Entry-Exit System;[24] and the Integrated Return Management Application (IRMA) to improve

[17] Communication from the European Commission to the Council and the European Parliament on EU Return Policy, COM/2014/0199 final, page 30.

[18] ibid.

[19] Communication from the European Commission to the Council and the European Parliament on EU Action Plan on Return, COM(2015) 453 final, 9 September 2015.

[20] Annex to the Commission Recommendation establishing a common 'Return Handbook' to be used by Member States' competent authorities when carrying out return related tasks, C(2017) 6505, 27 September 2017.

[21] Commission Recommendation of 7 March 2017 on making returns more effective when implementing the Directive 2008/115/EC of the European Parliament and of the Council, C(2017) 1600 final.

[22] Regulation (EU) 2016/1953 of the European Parliament and of the Council of 26 October 2016 on the establishment of a European travel document for the return of illegally staying third-country nationals, and repealing the Council Recommendation of 30 November 1994, [2016] OJ L311/13.

[23] Regulation (EU) 2018/1860 of the European Parliament and of the Council of 28 November 2018 on the use of the Schengen Information System for the return of illegally staying third-country nationals, [2018] OJ L312/1.

[24] Regulation (EU) 2017/2226 of the European Parliament and of the Council of 30 November 2017 establishing an Entry/Exit System (EES) to register entry and exit data and refusal of entry data of third-country nationals crossing the external borders of the Member States and determining the conditions for access to the EES for law enforcement purposes, and amending the Convention implementing the Schengen Agreement and Regulations (EC) No 767/2008 and (EU) No 1077/2011, [2017] OJ L327/20.

cooperation between Member States, now part of the newly revised European Border and Coastguard Regulation. In 2016, a Commission Communication on establishing a new Migration Partnership Framework[25] aimed at making cooperation on return and readmission conditional to other forms of cooperation with third countries in other key policy areas, including development cooperation, trade and visa facilitation. The 2017 Recommendation on making returns more effective urged Member States to harmonise their approaches on standards for returns, including through increased use of detention and lowering of procedural safeguards. The impact of these recommendations on Member States' return rates has not been comprehensively assessed to date by the European Commission.

As part of his 2017 State of the Union Letter of Intent, the then President of the Commission, Juncker, announced that by the end of 2018 the Commission would present 'targeted measures to promote a more effective approach to returns'. Such 'targeted measures', published on 12 September 2018, included further amendments to the European Border and Coast Guard's mandate in the area of returns and a full recast of the Return Directive, in the absence of an impact assessment providing guidance and reasoning to the EU co-legislators in terms of policy objectives vis-a-vis policy choices. The lack of an evidence base for the proposed recast has been highlighted by the European Parliamentary Research Service in its substitute impact assessment of the proposed recast Return Directive as requested by the European Parliament's Committee on Civil Liberties, Justice and Home Affairs (LIBE). The assessment considered the main expected impacts of the key provisions of the Commission proposal, focusing on the social, human rights and financial impacts, as compared to the status quo and concluded, inter alia, that there is no clear evidence supporting the Commission's claim that its proposal would lead to more effective returns of irregular migrants.[26] The lack of an evidence base is part of a worrying and increasing trend in EU legislative processes in the field of asylum, migration and border management overall, with none of the seven legislative proposals composing the Common European Asylum System reform presented by the European Commission between May and July 2016 having been accompanied by an impact assessment.

The Commission describes the recast Return Directive as a 'targeted review' intended to speed up return procedures, make more links between asylum and return procedures, and reduce the risk of absconding, whilst protecting individuals' fundamental rights. The Commission seeks to justify the proposed changes as needed to increase the effectiveness, intended in absolute quantitative terms, of returns, but fails to assess the unwarranted impact that new proposed provisions, in particular those introducing a more systematic use of detention and swift border

[25] European Commission Communication on establishing a new Partnership Framework with third countries under the European Agenda on Migration, 7 June 2016.

[26] K Eisele and E Muir, 'The Proposed Return Directive (recast) substitute impact assessment' (European Union, European Parliamentary Research Services, 2019).

procedures, would have in terms of discouraging cooperation with Member States' authorities and actually encouraging absconding. For example, studies carried out in France show that the vast majority of returnees are effectively returned in the first few days, and that the impact on return rates of an extension of the maximum periods of detention from 45 to 90 days will be low.[27] Similar evidence in Italy shows that periods of detention longer than 30–60 days were not securing an increase in the return rate if the return had not been possible until then.[28]

Furthermore, the recast proposal aims at accelerating return procedures through the creation of a border procedure, where no period for voluntary departure would be granted as a rule; shorter time limits would be imposed for lodging an appeal and detention would be largely applied. This would likely further increase the risk of absconding and discourage returnees' cooperation. This risk is also highlighted in the 2016 European Migration Network report on the return of rejected asylum seekers, where it is noted that:

> [T]he focus and rationale behind policies and measures vary quite significantly and without evaluative evidence it is difficult to draw conclusions as to which practices are more effective. However, the practice of drastically removing rights following a rejection and/or return decision may increase the likelihood of absconding, or at least of rejected asylum seekers falling out of contact with the authorities thus affecting the feasibility and effectiveness of return operations. It may also be likely to increase the likelihood of destitution.[29]

One aspect that has remained untouched but that is indirectly affected by other changes – in particular the ones limiting possibilities for voluntary departure – proposed by the European Commission in its recast proposal and which deserves particular attention when measuring the impact of existing legislation setting out common standards on returns on having the stated effect of deterring irregular migration, is the obligation on Member States to issue entry bans to individuals when adopting return decisions. As a general rule, article 11 of the current Return Directive obliges Member States to issue entry bans for a maximum of five years running from the day in which the person concerned has effectively left the territory of Member States, alongside return decisions if no period for voluntary departure has been granted, or if an individual has not complied with the obligation to return. The Directive allows for various specific exceptions concerning the length of the entry ban and allows Member States to impose an entry ban – but does not oblige them to do so – even in cases where a period for voluntary departure has been granted or the person has voluntarily complied with an obligation to return. As the Directive allows Member States a wide margin of discretion, there

[27] La Cimade, 'Décryptage du projet de loi asile et immigration', July 2018.

[28] Senato della Repubblica, Commissione straordinaria per la tutela e la promozione dei diritti umani, 'Rapporto Sui Centri Di Identificazione ed Espulsione in Italia', July 2014.

[29] EMN Synthesis Report for EMN Focussed Study 2016, the Return of Rejected Asylum Seekers, Challenges and Good Practice, 3 November 2016, 4.

is currently no convergence in the length and grounds for issuing entry bans.[30] Article 13 of the recast proposal does not alter the obligation on Member States to issue entry bans and further allows national authorities to issue entry bans when the 'illegal stay is detected in connection with border checks carried out at exit'. It is to be highlighted that the recent reform of the Schengen Information System prescribes that entry bans issued in accordance with the Return Directive must be accompanied by the automatic introduction of an alert on refusal of entry or stay in the system.[31] The issuance of entry bans upon exit, may have the unwarranted effects of discouraging cooperation in terms of voluntary returns – as an entry ban may still be imposed upon exit – and potentially increase attempts of undetected exit or demands for extra- or intra-EU smuggling. It is interesting to note that, conversely, in its partial general approach covering all aspects of the proposal except those relating to the border procedure, reached at the Justice and Home Affairs meeting of 6/7 June 2019, the Council proposed to extend the maximum duration of entry-bans from five to 10 years, thus confirming Member States' main focus in recent years on stemming irregular migrant flows, with little or no regard for the proposal's potential impact on enhancing irregular migrant stocks as a consequence of de facto discouraging voluntary departures and voluntary returns.

C. The Common European Asylum System (CEAS) and its Proposed Reform: Risks of Precariousness of Status and Punitive Approach

Rooted in articles 67(2), 78 and 80 TFEU and in article 18 of the EU Charter of Fundamental Rights, the EU's aim to develop a common policy on asylum has undergone a significant evolution since the previous intergovernmental cooperation on asylum was brought into the EU's institutional framework under the 1993 Treaty of Maastricht. It was with the Treaty of Amsterdam in 1999 that EU institutions were mandated with drawing up legislation in the area of asylum, following an approach in two phases as decided by the European Council with the adoption of the Tampere Programme in October 1999. A first phase of negotiations on the Common European Asylum System (CEAS) was carried out from 1999 to 2004, and resulted in the establishment of the criteria and mechanisms for determining the Member State responsible for examining asylum applications (replacing the intergovernmental 1990 Dublin Convention), the first establishment of Eurodac

[30] European Migration Network, 'The effectiveness of return in EU Member States 2017', 2017, 77–85.

[31] Art 24(1)(b), Regulation (EU) 2018/1860 of the European Parliament and of the Council of 28 November 2018 on the use of the Schengen Information System for the return of illegally staying third-country nationals, [2018] OJ L312/1.

(the European Asylum Dactyloscopy Database) for storing and comparing fingerprint data of asylum seekers, minimum standards for the reception of asylum seekers, qualifications for international protection and procedures for granting and withdrawing refugee status. The Hague Programme, adopted in November 2004, called for the second-phase measures to be negotiated by the end of 2010, with the aim of going beyond minimum standards and establishing a single asylum procedure comprising common guarantees and a uniform status for those granted protection. The second phase concluded in 2012 with the adoption of the existing Qualification Directive,[32] which entered into force in January 2012; the Eurodac Regulation;[33] the Dublin III Regulation;[34] the Reception Conditions Directive;[35] and the Asylum Procedures Directive,[36] which all entered into force in July 2013, causing their delayed transposition in mid-July 2015 to coincide with the peak of increased spontaneous arrivals of asylum seekers at the external borders of the European Union.

It has to be highlighted that, since the entry into force of the Treaty of Lisbon in December 2009, article 80 of the TFEU explicitly provides for the principle of solidarity and fair sharing of responsibility between Member States and measures on asylum are no longer aiming at establishing minimum standards, but at creating a common system comprising a uniform status and uniform procedures. The essential elements of such common system are: a uniform status of asylum and of subsidiary protection; a common system of temporary protection; common procedures for the granting and withdrawing of uniform asylum or subsidiary protection status; criteria and mechanisms for determining which Member State is responsible for considering an application; standards concerning reception conditions; and partnership and cooperation with third countries.

[32] Directive 2011/95/EU of the European Parliament and of the Council of 13 December 2011 on standards for the qualification of third-country nationals or stateless persons as beneficiaries of international protection, for a uniform status for refugees or for persons eligible for subsidiary protection, and for the content of the protection granted, [2011] OJ L337/9.

[33] Regulation (EU) No 603/2013 of the European Parliament and of the Council of 26 June 2013 on the establishment of 'Eurodac' for the comparison of fingerprints for the effective application of Regulation (EU) No 604/2013 establishing the criteria and mechanisms for determining the Member State responsible for examining an application for international protection lodged in one of the Member States by a third-country national or a stateless person and on requests for the comparison with Eurodac data by Member States' law enforcement authorities and Europol for law enforcement purposes, and amending Regulation (EU) No 1077/2011 establishing a European Agency for the operational management of large-scale IT systems in the area of freedom, security and justice, [2013] OJ L180/1.

[34] Regulation (EU) No 604/2013 of the European Parliament and of the Council of 26 June 2013 establishing the criteria and mechanisms for determining the Member State responsible for examining an application for international protection lodged in one of the Member States by a third-country national or a stateless person, [2013] OJ L180/31.

[35] Directive 2013/33/EU of the European Parliament and of the Council of 26 June 2013 laying down standards for the reception of applicants for international protection, [2013] OJ L180/96.

[36] Directive 2013/32/EU of the European Parliament and of the Council of 26 June 2013 on common procedures for granting and withdrawing international protection, [2013] OJ L180/60.

Due to the increased arrivals as of 2014, the European Commission issued the European Agenda on Migration in May 2015 and proposed several measures to manage spontaneous arrivals including through the so-called hotspot approach: setting up migration management support teams composed of the European Asylum Support Office (EASO), the European Border and Coast Guard Agency (Frontex) and the European Union Agency for Law Enforcement Cooperation (Europol).

Besides offering the first conceptualisation of the hotspot approach, the European Agenda on Migration also called for a reform of the CEAS, which was presented as a set of two packages of legislative proposals in May and July 2016 and on which the EU co-legislators have not managed to find an agreement to date, due to the stalemate in Council. The set of legislative initiatives sought to promote further harmonisation of the EU asylum acquis by proposing directly applicable regulations instead of directives (with the one exception of the Reception Conditions Directive). The seven proposals included: a new Asylum Procedures Regulation;[37] a Qualifications Regulation;[38] a Dublin recast Regulation;[39] a Eurodac recast Regulation;[40] a Reception Conditions recast Directive;[41] a new Regulation establishing a European Asylum Agency[42] – to replace EASO and; a new Regulation establishing an EU Resettlement Framework.[43]

[37] Proposal for a Regulation of the European Parliament and of the Council establishing a common procedure for international protection in the Union and repealing Directive 2013/32/EU, COM(2016) 467 final 2016/0224 (COD), 13 July 2016.

[38] Proposal for a Regulation of the European Parliament and of the Council on standards for the qualification of third-country nationals or stateless persons as beneficiaries of international protection, for a uniform status for refugees or for persons eligible for subsidiary protection and for the content of the protection granted and amending Council Directive 2003/109/EC of 25 November 2003 concerning the status of third-country nationals who are long-term residents, COM(2016) 466 final 2016/0223 (COD), 13 July 2016.

[39] Proposal for a Regulation of the European Parliament and of the Council establishing the criteria and mechanisms for determining the Member State responsible for examining an application for international protection lodged in one of the Member States by a third-country national or a stateless person (recast), COM/2016/0270 final/2 – 2016/0133 (COD), 4 May 2016.

[40] Proposal for a Regulation of the European Parliament and of the Council on the establishment of 'Eurodac' for the comparison of fingerprints for the effective application of [Regulation (EU) No 604/2013 establishing the criteria and mechanisms for determining the Member State responsible for examining an application for international protection lodged in one of the Member States by a third-country national or a stateless person], for identifying an illegally staying third-country national or stateless person and on requests for the comparison with Eurodac data by Member States' law enforcement authorities and Europol for law enforcement purposes (recast), COM(2016) 272 final 2016/0132 (COD), 4 May 2016.

[41] Proposal for a Directive of the European Parliament and of the Council laying down standards for the reception of applicants for international protection (recast), COM(2016) 465 final 2016/0222 (COD), 13 July 2016.

[42] Proposal for a Regulation of the European Parliament and of the Council on the European Union Agency for Asylum and repealing Regulation (EU) No 439/2010, COM/2016/0271 final – 2016/0131 (COD), 4 May 2016.

[43] Proposal for a Regulation of the European Parliament and of the Council establishing a Union Resettlement Framework and amending Regulation (EU) No 516/2014 of the European Parliament and the Council, COM/2016/0468 final – 2016/0225 (COD), 13 July 2016.

Despite having a much needed reform of the Dublin system at its core, the 2016 CEAS reform as proposed by the European Commission included provisions significantly lowering protection standards, leading to precariousness of status and adopting in large part a punitive approach introducing both procedural and material sanctions for non-compliance with different requirements at various stages of the asylum procedure or sanctioning unauthorised onward movements from one Member State to another Member State (commonly referred to by the European Commission as 'secondary movements').

i. The Proposed Qualifications Regulation: Precariousness of Status and Enhanced Risks of Irregularity

A particularly contentious point as part of the negotiations on the Qualifications Regulation, which have stalled after a provisional compromise text agreed between the Bulgarian Presidency and the European Parliament had not been endorsed by the Council, has been the Commission's proposal for a mandatory review of the continued need for international protection of status holders on the occasion of the renewal of their residence permit. In particular, articles 15 and 21 of the proposed Qualification Regulation propose a mandatory review of status upon the renewal of a residence permit or when guidance from the EU Agency for Asylum suggests a significant change in the country of origin that could impact protection needs of the person. The introduction of such mandatory review of a protection status, would have the particularly detrimental impact of pushing beneficiaries of international and subsidiary protection into a situation of precariousness of status, having direct consequences on their security of status and enhanced risk of falling into irregularity.

ii. The Punitive Approach Towards Unauthorised Movements in the CEAS Reform: Discouraging Cooperation with National Authorities

The proposed reform of the Common European Asylum System introduces a set of both material and procedural sanctions against asylum applicants irregularly moving from one Member State to another Member State (commonly referred to by the European Commission as 'secondary movements').

The Dublin Regulation recast introduces, in its article 5, specific sanctions for applicants who do not remain in the Member State of first entry. Sanctions include: the mandatory use of the accelerated procedure upon return to the responsible Member State; withdrawal of reception conditions save for emergency health care if the applicant absconds; and the procedurally very serious consequence of the inadmissibility of information submitted after the Dublin interview. Such sanctions are not only disproportionate in response to the conduct they attempt to deter, but are also risking having the opposite, unwanted effect of discouraging cooperation with national authorities responsible for the processing of asylum applications and further absconding.

Similarly, the punitive approach to secondary movements of asylum seekers envisaged by the Commission in the recast Reception Conditions Directive amounts to the exclusion from general material reception conditions of asylum seekers engaging in secondary movements. Excluding asylum seekers from access to reception conditions risks pushing them into destitution and irregularity, as also noted by civil society organisations working on the CEAS reform.[44]

Against this backdrop, and in order to address the stalemate of the Common European Asylum System reform, the President of the European Commission, Ursula von der Leyen, has included in her political guidelines for the next European Commission (2019–24) and in the 2020 Commission Work Programme the intention of proposing a New Pact on Migration and Asylum, including the relaunch of the Dublin reform.[45] It remains to be seen how the Commission will ensure that any new proposal is rooted into solid evidence base, by providing duly impact assessments measuring ex ante the potential impacts of proposed legislation, in particular for what relates to the unwarranted effects of creating more exclusion, precariousness of status and irregularity of migrants and asylum seekers, which would be derived by the CEAS reform and Return Directive recast proposals currently on the table of the co-legislators.

IV. Conclusions

Irregular migration is a complex and dynamic phenomenon, fast-changing and, most importantly, caused by a multiplicity of reasons, often intersected. During their migration journey, at different points in space and time, migrants may fall in an irregular situation as a consequence of loss of status for reasons such as unemployment, end of a relationship or refusal of a residence permit renewal or asylum application.

While policy-makers maintain their focus on developing measures aimed at contrasting irregular migration intended as irregular entry, little or no attention is given by the EU legislators to the need to develop measures aimed at preventing irregular migration, meaning loss of status and providing migrants in an irregular situation with the possibility and adequate incentives to obtain a regular status. This approach would be in line with the commitments embraced by the international

[44] See, eg: ECRE Comments on the Commission Proposal to recast the Reception Conditions Directive COM(2016) 465, October 2016, 21.

[45] Ursula von der Leyen, 'A Europe that strives for more. My agenda for Europe', political guidelines for the next European Commission 2019–24 and Annexes to the Adjusted Commission Work Programme 2020 COM(2020) 440 final, 27 May 2020, line 32.

community on the global level with the adoption of the Global Compact on Safe, Orderly and Regular Migration in December 2018.[46]

In line with article 79 TFEU the prevention of irregular migration should be one of the guiding aims of the Union's common migration policy. Measures preventing the loss or precariousness of status and encouraging cooperation with national authorities would support achieving a coherent migration policy at EU level and the overall reduction of irregular migration in the European Union. Such measures should include the following.

A. Promoting Security of Status as Part of the Asylum Acquis

Risk of loss of status as part of measures comprising the asylum acquis and its ongoing reform should be addressed. In this sense, access to long-term refugee status should be prioritised over access to subsidiary protection and measures such as the mandatory review of status upon renewal of a residence permit or ex officio in case of changes of the situation in the country of origin would be counterproductive as bearing the unwarranted effect of leading to more irregularity in the medium/long-term.

B. Providing Adequate Flexibility in Terms of Convertibility of Status

Policies allowing for in-country regularisation or switching of residence status in-country – for instance from student to work residence permit – should be promoted or facilitated. Policy-makers should prioritise the adoption of measures that do not create dependency of status between the visa or residence permit holder and the third country national as is often the case for instance for work permits tied to one employer.

C. Prioritising and Incentivising Voluntary Departures and Voluntary Returns Over Forced Removals

Improving the effectiveness of the return procedure has been one of the priorities of the European Commission and Member States in recent years. To this end, the prioritisation of voluntary departures and voluntary returns would serve the

[46] See especially: Objective no 5 of the Global Compact on Safe, Orderly and Regular Migration: UN General Assembly Resolution adopted on 19 December 2018 (A/73/L.66).

purpose of ensuring better effectiveness of the return acquis. Yet, existing measures and ongoing reform proposals do not seem to translate this into practice. On the contrary, the Return Directive recast proposed by the European Commission in September 2018 increases the use of detention and application of entry bans, thus de facto discouraging voluntary departures and voluntary returns and increasing irregularity.

D. Prioritising Access to Fundamental Rights Over Migration Enforcement

Migrants' access to fundamental rights should be ensured through the establishment of 'firewalls' aimed at avoiding the exchange of data concerning a migrant's status when seeking to access services, including justice, healthcare and education.[47] This would ensure a real prioritisation of migrants' fundamental rights over immigration enforcement and control.

[47] This has also been highlighted by the Council of Europe's European Commission Against Racism and Intolerance (ECRI) in its general policy recommendation no 16 on safeguarding irregularly present migrants from discrimination, adopted on 16 March 2016.

PART II

The Criminalisation of Migration: National, European and Comparative Perspectives

6

Crimmigration in Spain

JOSÉ A BRANDARIZ [1]

I. Introduction

In the last years, the Spanish migration law enforcement system seems to have come of age. Against the backdrop of significant immigration flows and relevant contingents of undocumented residents,[2] the Spanish Ministry of the Interior carried out scores of deportations in the first decade of this century.[3] Nonetheless, back then migration enforcement practices were largely unplanned and focused on the short run.[4]

This has remarkably changed over the last decade. The dire consequences of the financial crisis initiated in 2008 led to a significant decrease of immigration flows, which gradually moved towards Central and Eastern Mediterranean areas. This new scenario alleviated the pressure put on the Spanish migration control system, thereby facilitating its reorganisation. More precisely, over the last decade this apparatus has undertaken two critical transformations. First, its scale has been notably downsized. Second, it has gone a long way in organising its selective operation.

[1] This chapter is partially based on the homonymous paper presented at the *International Conference 'Managing Migration through Criminal Law Tools'* (Milan, Italy, December 2018), organised by the University of Milan. I wish to thank Gian Luigi Gatta, Stefano Zirulia and Valsamis Mitsilegas for having invited me to take part in that conference. Daniel Quinteros, and Roberto Dufraix for their insightful comments that have assisted me in refining this article. I owe a special debt of gratitude to my University of A Coruna colleague Cristina Fernández-Bessa, who as usual provided many thoughful suggestions. A vast number of ideas and conclusions contained in this paper are her own. This chapter has been backed by the research actions DER2017-82390-R and ED431C2019/18, granted by Spanish institutional bodies to the research group ECRIM of the University of A Coruna, Spain.

[2] C Carrasco Carpio, 'Mercado de trabajo e inmigración' in A Izquierdo Escribano (ed), *El modelo de inmigración y los riesgos de exclusión* (Madrid, Foessa, 2008); D Moffette, *Governing Irregular Migration: Bordering Culture, Labor, and Security in Spain* (Vancouver, UBC Press, 2018).

[3] C Fernández Bessa, *El dispositiu de deportació: Anàlisi criminològica de la detenció, internament i expulsió d'immigrants en el context espanyol* (University of Barcelona, Unpublished PhD Dissertation, 2016; diposit.ub.edu/dspace/bitstream/2445/97108/1/CFB_TESI.pdf).

[4] ibid.

This chapter aims to scrutinise in detail this relevant shift, which is the main focus of its last section. This analysis is inscribed, though, within the framework of the international academic debate on the recent changes of national deportation models. Specifically, the following section examines the implications of the 'crimmigration thesis'[5] on the deportation field, as well as its nexus with the so-called 'deportation gap'. Subsequently, this article explores two critical national cases, namely the US and the UK, the evolution of which appears to resonate with – and, therefore, contribute to grasp – what has occurred in Spain.

II. The Deportation Gap and the Crimmigration Thesis

Generally, law enforcement systems are effective in enforcing legal sanctions. Evidently, in the vast majority of national jurisdictions, a judicial decision handing down an unsuspended prison sentence results in the incarceration of the sentenced individual. Thus, the effectiveness of law enforcement agencies in enforcing penalties and other legal consequences is justifiably taken for granted.

This is not the case, however, in the field of migration control policies. With very few exceptions, national authorities have a hard time in enforcing all – or, even a significant percentage – of the issued deportation orders. In other words, many countries face significant obstacles in carrying out deportation measures, which leads to low or very low enforcement rates.

The causes of this phenomenon, which is widely known by EU and national political institutions,[6] are variegated and their analysis falls beyond the scope of this chapter. Yet, in this regard the logistical obstacles hampering the detection and identification of potentially deportable non-citizens, the legal obstacles impeding the return of foreing individuals to either countries in which their life of physical integrity might be under threat or to nations with which no repatriation agreements have been concluded, and the financial obstacles arising from the huge resources required by an effective deportation system should be particularly taken into consideration.[7]

[5] J Stumpf, 'The Crimmigration Crisis: Immigrants, Crime, and Sovereign Power' (2006) 56 *American University Law Review* 367.

[6] See on this the Commission Recommendation (EU) 2017/432 of 7 March 2017 on making returns more effective when implementing Directive 2008/115/EC of the European Parliament and of the Council ([2017] OJ L66).

[7] A Ellermann, *States against Migrants: Deportation in Germany and the United States* (Cambridge, Cambridge University Press, 2009); D Kanstroom, *Aftermath: Deportation Law and the New American Diaspora* (New York: Oxford University Press, 2012); Moffette, above n 2; N Peutz and N De Genova, 'Introduction' in N De Genova and N Peutz (eds), *The Deportation Regime: Sovereignty, Space, and the Freedom of Movement* (Durham, Duke University Press, 2010).

This phenomenon has been termed 'deportation gap' by the academic literature, which has especially stressed the consequences of these ineffective deportation policies on the living conditions of non-citizens.[8] An additional analytical framework, the so-called 'deportability thesis', approaches this gap by claiming that it is not deportation as such, but its constant and latent threat, which disciplines migrant groups and individuals. This perspective, therefore, nuances the alleged ineffectiveness of forced return policies.[9]

EU removal practices are the best evidence of this deportation gap. Since 2008, when Eurostat began to disclose data on issued and enforced deportation orders, this phenomenon became particularly evident. As illustrated by Table 1, despite the huge resources allocated to border control policies, EU national systems are remarkably affected by this shortcoming.

Table 1 Deportations enforced in EU Member States and national enforcement rates, 2008–2018

EU Member State	Enforced deportation orders	% of issued deportation orders	EU Member State	Enforced deportation orders	% of issued deportation orders
UK	551,360	88.1%	**Netherlands**	102,445	33.6%
Greece	327,655	34.9%	**Italy**	65,105	16.3%
Germany	319,630	76.6%	**Belgium**	63,360	17.3%
France	203,675	21.5%	**Austria**	62,680	63.6%
Spain	202,100	32.5%	**Hungary**	35,735	44.3%
Poland	133,380	86.8%	**Other MMSS**	227,945	49.2%
Sweden	128,590	65.7%	**Total**	2,423,660	43.2%

Source: Eurostat (ec.europa.eu/eurostat/web/asylum-and-managed-migration/data/database).[10]

These data lay bare the salience of the analysed gap. Whilst some EU Member States such as the UK, Poland and Germany manage to enforce the majority of the issued removal orders, a number of top deporting countries (Greece, France and Spain, as well as the Netherlands, Italy and Belgium) do not carry out more than

[8] MJ Gibney, 'Asylum and the Expansion of Deportation in the United Kingdom' (2008) 43 *Government and Opposition* 146; Ellermann, above n 7; S Rosenberger and C Küffner, 'After the Deportation Gap: Non-Removed Persons and their Pathways to Social Rights' in R Hsu and C Reinprecht (eds), *Migration and Integration: New Models for Mobility and Coexistence* (Wien, Vienna University Press, 2016).

[9] N De Genova, 'Migrant "Illegality" and Deportability in Everyday Life' (2002) 31 *Annual Review of Anthropology* 419; Peutz and De Genova, above n 7.

[10] These data do not take into account deportations targeting EU citizens, since Eurostat do not supply statistical information on this type of removals.

one third of the issued repatriation measures. In short, the deportation gap is a critical trait of the deportation landscape, which leads many national migration enforcement systems to operate in a highly selective way.

A body of scholarship has claimed that the increasing awareness on this institutional conundrum coincided with a growing political concern to both scale up removal policies and improve their effectiveness, in what has been called the 'deportation turn'.[11] However, in order to scrutinise in detail the relation of migration enforcement changes and the deportation gap an additional theoretical perspective should be brought to the fore, that is, the so-called 'crimmigration thesis'.

As is widely known, in an article published in 2006, Juliet Stumpf set the groundwork for the development of an innovative approach to the field of migration control that since then has been called the 'crimmigration thesis'. She claimed that migration law enforcement policies are currently characterised by an increasing convergence of migration law and criminal law, which has a significant impact in defining and setting the boundaries of belonging and alienness, of inclusion and exclusion.

Embracing this analytical framework, a broad number of papers and publications have scrutinised the main tenets and components of what may be called the crimmigration turn.[12] Nancy Wonders argues that this merging of migration law and criminal law has led to the enaction of legal norms reinforcing the deportability of sentenced foreigners, to implement policies and strategies aimed at criminalising immigration, especially irregular immigration, and to the interweaving of

[11] A Bloch and L Schuster, 'At the Extremes of Exclusion: Deportation, Detention and Dispersal' (2005) 28 *Ethnic and Racial Studies* 491; L Fekete, 'The Deportation Machine: Europe, Asylum and Human Rights' (2005) 47 *Race & Class* 64; Gibney, above n 8; D Kanstroom, *Deportation Nation: Outsiders in American History* (Cambridge, Harvard University Press, 2007); L Schuster, 'A Sledgehammer to Crack a Nut: Deportation, Detention and Dispersal in Europe' (2005) 39 *Social Policy & Administration* 606.

[12] KF Aas, '"Crimmigrant" Bodies and Bona Fide Travelers: Surveillance, Citizenship and Global Governance' (2011) 15 *Theoretical Criminology* 331; KF Aas, 'The Ordered and the Bordered Society: Migration Control, Citizenship, and the Northern Penal State' in KF Aas and M Bosworth M (eds), *The Borders of Punishment: Migration, Citizenship, and Social Exclusion* (Oxford, Oxford University Press, 2013); CC García Hernández, *Crimmigration Law* (Chicago, American Bar Association, 2015); R Koulish, 'Sovereign Bias, Crimmigration, and Risk' in MJ Guia, R Koulish and V Mitsilegas (eds), *Immigration Detention, Risk, and Human Rights: Studies on Immigration and Crime* (New York, Springer, 2016); D Quinteros, '¿Nueva "crimigración" o la vieja economía política del castigo? Dos aproximaciones criminológicas para entender el control punitivo de la migración en Chile' (2016) 17 *Astrolabio* 81; J Stumpf, 'The Process is the Punishment in Crimmigration Law' in KF Aas and M Bosworth (eds), *The Borders of Punishment: Migration, Citizenship, and Social Exclusion* (Oxford, Oxford University Press, 2013); J Stumpf, 'Crimmigration: Encountering the Leviathan' in S Pickering and J Ham (eds), *The Routledge Handbook on Crime and International Migration* (London, Routledge, 2015); JM Chacon, 'Managing Migration through Crime' (2009) 109 *Columbia Law Review* 135; JM Chacon, 'Overcriminalizing Immigration' (2012) 102 *Journal of Criminal Law and Criminology* 613; V Mitsilegas, *The Criminalisation of Migration in Europe: Challenges for Human Rights and the Rule of Law* (New York, Springer, 2015).

border control and the criminal justice system.[13] Ben Bowling,[14] in turn, points out that crimmigration policies encompass legal reforms, monitoring and surveillance technologies, policing models and *imm-carceration* schemes. In elaborating these perspectives, Joanne van der Leun and Maartje van der Woude[15] convincingly highlight that the crimmigration turn does not only affect the legal field; it has, in effect, a social dimension, and its impact is felt in the political discourses that associate immigration with crime. In addition, these Dutch scholars[16] conclude that crimmigration changes are epitomised by measures aimed at criminalising (particularly, irregular) immigration, excluding 'unwanted' foreign nationals, integrating migration issues within the criminal law order, expanding deportation powers with regard to criminally convicted non-citizens, and detaining immigrants.

As can be seen, these various descriptions of the crimmigration turn make reference to the adoption of removal measures as a tool to curb criminal activities. In fact, Stumpf[17] has synthetised her crimmigration thesis in two main aspects, that is, the expansion of crime-related deportation powers and the creation of immigration crimes to regulate migration flows.[18] The first dimension is what concerns our analysis. In short, the question to be posed is if, and to what extent, this aspect of the crimmigration turn can be understood as a way to address the long-lasting deportation gap.

This gap-crimmigration nexus was conspicuously pointed to by an Immigration and Customs Enforcement (ICE) Memorandum published in March 2011 by John Morton,[19] then director of this US migration law enforcement agency. More unambiguous than top officials normally are, Morton pointed out:

> ICE is charged with enforcing the nation's civil immigration laws. This is a critical mission … ICE, however, only has resources to remove approximately 400,000 aliens per year, less than 4 percent of the estimated illegal alien population in the United States. In light of the large number of administrative violations the agency is charged with addressing and the limited enforcement resources the agency has available, ICE must prioritize the use of its enforcement personnel, detention space, and removal resources

[13] N Wonders, 'Sitting on the Fence – Spain's Delicate Balance: Bordering, Multiscalar Challenges, and Crimmigration' (2017) 14 *European Journal of Criminology* 7.

[14] B Bowling, 'Epilogue: The Borders of Punishment: Towards a Criminology of Mobility' in KF Aas and M Bosworth (eds), *The Borders of Punishment: Migration, Citizenship, and Social Exclusion* (Oxford, Oxford University Press, 2013).

[15] J van der Leun and M van der Woude, 'A Reflection on Crimmigration in the Netherlands' in MJ Guia, M van der Woude and J van der Leun (eds), *Social Control and Justice: Crimmigration in the Age of Fear* (Den Haag, Eleven, 2013); M van der Woude, J van der Leun and J Nijland, 'Crimmigration in the Netherlands' (2014) 39 *Law and Social Inquiry* 560.

[16] van der Woude, van der Leun and Nijland, above n 14.

[17] Stumpf, above n 11 (both references).

[18] A Aliverti, *Crimes of Mobility: Criminal Law and the Regulation of Immigration* (London, Routledge, 2013).

[19] *Civil Immigration Enforcement: Priorities for the Apprehension, Detention, and Removal of Aliens*; www.ice.gov/doclib/news/releases/2011/110302washingtondc.pdf.

> to ensure that the removals the agency does conduct promote the agency's highest enforcement priorities, namely national security, public safety, and border security.

As will be subsequently addressed, this Memorandum led the US administration to prevailingly target a set of migrant groups, allegedly characterised by their inherent dangerousness. This political document did not openly mention the deportation gap, despite its impact on the US deportation apparatus.[20] However, the ICE Memorandum realistically acknowledged the limited scope of the migration control agencies' resources and, hence, put in place a model to organise ICE's selective intervention. In this regard, it set up a utilitarian – and, as will be pointed out later, crimmigration-like – response to the concerning and unmanageable deportation gap. Certainly, the preference order set by the Memorandum may be considered entirely reasonable in terms of the efficiency and effectiveness of public policies. Since no jurisdiction is capable of deporting either all irregular migrants or even those detected by law enforcement agencies, it may be seen as rational to organise the operation of the deportation apparatus according to a sort of hierarchy of otherness. Consequently, the next section will scrutinise if realist stances such as that championed by John Morton have had an impact on the deportation field, by exploring two critical national cases.

III. Crimmigration and Deportation Changes: Two National Cases

Although national governments have hardly been so outspoken as Morton's ICE was, the concerns addressed by that 2011 Memo have an international reach. This section is devoted to examine whether the reorganisation of the selectiveness of deportation systems advocated by that policy document has actually had consequences on the ground. For these purposes, two national cases will be explored, namely the USA and the UK. These cases have not been randomly selected. The USA arguably features the widest-encompassing deportation system of all Global North jurisdictions;[21] additionally, it is the country in relation to which the crimmigration thesis was elaborated.[22] Britain, in turn, has the most developed deportation apparatus of all EU Member States (see Table 1).

In the US, the legal basis for the crimmigration turn was set by the almost simultaneous passage in 1996 of the Illegal Immigration Reform and Immigrant

[20] Ellermann, above n 7.

[21] The US administration enforced 3.73 million removals from 2008 to 2017, whereas EU national deportation systems carried out 2.23 million returns over the same period (sources: Eurostat and DHS Immigration Enforcement Actions; www.dhs.gov/immigration-statistics/enforcement-actions).

[22] V Barker, J van der Leun and M van der Woude, 'Introduction: Crimmigration in Europe' (2017) 14 *European Journal of Criminology* 3; van der Leun and van der Woude, above n 14.

Responsibility Act (IIRIRA; sections 321–34) and the Antiterrorism and Effective Death Penalty Act (AEDPA; sections 431–43), which scaled up the scope of the detention and deportation measures targeting so-called 'criminal aliens'.[23] Specifically, this new legal framework broadened the catalogue of aggravated felonies (section 440 AEDPA, section 321 IIRIRA), criminal offences leading to mandatory removal when committed by non-citizens. Since then, aggravated felonies encompass all felonies and misdemeanours punishable with a prison sentence of one year or more.[24] Furthermore, these aggravated felonies are applied to undocumented immigrants and documented immigrants alike, regardless of the social and family bonds in the US and the time in which they left their home country.[25]

Beyond these normative reforms, as is usual in a field logistically so complex as that of migration law enforcement, the crimmigration turn was essentially driven by extra-legal factors. The xenophobic scenario triggered by the September 2001 terror attacks was particularly crucial.[26] This new political landscape resulted in an exponential increment of the resources allocated to migration control agencies,[27] which expanded the deportation and – especially – detention capabilities of the US system.[28]

An efficient deportation apparatus, though, requires supplementing financial resources with public policies aimed at easing and speeding up removal procedures. In this regard, US agencies have implemented two significant innovative practices over the last 20 years. First, as was previously mentioned, they passed a number of memoranda setting priorities in detecting, apprehending and returning non-citizens. These guidelines, which were in force from 2011 to 2017, gave preference to the detention and removal of migrants that either may allegedly be a threat for national security or perpetrate criminal offences, especially serious crimes.[29]

[23] A Armenta, *Protect, Serve, and Deport: The Rise of Policing as Immigration Enforcement* (Oakland, University of California Press, 2017); TM Golash-Boza, 'Structural Racism, Criminalization, and Pathways to Deportation for Dominican and Jamaican Men in the United States' (2017) 44 *Social Justice* 137; Kanstroom, above n 7.

[24] TM Golash-Boza, *Deported: Immigrant Policing, Disposable Labour, and Global Capitalism* (New York, New York University Press, 2015) Kanstroom, above n 10; P Macías-Rojas, *From Deportation to Prison: The Politics of Immigration Enforcement in Post-Civil Rights America* (New York, New York University Press, 2016).

[25] Golash-Boza, above n 23; Kanstroom, above n 7; MK Dingeman-Cerda and SB Coutin, 'The Ruptures of Return. Deportation's Confounding Effects' in C Kubrin, MS Zatz and R Martínez Jr (eds), *Punishing Immigrants* (New York, New York University Press, 2012); SS Wadhia, *Beyond Deportation: The Role of Prosecutorial Discretion in Immigration Cases* (New York, New York University Press, 2015).

[26] Armenta, above n 22; Kanstroom, above n 7; Wadhia, above n 24.

[27] Golash-Boza, above n 22; Kanstroom, above n 7.

[28] Macías-Rojas, above n 23; R Koulish, *Immigration and American Democracy* (New York, Routledge, 2010); A Sampaio, *Terrorizing Latina/o Immigrants* (Philadelphia, Temple University Press, 2015).

[29] The last of these memoranda, published by ICE in November 2014 (*Policies for the Apprehension, Detention and Removal of Undocumented Immigrants*; www.dhs.gov/sites/default/files/publications/14_1120_memo_prosecutorial_discretion.pdf), which was formally abrogated by the

Second, this selective model was coupled with the implementation of a series of programmes geared towards enhancing cooperation and information exchange among law enforcement agencies, with a view to improve the detection of deportable aliens, especially those falling under memoranda categories. These programmes, such as the CAP (Criminal Aliens Program), the S-Comm (Secure Communities Program) and the so-called 287(g) agreements (named after the corresponding section of the Immigration and Nationality Act),[30] sought to refine the collaboration of migration law enforcement agencies and police corps, namely local and state police units.[31]

Since the onset of the century, the main consequence of the aforementioned financial, organisational and logistical measures has been the salient increase in the number of enforced removals (*post-entry control*), that is, forced repatriations that are not the immediate result of an arrest carried out within the border area (in contrast to *returns*; *extended border control*).[32] As illustrated by the available data (Table 2), both the number of enforced removals and that of detentions significantly mounted all thoughout the Obama administration, with the exception of its last years.[33]

Table 2 Detentions and removals carried out in the US, 2006–2018 (in thousands)

	2006	2007	2008	2009	2010	2011	2012	2013	2014	2015	2016	2017	2018
Detentions	256.8	311.1	378.6	383.5	358.4	421.3	464.2	440.5	425.7	307.3	352.9	323.6	396.4
Removals	281	319.4	359.8	391.3	382.5	390.5	415.7	432.4	405.6	326.4	333.6	295.4	–

Sources: DHS. Immigration Data and Statistics; ICE Statistics (www.ice.gov/statistics).

An additional result of the legal and policy changes put in practice by the US administration is more closely associated with the dimension of the crimmigration turn which, in line with the aforementioned ICE memoranda, leads to giving preference to the deportation of criminally convicted migrants. However, the outcome of this selective organisation of the system has been ambivalent.[34]

Executive Order No. 13768 passed in January 2017 (Armenta, above n 22), set a three-level hierarchy of priorities: a) Priority 1: threats to national security, border security, and public safety; b) Priority 2: individuals perpetrating misdemeanours and new immigration offenders; c) Priority 3: other immigration breaches. Level 1 targeted non-citizens involved in terrorism crimes, other criminal offences that may threaten national security, and serious non-immigration crimes, as well as immigrants participating in criminal organisations and criminal gangs, and aliens sentenced for committing aggravated felonies, but also irregular border-crossers (Koulish, above n 11). See Macías-Rojas, above n 23; Sampaio, above n 27; Wadhia, above n 24.

[30] Armenta, above n 22; Kanstroom, above n 7.

[31] See Macías-Rojas, above n 23; Sampaio, above n 27.

[32] See on this Kanstroom, above nn 7 and 10.

[33] Golash-Boza, above n 23; M Gottschalk, *Caught: The Prison State and the Lockdown of American Politics* (Princeton, Princeton University Press, 2015); Kanstroom, above n 7.

[34] Kanstroom, above n 7; Sampaio, above n 27; Wadhia, above n 24.

Table 3 Criminal removals and non-criminal removals enforced in the US, 2006–2017 (in thousands)

	2006	2007	2008	2009	2010	2011	2012	2013	2014	2015	2016	2017
Non-criminal removals	185.2 (65.9%)	219.4 (68.7%)	262.7 (73%)	263 (67.2%)	211.5 (55.3%)	199.8 (51.4%)	215.7 (51.9%)	233.9 (54.1%)	233.0 (57.4%)	187.4 (57.4%)	204.4 (59.2%)	174.1 (58.9%)
Criminal removals	95.8 (34.1%)	100 (31.3%)	97.1 (27%)	128.3 (32.8%)	171.0 (44.7%)	189.7 (48.6%)	200 (48.1%)	198.5 (45.9%)	172.6 (42.6%)	139.0 (42.6%)	136.2 (40.8%)	121.3 (41.1%)

Source: DHS (www.dhs.gov/immigration-statistics/enforcement-actions).

Indeed, these US Department of Homeland Security data lay bare that the immigration enforcement strategies aimed at giving prevalence to the removal of allegedly dangerous individuals have partially failed. From 2006 to 2017, only 40.4 per cent of the deportees had a criminal conviction, and whilst this percentage rapidly escalated from the late 2000s to the early 2010s it has declined in the last years. Moreover, the vast majority of these deported offenders were far from having high-risk profiles.[35] From 2010 to 2017, roughly 2/3 of these deported offenders had been sentenced for minor crimes, namely immigration violations (27.2 per cent), drug crimes (19.3 per cent), and traffic offences (17.3 per cent).[36]

In short, the US case shows the strengths as well as the weaknesses of a crimmigration strategy apparently seeking to address the long-lasting obstacle put by the deportation gap.[37] Yet, this is not the only national system undertaking a reorientation of its deportation apparatus. This change may be further explored by taking into account the UK case.

The British migration law enforcement system has also been increasingly focused on the deportation of sentenced foreigners over the last decade.[38] The starting point of this shift can be easily dated. In April 2006, the UK Home Office acknowledged that over a seven-year period some one thousand foreign prisoners had been released without being considered for post-release removal measures.[39] The subsequent public scandal forced the Home Office Secretary to resign and

[35] Armenta, above n 22; Golash-Boza, above n 23.

[36] Source: DHS Immigration Enforcement Actions (www.dhs.gov/immigration-statistics/enforcement-actions).

[37] Wadhia, above n 24.

[38] M Bosworth, 'Deportation, Detention and Foreign-National prisoners in England and Wales' (2011) 15 *Citizenship Studies* 583; S Turnbull and I Hasselberg, 'From Prison to Detention: The Carceral Trajectories of Foreign-National Prisoners in the United Kingdom' (2017) 19 *Punishment & Society* 135.

[39] Aliverti, above n 17; HS Bhui, 'Alien Experience: Foreign National Prisoners after the Deportation Crisis' (2007) 54 *Probation Journal* 368; E Kaufman, 'Hubs and Spokes: The Transformation of the British Prison' in KF Aas and M Bosworth (eds), *The Borders of Punishment: Migration, Citizenship, and Social Exclusion* (Oxford, Oxford University Press, 2013); E Kaufman, *Punish and Expel: Border Control, Nationalism and the New Purpose of the Prison* (Oxford, Oxford University Press, 2015); F Pakes and K Holt, 'Crimmigration and the Prison: Comparing Trends in Prison Policy and Practice in England & Wales and Norway' (2017) 14 *European Journal of Criminology* 63; E Kaufman and M Bosworth, 'The Prison and National Identity: Citizenship, Punishment and the Sovereign State' in D Scott (ed), *Why Prison?* (Cambridge, Cambridge University Press, 2013).

set the conditions for the eventual passage of the UK Borders Act 2007 in October 2007. This new statute significantly widened deportation powers. Specifically, it made all foreign prisoners potentially eligible for judicial orders imposing post-prison removals. In addition, the UK Borders Act 2007 (section 32) made these removal orders mandatory in the case of foreign prisoners sentenced to one year of imprisonment or more, and to two years of imprisonment or more in the case of EU and European Free Trade Agreement national prisoners.[40]

As it happened in the US, the crimmigration turn went far beyond this legal reform. It was crucially fuelled by the implementation of a number of measures and programmes aimed at detecting deportable non-citizens in 2009.[41] On the one hand, the prison service and the migration enforcement agency (UK Border Agency, from 2013 split into two new agencies, UK Border Force and Immigration Enforcement) concluded cooperation agreements geared towards facilitating forced repatriation procedures, focusing on information exchange and the access of border control officers to prison facilities.[42] On the other hand, again with a view to facilitate the detection of deportable aliens, the British prison service concentrated foreign national inmates in a small number of prisons, in which they remain under custody until serving their sentence, awaiting for a subsequent deportation order to be enforced.[43]

In addition, in order to give preference to the removal of foreign inmates with high-risk profiles, the UK Home Office implemented so-called 'harm' protocols setting enforcement priorities, in which only category A (highest harm) deportees encompass serious criminal offenders, rather than migration violators.[44]

The available data illustrate that these various innovations have only partially transformed UK deportation practices. The number of deportations involving former foreign national prisoners has significantly risen over the last decade – mainly due to the relevant increase of the removals targeting former EU national

[40] Aliverti, above n 17; Bosworth, above n 37; MJ Gibney, 'Deportation, Crime, and the Changing Character of Membership in the United Kingdom' in KF Aas and M Bosworth (eds), *The Borders of Punishment: Migration, Citizenship, and Social Exclusion* (Oxford, Oxford University Press, 2013).

[41] Pakes and Holt, above n 38.

[42] Bosworth, above n 37; Kaufman, above n 38 (both references); Kaufman and Bosworth, above n 39.

[43] Aliverti, above n 17; M Bosworth, 'Border Criminology and the Changing Nature of Penal Power' in A Liebling, S Maruna and L McAra (eds), *The Oxford Handbook of Criminology* 6th edn (Oxford, Oxford University Press, 2017); Pakes and Holt, above n 38; Turnbull and Hasselberg, above n 37.

[44] This 'harm matrix' sets the following classification: a) Category A (highest harm): criminal offences, including serious crimes such as terrorism, homicide, rape, trafficking in human beings, drug crimes, violent crimes and child abuse; b) Category B (high harm): other crimes, namely migration offences such as working without a permit, fraudulent asylum request and forgery of identity documents; c) Category C (medium harm): other violations, including minor immigration breaches, welfare abuse and anti-social behaviour; d) Category D (low harm): other minor violations, including shoplifting (Home Office (2019) *User Guide to Home Office Immigration Statistics* (assets.publishing.service.gov.uk/government/uploads/system/uploads/attachment_data/file/781065/user-guide-immigration-statistics.pdf). See Aliverti, above n 17.

inmates[45] – but they still make up a minor part of the deportation model (see Table 4). This is unsurprising, since British migration enforcement agencies promoted the expansion of the repatriation system in its entirety, among other means by setting quantitative deportation quotas.[46]

Table 4 Criminal and non-criminal deportations carried out in the UK, 2009–2018

	2009	2010	2011	2012	2013	2014	2015	2016	2017	2018
Criminal deportations	5,528 (14.5%)	5,344 (12.7%)	4,649 (11.2%)	4,765 (10.8%)	4,993 (11.0%)	5,286 (13.2%)	5,768 (13.8%)	6,171 (15.6%)	6,113 (18.8%)	5,209 (21.8%)
Non-criminal deportations	32,524 (85.5%)	36,624 (87.3%)	36,833 (88.8%)	39,545 (89.2%)	40,496 (89.0%)	34,893 (86.8%)	36,111 (86.2%)	33,455 (84.4%)	26,438 (81.2%)	18,680 (78.2%)

Source: UK National Statistics. Immigration Statistics (www.gov.uk/government/statistics/immigration-statistics-year-ending-december-2018-data-tables).[47]

Risk assessment should also be taken into consideration. From 2009 to 2018, only 10.5 per cent of the evaluated deportations (8 per cent of all deportations, including non-assessed removals) were classified as highest harm (category A) removals.[48]

The examination of the UK case leads to two relevant conclusions. First, also in Britain crime-related deportations have gained traction in the recent past. In fact, in the framework of a downsizing of this national migration enforcement apparatus, they have augmented its relative share. Second, the crimmigration shift cannot be understood as a response to the deportation gap. As was previously mentioned (see Table 1), the UK features the highest enforcement rate of all EU Member States, close to 90 per cent in the last years. In Britain, therefore, the deportation gap is a relatively minor problem. This stands in contrast with the Spanish situation, a jurisdiction that, in line with other European States such as Belgium,[49] Norway[50] and Sweden,[51] has also witnessed an increasing effort to enforce crime-related deportations.

[45] S Turnbull, 'Immigration Detention and the Racialized Governance of Illegality in the United Kingdom' (2017) 44 *Social Justice* 142.

[46] L Fekete, *A Suitable Enemy: Racism, Migration and Islamophobia in Europe* (London, Pluto Press, 2009); Kaufman 2015, above n 38.

[47] These data include both forced removals and the so-called 'voluntary' returns, because some former prisoners are repatriated under 'voluntary' return schemes.

[48] Source: UK National Statistics. Immigration Statistics (www.gov.uk/government/publications/immigration-statistics-year-ending-december-2019/how-many-people-are-detained-or-returned#data-tables).

[49] L Breuls, 'Portraying Forced Removal As a Means for Crime Control. On Immigration Policy Communication in Belgium' (2017) 44 *Lo Squaderno* 44, 39.

[50] KF Aas, 'Bordered Penality: Precarious Membership and Abnormal Justice' (2014) 16 *Punishment & Society* 520.

[51] V Barker, *Nordic Nationalism and Penal Order: Walling the Welfare State* (Abingdon, Routledge, 2018).

IV. The Crimmigration Turn of the Spanish Deportation Regime

In effect, in line with what has been theorised by the crimmigration thesis, also in Spain the utilisation of deportation measures for crime prevention purposes has gained currency over the last decade.[52] The analysis of the US and UK cases contributes to shed light on this change, because the Spanish shift is consistent with what has happened in those Global North Jurisdictions.

As any other EU Member State, the Spanish legal order regulates various types of removal orders. Initially, the Spanish 2000 Foreigners' Law (Article 57(1)) sanctions with an administrative removal order a range of serious migration law breaches (Articles 53–54), by far the most relevant being the irregular residence in Spain (Article 53(1) of the Spanish Foreigners' Law).

In addition, Spanish legal provisions set a number of removal orders based on crime and criminal activities. First, there is the criminal deportation order (Article 89 of the Penal Code) that is imposed to non-citizens sentenced to one year of imprisonment or more, in partial or total substitution of the prison sentence. Second, Article 57(2) of the Foreigners' Law mandates the removal of foreign nationals with criminal records of a previous sentence, handed down either in Spain or elsewhere, of one year of imprisonment or more.[53] Moreover, as in any other EU Member State (see Articles 27–33 of the Citizens' Rights Directive – Directive 2004/38/EC of 29 April 2004; OJ [2004] L158; CRD), the forced (administrative) return of EU citizens and their kin is also related to safety concerns, namely to public policy and public security grounds (Article 15 of the Spanish Royal Decree No 240/2007, of 16 February 2007).

The regulation of these various types of removal orders has been hardly modified over the last decade. Both deportation orders based on criminal records and removal orders of EU nationals have not been reformed in the recent past. By contrast, criminal deportation orders have been legally modified three times since 2003. These reforms have generally sought to expand the scope of these crime-related deportation orders. Specifically, the most recent modification, which was enacted in March 2015 (Organic Law No 1/2015), made these removal measures applicable not only to irregular migrants but also to documented foreigners and even to EU citizens.[54] The legal salience of this reform is undeniable. However, the

[52] JA Brandariz, 'Crimmigration Policies and the Great Recession: Analysis of the Spanish case' in MJ Guia, R Koulish and V Mitsilegas (eds), *Immigration Detention, Risk And Human Rights* (New York, Springer, 2016); C Fernández Bessa, 'Il panorama dei centri di internamento per stranieri in Spagna: Dal controllo delle frontiere alla gestione della criminalità' (2013) 8 *Antigone* 68; Fernández Bessa, above n 3.

[53] E Larrauri, 'Antecedentes penales y expulsión de personas inmigrantes' (2016) 2 *InDret* 1.

[54] D Boza Martínez, *La expulsión de personas extranjeras condenadas penalmente: El nuevo artículo 89 CP* (Cizur Menor, Thomson Reuters Aranzadi, 2016); E García España, 'La expulsión como sustitutivo de la pena de prisión en el Código Penal de 2015: ¿De la discriminación a la reinserción?' (2016) 18-07 *Revista Electrónica de Ciencia Penal y Criminología* 1;

available data suggest that the crimmigration turn has not been prompted by this legal change. Although the 2015 legal amendment notably widens the reach of criminal deportation orders, it has not given rise to a significant expansion of the deportation regime.[55] In the framework of an immigration enforcement scheme that has been constantly downsizing over the last decade (see Table 5 below), the aim of this reform seems to be focused on refining the internal coherence of the legal order, by harmonising the regulation of the three types of crime-related and security-related deportation orders.

The crimmigration turn, though, may be easily traced in the field of political discourses. Since the right-wing Popular Party came into office in December 2011, the Spanish Ministry of the Interior crafted a narrative emphasising that 'criminal' migrants were the almost exclusive target of detention and deportation measures.[56] This official rhetoric was based on a transformation that predated the change of government and pertains to the range of organisational reforms (better said, managerial reforms)[57] that have enabled the turn of the deportation regime, that is, the creation of the so-called 'qualified deportations' in 2008. This non-legal notion was defined by the Ministry of the Interior in securitarian terms.[58] Although its definition was slightly altered over the years, the official rhetoric essentially described qualified deportations as removals targetting 'criminal aliens with numerous criminal and/or judicial records that are involved in terrorism crimes, organised crime, violence against women or any other most serious criminal act, and put under threat public security'.[59]

This political narrative is evidently hyperbolic, since the Spanish Ministry classifies as 'qualified deportations' removals targeting migrants that are neither hardened lawbreakers nor even sentenced criminal offenders.[60] In fact, the

[55] In contrast to the mentioned legal reform, the number of criminal deportation orders issued by Spanish courts has significantly decreased in the last period. On average, 2,032 criminal removal orders were issued per year from 2008 to 2014, before dwindling to 1,055 from 2015 to 2017 (Source: Spanish Statistical Office [INE], www.ine.es/dyngs/INEbase/es/operacion.htm?c=Estadistica_C&cid=1254736176793&menu=resultados&idp=1254735573206). It is not evident, though, whether these data are wholly reliable or not, since some some empirical studies (see P Martín Escribano, *La expulsión del extranjero del artículo 89 del Código Penal: Análisis jurídico-penal y criminológico* (University of Girona, Unpublished PhD Dissertation, 2015; www.tdx.cat/bitstream/handle/10803/361400/tpame1de1.pdf?sequence=5)) suggest that the number of issued orders is most likely higher than that published by the INE.

[56] Brandariz, above n 50. See also T Sust, 'El Gobierno primará el ingreso de foráneos con delitos en los CIE' *El Periódico de Catalunya*, 1 May 2012 (www.elperiodico.com/es/noticias/sociedad/gobierno-primara-ingreso-foraneos-con-delitos-los-cie-1731042). I Ulloa Rubio, 'El desafío de garantizar la seguridad pública: El modelo de seguridad pública' (2012) 7–8 *Seguridad y ciudadanía: Revista del Ministerio del Interior* 13.

[57] JA Brandariz and C Fernández Bessa, 'The Managerial Turn: The Transformation of Spanish Migration Control Policies since the Onset of the Economic Crisis' (2017) 56 *The Howard Journal of Crime and Justice* 198.

[58] Boza Martínez, above n 52.

[59] Ministry of the Interior press release of 29 April 2014; www.interior.gob.es/prensa.

[60] Campaña estatal por el cierre de los CIE (2014) *Paremos los vuelos: Las deportaciones de inmigrantes y el boicot a Air Europa* (Oviedo: Cambalache); Fernández Bessa, above n 3; M Martínez Escamilla,

Spanish administration includes within this category the coercive repatriation of both individuals with so-called 'police records' (i.e., records of police arrests that did not lead to either an indictment or a conviction) and migrants previously fined for their irregular status.[61]

However, despite its deceitful nature, the 'qualified deportations' category has served two intertwined key goals which stem from both political and managerial concerns. On the one hand, this category and the corresponding political discourse has been undeniably useful for political communication purposes.[62] On the other hand, in the framework of a selective system permanently affected by a significant deportation gap, the 'qualified deportations' guideline has operated as a criterion of managerial reorganisation[63] seeking to ensure that the Spanish deportation model is as politically – and legally – robust and unchallengeable as possible, which in the Ministry of the Interior's viewpoint can be achieved by portraying the vast majority of forced returns as 'qualified', i.e., as related to crime and security issues. From this political and managerial perspective, it is unsurprising that the Spanish Ministry has managed to ensure that qualified deportations have stood for more than 70 per cent of all enforced removals since the beginning of the decade.[64]

The adoption of this managerial guideline is not the only organisational measure that has enabled the crimmigration turn of the Spanish deportation. Qualified deportations have been coupled with the creation in 2009 of the Brigade for the Deportation of Foreign Criminals (BEDEX for its initials in Spanish; since 2012 renamed as Service, SEDEX) within the Spanish National Police, to boost the enforcement of qualified deportations,[65] which has been a crucial aspect of recent changes.

In sum, the crimmigration turn of the Spanish deportation apparatus was heralded by a renewed official rhetoric and was brought about by managerial and organisational alterations of the migration law enforcement system.

The available data unambiguously confirm the shift forecasted by these reforms and changes. The crimmigration shift has occurred in the context of an overall

Mujeres en el CIE: Género, inmigración e internamiento (Donostia-San Sebastián, Tercera Prensa, 2013); M Martínez Escamilla, 'Centros de Internamiento para Extranjeros: Estado de la cuestión y perspectivas de futuro' (2016) 18–23 *Revista electrónica de Ciencia penal y Criminología* 1; Moffette, above n 2.

[61] Boza Martínez, above n 52; Martínez Escamilla 2013, above n 58; Moffette, above n 2; E Sainz de la Maza Quintanal, *'Ultima Ratio': El proceso de expulsión de inmigrantes en situación irregular En España* (Complutense University of Madrid, Unpublished PhD Dissertation, 2015; eprints.ucm.es/34472/).

[62] Boza Martínez, above n 52; Campaña Estatal por el Cierre de los CIE, above n 58; Moffette, above n 2.

[63] Brandariz and Fernández Bessa, above n 55.

[64] JA Brandariz and C Fernández Bessa, 'La crimigracion en el contexto español: El creciente protagonismo de lo punitivo en el control migratorio' in A López-Sala and D Godenau (eds), *Estados de contención, estados de detención: El control de la inmigración irregular en España* (Barcelona, Anthropos, 2017).

[65] Boza Martínez, above n 52; Ministerio del Interior (2010) *Balance de la lucha contra la inmigración ilegal 2009* (www.interior.gob.es/gl/prensa/balances-e-informes/2009); Sainz de la Maza, above n 59.

contraction of the Spanish deportation apparatus.[66] As illustrated in Table 5, the number of both issued and enforced deportation orders has almost constantly and remarkably declined since the onset of the economic crisis, which resulted in a significant reduction of immigration flows.[67] From 2008 to its nadir in 2016, the number of enforced returns plummeted by an impressive 65.8 per cent, whilst that of issued orders dwindled by a no less significant 66.4 per cent. Both indicators have risen in the last two years, specially that of issued orders, arguably as a result of the relatively relevant number of (failed) asylum requests received in the recent past.[68] Furthermore, these data demonstrate that the Spanish deportation system has always operated in a highly selective way,[69] especially in 2018, when the enforcement rate has attained its lowest level, for reasons related to the management of the asylum system.

Table 5 Deportation orders issued and enforced in Spain, 2008–2018

	2008	2009	2010	2011	2012	2013	2014	2015	2016	2017	2018
Issued deportation orders	82,940	103,010	78,920	73,220	60,880	32,915	42,150	33,495	27,845	27,340	59,255
Enforced deportation orders	29,785	28,865	21,955	23,350	18,865	17,285	15,150	13,315	10,185	10,785	12,560
Enforcement rate	35.9%	28.0%	27.8%	31.9%	31.0%	52.5%	35.9%	39.8%	36.6%	39.4%	21.2%

Source: Eurostat.

Although the Spanish system has followed a declining path, this has not equally affected all types of deportation orders. On the contrary, against the backdrop of this downsizing, the migration enforcement apparatus has managed to give preference to crime-related deportations. Therefore, to ascertain the impact of the crimmigration turn in Spain the available data should be broken down by type of removal order.

[66] Boza Martínez, above n 52; D Boza Martínez, 'El internamiento de personas extranjeras: Más allá de los límites de la privación de libertad' in A López-Sala and D Godenau (eds), *Estados de contención, estados de detención: El control de la inmigración irregular en España* (Barcelona, Anthropos, 2017); Fernández Bessa, above n 3; Moffette, above n 2; E Sainz de la Maza, 'Actores y dinámicas en la puesta en práctica de las deportaciones' in A López-Sala and D Godenau (eds), *Estados de contención, estados de detención: El control de la inmigración irregular en España* (Barcelona, Anthropos, 2017).

[67] On average, Spain received 614,727 international immigrants per year from 2000 to 2008. From 2009 to 2015, this number plummeted to 336,770 migrants per year, before slightly rising since 2016 (source: Eurostat; ec.europa.eu/eurostat/web/population-demography-migration-projections/data/database).

[68] The Spanish administration received, on average, 3,293 asylum applications per year from 2008 to 2014, whilst 30,298 applications have been annually filed in the subsequent four years (source: Eurostat; ec.europa.eu/eurostat/web/asylum-and-managed-migration/data/database).

[69] JA Brandariz, *Sistema penal y control de los migrantes: Gramática del migrante como infractor penal* (Granada, Comares, 2011); Fernández Bessa, above n 3.

Table 6 Deportations enforced in Spain, divided by legal categories, 2008–2017

	Crime-related deportations		*Security-related deportations*	*Non crime-related and non security-related deportations*		
	Criminal deportations	**Administrative removals: criminal records**	**Administrative removals: EU citizens**	**Administrative removals: irregular residence**	**Other administrative removals**	**Total**
2008	634 (6.0%)	908 (8.6%)	21 (0.2%)	9,003 (84.8%)	50 (0.5%)	10,616 (100%)
2009	1,446 (10.9%)	534 (4.0%)	11 (0.1%)	11,223 (84.5%)	64 (0.5%)	13,278 (100%)
2010	1,799 (15.7%)	951 (8.3%)	27 (0.2%)	8,642 (75.4%)	35 (0.3%)	11,454 (100%)
2011	2,301 (20.3%)	1,365 (12.0%)	57 (0.5%)	7,608 (67.0%)	27 (0.2%)	11,358 (100%)
2012	2,309 (22.8%)	1,466 (14.5%)	166 (1.6%)	6,148 (60.7%)	41 (0.4%)	10,130 (100%)
2013	2,105 (23.4%)	1,425 (15.9%)	208 (2.3%)	5,218 (58.1%)	28 (0.3%)	8,984 (100%)
2014	1,916 (24.9%)	1,467 (19.1%)	269 (3.5%)	4,029 (52.4%)	15 (0.2%)	7,696 (100%)
2015	1,951 (28.4%)	1,431 (20.8%)	398 (5.8%)	3,075 (44.8%)	14 (0.2%)	6,869 (100%)
2016	1,348 (26.7%)	1,174 (23.2%)	374 (7.4%)	2,145 (42.5%)	10 (0.2%)	5,051 (100%)
2017	988 (24.4%)	852 (21.0%)	427 (10.5%)	1,685 (41.6%)	102 (2.5%)	4,054 (100%)

Sources: Spanish Ministry of the Interior; National Mechanism for the Prevention of Torture (NMPT).[70]

These data are particularly telling. They show that, mirroring the aforementioned official discourse, the Spanish deportation system has been increasingly geared towards the prevailing enforcement of deportations either related to crime or driven by security concerns. Thus, removals based on the administrative offence of irregular residence have been losing their long-standing prominence. Whereas in 2008 and 2009 they accounted for almost 85 per cent of the enforced deportations, this percentage was halved by 2017 (41.6 per cent). Despite this sharp decline, these administrative removals continue to be the most frequently enforced type of repatriation. This enduring importance can be grasped by taking into account the system's efficiency needs. In recent years, the Spanish deportation model

[70] The 2008–16 data have been provided by the Spanish Ministry of the Interior, after having submitted a request via the Transparency Portal (transparencia.gob.es). The 2017 data have been published by the NMPT (www.defensordelpueblo.es/informe-mnp/mecanismo-nacional-prevencion-la-tortura-informe-anual-2017/). These data differ from those of Table 5 because for these purposes the Spanish Home Office do not take into account several types of forced returns, especially accelerated returns (*devoluciones*), the number of which has been risen in the last years.

has been increasingly concentrated on the enforcement of the so-called 'express deportations',[71] which in turn has led to the growing irrelevance of the detention facilities as critical sites to prepare repatriations.[72] This scheme cannot disregard completely the use of removal orders based on the offence of irregular migration.[73] In fact, the pressure to rapidly load a collective transportation of return compels the Spanish police to capture and arrest deportable foreigners with previously issued and immediately enforceable deportation orders, many of whom are based on the migration breach of irregular residence.

However, the persistent salience of these removals based on migration law breaches cannot be completely disconnected from crimmigration concerns. On the contrary, there is evidence that these low-profile removals are being used to tackle petty crimes committed by undocumented non-citizens. These deportation practices, therefore, operate as a cost-effective – albeit, highly questionable – strategy to cope with minor criminal activities, circumventing the lengthy, resource-consuming, and evidently more rights-based criminal adjudication processes.[74]

In addition, the data presented in Table 6 illustrate the increasingly relevant role played by crime-related deportations. Both criminal deportations and administrative removals based on criminal records have consistently increased their share within the deportation system. Criminal deportations accounted for an insignificant 6.0 per cent of all forced returns in 2008, whilst they have stood for more than 20 per cent since 2012. This escalation is especially significant. In contrast to the low general enforcement rate, INE data on issued criminal deportations show that, at least in this segment of the deportation system, the number of enforced orders largely matches that of issued orders since 2010. The Spanish government, therefore, seems to have striven to enforce all criminal deportation orders. Also the number of administrative removals based on criminal records has significantly risen in the last 10 years. They accounted for 8.6 per cent of all enforced deportations in 2008 and 4.0 per cent in 2009, but they escalated to more than 20 per cent since 2015. The two types of crime-related deportations combined have come to account for roughly half of all enforced returns in the last three years.

[71] Martínez Escamilla 2013, above n 58; Pueblos Unidos, *CIE y expulsiones exprés: Informe anual 2014* (Madrid, Pueblos Unidos, 2015; pueblosunidos.org/wp-content/uploads/InformeCIE2014.pdf); Sainz de la Maza, above n 64; HC Silveira Gorski, 'La *Legalarbitrariedad* como mecanismo jurídico de control de la inmigración irregular' (2017) 12 *Crítica penal y poder* 34.

[72] The number of migrants annually confined in detention facilities dwindled by 66.8 per cent from 2008 to 2017 (Sources: Brandariz and Fernández Bessa, above n 62; Spanish National Mechanism for the Prevention of Torture [MNPT], www.defensordelpueblo.es/informes/resultados-busqueda-informes/?tipo_documento=informe_mnp). What is more, the number of deportations carried out from detention facilities plummeted from 60.1 per cent of all deportations in 2011 to 43.7 per cent in 2016 (Source: MNPT, www.defensordelpueblo.es/informes/resultados-busqueda-informes/?tipo_documento=informe_mnp).

[73] Brandariz and Fernández Bessa, above n 55.

[74] R Carranco, 'Los identificados en la operación contra los robos en el metro de Barcelona acumulan 185 detenciones y 667 denuncias' *El País*, 29 August 2019 (elpais.com/ccaa/2019/08/28/catalunya/1567006166_095200.html).

Additionally, a third sub-field of the deportation system has substantially expanded in the recent past. This third type of removal practices makes up the last – and most unacknowledged – component of the crimmigration turn: the deportation of EU citizens and their relatives. This return measure soared from an insignificant 0.1–0.2 per cent of all coercive repatriations in the late 2000s to more than 10 per cent in 2017. This striking change is particularly concerning, since both Spanish and EU legal provisions regulate these return orders as a measure to be taken only in the most exceptional cases.[75] Although the politically controversial nature of these deportation practices may explain that the Spanish Ministry of the Interior never mentioned them within its rhetoric of qualified deportations, its recent increase is a telling manifestation of the crimmigration turn. The deportation of EU nationals and their kin is both legally and practically associated to security concerns. Article 15 of the Royal Decree No 240/2007 and Articles 28, 31 and 33 of the CRD set a variety of safeguards regarding the enforcement of these deportation orders, which can only be based in 'serious' reasons of public order and public security. In addition, migration policing strategies resonate with this legal regulation. In line with what has been pointed out with regard to deportation practices targeting undocumented migrants, there are evidences that both in Spain and elsewhere CRD returns are being used, as a legal tool more expeditious than criminal law measures, to deal with petty crimes and misdemeanours allegedly perpetrated by EU citizens.[76]

In sum, the Spanish deportation system has been affected by the crimmigration turn, a change that had already been witnessed in other Global North jurisdictions, such as the US and the UK. Beyond this cross-national trend, the next section explores what factors have contributed to this turn in the Spanish case.

V. Conclusion

In the US case, crimmigration programmes giving preference to the enforcement of crime-related deportations have been officially advocated by stressing their contribution to the decline of the correctional population, which is especially needed in a period of prison overcrowding and mass incarceration.[77] This purposeful policy seems to have succeeded, since the expansion of the deportation regime

[75] JA Brandariz and C Fernández-Bessa, 'A Changing and Multi-Scalar EU Borderscape: The Expansion of Asylum and the Normalisation of the Deportation of EU and EFTA Citizens' 9 *Crime, Justice and Social Democracy* (forthcoming).

[76] I Vrăbiescu, 'Devised to Punish: Policing, Detaining and Deporting Romanians from France' (2019) *European Journal of Criminology* (online first).

[77] Macías-Rojas, above n 23.

fostered by the Obama Administration has been concomitant to the first reduction of the prison population witnessed in the USA over the last four decades.[78]

In Spain, on the contrary, the diminution of correctional spending has not apparently been the main driver of the crimmigration turn.[79] Certainly, also in Spain the expanded enforcement of deportations associated to crime has been simultaneous to a significant decrease of the number of foreign prisoners.[80] Nonetheless, this reduction has been caused by various factors, and the intensive utilisation of crime-related deportations has only been one of them. Interestingly, the number of non-citizens arrested, convicted and sentenced to prison terms has dwindled, and this has also contributed to the decline in the number of incarcerated foreigners.[81]

Therefore, the main triggering factors of the Spanish crimmigration turn are related to the political legitimation and managerial reorganisation of migration enforcement activities. The Spanish apparatus of border and migration management has been highly criticised over the last decade, in stark contrast to any other field of law enforcement policies. Criticisms have been especially voiced by human rights and pro-migrant rights groups, and have been largely focused on racist policing and the confinement of poor foreigners in detention facilities.[82] Yet, no less effective have been the critiques aired by police unions, which in several occasions have bitterly questioned the Spanish Ministry of the Interior's policies in this field. This tricky context led the Spanish government to craft new political narratives, in order to secure the public legitimation of its migration control scheme.

[78] The US incarceration rate has declined from 758 prisoners per 100,000 inhabitants in 2007 to 666 in 2016 (source: Bureau of Justice Statistics; www.bjs.gov/index.cfm?ty=tp&tid=11). This prison downsizing seems to have followed unabated in the last two years; yet, no total correctional population data have been disclosed since 2016. See H Aviram, *Cheap on Crime: Recession-Era Politics and the Transformation of American Punishment* (Berkeley, University of California Press, 2015); A De Giorgi, 'Five Theses on Mass Incarceration' (2015) 42 *Social Justice* 5; Gottschalk, above n 32.

[79] See though D Jiménez Franco, *Mercado-Estado-cárcel en la democracia neoliberal española* (Barcelona, Anthropos, 2016).

[80] The foreign correctional population plummeted by 40.2 per cent from its apex in May 2010 to May 2019. By contrast, the number of Spanish prisoners decreased by 13.3 per cent over the same period (source: Spanish Prison Service, www.institucionpenitenciaria.es/web/portal/documentos).

[81] JA Brandariz, '¿Historia de Dos Continentes? Comparación del reciente descenso de la población penitenciaria en EE.UU. y España' (2017) XII *Studi Sulla Questione Criminale* 151.

[82] I Barbero González and C Fernández Bessa, 'Beyond Surveillance: Racial profiled detention practices in everyday life' in WR Webster et al (eds), *Living in Surveillance Societies: The State of Surveillance* (Seattle, CreateSpace, 2013); L Escudero, S García and N Slepoy, 'Los controles de identidad como expresión de la seguridad diferencial' in D Ávila and S García (eds), *Enclaves de riesgo: Gobierno neoliberal, desigualdad y control social* (Madrid, Traficantes de Sueños, 2015); Fernández Bessa, above n 3, C Fernández Bessa, 'A Theoretical Typology of Border Activism: From the Streets to the Council' (2019) 23 *Theoretical Criminology* 156; A López-Sala and D Godenau, 'Introducción: El estudio del control migratorio en España' in A López-Sala and D Godenau (eds), *Estados de contención, estados de detención: El control de la inmigración irregular en España* (Barcelona, Anthropos, 2017); D Moffette, 'Governing Immigration through Probation: The Displacement of Borderwork and the Assessment of Desirability in Spain' (2014) 45 *Security Dialogue* 262; Sainz de la Maza, above n 64.

In this sense, as has been previously mentioned, the qualified deportations discourse that branded detained and deported migrants as criminal aliens was a simple, albeit potentially fruitful, communicative resource.[83]

Additionally, the crimmigration turn cannot be disconnected from the efficiency-oriented managerialisation of the entire Spanish migration enforcement system.[84] This managerial reorganisation aimed to tackle two major challenges affecting this sub-system of penal policies. On the one hand, there is the enduring and consistent deportation gap, with its consequences in terms of ineffective removal practices.[85] On the other hand, this managerial shift is especially coherent with the markedly resource-consuming nature of the migration law enforcement system.[86] Most likely, in the pre- financial crisis period this burdensome trait of the system was not especially pressing. Yet, since public deficit began to be considered a critical public problem in 2008–10, the need to set in motion cost-efficient law enforcement practices has been as urgent as ever.

This managerial transformation has gone beyond the deportation field, since it has notably affected the organisation of migration policing and the use of detention facilities.[87] Yet, in this cost-efficient framework the preference given to deportations of foreigners characterised by an alleged criminal or dangerous profile is wholly meaningful. This sort of hierarchy of otherness appears to be all the more reasonable in a period of stark reduction in the number of enforced deportations.

Crimmigration policies enable the consolidation of racially and ethnically biased models of migration enforcement.[88] Yet, both for their contribution to reduce the correctional population and for their ability to articulate deportation priorities, crimmigration policies are also especially consistent with the aims and rationales of managerial penality. This symbiotic co-existence of penal managerialism and crimmigration is one critical conclusion that can be inferred from the recent shift of the Spanish migration enforcement regime.

[83] Martínez Escamilla 2013, above n 58; see also Golash-Boza, above n 23; Macías-Rojas, above n 23.

[84] Brandariz and Fernández-Bessa, above n 55.

[85] Fernández Bessa, above n 3; E García España, 'Extranjeros presos y reinserción: Un reto del siglo XXI' in AI Cerezo Domínguez and E García España (eds), *La prisión en España: Una perspectiva criminológica* (Granada, Comares, 2007); M Monclús Masó, *La gestión penal de la inmigración* (Buenos Aires, Del Puerto, 2008).

[86] K Calavita, 'A "Reserve Army of Delinquents": The Criminalization and Economic Punishment of Immigrants in Spain' (2003) 5 *Punishment & Society* 399.

[87] One piece of good evidence of the managerial reorganisation of migration enforcement is the Circular No. 6/2014 of the Spanish National Police, of 11 July 2014, which sought to both efficiently reorientate and restrain the utilisation of detention facilities for deportation purposes. See Boza Martínez, above n 64; Brandariz and Fernández Bessa, above n 55; Moffette, above nn 2 and 79; Sainz de la Maza, above n 64.

[88] JA Brandariz and C Fernández Bessa, '"Perfiles" de Deportabilidad: El sesgo del sistema de control migratorio desde la perspectiva de la nacionalidad' (2017) 37 *Estudios penales y criminológicos* 307.

Beyond these situated conclusions, more comparative research is needed to explore the general drivers and the contextual determinants of the crimmigration turn in the field of deportation policies and practices. This chapter has examined the nexus between crimmigration rationales and the pressing need to reorganise national deportation systems. This perspective addresses a 'why' question on the momentum gained by efficiency and legitimacy-driven modes of articulating removal strategies. However, it is evident that the link between crimmigration policies and migration enforcement shortcomings such as the deportation gap does not equally affect all Global North jurisdictions. As has been previously pointed out, the UK deportation system is largely immune to systemic ineffectiveness and inefficiency problems. This lays bare that, beyond a general why question, the crimmigration turn in the deportation field calls for a closer and nationally focused look, so as to subsequently consolidate a meaningful body of research in comparative deportation studies. By undertaking this academic endeavour, scholars working in this field may cement a fine-grained exploration of the – arguably, diverse – 'proximate' factors that have given birth to the crimmigration-driven removal strategies in any given jurisdiction, as a first step to set a really cross-national dialogue on this border criminology field.

7

Ethnicity Based Immigration Checks

*Crimmigration and the How of Immigration and Border Control**

MAARTJE VAN DER WOUDE

I. Introduction

Amidst the global Coronavirus pandemic, countries are taking far-reaching measures in trying to protect the nation state and its members. Within the European Union, Member States are taking different approaches when it comes to curbing mobility and thus potentially preventing the virus from spreading: some have fully 'closed' their intra-Schengen and external borders, which means that no one gets in without being checked at the physical border and that those who cannot prove to have a reason to be in the country will be refused entry, whereas others have implemented an entry-ban for people travelling from certain countries that are considered to be COVID-19 high risk areas.[1] The latter means that the borders are still 'open' for those travelling from non-risk countries. At the time of writing this chapter, Germany, France and Belgium for instance have fully closed their borders, whereas the Netherlands and some other countries have taken the other approach. Making decisions about who is allowed to enter and who is not because they might be a potential risk seems to be more crucial than ever. These decisions on how to assess whether or not a person should be allowed to enter into a country tie in to a large, critical, body of scholarship on profiling and risk assessments. Whereas it seems rather clear cut that in trying to prevent people to further spread COVID-19 throughout Europe risk indicators would be based on various aspects of someone's health: does the person appear to be sick, are they coughing, do they have a fever etc, finding indicators to guide this process of decision-making in the context of immigration and border control in non-pandemic times seems to be more challenging. This is illustrated by a court case that was filed against the

* This work is part of the 5-year research project "Getting to the Core of Crimmigration" (project number 452-16-003), which is financed through the VIDI research scheme by the Dutch Science Council (NWO). The author is project coordinator and principal investigator.

[1] See for instance: https://euobserver.com/coronavirus/147742.

Royal Netherlands Marechaussee (RNM) early 2020 by human rights organization Amnesty International, the lawyers for human rights committee NJCM and two Dutch people who claim to have been checked repeatedly on entering the Netherlands because of the colour of their skin.[2] A case that, although it focuses on the Netherlands and the Royal Netherlands Marechaussee, might have significant implications for the ways in which border agencies across the EU make their decisions on whom to stop and check.

The RNM is a paramilitary organisation responsible for, amongst many other things, the implementation of the Schengen Borders Code (SBC). This means that they are tasked with carrying out border checks at the external borders of the Netherlands – which is mostly at the international airports and ports – but they are also tasked with the monitoring of the intra-Schengen borders based on article 23 of the SBC.[3] Based on this provision and a limited but rather vast line of jurisprudence coming from the Court of Justice of the EU (CJEU), European Member States are allowed to carry out immigration control or crime control checks in a spatially designated area *around* the physical border. Yet, these checks have to meet certain requirements to prevent them from in reality being actually a hidden form of border control. That the latter seems to be a matter of semantics will be discussed more in depth later on, as research has shown that, especially in times of perceived or actual 'crisis', the notion of 'open' borders in Europe is, and has always been, rather relative.[4] As already alluded to, another aspect that has always been strongly questioned by scholars and NGOs is the way in which, at the border but also more in general, decisions to stop and check are largely, and perhaps even predominantly, based on racial stereotypes and therewith a form of (in)direct discrimination. In the case that was filed against the RNM, Amnesty International and the NJCM claim that ethnicity as a selection criterion is discriminatory and not based on any objective or justifiable grounds. The RNM admit that ethnicity forms part of its controls, which are aimed at combating illegal immigration, passport fraud and human trafficking but denies it is the *only* reason to stop people. By bringing together literature on ethno-racial profiling and crimmigration as well as insights from ethnographic fieldwork done with the RNM, this chapter will address the question to what extent it is *possible* and also *desirable* for agencies tasked with the implementation of article 23 SBC checks to

[2] See Amnesty International's press release from 26 Feb 2020: www.amnesty.nl/content/uploads/2020/02/Press-Release_Dutch-border-police-in-court-for-ethnic-profiling.pdf?x10542.

[3] Regulation (EU) 2016/399 of the European Parliament and of the Council of 9 March 2016 on a Union Code on the rules governing the movement of persons across borders (Schengen Borders Code).

[4] R Bueno Lacy and H van Houtum, 'Lies, Damned Lies and Maps: The EU's Cartopolitical Invention of Europe' in A Cooper (ed), *Where are Europe's New Borders?: Critical Insights into Contemporary European Bordering* (Abingdon, Routledge, 2017); Adam K Webb, 'When Open Borders Must Stay Open: Expectations and Freedom of Movement' (2019) 51(2) *Polity* 202–30; Desmond Dinan, 'Debating Europe's Future' (2019) 34(4) *Irish Political Studies* 490–506; S Mau, H Brabandt, L Laube and C Roos, *Liberal States and the Freedom of Movement: Selective Borders, Unequal Mobility* (Basingstoke, Palgrave Macmillan UK, 2012).

not, partially, base their decision to stop people based on their (perceived) ethnicity and/or race. In so doing, the article will also further elaborate upon Weber and McCulloch's observation that the crimmigration thesis is especially useful in understanding the *how* of immigration and border control.[5]

II. Europe's 'Open' Borders

The differences between the MS in their responses to the Corona crisis are illustrative for the different ways in which MS have managed cross-border mobility within the Schengen Area even *before* the crisis. While the so deeply cherished and often lauded principle of free movement has always proven to be problematic and to trigger nationalistic tendencies and measures when it comes to the free movement of *people*, it is just in times of crisis when the tension that surrounds the principle becomes painfully clear. The so-called European migration crisis brought to the fore the fundamental lack of EU solidarity and absence of a collective response to the humanitarian and political challenges imposed by the influx. It also further laid bare the limitations of common border control and migration and refugee burden-sharing systems that had never been wholly and satisfactorily implemented.[6] Nevertheless, it is important to realise that other than what is often thought or imagined, especially by a non-European audience, the implementation of the Schengen Agreement was never meant to deprive countries from all forms of border management: the true 'free' movement of people was seen as too risky in the light of the national security of the Member States. Therefore, from the very onset, the original Member States negotiated so-called compensatory measures: measures that were implemented to counter the risk(s) posed by doing away with permanent intra-Schengen border checks.[7] Besides the use of systems such as the Schengen Information System (SIS) or the European Dactylographic System (Eurodac) – systems used to collect and exchange (biometric) information on people travelling through or trying to enter into the European Union[8] – the

[5] L Weber and J McCulloch J, *Penal power and border control: Which thesis? Sovereignty, governmentality, or the pre-emptive state? Theoretical Criminology*. Epub ahead of print 9 October 2018. Weber, L., & McCulloch, J. (2019). Penal power and border control: Which thesis? Sovereignty, governmentality, or the pre-emptive state? Punishment & Society, 21(4), 496–514. https://doi.org/10.1177/1462474518797293.

[6] KM Greenhill, 'Open Arms Behind Barred Doors: Fear, Hypocrisy and Policy Schizophrenia in the European Migration Crisis' (2016) 22(3) *European Law Journal* 317–32.

[7] TJM Dekkers, MAH van der Woude and JP van der Leun, 'Exercising Discretion in Border Areas: On the Changing Social Surround and Decision Field of Internal Border Control in the Netherlands' (2016) 2(4) *International Journal of Migration and Border Studies* 382–402.

[8] For more information on these systems: MJ Pedersen, 'The Intimate Relationship between Security, Effectiveness, and Legitimacy: a New Look at the Schengen Compensatory Measures (2015) 24(4) *European Security* 541–59.

Schengen Borders Code[9] also made clear that MS would still have a way to monitor their intra-Schengen border regions. True, as a result of article 20 SBC, '[i]nternal borders may be crossed at any point without a border check on persons, irrespective of their nationality, being carried out', yet article 23 SBC reads:

> 'The abolition of border control at internal borders shall not affect the exercise of police powers by the competent authorities of the Member States under national law, insofar as the exercise of those powers does not have an effect equivalent to border checks.

Article 23 thus allows countries to exercise police powers – and to carry out identity and immigration checks in intra-Schengen border zones – as long as: (1) the exercise of these powers cannot be considered equivalent to the exercise of border checks, (2) the police measures do not have border control as an objective, (3) are based on general police information and experience regarding possible threats to public security and aim, in particular, to combat cross-border crime, and lastly (4) as long as the measures are devised and executed in a manner clearly distinct from systematic checks on persons at the external borders and are carried out on the basis of spot-checks.[10]

A. Autonomous Member States

When looking at article 23 SBC through a legal lens, it is clear that the article provides Schengen Member States a lot of discretionary space in how to actually implement and use the article within their national borders. Of course, at face value there seem to be some limitations put in place as to how these checks can be performed, but without the presence of a strong and functional objective and effective monitoring system, Member States still have a lot of autonomy when it comes to performing so-called 'article 23' checks.[11] In terms of 'checks and

[9] Regulation (EU) 2016/399 of the European Parliament and of the Council of 9 March 2016 on a Union Code on the rules governing the movement of persons across borders (Schengen Borders Code).

[10] MAH van der Woude, 'Border Policing in Europe and Beyond: Legal and International Issues' in M den Boer (ed), *Comparative Policing from a Legal Perspective* (Cheltenham, Edgar Elgar Publishing, 2018) 255–71.

[11] The objectivity and effectiveness of the new and the old 'Schengen Evaluation system' has been contested by several authors and institutions e.g., European Parliament's Policy Department for Citizen's Rights and Constitutional Affairs, *Internal border controls in the Schengen area: is Schengen crisis-proof?* European Parliament Study for the LIBE committee. Research Administrator D Neville, 2016; E De Capitani, 'The Schengen System after Lisbon: from Cooperation to Integration (2014) 15(1) *Academy of European Law (ERA) Forum* 101–18; Y Pascouau, 'The Schengen Governance Package: the Subtle Balance between Community Method and Intergovernmental Approach' European Policy Centre, Discussion Paper, 2013; MAH van der Woude and P van Berlo, 'Crimmigration at the Internal Borders of Europe? Examining the Schengen Governance Package' (2015) 11(1) *Utrecht Law Review* 61–79. For a pilot study on the effectiveness and the objectivity of the SES see: J Kaasik and S Tong, 'The Schengen Evaluation Mechanism: Exploring the Views of Experts in the Field of Police Cooperation' (2019) 18 *European Law Enforcement Research Bulletin* 53–69.

balances', over the years, the discretionary space – or room for interpretation left in the wording of article 23 SBC – has also been discussed by the CJEU in several cases against Germany, France and the Netherlands.[12] This limited line of case law shows that the CJEU seems to follow a rather clear and strict line of reasoning by consistently stating that the national framework that Member States use to act in line with article 23 SBC must 'guide the discretion that national authorities enjoy in the practical application of their powers' and prevent these checks from being a 'veiled' form of permanent border control and therewith explicitly at odds with the principle of free movement. The CJEU further states that the checks should be carried out randomly and based on 'general police information' and 'experiences regarding possible threats to public security' and in so doing repeating the wording of the SBC. It is therefore safe to say that both on the legislative level – the wording of the Schengen Borders Code – as well as on the level of the judiciary there doesn't seem to be the tendency to want to be more clear about the conditions under which article 23 checks can be carried out: the conditions remain very open and rather vague and leave room for narratives of the unwanted and potential dangerous or criminal 'other' to play a role in street-level decision-making in these border areas. And, as will be discussed in section III, it is precisely at this level – the street level – where discretionary decisions can play a crucial role in the process of crimmigration.

B. Intra-Schengen Crimmigration Assemblages

It is interesting to see that whereas there is a lot of research addressing the discretionary powers of law enforcements agencies operating within the borders of a nation state as well as an ever growing body of empirical research on crimmigration, the research on the discretionary powers of border officials – let alone on article 23 checks specifically – is rather limited still.[13] This is of course understandable as the type of research that it would require to really observe and unravel how decisions are being made, qualitative fieldwork for a longer period of time,

[12] CJEU 19 July 2012 C-278/12 *Adil*, ECLI: C: 2012:508 (against the Netherlands); CJEU 22 June 2010, C-188/10 *Melki & Abdeli*, ECLI: C: 2101:363 (against France); CJEU 21 June 2017, C-9/16, ECLI:EU:C:2017:483 (against Germany).

[13] With the exception of: K Côté-Boucher, 'The Paradox of Discretion: Customs and the Changing Occupational Identity of Canadian Border Officers (2015) *British Journal of Criminology* 1–19; Sara Casella Colombeau, 'Policing the Internal Schengen Borders – Managing the Double Bind between Free Movement and Migration Control' (2017) 27(5) *Policing and Society* 480–93; Irene I Vega, 'Empathy, Morality, and Criminality: the Legitimation Narratives of US Border Patrol Agents' (2018) 44(15) *Journal of Ethnic and Migration Studies* 2544–61; A Amenta, *Protect, Serve, and Deport The Rise of Policing as Immigration Enforcement* (Berkeley, University of California Press, 2017); A Pratt, 'Between a Hunch and a Hard Place: Making Suspicion Reasonable at the Canadian Border' (2010) 19 *Social & Legal Studies* 461–80; A Pratt and SK Thompson, 'Chivalry, Race and Discretion at the Canadian Border' (2008) 48 *British Journal of Criminology* 620–40.

would require a level of access that many border agencies would not feel comfortable allowing. In an attempt to nevertheless get a little bit more clarity about what various EU countries are doing in their border areas with either Schengen or non-Schengen states, in June 2018 a brief survey was launched with the help of the Dutch National Contact Point (DNCP) of the European Migration Network (EMN).[14] Countries in principle have the obligation to respond to a so-called query sent by the EMN and there is also a financial compensation once a response is submitted, which should incentivise European Member States to react. Out of the 27 countries that the European Union is made up of, 21 countries responded. The six question-long survey questioned the Member States about Intra-Schengen border monitoring and border control, with the aim to provide a first insight into the extent to which the 'law in the books' – the Schengen Borders Code – resulted in similarities or differences between the 'law in action' in the different countries. The survey, among other things, shows that all countries that responded, as far as they were Schengen signatories, are indeed doing 'something' in their intra-Schengen border zones.[15] This immediately illustrates the false premise of free movement in the Schengen area. The EMN data reveal considerable variety in the institutional arrangements related to border policing and immigration control. Criminal justice and immigration elements form a number of assemblages in the various countries.[16] These arrangements are marked by a growing intersection between immigration control and criminal justice termed by Bowling and Westenra,[17] Guia et al[18] and Stumpf[19] as 'crimmigration control'. This is clearly reflected by the described aim of the different bordering practices that are being deployed. All countries report that the measures are driven by a logic of risk for national security and the prevention of crime and irregular migration. With an increased pressure on the external borders of the European Union, countries – especially those who can be seen as so-called destination countries – are feeling the pressure to more closely monitor their intra-Schengen border zones. In justifying their action they actively adopt a language of risk and develop rhetorical campaigns based on fear, such as the 'war on terrorism' or the 'war on migration', in order to

[14] A summary of the findings of the query can be found at the website of the EMN: https://ec.europa.eu/home-affairs/sites/homeaffairs/files/2018.1303_-_intra-schengen_border_monitoring_and_border_control.pdf.

[15] The countries that responded were: Austria, Belgium, Croatia, Cyprus, Czech Republic, Estonia, Finland, Germany, Hungary, Italy, Latvia, Lithuania, Luxembourg, Netherlands, Poland, Slovak Republic, Slovenia, Sweden, United Kingdom, Norway.

[16] KF Aas, 'The Ordered and the Bordered Society: Migration Control, Citizenship and the Northern Penal State' in KF Aas and M Bosworth (eds), *The Borders of Punishment: Migration, Citizenship and Social Exclusion* (Oxford, Oxford University Press, 2013) 21–39.

[17] B Bowling and S Westenra, 'Racism, Immigration and Policing' in M Bosworth, A Parmar and Y Va'zquez (eds), *Race, Criminal Justice and Migration Control: Enforcing the Boundaries of Belonging* (Oxford, Oxford University Press, 2017) 61–77.

[18] MJ Guia, M van Der Woude and J van Der Leun (eds), *Social Control and Justice: Crimmigration in the Age of Fear* (The Hague, Eleven International Publishing, 2013).

[19] J Stumpf, 'The Crimmigration Crisis: Immigrants, Crime and Sovereign Power' (2006) 56(2) *American University Law Review* 367–419.

foster the securitisation of national and transnational spaces and to provide an enduring excuse for ethno-racial othering and the potential violation of European rules and regulations.[20]

C. The Securitization of Migration and 'Open' Borders in the European Union

The strong language of risk, prevention and precaution that was visible in the answers to the EMN survey fits in seamlessly with a broader trend that has been visible within criminal justice for the past decades. Scholars have voiced their concerns about the rise of the preventative state and the development of a culture of control in which actuarial risk assessments and preventative and proactive coercive powers are used to manage rising fears and concerns about crime.[21] Both types of powers are meant to reduce (potentially) harmful behaviour to a tolerable level and coercive in the sense that people are forced, or at least feel rationally pressured, to comply with them if they don't want to get into trouble.[22] The difference between the two types of powers is that preventative powers usually require some degree of reasonable suspicion, whereas that is not the case for proactive powers. The latter are seen as powers that can be used at all times to 'check' whether people are obeying the rules. As a result of the growing securitisation of migration, these developments are no longer limited to the realm of criminal law and criminal justice, but also seeped into the realm of immigration law and even more broadly, immigration control and the management of mobility: in most countries proactive powers are used to check whether people in intra-Schengen border regions are carrying valid identification.

Securitisation theory has been proven very helpful to make sense of the shifts in the discourse on and the practice of migration and border control as the theory provides a powerful explanatory framework for understanding how security is a performative and intersubjective process between the securitising actor and the audience. In other words, securitisation theory has helped to understand how the mediatisation and politicisation of migration, mobility and borders feed into people's already existing fears and anxieties that things that are beyond their control. And what is more frightening than an unknown – in size – flow of unknown – in terms of their intention – people? The late German sociologist Ulrich Beck already mentioned that risk societies, societies that are preoccupied with the calculation and the prevention of risks, are by nature also scapegoat societies.[23] By this he

[20] J McCulloch and J Tham, 'Secret State, Transparent Subject: The Australian Security Intelligence Organization in the Age of Terror' (2005) 38 *Australian and New Zealand Journal of Criminology* 400–15.

[21] A Ashworth and L Zedner, *Preventive Justice* (Oxford, Oxford University Press, 2014).

[22] ibid, 6.

[23] U Beck, *Risk Society Towards a New Modernity* (London, Sage Publications Ltd, 1992).

means that especially in those cases where it is very difficult to pinpoint a clear entity to hold responsible for a potential risk – or a feared risk – individuals and societies will automatically seek a scapegoat to bear the brunt of the fears and anxieties. Often the scapegoat will be a (group of) 'other(s)' that already stands out within society because of their difference(s) from the dominant population. These differences will often be differences along the lines of race, religion and class.[24] When applying the lens of securitisation theory to the many discourses on migration and mobility in the context of the European Union, entwined linkages between crime and migration were – as mentioned earlier – already visible during the initial deliberations about the Schengen Agreement, but were only further intensified in the wake of a range of terrorist attacks in various European countries in the 2000s.[25] The call to further fortify the external borders of the European Union only grew stronger and more urgent. In that sense it is understandable that when it became clear during the Arab Spring in 2011, and the migratory flows as a result of that, that Europe wasn't the 'fortress' it thought or hoped it would be, several Member States started to panic. In public and political discourse at the time constructed displacement flows from the Southern Mediterranean as an 'invasion' of Europe.[26] Migrants' arrivals from Tunisia and Libya led to reinstating border checks and to a temporary suspension of French-Italian Schengen cooperation, with other countries following soon as the numbers of migrants from predominantly Syria, but also other countries in the horn of Africa, continued to grow. These concerns prompted Sweden, Germany, France, Denmark and Austria to suspend Schengen temporarily whereas other countries such as Slovenia and Austria have sought to block migration flows by building metal fences. Throughout the whole of Europe, forms of migration management have emphasised tightened border controls, patrolling and surveillance.[27]

Public discourses also play a vital role in the production of a securitized knowledge on migration. Public discourses provide a powerful vector for 'dramatizing' and 'performing' migration as a security threat. They moreover turn an 'emergency

[24] U Beck, 'The Terrorist Threat: World Risk Society Revisited' (2002)19(4) *Theory, Culture & Society* 39–55.

[25] V Mitsilegas, 'Border Security in the European Union: Towards Centralised Controls and Maximum Surveillance' in A. Baldaccini et al (eds), *Whose Freedom, Security and Justice? EU Immigration and Asylum Law & Policy* (Oxford, Hart Publishing, 2007).

[26] A Barry, 'Europe's Dilemma: Immigration and the Arab Spring' *Foreign Policy in Focus* (25 May 2012), http://fpif.org/europes_dilemma_immigration_and_the_arab_spring/; H de Haas, 'Europe's tiny refugee burden: Putting the Libyan migration crisis into perspective' (13 April 2011), http://heindehaas.blogspot.com/2011/04/europes-tiny-refugee-burden-putting.html.

[27] MAH van der Woude, 'Euroskepticism, Nationalism, and the Securitization of Migration in the Netherlands' in R Koulish, MAH van der Woude (eds), *Crimmigrant Nations: Resurgent Nationalism and the Closing of Borders* (Chicago, Fordham University Press, 2020) 227–48; K Franko, MAH van der Woude and V Barker, 'Beacons of Tolerance Dimmed? Migration, Criminalization, and Inhospitality in Welfare States' in SKN Bendixsen and T Wyller (eds), *Contested Hospitalities in a Time of Migration: Religious and Secular Counterspaces in the Nordic Region. Religion, Resistance, Hospitalities (RRH): Interpretation, Analysis, and Documentation* (Abingdon, Routledge, 2019) 55–75.

situation' shaped as such by policymakers into a consequential act[28] with 'real life' implications for the public sphere. They also provide an enabling terrain on which policy agendas inimical to migrants' interests thrive. Public debates about whether refugee arrivals are a threat to societal security and identity have proliferated, leading to a concerning upsurge of nationalistic discourse and the election of politicians representing a discourse of nationalism, exclusion and racism.[29] As Bosworth et al observe:

> The high octane public and political debates over immigration, particularly in relation to asylum seekers have often been marked by emotionally and exclusionary use old racial, gendered and religious tropes. The deserving and the undeserving, the genuine and the bogus are elided in an exclusionary push justified by unbridled electoral and populist politics.[30]

As Fakhoury notes, although various European platforms have contested the depiction of migrants and refugees as a liability,[31] a general receptiveness to 'uttering' migration as a security threat has been crucial to the securitisation move. Migrants are seen as a threat to societal security and bordering practices as an important defence mechanism to ensure the survival of national cultures.[32] The so-called migration 'crisis' in Europe thus seems to have highlighted the ever present tension between the opportunities and the risks that are inherent to the openness that Europe, and in particular the Schengen area, aims to represent. The migration crisis has led to various kinds of mobilisations of the most regressive and reactionary features of 'Europeanness': the protection of the national or supranational territory, the protection of the European people – read white European[33] – as well as rejection of the non-European other.

III. Crimmigration and the *How* of Immigration and Border Control

Whereas the literature on the securitisation of migration aims to illustrate how the public and political discourse of migration has become so intermixed with the topic of crime, the literature on crimmigration highlights how this translates into

[28] Anna Triandafyllidou, 'A "Refugee Crisis" Unfolding: "Real" Events and Their Interpretation in Media and Political Debates' (2018) 16(1–2) *Journal of Immigrant & Refugee Studies* 198–216.

[29] R Koulish and MAH van der Woude (eds), *Crimmigrant Nations: Resurgent Nationalism and the Closing of Borders* (Chicago, Fordham University Press, 2020).

[30] M Bosworth, K Aas and S Pickering, 'Punishment, Globalization and Migration Control: "Get Them the Hell Out of Here"' (2018) 20(1) *Punishment & Society* 34–53.

[31] Tamirace Fakhoury, 'Securitising Migration: The European Union in the Context of the Post-2011 Arab Upheavals' (2016)51(4) *The International Spectator* 67–79.

[32] S Sassen, *Guests and Aliens* (New York, New Press, 1999).

[33] U Linke, *German Bodies: Race and Representation after Hitler* (Philadelphia, University of Pennsylvania Press, 1999); DT Goldberg, 'Racial Europeanisation' (2006) 29(2) *Ethnic and Racial Studies* 331–64.

concrete legal measures and legal practices. That being said, looking at scholarship on crimmigration, it is not always clear how and if authors precisely distinguish between the two phenomena. This is to be explained by the fact that the term 'crimmigration',[34] although now widely used by scholars, still remains quite ambiguous and is also increasingly contested.[35] In its broadest sense, it describes a postulated blurring or fusion of functional, normative and discursive barriers between crime control and immigration control. There are many typologies of this convergence, most of which have emerged from the USA, which will not be fleshed out in this chapter as there is ample scholarship out there that does so. In finding explanations for the blurring of criminal law and migration law, Stumpf – who coined the term in 2006 – argues that membership theory, as applied within the legal system, produces categories of excluded and included individuals defined on the basis of a 'decision maker's vision of who belongs'. The decision-maker's vision, and his or her subsequent decision based on that vision, is therefore key in driving the 'crimmigration apparatus'. It is therefore understandable that Motomura claims that the discretion to stop persons is the strongest driver behind the process of crimmigration,[36] since it enables racial profiling and makes street-level officers responsible for funnelling immigrants into systems dealing with immigration crime or criminal violations. His assessment of the pivotal importance of street-level decision-making in the process of crimmigration is widely shared among scholars, who often link it to selectivity based on racial stereotypes.[37] Although there are competing perspectives as to what discretionary decision matters most in driving the process of crimmigration, this chapter focuses on the implications of the earlier mentioned proactive discretionary decisions made by street-level border officials.[38] When analysing the explanatory nature of the crimmigration perspective, Weber and McCulloch reached the conclusion that it is especially helpful in getting a better understanding of the mechanisms, or technologies, of immigration and border control: the *how* of immigration and border control.[39] Weber and McCulloch see the development of 'crimmigration law' as answering this question and, while referring to Stumpf, observe that the creation of crimmigration laws and practices can be explained by referring to the fact that both criminal law and immigration law are exclusionary in nature and therefore together a potent combination

[34] Stumpf, above n 19.

[35] G Hudson, 'Does Crimmigration Theory Rest on a Mistake?' (2018) 4(4) *International Journal of Migration and Border Studies* 303–25.

[36] H Motomura, 'The Discretion that Matters: Federal Immigration Enforcement State and Local Arrests and the Civil-Criminal Line' (2011) 58 *UCLA Law Review* 1819–58.

[37] CCG Hernandez, 'Creating Crimmigration' (2013) 6 *Brigham Young University Law Review* 1457–516; R Koulish, *Immigration and American Democracy: Subverting the Rule of Law* (New York, Routledge, 2010); TA Miller, 'Blurring the Boundaries Between Immigration and Crime Control After September 11th' (2005) 25(1) *Boston College Third World Law Journal* 81–123; Stumpf, above n 19.

[38] MAH van der Woude and JP van der Leun, 'Crimmigration Checks in the Internal Border Areas of the EU: Finding the Discretion that Matters' (2017) 14(1) *European Journal of Criminology* 27–45.

[39] Weber and McCulloch, above n 5.

to permanently cast out unwanted elements from societies. Yet, whereas this observation is very true, it seems to overlook the fact that it is through the conscious creation of discretionary space within the law(s) that this exclusionary effect gets to be executed. When thinking back to Motomura's statement on the role and impact of the creation of discretionary preventative and proactive powers for street-level officials in fuelling the process of crimmigration, the notion of discretion would deserve a more central role in arguing why the crimmigration thesis explains the *how* of immigration and border control. The importance of discretion is also highlighted by Sklansky who claims that crimmigration cannot be viewed separately from a broader trend of what he calls 'ad hoc instrumentalism'.[40] With this he means a way of thinking about the law and legal authorities in which formal distinction between legal domains is of secondary importance and government officials can simply choose the most effective instrument for solving a problem in each individual case. According to Sklansky, this way of thinking is strongly influenced by skepticism with regard to the necessity and possibility of limiting the discretionary decision-making power of street-level officials. Sklansky notes that such an instrumental approach to law is intrinsically linked to crimmigration. Due to the increasing intertwinement of criminal enforcement and immigration control, street-level officials have a broader spectrum of possibilities to stop or investigate a person, which increases their discretionary power. He mentions that street-level officials are increasingly equipped with a toolbox of legal instruments that they can use to deal with unwanted individuals, whether they are criminals or migrants. Given the instrumental considerations and the emphasis on effectiveness, enforcement this way not only takes on a strong ad hoc character but the procedural safeguards retire to the background as well. Furthermore, the many options available to enforcers can quickly lead to a lack of transparency, because 'this way, little or no insight is provided into the grounds on which individual street-level officers base their choices and decisions' and these officers often face little accountability for their actions as long as formal complaints are filed.[41]

The nature of proactive checks and powers as explained above as well as the absence of the necessity for there being a reasonable of suspicion, contribute to the possibility that other factors and stereotypes will consciously, or unconsciously, start to play a role in the decision-making process. The long standing line of literature on the way in which so-called 'street-level bureaucrats' deal with the challenges of their work – especially in the absence of clear rules and when having to act under quite some pressure and competing political, organisational and personal priorities – has proven that many factors *other* than the legal rules play a role in

[40] DA Sklansky, 'Crime, Immigration, and Ad Hoc Instrumentalism' (2012) 15(2) *New Criminal Law Review* 157–223.

[41] JP van der Leun, MAH van der Woude and S de Ridder, 'Crimmigratie in de Lage Landen: Smeltende Grenzen?' (2013) 11(3) *Strafblad* 221–28, 227.

their decision-making processes.[42] In their research on judicial decision-making, Tillyer and Hartley point to the fact that street-level officials – judges, prosecutors and police officials – tend to fall back on perceptual shorthands in their work, especially when having to make decisions under time pressure and based off of very little information.[43] As another example of using stereotypes and mental shorthands when making decisions Steffensmeier and colleagues' focal concerns theory argues that in the absence of complete information or unlimited time to make decisions, judges develop a 'perceptual shorthand' based on prior experience and stereotypical attributions to compensate for the uncertainty present in court decisions (e.g., who is dangerous and who is not).[44] These perceptual shorthands can furthermore be organised into three focal concerns. The three focal concerns are, the offender's blameworthiness and the degree of harm caused the victim, protection of the community, and practical implications of sentencing decisions. In the context of the previously described preventive turn within criminal justice but also in immigration and border control, a development that goes hand in hand with the creation and usage of more preventative and proactive powers based in an attempt to identify and contain risks and 'would be' risks as early as possible, the protection of the community is most likely to play the most dominant role in the decisions made by street-level border officials. This means that any conscious or (un)conscious (implicit) biases and/or preconceptions on what a 'would be' risk would look like will affect their daily decision-making processes and therewith impact the lives of those on the receiving end of these decisions. Based on a convincing line of international research into the decisions of police and judicial authorities, we know that shorthands can contribute to the development or maintenance of cognitive illusions due to the erroneous existence of certain ethnic, racial or national stereotypes.[45] Since this is undeniably *contra legem* and highly problematic, in the context of migration and border control it might be a justified question how it is possible not to let a person's perceived race or ethnicity play a role in the decision to stop someone. This is clearly a very unpopular question to ask, but as will be illustrated by the case of the Netherlands, a key question: not just in the light of the pending court case against the Royal Netherlands Marechaussee, but also in the light of proactive immigration and border control in general.

[42] J Black, *Managing Discretion* (Unpublished manuscript, London School of Economics, 2001) (www.lse.ac.uk/law/people/academic-staff/julia-black/Documents/black21.pdf); P Hupe and M Hill, 'Positioning Street-Level Bureaucracy Research' in *Research Handbook on Street-Level Bureaucracy* (Cheltenham, Edward Elgar Publishing, 2019); K Hawkins, *The Uses of Discretion* (Oxford, Oxford University Press, 1992).

[43] R Tillyer and RD Hartley, 'Driving Racial Profiling Research Forward: Learning Lessons from Sentencing Research' (2010) 38(4) *Journal of Criminal Justice* 657–65.

[44] D Steffensmeier, JT Ulmer and J Kramer, 'The Interaction of Race, Gender, and Age in Criminal Sentencing: The Punishment Cost of Being Young, Black, and Male' (1998) 36(4) *Criminology* 763–98.

[45] MA Alexander, *The New Jim Crow: Mass Incarceration in the Age of Colorblindness* (New York, The New Press, 2012); K Glover, *Racial Profling. Research, Racism and Resistance* (Plymouth, Rowman & Littlefeld Publishers, 2009); CL Schneider, 'Police Power and Race Riots in Paris' (2008) 36(1) *Politics and Society* 133–59; P Quinton, 'The Formation of Suspicions: Police Stop and Search Practices in England and Wales' (2011) 21(4) *Policing and Society* 357–68.

IV. The Dutch Approach Towards Article 23 SBC

In finding an answer to this chapter's leading research question, in this section where the Dutch approach towards article 23 SBC will be discussed, data will be used from an elaborate case study that was carried out in the Netherlands. Between March 2013 and November 2015, a team of three researchers observed the daily practice of street-level officials from the Royal Netherlands Marechaussee who were tasked with performing article 23 SBC checks in the border regions with Belgium and Germany. During this period the research team collected observational data on the stop and checks of the vehicles – and the persons in them – they conducted informal and formal (focus group) interviews with street-level and management level officials working in the Royal Netherlands Marechaussee and analysed a broad variety of legal and policy documents. As the data collected as part of this unique field study has been discussed in a variety of international publications already, this chapter will partially draw from these previous publications.[46]

The Dutch have named the national law interpretation of Article 23 of the Schengen Borders Code 'Mobile Security Monitoring' (MSM).[47] Based on article 50 of the Aliens Law (Vreemdelingenwet) and article 4.17a of the Aliens Decree (Vreemdelingenbesluit), the RNM has the authority to patrol in a 20 kilometre zone around the Dutch-German and Dutch-Belgian borders. In this 20 kilometre zone, people entering Dutch territory (either by plane, train or motor vehicle) can be asked for their identification papers as well as residence permits to establish their identity, nationality and legal status, without the necessity of there being any reasonable presumption of undocumented residence. The goal of the MSM is to combat irregular migration into the country as well as certain forms of cross-border crime such as human smuggling and identity fraud. As a result of two rulings of the Court of Justice for the EU – the *Melki/Abdeli* case and the *Adil* case – the frequency and intensity of the MSM have been limited. According to article 4.17a section 4, checks on the road can be carried out for six hours a day with a maximum of 90 hours a month. Limitations also apply to the number of trains and planes that can be checked on a daily and a monthly basis. According to the Court, the limitations that have been put in place are sufficient to guarantee that the practical exercise of the power to carry out identity controls in border areas did not have an effect equivalent to border checks.

[46] TJM Dekkers, *Mobility, control and technology in border areas: Discretion and decisionmaking in the information age* (PhD Thesis, Leiden University, The Netherlands, 2019); MAH van der Woude, J Brouwer and TJM Dekkers, *Beslissen in grensgebieden: een onderzoek naar het Mobiel Toezicht Veiligheid zoals uitgevoerd door de Koninklijke Marechaussee* (Den Haag, Boom Criminologie, 2016); J Brouwer, *Detection, Detention, Deportation. Criminal Justice and Migration Control through the Lens of Crimmigration* (Den Haag, Eleven International Publishing, 2020).

[47] van der Woude and van der Leun, above n 38; MAH van der Woude and J Brouwer, 'Searching for "Illegal" Junk in the Trunk: Underlying Intentions of (Cr)Immigration Controls in Schengen's Internal Border Areas' (2017) 20(1) *New Criminal Law Review* 157–79.

As mentioned, according to the applicable national legal framework, no reasonable presumption of illegal residence is required for stopping persons in the context of an MSM.[48] Article 4.17a paragraph 2 of the Aliens Decree states that the MSM 'is conducted on the basis of information or experiential data on illegal residence after crossing the border'. There is no further specification of the nature of the information or experiential data, which creates considerable discretion for street-level RNM officers in the selection of persons and vehicles and therewith also a real risk of selection based on ethnicity and nationality. The previously mentioned research into the MSM has indeed shown that RNM officials, amongst other things, indeed base their decision to stop and pull over a car for inspection on the external characteristics of the occupants of the vehicle, but also on the licence plate as an indicator of nationality.[49] To justify this, street-level RNM officers explain that both ethnicity and nationality are relevant indicators in the light of the central aim of the MSM: combating irregular migration into the Netherlands. Before discussing to what extent this justification holds ground, it is important to take a closer look into the 'law in action' based on the previously mentioned fieldwork.

A. Targeting Irregular Migration …

The decision to select persons and vehicles for a check, as observed by the researchers, was usually made by an RNM officer on a motorcycle who selected 'interesting' vehicles just after the border. He or she then directed the vehicle to a control location further inland, where other officers carried out the actual control by checking the identity papers of the persons stopped. Other times officers would drive around in vehicles and carry out both the stop and the control themselves. Because traffic normally passed at high speed, officers frequently indicated there was very little opportunity for a thorough examination of the passing vehicles and its passengers. They had to decide within a split second whether to select a vehicle or not, some- times without a clear view of the passengers due to darkness or bad weather. Officers were therefore usually only able to see very basic features of the passengers, such as a beard, skin colour or certain clothing. They furthermore had little to no prior information on the vehicles that were passing. Although most shifts started with a briefing in which attention was paid to wanted persons, this information was often provided by the police and usually not so much related to illegal migration or migration-related offences. Officers repeatedly stated that they believed this would not be very useful anyway, as the realities on the street cannot

[48] Vreemdelingencirculaire 2013, A2/2.

[49] MAH van der Woude, J Brouwer And TJM Dekkers, *Beslissen in grensgebieden: een onderzoek naar het Mobiel Toezicht Veiligheid zoals uitgevoerd door de Koninklijke Marechaussee* (Den Haag, Boom criminologie, 2016).

be captured in formal training or written instructions. As one officer said, 'you really only learn it when you are at the workplace'. In general, officers relied on their own judgements about how to filter out potential unauthorised immigrants. Besides the nationality of the licence plate, the number of passengers and the state of the vehicle, they strongly relied on skin colour as a visible marker of 'foreignness' to detect potential unauthorised immigrants. Almost all RNM officers we met were white males and perceived non-whiteness as an important indicator of foreignness. In practice this meant that during our observations primarily black or Arab-looking people were stopped.

Over the course of the fieldwork, numerous stops were justified by officers on the basis that the vehicle looked rather old, was of a particular brand or had a foreign licence plate, in combination with the 'foreign appearance' of the driver and passengers. An interaction between one of the researchers and an officer that occurred during the observations can illustrate this. When the researcher asked the motor driver why he had selected a particular vehicle, he responded by asking whether the researcher had seen the licence plate. After the researcher saw that it was a Belgian licence plate, the officer asked him in a rhetoric tone whether he thought the two passengers – who had Arabic features – looked Belgian to him. The officer then continued by saying that of course it was possible they were, but that he was nonetheless curious to check, also because they came into the Netherlands from Germany in a vehicle with a Belgium licence plate. Whereas skin colour was thus an important factor behind immigration-related stops, sometimes other factors were employed to infer 'foreignness'. During one control, researchers were in a car with two officers after dark, when the officers decided to follow a vehicle with Dutch licence plates. As they had not been able to see inside the vehicle they checked the licence plate in the systems. When they heard that the vehicle was registered by someone with an African sounding name, the driver said 'that is a name we can work with' and decided to stop the vehicle for a check.

B. … Through Ethno-Racial Profiling?[50]

Although most RNM officers were aware of the sensitivity of using racial or ethnic categories as a factor in their decisions and societal concerns about discrimination, they nonetheless often freely admitted that these categorizations played a role in their selection. As one of them said:

> When people ask if we select on the basis of skin colour, then we have to readily admit that. Somebody's skin colour is for us the first sign of possible illegality. But, because we select on the basis of skin colour does not automatically mean that we discriminate.

[50] This section is based on an article that was previously published in Dutch: MAH van der Woude, TJM Dekkers and J Brouwer, 'Over crimmigratie en discretionair beslissen binnen het Mobiel Toezicht Veiligheid … of Vreemdelingen … of Veiligheid?' (2015) 14(2) *Tijdschrift voor Veiligheid* 19–35.

Such openness was always coupled with a resolute denial that this selection criterion was driven by any racist intentions or motives. Instead, officers argued that their specific task of preventing illegal immigration leaves them little choice but to base their stops at least partially on skin colour as proxy of being a migrant. Indeed, they saw it as inherent to their work in the context of immigration law. Respondents emphasised their intentions rather than the outcomes. And as one officer explained:

> It is also the fact that many of those countries have a visa requirement. Look, we did not invent the visa requirement for Africa. That by chance it is black people that come from there is not our fault, that is what we have to control, if there had been living only white people that had visa requirements we would have been checking white people.

Such statements are in line with Satzewich and Shaffir's argument that 'the occupational culture enables the police to draw upon a vocabulary of explanations [that] permits them to deny responsibility when faced with the allegations that their profiling is racially motivated'.[51] According to them these kind of rationalisations help officers deal with possible feelings of guilt or shame, and generally offer a better explanation for police behaviour than intentional racism.

At the political level, concerns with respect to potential discrimination during the MSM have continuously been countered with reference to professionalism. Officers are supposed to act on the basis of more objective criteria rather than solely rely on appearance.[52] RNM officers indeed regularly pointed out that stops were based on a combination of factors and not appearance alone. The origin of the licence plate, the number of passengers, their clothing, other appearance-related factors and sometimes their behaviour were all factors that could play a role in the decision to stop a vehicle. In the debate on ethno-racial profiling there is disagreement about whether markers for ethnic categories are never allowed to play a role in decisions to stop, or whether it is acceptable when these markers are combined with other factors informing a decision.[53] Such considerations were also found among RNM officers: 'Naturally we are here to find illegal immigrants, so somebody's appearance and skin colour are important factors. Of course these are not allowed to be the only factors, I also know that and I agree with that'. More elaborate combinations of factors were also presented. For example, one officer gave a more detailed description of how a combination of factors could be invoked to stop a vehicle with North-African looking persons, drawing on knowledge and ideas about illegal immigration patterns.

[51] V Satzewich and W Shaffir, 'Racism versus Professionalism: Claims and Counter-Claims about Racial Profiling' (2009) 51(2) *Canadian Journal of Criminology and Criminal Justice* 199–226, 231.

[52] TJM Dekkers and MAH van der Woude, 'Acceptance Denied: Intelligence-led Immigration Checks in Dutch Border Areas' (2016) 4(2) *European Journal of Policing Studies* 242–65.

[53] MR Smith, 'Depoliticizing Racial Profiling: Suggestions for the Limited Use and Management of Race in Police Decision-Making' (2004) 15 *George Mason University Civil Rights Law Journal* 219–60.

> You notice that we get a lot of cars from France, Spain, Italy, those are interesting for us. There are of course a lot of people from North-Africa, Algerians and Moroccans who don't have their documents straight. It is simply known that they often come here with family members illegally so if you see something like that coming it is just interesting. When it is somebody driving alone it is less interesting, but if it is several people with North-African appearance you make sure to stop it.

At the same time, it was somewhat contradictory that although licence plates were the main other indicator of 'foreignness', a relatively large number of vehicles that we observed being stopped had Dutch licence plates. During our observations it regularly seemed that a 'foreign appearance' was the primary or only reason for a stop, especially when vehicles had a Dutch licence plate. For example, one time an officer indicated he had stopped a vehicle because he had the feeling 'it was not right'. When asked if he could explain that feeling, he responded that 'those three guys [the passengers, MW]' had aroused his interest. After talking a bit more, it became clear that he found it striking that three men with, according to the officer, 'clearly non-Dutch facial features' were driving a vehicle with a Dutch licence plate.

C. Crimmigrant Stereotypes[54]

Although the MSM is primarily aimed at preventing illegal entry and stay, there is a lack of clarity about what exactly falls within the official aims RNM officers are also tasked with, combating 'migration related forms of crime'.[55] Although this ambiguity was rarely considered an issue by officers, who generally seemed more interested in fighting crime than controlling illegal immigration, it had a large impact on the factors influencing officers' decisions. The focus on crime resulted in different groups being targeted. Various RNM officers expressed the idea that 'Moroccan', or more generally 'North-African', young men were disproportionally involved in – especially drugs-related – crime. This resonates with the study of Bonnet and Caillault, who found that Dutch regular police officers were heavily concerned with 'Moroccans' being involved in criminal behaviour.[56] RNM officers pointed to arrest and prison statistics as concrete evidence of this overrepresentation. Thus while North-African looking people were regularly stopped because of potential illegal entry or stay, especially when their car had a foreign licence plate, officers also indicated a few times that a stop involving young Moroccan-looking

[54] This section is based on the article: J Brouwer, MAH van der Woude and JP van der Leun, '(Cr) immigrant Framing in Border Areas: Decision-Making Processes of Dutch Border Police Officers (2018) 28(4) *Policing and Society* 448–63.

[55] See more about this ambiguity: van der Woude and Brouwer, above n 48.

[56] F Bonnet and C Caillault, 'The Invader, the Enemy Within and They-Who-Must-Not-Be-Named: how Police Talk about Minorities in Italy, the Netherlands and France' (2014) 38(7) *Ethnic and Racial Studies* 1–17.

men was primarily based on crime-related reasons. A North-African background could thus be a factor in stops both related to migration control and crime control. However, in the Netherlands there is a large population with a Moroccan background that can no longer be seen as foreigners or immigrants. Instead, they are typically born in the country and hold Dutch citizenship; Moroccan is usually seen as an ethnic, rather than national, category. As such, the ambiguity about the exact aim of the MSM on a political and policy level translates into the targeting of groups that are not necessarily interesting in the context of what is supposed to be primarily an instrument of migration control.

Although North-African young men were regularly linked to various forms of crime, most commonly and openly associated with criminal behaviour were people from CEE countries – primarily Bulgarians and Romanians, to a lesser extent also Hungarians and Polish. Such perceptions were usually said to constitute 'known facts' and being based on 'evidence'.

> I think that there is just evidence that if you say 'human trafficking', those are Bulgarians, it is just like that.
>
> No but if a Romanian is driving a vehicle with an Italian license plate then you already know something is not alright. They drive through all of Europe to commit criminal offenses and that is also proven.

During the observations, a relatively large number of vehicles with Eastern European licence plates were stopped, and officers regularly indicated that a Bulgarian or Romanian licence plate was already sufficient reason for them to make a check. Although other Eastern European countries were sometimes also mentioned – in particular Albania – the relatively high number of vehicles from Poland, Bulgaria and Romania that drive to the Netherlands meant that they were most often stopped. The targeting of these groups was primarily based on the origin of the licence plate, as this was an easy visible marker and the nationality of individuals from Eastern European Member States are generally harder to recognise on the basis of physical characteristics. Nonetheless, officers said it was a particular challenge to also be able to select Eastern European people when they were driving a vehicle with another licence plate, something that regularly happened. For example, during one of the controls researchers were sitting in the back of the vehicle when a car with a German licence plate was stopped. According to the officer he had stopped the car because he believed the driver and passengers to be Albanian, and Albanians were often involved in crime in the Netherlands. Justifications for such stops were based on the merging of a variety of crime risks that range from mobility-related offences such as human trafficking and false identification papers to more mundane crimes as pickpocketing and theft.

> That has to do with crime there. We have come across a lot of false documents from Romanians and Bulgarians, many false ID-cards and that is one of our priorities.
>
> And the Bulgarians and the Romanians and especially the Bulgarians are known for false papers and Romanians too, but Romanians are also well known for pickpocketing etcetera, human trafficking.

Overall, there was a common understanding among RNM officers that 'there is almost always something wrong' with members of these groups in the border areas concerned. This led to extreme statements proclaiming that nine out of 10 times Eastern European drivers have burglary tools in their trunk, or that Romanian looking people in a vehicle with a British or Spanish licence plate were nine out of 10 times thieves.

These 'profiles' were based on shared ideas rather than on information provided by the organisation. At the same time, it was interesting to note that such common-sense profiles were far from static. Nationalities that used to be targeted quite frequently could become less interesting over time, as during our research was the case with people from Poland. While Polish vehicles were considered interesting for various crime-related reasons in earlier years, respondents regularly stated that this was now much less the case. Although they were sometimes mentioned in the same breath with Bulgarians and Romanians, other times clear distinctions were made and it was argued that Polish people nowadays mostly came here to work and had their papers in order. As one officer noted: 'in the beginning we checked them quite a lot. Those vans and stuff. But it turns out that most of it is work-related'. That did not necessarily translate into practice though, as we still quite regularly observed Polish vehicles being checked during the controls. However, officers were now much less positive about the likelihood of actually encountering something wrong than they were in the past.

This normalcy of nationality as a proxy for a high risk background reflects the findings of Pratt and Thompson,[57] who argued in their study on Canadian border officials that 'while race is an unacceptable basis of discretionary risk assessment at the border, nationality is continually reproduced as a legitimate consideration'. Dutch border police officers equally seemed to find that assumed nationality (often based on licence plates) was far less controversial as a (partial) selection criteria than ethnic or racial features, especially for crime-related stops.

V. Ethnicity and Race as Problematic Indicators for Immigration Control?[58]

The empirical insights presented in the previous section touch upon a complicated discussion about whether ethno-racial profiling is about intentions or outcomes and therewith also on the very core of the legal case that was filed against the Royal Netherlands Marechaussee. Obviously the practices that were observed in the research result in ethnic disparities among those who are stopped during the

[57] Pratt and Thompson, above n 13, 632.

[58] PR Rodrigues and MAH van der Woude, 'Proactieve politiecontrole en onderscheid naar etniciteit of nationaliteit; (2016) 91(32) *Nederlands Juristenblad* 2294–302.

MSM and may send a message of non-belonging to the relatively large number of legal residents or citizens that are stopped on account of their 'foreign appearance'. At the same time this does not directly mean that RNM officers are driven by beliefs about the inferiority of certain groups of people. Alpert et al note that certain organisational or legal factors 'can lead to discriminatory policing without individual-level discrimination'.[59] This seems particularly true for proactive forms of border policing aimed at preventing illegal immigration; it is the instrument that leaves individual officers little choice but to use their powers in a discriminatory way, with skin colour playing an important role.

Although it is understandable how race and ethnicity as well as proxies thereof – most importantly, licence plates – *can* play a role in discretionary decisions made by street-level officials tasked with immigration and border control, it is the question to what extent these factors are legally allowed to play a role at all in their decision-making.

Race as a legal concept is enshrined in the International Convention on the Elimination of All Forms of Racial Discrimination (ICERD). Article 1 paragraph 1 of the convention reads that race should also be understood to include skin colour, descent and ethnic or national origin. Nationality is excluded, although the treaty does prohibit discrimination against a certain nationality (Article 1, paragraph 3). Signatory States to the convention are in principle permitted to distinguish between nationals and foreign nationals (Article 1, paragraph 2). In addition, 'race' is mentioned in the non-discrimination clauses of, inter alia, the International Covenant on Civil and Political Rights (Article 26 ICCPR) and the ECHR (Article 14). Nationality is lacking as a ground for discrimination in these treaties, but this is covered by the jurisprudence on the open norm 'on any ground', as a result of which this form of discrimination also falls within the scope of the clause.[60]

A complicating factor is that European Union law applies to immigration and border control actions, which is the case with regard to the MSM as carried out by the RNM. Under EU law discrimination based on race and nationality is prohibited based on article 21 of the EU Charter. Furthermore, article 18 of the Treaty on the functioning of the European Union reads: 'Within the scope of application of the Treaties, and without prejudice to any special provisions contained therein, any discrimination on grounds of nationality shall be prohibited'. It is disputed whether this provision only concerns the protection of the nationality of EU nationals, because it can be argued that the provisions on border control (Article 77), asylum (Article 78) and regular residence and the prevention of illegal residence and human trafficking (Article 79) third-country nationals also

[59] GP Alpert, JM MacDonald and RG Dunham, 'Police Suspicion and Discretionary Decision Making During Citizen Stops' (2005) 43(2) *Criminology* 407–34.

[60] EHRM 16 september 1996, 17371/90 (Gaygusuz/Oostenrijk), NJCM-Bulletin. 1997, nr. 4, p. 461-474, m.nt. Groenendijk

fall within the scope of Article 18 of the Treaty on the functioning of the European Union.[61] Up until today, the CJEU has not yet ruled on this.

Also, a distinction needs to be made between direct and indirect discrimination. Direct discrimination is happening when someone is treated differently based on one of the so-called protected characteristics such as skin colour.[62] Indirect discrimination is at play when a criterium is being applied in such a way that it is disproportionately disadvantageous for persons who are protected against direct discrimination. For example, if a disproportionately large number of cars with a Polish licence plate are stopped, this will predominantly affect Polish people. Indirect discrimination is sometimes used to disguise someone's *actual* intentions. In these cases, the CJEU speaks of 'disguised discrimination'.[63] Both under European Union law and under the various human rights treaties it is less likely for direct forms of discrimination to be justified than for forms of indirect discrimination. Under European Union law, such justification should lie in a legal exception and under the case law of the European Court of Human Rights (ECtHR) there is no objective justification for discrimination on ethnic grounds only in the case of disputed police actions.[64] It is less likely to find justified exceptions for racial discrimination than for discrimination based on nationality. In addition to that, the CJEU tends to equate indirect racial discrimination based on unsubstantiated prejudice with direct racial discrimination.[65] When it comes to objective justifications for indirect discrimination it has to be proven that the distinction is made in order to pursue a legitimate goal and that the means to achieve the goal must be appropriate and necessary.

It is therewith safe to conclude that it will be very difficult, if not impossible, to find an objective justification for direct discrimination based on race. This could be the case with indirect discrimination, as long as the indirectly discriminatory actions are not driven by stereotypical perceptions about certain populations.[66] Making distinctions based on nationality can more easily be justified than distinctions based on race. The ECtHR states that it is necessary in these cases to prove that there were 'very weighty reasons' to do so.[67] What is difficult to assess is the extent to which these characteristics – race and nationality – *can* play a role when they are *part* of a composed range of characteristics guiding a decision. There still seems to be some room for negotiation there, some discretionary space for the courts to further specify.

[61] E Brouwer and K de Vries, 'Third-Country Nationals and Discrimination on the Ground of Nationality: Article 18 TFEU in the Context of Article 14 ECHR and EU Migration Law: Time for a New Approach' in M van der Brink, S Burri and J Goldschmidt (eds), *Equality and Human Rights: Nothing But Trouble* (Utrecht, Netherlands Institute of Human Rights (SIM), 2015) 139–41.

[62] Other protected characteristics are: Age, Disability, Gender, Marriage and civil partnership, Pregnancy and maternity, Religion and belief, Sex, Sexual orientation.

[63] HvJ EU 12 februari 1974, C-152/73 (*Sotgiu*), r.o. 11.

[64] EHRM 13 december 2005, 55762/00 en 55974/00 (*Timishev/Rusland*), r.o. 58.

[65] HvJ EU 16 juli 2015, C-83/14 (*Chez*), JV 2015/308, m.nt. Rodrigues.

[66] EHRM 24 mei 2016, 38590/10 (*Biao/ Denemarken*).

[67] EHRM 8 april 2014, 17120/09 (*Dhahbi/Italië*), r.o. 48.

When looking at the specific goal of the MSM – preventing irregular migration into the Netherlands – it is clear that this goal is related to preconceptions of someone's legal status. Given the fact that the MSM is carried out in the form of spot checks in intra-Schengen Border areas, it seems very difficult to imagine how someone's perceived nationality or ethnicity cannot play a role in the decision-making process in combination with less problematic factors such as someone's behaviour, the looks of the car, etc. Contrary to the racial profiling of potential 'criminals' by the regular police, one could argue that taking into account the characteristic(s) race and/or nationality by the RNM while performing the MSM is crucial to properly perform their statutory task and that this task cannot be performed based on decisions based only on neutral criteria and non-protected characteristics. Having said this, it is clear that allowing this in practice will cause many problems, especially with regard to proving that race and/or nationality were indeed part of a composed range of factors leading up to the decision to stop and search a vehicle or a person and not the *only* reason. As illustrated by the excerpts from the fieldwork, there are strong stereotypes amongst street-level RNM officials with regard to the involvement of certain populations in behaviours that would fall within the legal mandate of the MSM. And in practice it can be difficult to establish to what extent a decision is predominantly – and initially – fuelled by these stereotypes after which street-level RNM officials will also try to find other factors to support their decision, or whether the decision is indeed based on a more holistic assessment in which race and/or nationality are just one of many factors that are taken into consideration. It remains to be seen what the Dutch Court will decide and how they will motivate their decision.

VI. Concluding Reflections

As observed by Carrera, 'crises' are well known to serve as political catalysts for the adoption of previously existing and controversial ideas, offering new momentum for their expedited adoption in the name of emergency.[68] The so-called European migration crisis definitely seemed to have served that purpose and it remains to be seen to what extent the global Corona-crisis will also leave its mark on migration and border control. Some critics are saying that it might even be the end of Schengen as we know it.

What this chapter has illustrated is that the Schengen as we know it, has always been less 'open' than its main underlying principle – the principle of free movement – implied it was. The mobility of people has always been securitised

[68] S Carrera, 'The 20 Years Anniversary of the Tampere Programme: Securitization, Intergovernmentalism and Informalization' (2010) 27(1) *Maastricht Journal of European and Comparative Law* 3–9.

and therefore monitored. Whereas this might not have been very visible before, the European migration crisis has made it clear that Member States are willing to go 'all out' in an attempt to protect their borders against unwanted others. A rhetoric of exclusion and othering underpins European and national debates on mobility, leading to the further blurring and fusion of functional, normative and discursive barriers between crime control and immigration control.

The blurring of the boundaries between crime control and immigration control – and the ways in which that subsequently affects the actions of street-level immigration and border officials – is illustrated by the analysis of the MSM in the Netherlands. The proactive discretionary power to stop a vehicle or a person to check whether or not they are entering the Netherlands with a valid status – so 'legally' – creates room for 'crimmigrant' stereotypes to roam freely. The Dutch case illustrates that – like in other countries – 'nationality' and 'ethnicity' have become proxies for race, for focusing on the non-native 'other'. Whereas this is a problematic observation from the standpoint of non-discrimination, it touches upon a more fundamental question: the question whether measures of immigration and border control in a time where migration is highly securitised, politicised and mediatised can in fact be enforced without such stereotypical images playing a role at all.

Current times and current crises force us to rethink the notion of Schengen as well as perhaps the notion of Europe. Whereas the idea behind the European Union is said to be solidarity, again, the increased emphasis on security seem to take Member States in another direction: one of national sovereignty and the preservation of national identity in which there might not even be the need for article 23 SBC checks anymore.

8

Crimmigration in Greece

A Story of Exceptional Derogations from the Rule of Law within a Permanent Situation of Emergency

NIKOLAOS CHATZINIKOLAOU

I. Main Features of Greek Criminal Law

In July 2019, the new Criminal Code (CC) and the new Code of Criminal Procedure (CCP) entered into force in Greece.[1] These legislative texts do not constitute a paradigm shift since they substantially share the same structure and main notions with the prior codes, all belonging to the continental criminal law tradition. However, the new codes introduce many changes. As far as substantive criminal law is concerned, the most decisive change has to do with the system of criminal sanctions. Its declared objective was particularly the de-escalation of the prescribed sanctions and the proportional reformation of the conditional release regulation in order to decrease the difference between the imposed sentence and the actual time that is being served by the offender.

The Greek CC classifies crimes in two categories: felonies and misdemeanours while it repealed the third category of crimes, infractions. Each crime is labelled depending on the penalty prescribed for it, notwithstanding any applicable mitigating circumstances. Accordingly, article 18 CC provides that a felony is an unlawful act punishable by imprisonment of five to 15 years (long-term imprisonment) or life imprisonment; a misdemeanour is an unlawful act punishable by imprisonment of 10 days to five years (short-term imprisonment), juvenile detention, community service or pecuniary fine. The above custodial penalties are mitigated in the presence of certain circumstances, such as attempt, indirect aiding or abetting, and, notably, mitigating circumstances (article 84 CC).

[1] Statutes No 4619/2019 and 4620/2019 respectively.

Despite its idiosyncrasy, the Greek sanction system can be regarded as a 'dualistic' or 'two-track' one, its two 'tracks' being penalties and measures of reform and security. From the crimmigration perspective, it is important to highlight the repeal of judicial expulsion. The previous CC prescribed this sanction as a security measure against foreigner offenders that completed or replaced, under specific circumstances, the custodial sentence. The identity of expulsion as a safety measure was seriously challenged in theory.[2] However, it is not likely that the repeal of this provision reinforces the rule of law since all relevant issues are transferred to the administrative expulsion which can still be imposed as a reaction to the conviction, acquittal or even prosecution of a foreigner, without the safeguards that were formerly prescribed by the previous CC. Administrative expulsion is within the domain of police and can be controlled judicially only after its imposition by the authorities.[3]

II. Turning Points of Criminal Suppression of Irregular Migration in Greece

A. Introduction

Ever since the establishment of the modern Greek state in the beginning of the nineteenth century up until the end of the twentieth century, Greece has traditionally been an emigration country.[4] During times of financial crisis, the pursuit of better living conditions led to mass emigration of large sections of the Greek population to other European countries, the USA and elsewhere.[5] This phenomenon repeated itself during the current financial crisis affecting especially the youngest and highly educated Greeks (brain drain). There were also times when sections of Greek population were forced to flee their country because of political reasons, the most recent example being the military dictatorship that lasted for seven years and ended in 1974. A partly reverse situation was the integration of Greek natives of Asia-Minor that took place during the Greek inter-war period, as a result of

[2] See, e.g., N Chatzinikolaou, *Η απέλαση αλλοδαπού ως κύρωση του ποινικού δικαίου* (*The expulsion of aliens as a criminal sanction*) (Thessaloniki, Sakkoulas, 2006) 68–204.

[3] See, e.g., I Symeonides, *Η διοικητική απέλαση* (*The administrative expulsion*) (Thessaloniki, Sakkoulas, 2008).

[4] N Diamandouros (preface in M Pavlou and D Christopoulos (eds), *Η Ελλάδα της μετανάστευσης* (*Greece of immigration*) (Athens, Kritiki, 2004) 12) points out that because of this historical experience the term 'immigration' in Greek language is correlated with the phenomenon of leaving a country. In fact, this is the reason why the word 'emigrate' has no distinguishable term in Greek language.

[5] For a broader approach see M Mazower (ed), *After the War was Over – Reconstructing the Family, Nation and State in Greece, 1943–1960* (Princeton and Oxford, Princeton University Press, 2000); N Sitaropoulos, *Immigration Law an Management in Greece* (Athens-Komotini, AN Sakkoulas, 2003) 12–14, R Evans, *Η επιδίωξη της ισχύος– Ευρώπη 1815–1914* (*The pursuit of power – Europe 1815–1914*) (Athens, Alexandreia, 2018) 408–10.

Greece's defeat in Greco-Turkish war. However, this was the case of a partly agreed population 'exchange' between Turkey and Greece.

Greek immigration policy remained thus unchanged for almost 60 years,[6] although, according to published case-law, there were hardly any cases where the criminal sanctions prescribed by statute No 4310/1929 were enforced. The aforementioned law introduced lenient sanctions for the facilitation of illegal entry, most of them of pecuniary nature.[7]

B. The Gradual Toughening of Criminal Suppression

This situation started changing in 1991. The legislation's toughening was the result of mass unauthorised entries of hundreds of thousands of people who mainly came through the Albanian-Greek border, that was triggered by the political changes in Albania and the Balkans after the collapse of the 'real socialism' regimes.[8] Therefore, the legislative framework was amended several times with the adoption and implementation of statutes No 1975/1991, 2910/2001 and 3386/2005. Throughout this period, the fact that Greece has transformed from an emigration country to a host country for immigrants[9] is being used as an excuse for the toughening of the legislation. However, the portrayal of the increased migration flows in the early 1990s as an exceptional situation, should be approached carefully since it is sometimes connected to the justification of 'emergency legislation'[10] that remains in force for over 30 years; thus, aliens' presence in the country is being regarded in the same context rather as a crisis situation and not as a normal condition which legislators, society and the justice system should approach within the rule of law.[11]

Up until the middle of the previous decade, there was a gradual strengthening of the penal framework concerning the unlawful action of migrant smuggling with the use of any means of transportation combined with the criminalisation of

[6] See inter alia Sitaropoulos, above n 5, 12.

[7] See P Dagtoglou, 'Die Rechtstellung von Ausländern nach staatlichen Recht und Völkerrecht in Griechenland' in J Frowein and T Stein (Hrsg), *Die Rechtstellung von Ausländern nach staatlichen Recht und Völkerrecht* (Berlin, Springer Verlag, 1987) pt I 529.

[8] Another important flow of immigrants during the same period involved those of Greek origin from the former Soviet Union; see R Fakiolas, 'Η ενσωμάτωση των Ελληνοποντίων στην ελληνική κοινωνία' ('The integration of Pontic Greeks in Greek society') in G Amitsis and G Lazaridi (eds), *Νομικές και κοινωνικοπολιτικές διαστάσεις της μετανάστευσης στην Ελλάδα* (*Legal and Socio-Political Dimensions of Immigration in Greece*) (Athens, Papazissi, 2001) 129–55.

[9] Explanatory reports of the three aforementioned laws, all available at www.hellenicparliament.gr.

[10] See S Georgoula, 'Η νέα μεταναστευτική πολιτική στην Ελλάδα και η νομιμοποίησή της' ('The new immigration policy in Greece and its legalization') in A Marvaki, D Parsanoglou and M Pavlou (eds), *Μετανάστες στην Ελλάδα* (*Immigrants in Greece*) (Athens, Ellinika Grammata, 2001) 199; Ch Konstandinidou, *Κοινωνικές αναπαραστάσεις του εγκλήματος – Η εγκληματικότητα των αλβανών μεταναστών στον αθηναϊκό τύπο* (*Social depictions of crime – Albanians criminality in Athens' press*) (Athens, AN Sakkoulas, 2001) 100.

[11] See also Sitaropoulos, above n 5, 73.

unauthorised entry. However, during this period all these crimes remained misdemeanours, with prescribed sanctions gradually getting tougher. The effectiveness of the criminal sanctions was supported by exceptional provisions and similar interpretation of either concurrence rules or appeals' suspensory effect, which are discussed below.

Apart from the direct provisions of criminal nature, there was a general difficulty in handling irregular migration on an administrative level. As a result, large groups of foreigners were found *in limbo*. An inflexible legal framework of provisions concerning the acquisition of a residence permit was introduced but its implementation was impossible from the start, in part due to lack of an appropriate administrative culture. Consequently, even though hundreds of thousands of migrants were working in Greece, very few had a residence permit and could thus enjoy even the basic individual and social rights. According to the data provided by the Ministry of Employment (1993), two years after statute No 1975/1991 was put into force, there were 30,000 legal immigrants (including 3,000 European Union nationals) and 300,000 irregular immigrants in Greece.[12] The relevant Common Ministerial Decision of Ministers of Foreign Affairs, Employment and Public Order ('maximum number of foreigners' work permits') was typical: even though the legislator accepted the extension of the immigration phenomenon in Greece, the maximum number of work permits was 40 for the city of Athens and 15 for the city of Thessaloniki. This situation favoured mass labour exploitation of these populations whose contribution to the substantial growth of the Greek economy of the time is widely recognised.[13]

Efforts were made to address this problem mainly through the implementation of successive programs of mass 'legalisation of migrants',[14] that provided a chance of acquiring residence permits to people that had irregularly entered the country as long as they proved a minimum period of actual residence and work and could afford to pay the fees required. Even though the application of these procedures faced serious problems leading to a constant alteration of the foreigners' legal status,[15] the relevant provisions contributed to the smoother integration of first-generation immigrants. The ultimate consequence of this development

[12] See Z Papasiopi-Passia, 'Νόμιμη και παράνομη εργασία στην Ελλάδα' ('Legal and illegal employment in Greece') in Hellenic Society of International Private Law, *Το νομικό καθεστώς των αλλοδαπών στην Ελλάδα* (*Legal status of foreigners in Greece*) (Athens, Private Edition, 1995) 77–78.

[13] See, e.g., A Limperaki and Th Pelagides, *Ο «φόβος του ξένου» στην αγορά εργασίας: ανοχές και προκαταλήψεις στην ανάπτυξη* (*The 'fear of aliens' in labor market: tolerance and prejudice in evolution*) (Athens, Polis, 2000) 26, 72; Sitaropoulos, above n 5, 16; Th Lianos, 'Illegal Migrants to Greece and their Choice of Destination' (2001) *International Migration* 3, 15; K Simitis, *Πολιτική για μια δημιουργική Ελλάδα 1996-2004* (*Policy towards a creative Greece, 1996–2004*) (Athens, Polis, 2005) 272.

[14] See presidential order No 358 and 359/1997, art 66 of statute No 2910/2001 and art 91 of statute No 3386/2005.

[15] See, e.g., A Scordas, 'The Regularization of Illegal Immigrants in Greece' in Ph De Bruycker et al, *Regularizations of illegal immigrants in the EU* (Brussels, Bruylant, 2000) 343; Sitaropoulos, above n 5, 33–40; M Papantoniou-Frangouli and KM Leventi, 'The Legalization of Aliens in Greece' (2000) *International Migration Review* 950.

was the gradual improvement of nationality legislation during the current decade so that the second generation of immigrants will not have to deal with the same difficulties especially in enjoying their social rights.[16]

In general, during this period criminal and administrative control had to do with people, the vast majority of whom wished to pursue better living conditions in Greece, where, because of the steady economic development, there was an increased number of lower-paid employment positions that were reserved almost exclusively to foreigners.[17] Under these circumstances, external pressure for strict control became even weaker, while the results of the Schengen acquis were not yet fully apparent in Greece.

C. A Change of Approach: Transition to Felonies

During the European Parliament Election on the 7 June 2009 in Greece for the election of the national delegation to the European Parliament, the only political party that placed the 'fight' against irregular immigration at the core of its election campaign, Popular Orthodox Rally (LAOS[18]), doubled its percentage by climbing from the 4.12 per cent of the vote of the previous elections to 7.15 per cent. LAOS was not identical to the neo-Nazi political party 'Golden Dawn', that appeared dynamically in the political scene of the following decade, during a period of financial crisis in the Eurozone and Greece and played a leading role in anti-immigration rhetoric and actions. However, the election's results led to the first serious fracture of the Greek two party political system which had dominated the political scene for over four decades after the restoration of Democracy in 1974. Generally, during the election period that coincided in time with the first years of economic downturn in Greece, irregular immigration became a major political challenge. The main concern was the frustration of residents of an underdeveloped neighbourhood in Athens, Agios Pantelaemonas, caused by the overcrowding of irregular immigrants and the daily disturbances as a result of immigrants' inferior living conditions in an abandoned building (that was previously a court house). It seems that this data was later in fact reflected in a public opinion survey.[19]

A couple of days after the election results, at 20:00 on the 18 June 2009, amendment No 600/44 was proposed to the national delegation. This amendment introduced in a hasty manner drastic changes of criminal provisions for migrant smugglers that resulted in a dramatic toughening of criminal sanctions and a general

[16] See especially the provisions of statutes No 3838/2010 and No 4332/2015.

[17] See also Sitaropoulos, above n 5, 35.

[18] The acronym LAOS means 'people' in Greek.

[19] Research presented by the newspaper 'Kathimerini tis Kiriakis' on 21 June 2009, available at www.skai.gr/articles/news/politics/ΒαρόμετροΙουνίουτηςPublicIssue/. According to the data presented, 18 per cent of Greek nationals thought that immigration was the most serious national issue. Contrarily, only 2 per cent of the Greek population gave the same answer in the previous survey of the same company (Public Issue).

According to the statistics available, on 3 September 2019 there were 69,387 requests for asylum pending examination while the annual processing rate never exceeded 7,000, even though it was upgraded in 2017.[27] Despite the existing need for an actual improvement of the asylum system, a careful attempt to define the limits of refugees' protection is being made at the proposal, that was adopted by statute No 4636/2019: the explanatory report of the draft refers to

> closed borders, increased flows, lack of resources in Greece in order to receive every third-country national or stateless person and to international protection the aim of which is only to protect the 'downtrodden', as an ultimate humanitarian act and not to broaden the meaning of the word.[28]

The same restrictive approach was indirectly expressed earlier with the revision of provisions on Greek Appeal Committees on asylum. The composition of the Committees with administrative judges as a majority, that was established with article 86 of statute No 4399/2016, was attributed to the previous almost unanimous denial of Committees to consider Turkey as a safe third country, an interpretative approach that made the implementation of the EU-Turkey Statement extremely difficult.[29]

This restrictive approach reached its peak on the 2 March 2020 with the enforcement of a Legislative Decision issued by the President of the Hellenic Republic on the basis of the relevant Proposal of the Council of Ministers.[30] This urgent temporary legislative measure was a reaction to Turkey's decision to open its borders at the end of February 2020, that resulted in the gathering of a great number of immigrants and refugees at the Greek-Turkish borders along the river Evros, who aimed to enter the country. This legislative measure, that was published a few days before the completion of this contribution, mentions in its preamble that there is

> an extremely urgent and unpredictable need to face this unbalanced threat against state's security, that exceeds European and international law's justification about asylum procedure, in combination with the incapacity of examining the asylum requests within reasonable time.

According to the Legislative Decision:

> All asylum requests from people who illegally enter the country are postponed [for a month, after this measure is put into force]. People who illegally enter the country are returned, without listing, to the source country or their country of origin.[31]

[27] See data available at www.asylo.gov.gr.

[28] Explanatory report, above n 26, 20.

[29] See M Gliati, 'The Application of the EU-Turkey Agreement: A Critical Analysis of the Decisions of the Greek Appeal Committees' (2017) *European Journal of Legal Studies* 81–123.

[30] This is an extremely urgent legislative measure taken by the Council of Ministers which was later ratified by the Parliament. The Decision has been ratified by virtue of statute No 4681/2020.

[31] Art 1 para 1 of statute No 4681/2020.

III. Aberration from General Principles

During this development, legislation, interpretation and implementation of law on criminal suppression of irregular migration constantly deviates from generally accepted principles of Greek criminal law.

A. Transition to Felonies without Proper Justification

i. The Remaining Strict Sanctions – Architecture Problems

Statute No 4251/2014 which is currently in force repeats criminal provisions for migrant smugglers that were first prescribed in statute No 3386/2005 after its modification by statute No 3772/2009.

Specifically, according to article 29 paragraphs 5 and 6 of statute No 4251/2014 (Immigration Code):

> 5. Any person who intentionally assists a third-country national to enter or exit from the territory of Greece, who has not undergone the procedure described in article 5, should be punished with long-term imprisonment of no more than 10 years and a pecuniary fine of no less than 20.000 euros. If the offender was seeking financial gain or commits this unlawful act to make a living or regularly commits this unlawful act, he should be punished with long-term imprisonment of no less than 10 years and a pecuniary fine of no less than 50.000 euros.
>
> 6. Any person who intentionally assists a third-country national to illegally reside within the territory of Greece or hinders police investigation for the tracking, arrest and expulsion of this person, should be punished with short-term imprisonment of no less than one year and a pecuniary fine of no less than 5.000 euros. If the offender was seeking financial gain, he should be punished with short-term imprisonment of no less than two years and a pecuniary fine of no less than 10.000 euros.

According to article 30 paragraph 1 of statute No 4251/2014:

> Captains of ships, vessels or aircrafts and drivers of every means of transportation who transport to Greece from abroad third-country nationals who are not authorised to enter Greek territory or who are not allowed to enter Greek territory as well as any person who recruits these irregular immigrants at internal or external Greek borders in order to facilitate their transfer within Greek territory or the territory of any other EU member-state or any other third country or any person harbors these people, should be punished with:
>
> a) long-term imprisonment of no more than 10 years and a pecuniary fine of no less than 30.000 euros and no more than 60.000 euros per irregular immigrant,
> b) long-term imprisonment of no less than 10 years and a pecuniary fine of no less than 60.000 euros and no more than 100.000 euros per irregular immigrant, if the offender was seeking financial gain, or commits this unlawful act to make a living or regularly commits this unlawful act or if the unlawful act is committed by a repeat offender or a civil servant or a tourist/shipowner's/travel agent,

c) long-term imprisonment of no less than 15 years and a pecuniary fine of no less than 200.000 euros per irregular immigrant, if the unlawful act could lead to endangerment of life,
d) life imprisonment and a pecuniary fine of no less than 700.000 euros per irregular immigrant if the unlawful act of point (c) leads to death.

As a result, all unlawful acts of migrant smuggling remain characterised as felonies. As noted above, there was a general de-escalation of criminal sanctions after the new CC and its transitional provisions were entered into force, which affected for a while also statute No 4251/2014. Articles 83 (c) and 463 paragraph 3 CC[32] provided a similar de-escalation of penalties prescribed in special criminal laws, outside the CC. As a result of this provision, 'basic' offences of assisting in unauthorised entry and migrant smuggling are punished with imprisonment of no less than one year and no more than six years for each undocumented foreigner. There was also a slight softening of the penalties prescribed for the aggravated crimes of this statute that remained some of the toughest under the Greek penal legislation system and can even be compared with the penalties prescribed for the unlawful act of homicide.

But even this indirect de-escalation of the draconian penalties for migrant smuggling, after the new CC was entered into force, was partially cancelled four months later: by virtue of article 12 paragraph 6 of statute No 4637/2019, the general de-escalation of penalties prescribed in article 463 CC *does not apply* to the crime prescribed in article 30 of statute No 4251/2014. This is the last typical paradigm where smuggling of migrants is treated as an exception. The relevant explanation for the last-minute amendment of the original draft of the Statute mentions that:

> The exception of the crimes related to unlawful transportation of migrants from the de-escalation of penalties prescribed in Article 463 CC is justified by the fact that a possible reduction of these penalties will contribute to the increase of the -already many- cases of illegal migrant smuggling, a situation that is overtime considered as a severe social problem globally and especially during this period, since it takes place with high intensity.[33]

No further explanation is given why this justification does not apply to the crimes prescribed in article 29 of statute No 4251/2014.

Article 30 of statute No 4251/2014 provides criminal penalties for the traditional felonies of migrant smuggling, that refers to acts of transportation of irregular immigrants in or within the country by any means of transportation, though article 29 establishes the rather recent offence of facilitating of unauthorised

[32] The latter affirms that the offences remain felonies, although they are punished by a 'mixed' sentence (short- and long-term imprisonment).

[33] www.hellenicparliament.gr/UserFiles/bbb19498-1ec8-431f-82e6-023bb91713a9/11131013.pdf, 2.

entry or exit from the country. This last offence is based on the 2002/946/JHA Framework Decision[34] and the corresponding Directive 2002/90/EU,[35] legislative texts that both reflect an alternative approach to the same criminal behaviour, focusing on a generic notion of 'facilitation of unauthorised entry, transit and residence'.

These provisions were in fact copied and incorporated into national laws.[36] This methodology contributed to the creation of unclear legislative texts. The legislative process failed to detect the reasons why the Greek legal framework always paid attention to drivers, captains etc as principals of migrant smuggling. As a result, while the unauthorised transportation of a migrant is still prescribed as a criminal offence in article 30, the more general behaviours of facilitating unauthorised entry or exit, were also criminalised as felonies.[37]

Considering these decisions, every effort for a more systematic approach and application of the legislation in force faces plenty of difficulties. As a result, it is impossible to give a rational explanation for the gradation of criminal sanctions in similar cases. Stricter sanctions are prescribed e.g., when migrant smuggling is committed by a civil servant or a shipowner's or travel agent whereas these aggravating circumstances are not being taken into consideration at the crime of facilitating unauthorised entry or exit.

This inflationary approach sets boundaries on both providing different interpretations of the legislation and on applying it in an alternative way: if a criminal provision cannot be applied to a specific case, chances are that the other similar provision will be easily applied, resulting in a combination of crimes that multiply the unbearable consequences of an already blindly strict legislation.

In a legislative environment like this one, the judicial body plays an even more important and demanding role: judges are expected to conform to thoughtless legislative choices and safeguard the thoroughness and cohesion of criminal law in the most effective possible way. It is however doubtful whether the judicial body has fully met this demanding duty or not. The most typical examples of this situation, which are discussed below, are the application of the concurrence rules, the prescribed penalty 'for every transported person'[38] and the dubious characterisation of accessories as principals of migrant smuggling.[39]

[34] [2002] OJ L328/1.

[35] [2002] OJ L 328/17.

[36] See statutes No 3386/2005, 3536/2007 and 3772/2009, whose provisions were repeated in the last Code of Immigration and Social Integration.

[37] See N Chatzinikolaou, *Η ποινική καταστολή της παράνομης μετανάστευσης* (*The criminal suppression of illegal migration*) (Thessaloniki, Nomiki Vivliothiki, 2009) 173 ff.

[38] See the full bench of the Supreme Court's decision No 9/1995, (1996) *Poinika Chronika* 476 = (1996) *Iperaspissi* 759 with comments of D Kioupis and M Kaiafa-Gbandi respectively in favour of the 'real concurrence' doctrine. See also Supreme Court's decision No892/2001, (2002) *Poiniki Dikaiosini* 14 with comments of A Papadamakis.

[39] See e.g., Supreme Court's decision No 1237/1999, (2000) *Poinika Chronika* 618.

This unnecessary fragmentation of the offences seems to lead to some resignation and interpretative automation. The only guidelines are the elimination of every possible delimitation of criminal offences so that this excessive legislation that reinforces the suppression of this phenomenon in any way will be accompanied by a similarly excessive application of the law.

On the other hand, the unlawful acts of facilitating irregular residence have always been punished as misdemeanours, if there are not directly related with the unauthorised entry, i.e., if facilitation is not provided right after the entry of the migrant. Similarly, the unlawful acts of hiring undocumented workers or renting to undocumented foreigners are punished by the imposition of administrative fines. The corresponding criminal sanctions[40] are in fact rarely applied in comparison to the criminal sanctions against migrant smugglers. In this framework, there is no published case-law about cases of prosecution or imposition of administrative fines for providing e.g., food to undocumented foreigners.[41] These circumstances can be attributed to the difficulties that the Greek administration faces in the handling of the phenomenon, the difficulties in the actualisation of the returns and the lack of proper public infrastructure to host the undocumented foreigners. The relevant public servants thus recognise informally that such activity by society should not be criminalised. However, keeping these provisions in force puts many irregular migrants under exploitation conditions.[42]

ii. Migrant Smuggling, Assisting and Accessory to the Unauthorised Entry and Exit

Apart from the clarity and architectural problems, the most fundamental flaw of the criminal legislation in question is that it basically fails to provide convincing justification for the drastic toughening of criminal sanctions for the unlawful acts of migrant smuggling, assisting and accessory to the unauthorised entry and exit.

According to the explanatory reports of the statutes that shaped the legislative framework in force, the core of the justification for the toughening of criminal sanctions for migrant smugglers lies in issues such as the exploitation of the foreigners' need, the fact that the offender intends to make a profit of the immigrants' need while putting their life at risk. A statement of the competent Minister during the parliamentarian consultation of statute No 2910/2001 clarifies this reasoning, referring to the same provision which is now prescribed in Article 30 paragraph 1 of statute 4251/2014: 'this is a totally different offence … it deals with the *mass* transportation of illegal migrants,

[40] Arts 28 and 29 of statute No 4251/2014.

[41] See similar cases at Carrera, Mitsilegas, Allsop and Vosyliute, above n 25, 151.

[42] See the explanatory report of the new asylum legislation discussed above, n 26, 3.

it refers to perpetrators who *get rich from these shiploads*'.[43] Respectively, in one of the first attempts for the characterisation of migrant smuggling offences as felonies, the offenders were actually characterised as 'slave traders'.[44]

The same reasoning lies behind the provision about special investigative techniques for the effective prosecution of organised crime 'even if the preconditions described in articles 187 and 187A CC are not fulfilled'.[45] This choice implies that the unlawful acts in question are committed by offenders who systematically smuggle immigrants. This is also the case with the confiscation provisions as well as the high pecuniary fines that are being imposed in combination with the imprisonment.[46]

This policy choice should not itself be rejected. Neither should anyone support that the reversal of the traditional doctrine of complicity is always unjustified.[47] Generally speaking, the – exceptional – provision of stricter sanctions for accessories – compared with the sanctions for the perpetrator – of certain crimes is not that uncommon even in light of the Greek and continental doctrine of complicity.[48] However, this exceptional reversal of criminal liability rules should be sufficiently justified. The above-mentioned reasons, that are being used as an explanation for the toughening of criminal sanctions prescribed for the unlawful act of assisting irregular immigration, a behaviour like the concept of complicity, can provide a general argument towards this direction. However, it is not clear whether they can justify all the legislative choices concerning the relevant unlawful acts.

First, the term 'slave trader' is itself incapable of describing and approaching this specific criminal behaviour even on a policymaking level, as it clearly refers to the deprivation of the immigrants' freedom, an element not required by articles 29 and 30 of statute No 4251/2014. Relevant European texts about human trafficking have been incorporated into Greek legislation providing different offences than the ones of smuggling of migrants, while article 323A CC prescribes a stricter

[43] Minutes of Greek Parliament (Full bench), Session No ΡΜΓ, 20 June 2001, 6156, www.hellenicparliament.gr (emphasis added).

[44] Law proposal of 13 January 2003, www.hellenicparliament.gr.

[45] Art 30 para 7 statute no 4251/2014. Arts 187 and 187 A CC concern organised crime and terrorist acts.

[46] The financial penalty prescribed for the unlawful act of art 30 statute No 4251/2014 is still no less than 700,000 euros without a maximum limit.

[47] See K Vathiotis, 'Ιστορική εξέλιξη του νόμου περί αλλοδαπών: Μια εξέλιξη χωρίς εξέλιξη;' ('Aliens' Law historic development: a development without progress?') in A Sikiotou (ed), *Αλλοδαποί στην Ελλάδα* (*Foreigners in Greece*) (Komotini, AN Sakkoulas, 2008) 201; Chr Naidos, 'Προβλήματα συμμετοχής στην υποβοήθηση της παράνομης μετανάστευσης' ('Complicity problems on facilitation of irregular migrants' crimes') (2019) *Poinika Chronika* 172.

[48] See A Konstantinides, *Μορφές συμμετοχής στο έγκλημα ως αυτοτελή αδικήματα* (*Forms of Crime as separate offences*) (Komotini, AN Sakkoulas, 1982) 73, M Böse, 'Das Einschleusen von Ausländern: Teilnahme an Bagatellunrecht oder in hohem Maße sozialschädliches Verhalten?' (2004) *Zeitschrift für die gesamte Strafrechtswissenschaft* 680.

sanction when human trafficking is connected to the victim's unauthorised entry, stay or exit from the country.[49]

There is no such distinction in criminal provisions about smuggling of migrants, as the perpetrators do not need to meet the requirements of slave traders or exploit the people who are being transported. Whoever assists or transports, by using any means of transportation, third country nationals, is always treated more strictly than the person who is being assisted or transported. All these types of criminal conduct are punished as complete crimes with a maximum of long-term imprisonment. There is no distinction based on the severity of each criminal conduct since both providing of accommodation or assisting the irregular entry or exit and 'professional' smuggling of dozens of immigrants who are being crammed in trucks or boats are treated in the same way.

The pursuit of profit-making or the collection of profit that derives from smuggling is an aggravating circumstance to the basic felony in contrast to the Palermo Protocol against smuggling of migrants by land, sea and air,[50] according to which, the pursuit of profit is an element of the crime (article 3).

What is therefore missing is a legal provision with elements that can justify the abstention from the doctrine of complicity and a stricter criminal sanction than the one prescribed for the principal of the criminal conduct, i.e., the migrant's irregular entry or exit. This is a legislative deficit that has traditionally been observed in Greek legislative texts and is indirectly ratified by European legislation, according to which the pursuit of profit-making or the collection of profits are not elements of migrant smuggling.[51] This legislative trend has severe consequences in Greece because of the prescribed sanctions of extreme harshness.

The only objection to these arguments is the fact that sometimes, people who control the migration flows do control the foreigners' movements, the latter 'just being transported involuntarily'.[52] For this reason, as it's argued, they actually become principals and not just accessories to the offence. From a criminological point of view these thoughts may be correct when referring to the heads of international criminal networks for migrant smuggling. However, where the problem lies is the fact that according to migrant smuggling legislation, that is completely different than the human trafficking legislation, the offenders do not need to meet these prerequisites.

[49] See generally N Chatzinikolaou, M Kaifa-Gbandi, Ath Giannakoula and Th Papakyriakou, 'The Framework Decision on Combating Trafficking in Human Beings. Evaluating its Fundamental Attributes As Well As its Transposition in Greek Criminal Law' in A Weyembergh and V Santamaria (eds), *The Evaluation of European Criminal Law* (Brussels, Editions de l' Université de Bruxelles, 2009) 131–96.

[50] See Document A/RES/55/25.

[51] See Chatzinikolaou, above n 37, 41 ff; Carrera, Mitsilegas, Allsop and Vosyliute, above n 25, 2 ff.

[52] See e.g., E Symeonidou-Kastanidou, 'Η ιδιότητα του πρόσφυγα και η επιρροή της στο ποινικό δίκαιο κατά της παράνομης μετανάστευσης' ('The refugee status and its impact for the criminal law against illegal migration') (2018) *Poinika Chronika* 263 ff; cf K Chatzopoulos, 'Foreigners, I' in S Pavlou and T Samios (eds), *Special Criminal Laws* (Athens, P.N. Sakkoulas, 2020), 6 ff.

There is an enlightening decision of the misdemeanour's board[53] of Thessaloniki, that refers to the topic in question.[54] According to the facts that were established by the misdemeanour's board, the accused persons, a Spanish driver and his Greek partner who were in Greece for holidays, were arrested at the highway between Kavala and Thessaloniki because they were transporting four undocumented Palestinians. As the migrants stated, they had actually come in touch with a criminal network of migrant smugglers that transported them in a truck among merchandise and got them out of the truck just outside of Thessaloniki, having to walk to get to the city. According to the decision, the accused persons who picked the Palestinians up from the highway did not pursue any profit-making or collect any profit, having actually stated in their apologies that they transported the foreigners for humanitarian reasons 'to help the refugees' because they felt sorry for them, not knowing that this conduct was a criminal offence. According to the Prosecutor's submission, that did not provide further adequate justification and documentation, the defendants should not be brought before trial because 'the Palestinians did not pay to be transported; by contrast their transport by the accused persons was a coincidence since they did not know that their conduct was illegal'. However the opinion of the misdemeanour's board was that the 'pursuit of profit-making does not constitute an element of this specific crime', noting that the defendants had actually confessed to the crime so they must be brought before trial.

Even if we overlook the arising issues about the proper characterisation of the relevant criminal conduct, one should recognise that the main line of argument concerning the element of the pursuit of profit-making is coherent with the European and national legislative choices. The fact that this legislation leaves open the possibility of everyday behaviour of human solidarity being punished as a criminal offence is thus clearly emphasised. The complex interpretative effort to limit these provisions on the grounds of e.g. the foreigner's refugee status,[55] even if it is occasionally and silently adopted by Greek courts, cannot offer a stable and safe resort from the problem. Similarly, some Greek courts' tendency in everyday practice to soften the criminal treatment of offenders by applying mitigating circumstances in such cases cannot comprehensively solve the arising problem in question.[56]

B. Concurrence and Aggregation of Penalties

Up until the end of the last decade, during the gradual strengthening of criminal sanctions for migrant smugglers when these unlawful acts were still

[53] Despite its name, misdemeanour's board is competent to judge, after the end of the official interrogation of a felony, whether the defendant will be brought to trial or not.

[54] No 826/2019 (unpublished).

[55] See Chatzinikolaou, above n 37, 156 ff; *cf* Symeonidou-Kastanidou, above n 52, 263 ff.

[56] See also Carrera, Mitsilegas, Allsop and Vosyliute, above n 25, 59, with reference to Italy.

misdemeanours, the concurrence doctrine applicable in cases of migrant smuggling of more than one person was of high importance since it defined decisively the offender's criminal liability. The consideration of the concurrence doctrine drew more attention of both judges and scholars than the significance of the individual elements of the crime in question.[57]

The CC's general part always made a distinction between concurrence of crimes that result from multiple acts (the so called 'real' concurrence) and concurrence of crimes that result from one act. In the first case, the offender commits multiple crimes with multiple acts (e.g., the offender injures three persons with separate acts); in the other case, multiple crimes are committed with one single act (e.g., the offender injures a police officer who is trying to arrest him/her, committing both bodily injury and resistance against the authority). Since the commission of multiple crimes with multiple acts implies, according to the legislator, a more persistent and hostile attitude against the legal order, the aggregation of penalties can exceed the maximum sentence prescribed and reach 10 years in cases of short-term imprisonment and 25 years in cases of long-term imprisonment. After the new CC was put into force, the maximum sentence is eight years in cases of short-term imprisonment and 20 years in cases of long-term imprisonment. As a result, up until 2009, when migrant smuggling was still a misdemeanour, there was an important differentiation of criminal sanctions depending on the concurrence rules applicable, since a maximum sentence of five years could reach a sentence of 10 years if the crimes were committed with multiple acts. This issue remains equally important to this day, since, depending on the concurrence rule applicable, a maximum sentence of 10 years can reach a sentence of 20 years.

There was no question whatsoever about the fact that migrant smuggling of more than one person even if committed by the use of a single means of transportation results in concurrence of crimes and not concurrence of laws since the legislation in question clearly demonstrates that the prescribed sanction refers to 'each person that is being transported' a provision that was first prescribed by statute No 1941/1991 and was repeated in statutes No 1975/1991, 2910/2001 and 3386/2005. Under these circumstances it was argued that there is no way to support the alternative of concurrence of laws instead of concurrence of crimes since the legislation in question demands the imposition of an independent sanction for every person that is being illegally transported.[58]

[57] See for this general tendency regarding criminal provisions for migrants, Chatzinikolaou, above n 2, 3, with reference to article 74 of the previous CC.

[58] Compare M Kaiafa-Gbandi, 'Ο νέος Κώδικας Μετανάστευσης και οι διακεκριμένες μορφές της υποβοήθησης της παράνομης μετανάστευσης από τους «μεταφορείς»' ('The new Immigration Code and the aggravating circumstances of facilitating illegal immigration from "transporters"') in N Zaikos (ed), *Μετανάστευση και Δίκαιο* (*Law and Immigration*) (Thessaloniki, Annikoula, 2017) 87; according to this approach, which proposes a corrective interpretation of the relevant provisions as far as aggravating circumstances are concerned, when the aliens' lives might be at risk, the judge can then ignore the legislative provision that requires the imposition of an individual sentence for every person that is being illegally transported and impose only one sentence on the basis of the unlawful act's nature as a crime of common danger.

Thus, the concern focuses on the concurrence doctrine applicable in cases where the offender transported more than one undocumented immigrant in a single route. After a short period of ambivalence of the Greek Supreme Court Areios Pagos,[59] the grand chamber of the latter by virtue of decision No 9/1995 upheld the view that whenever more than one persons are being transported in a single route, the rules of 'real concurrence' are applicable and consequently the exceedance of the maximum prescribed sanction is possible.[60] Even though there was an important minority that did not support this interpretative version, this opinion has been well-established ever since.[61]

The one-dimensional justification of the Areios Pagos's opinion is indeed impressive. Its only argument was statute No 1941/1991's explanatory report, that depicted the legislator's will, not about the concurrence rules but about the maximum prescribed sentence.[62] It is also typical that the majority's opinion did not intend to take into consideration the minority's point of view that was previously expressed in Decision No 1226/1993 which led to the referral of the case to the grand chamber of the Court, according to which:

> the number of routes that took place is not critical. What is important is the facilitation of the immigrant's entry which is a complex process for each person that requires a different agreement of transportation, part of which is the usage of the means of transportation.[63]

Decision No 9/1995, which was only partly justified with reference to statute No 1941/1991's explanatory report is methodologically incorrect, as it is clear that the legislator's will itself is not enough to extend criminal liability and permit the application of the concurrence rules described in article 94 CC.[64]

When referring to later modifications of the legislative framework that adopted the 'real concurrence' doctrine, the unquestioning acceptance of the solution provided by the grand chamber of the Supreme Court, is highly problematic.[65] Apart from the fact that the argument about the explanatory report is inadequate, its later utilisation meets additional and unbeatable obstacles since in later statutes No 1975/1991, 2910/2001 and 3386/2005 there was no similar reference.

[59] See, e.g., Decisions No 1226/1993, (1994) *Iperaspissi* 797 with comment of A Papadamakis, No 1540/1994, (1995) *Iperaspissi* 485 with comment of M Kaiafa-Gbandi.

[60] (1996) *Iperaspisi* 759= (1996) *Poinika Chronika* 476 with comments of M Kaiafa-Gbandi and D Kioupis, respectively.

[61] See, eg decisions No 585/2006, (2006) *Poinikos Logos* 488, 87/2006, (2006) *Poiniki Dikaiossini* 805, 228/2003, (2003) *Poinikos Logos* 235, 33/2003, (2003) *Poinikos Logos* 65; see also Chatzinikolaou, above n 37, 106 ff.

[62] According to the amended art 19 para 2 of statute No 4310/1929 'the sentence imposed can be no more than 10 years in accordance to article 94 par. 1 CC'.

[63] See also the minority of judges on Decision No 1540/1994, above n 59.

[64] See M Kaiafa-Gbandi, *Εμβάθυνση στην Ποινική Νομολογία* (*Review on criminal jurisprudence*) 2nd edn (Thessaloniki, Sakkoulas, 2009) 234.

[65] See Chatzinikolaou, above n 37, 106 ff.

This is probably the reason why in some later Supreme Court decisions, there is no mention of the explanatory report's argument. By contrast, even though these decisions respect the opinion of the grand chamber of the Supreme Court, they point out that the criminal conduct in question consists of a complex process.[66] This argument is also incorrect since it does not take into consideration the legislative modifications that followed and attempts to make an argument out of statute No 1941/1991, which is no longer in force. However, it is obvious that the plurality of acts, that determines the concurrence rules, is directly linked to the elements of criminal conduct as they are described in the criminal legislation in force.[67] Statutes No 3386/2005 (article 88) and No 4251/2014 (article 30) leave no room for the opinion that when migrant smuggling of more than one person takes places in a single route the 'real concurrence' doctrine must be applied.

Even if we omit other aspects of the same interpretative problem, what we should point out is the fact that jurisprudence not only made no efforts to set some boundaries to this legislative harshness, but reinforced it instead, by referring to the common issue of concurrence, which is critical for the sentence that will be served by the offender.

This weak argumentation of the Supreme Court recalls the similarly weak legislative argumentation concerning the criminal sanctions prescribed. What is implied is that the 'emergency' and pressing nature of the migrant and refugee crisis justifies the deviation or limitation of general principles such as the concurrence rules.

C. Vagueness of Prescribed Pecuniary Fines – Exceptions from the Suspensory Effect of the Appeal

Statute No 4251/2014 was as problematic as the previous legislation in force concerning the prescribed pecuniary fines.

The pecuniary fine that is prescribed in combination with the deprivation of the offender's freedom is no less than 200,000 euros per transported person if the unlawful act puts life at risk and no less than 700,000 euros per transported person if the unlawful act resulted in death, in both cases without providing a maximum of the pecuniary fines. The recent modification of statute No 3772/2009 and, more

[66] See the Supreme Court's Decision No 892/2001, (2002) *Poiniki Dikaiossini* 15 with the comment of A Papadamakis. According to this decision,

> what is critical, when more than one person is being transported, is the facilitation provided to each person individually and not the amount of money paid by each person, since in some cases the amount of money is paid for the whole group of immigrants that are being transported.

[67] See, e.g., I Manoledakis, M Kaiafa-Gbandi and E Simeonidou-Kastanidou, *Ποινικό Δίκαιο – Επιτομή Γενικού Μέρους* (*Criminal Law: general part*) (Thessaloniki, Sakkoulas, 2005) 279.

recently, No 4251/2014, did not actually cause the problem, as this already existed in previous legislative texts.[68]

This problematic approach originates from Directive 2001/51/EU.[69] The latter provided alternatives for the minimum and maximum pecuniary fines for migrant smugglers. More specifically, the Member States could either prescribe an individual pecuniary fine of no less than 5,000 euros per migrant or prescribe a combined pecuniary fine of no less than 500,000 euros irrespective of the number of persons being transported.

The Greek legislator adopted a mixed model by prescribing specific frameworks of pecuniary fines per person for the unlawful acts described in points (a) and (b) of article 88 (statute No 3386/2005), a provision compatible with the Directive and a minimum pecuniary fine for the unlawful acts of points (c) and (d) of the same article, the last being no less than 500,000 euros and after the recent modification no less than 700,000 euros. However, Directive 2001/51/EU did not force Member States to prescribe equivalent pecuniary fines. It just defined the maximum and minimum limits, the minimum amount of which should be respected by Member States. The Greek legislator believed that copying the corresponding European legislative text would be enough. As a result, there is no maximum pecuniary fine for the unlawful acts of points (c) and (d) since their minimum limits exceeded the provisions of article 57 of the former CC. Each judge was and is thus free to impose any pecuniary fine if it is no less than the minimum amount prescribed.

This is a choice that raises concerns with regard to its constitutionality, since, according to a widely supported opinion, the Greek Constitution forces legislators to fully describe both the elements of each crime and the limits of the criminal sanction that could be imposed for each unlawful act.[70] If this is not the case, the *nullum crimen nulla poena sine lege certa* principle will not cover a dimension of critical importance for the citizens' needs.

This is a unique exception of Greek legislation, according to which, if the unlawful act of migrant smuggling results in negligent death, the prescribed sentence is stricter than the one prescribed for the unlawful act of homicide, making it the harshest criminal sanction in the Greek legal order.

A relevant and equally unique exception is described in article 30 paragraph 8 of statute No 4251/2014 concerning the suspensory effect of convictions for migrant smuggling.

[68] The only difference was the minimum number of pecuniary fines (100,000 euros and 500,000 euros respectively).

[69] [2001] OJ L187/45.

[70] See N Chorafas, *Ποινικό Δίκαιο* (*Criminal Law*) (Athens, P Sakkoulas, 1978) 57; G Mangakis in D Spinellis (ed), *Συστηματική Ερμηνεία του Ποινικού Κώδικα* (*Systematical Interpretation of Criminal Code*) (Athens, PN Sakkoulas, 2005) 27 no 41; N Androulakis, *Ποινικό Δίκαιο – Γενικό Μέρος, τ. I* (*Criminal Law: general part, part I*) 2nd edn (Athens, PN Sakkoulas, 2006) 131; A Eser in A Shönke and H Schröder (eds), *Strafgesetzbuch* 27th edn (Munich, CH Beck, 2006) § 1 no 23; Ch Mylonopoulos, *Ποινικό Δίκαιο, τ. I* (*Criminal Law part I*) (Athens, PN Sakkoulas, 2007) 84.

According to Greek legislation, in cases of long-term imprisonment, it is the judges that decide to provide the suspensory effect, a decision based on criteria described in the Greek Code of Criminal Procedure (CCP) such as permanent residence, recidivism risk etc. In the past, there were some limited cases of legislative prohibition of suspensory effect whose aim was to point out that the convicted person must suffer the deprivation of his/her freedom after conviction from the first-instance court. However, these provisions were not effective and caused additional problems in everyday practice, mainly because of the increase of applications for granting of the suspensory effect by the Court of Appeals. This is the reason why these provisions were repealed with statute No 3904/2010.

However, this exception was repeated in the Code of Immigration in 2014, without proper justification. Even though the enforcement of the new CCP in July 2019 possibly raises some doubts about the continuation of this exception, the provision points out the legislator's persisting concern to skip the application of general rules in the discussed crimes.

D. Criminalisation of Unauthorised Entry – Administrative Detention of the Foreigner under Expulsion

i. Unauthorised Entry and Exit from the Country

Unauthorised entry and exit from the country and their attempt were always a misdemeanour. When the new Code of Immigration was first presented, the repeal of this specific provision was proposed without success, since, after national delegation for statute No 3386/2005, it was decided to keep this criminal provision in force.

National courts often had to deal with the unlawful act of unauthorised entry up until the middle of 2000, developing a dynamic interpretative tendency in favour of refugees. National courts construed their refugee status determination decisions as recognising the already existing refugee status instead of establishing it for the first time. As a result, although such a defence was not successful during the 1990s, in the following years in many cases defendants were acquitted because courts had the opinion that irrespective of the administrative procedure, the accused person should be recognised as having the refugee status. In order to justify these decisions, national courts referred to elements such as a state of emergency or personal grounds for acquittal.[71]

Gradually, the importance of this unlawful act was diminished since most public prosecutors abstain from prosecution, in compliance with the provisions of article 83 paragraph 2 of statute No 3386/2005. In practice, the imposed sanctions

[71] For further documentation see Chatzinikolaou, above n 37, 95.

were all suspended, and foreigners were taken to Immigration Service so that administrative expulsion could be imposed.

In view of this development, today only aggravated crimes are being prosecuted, especially when the foreigner irregularly enters the country even though he or she is registered on the list of unwanted foreigners or in 'special' cases when the government wishes to continue the criminal procedure on the grounds of international relations. Such recent cases include the conviction of Turkish military personnel claimed asylum in Greece, after the failed 2016 Turkish coup d'état attempt on 15 July 2016. Since the Turkish government demanded their extradition, they were first convicted for the unlawful act of unauthorised entry. Finally, the Supreme Court of Greece refused to extradite the eight Turkish soldiers and granted asylum to the Turkish military personnel, as the Greek government's application to cancel this decision was overruled.[72]

The imposition of the extremely strict sentence of imprisonment of four years to the offenders of unauthorised entry, who managed to enter the country from the Greek-Turkish borders along the river Evros during the recent crisis, when Turkey opened its borders in the end of February 2020, has similar characteristics. Journalists revealed that local courts did not provide the offenders with suspension of their sentence or with suspensory effect.[73] As a result, the offenders were imprisoned. This is an extremely rare in practice decision regarding misdemeanours whose aim obviously was to 'send a message' to those still waiting at Greek borders.

Overall, except from such rather symbolic cases as the latter, in everyday practice the processing of cases for irregular entry, administrative detention included, is assigned to police officers, whose decisions can only be reviewed by administrative justice after the imposition of detention.

This turn of events led to the repeal of judicial expulsion, that was mentioned above. However, this development did not manage to reinforce the rule of law, as it traps refugees and migrants in a grey administrative zone where judicial protection is not always an option. This 'administrative' detention is of doubtful legality, as outlined below.

A recent case related to NGO activity was the administrative expulsion of a Danish member of an NGO. According to the press, although he was previously acquitted of the crime of attempting to facilitate illegal entry of migrants, he was arrested as unwanted and deported for 'secret reasons' for which he had not been informed.[74]

[72] See the full bench of Council of State's Decision No 1694/2018, (2018) *European Review on European Law* 579 with comment of E Fotiadou.

[73] See e.g., www.dikastiko.gr/%CF%80%CF%81%CF%89%CF%84%CE%BF-%CE%B8%CE%B5%CE%BC%CE%B1/fylakisi-4-eton-choris-anastoli-kai-prostimo-10-000-eyro-se-paranomoys-metanastes-toy-evroy/.

[74] See D Agelides and G Tessi, 'Ανεπιθύμητος στην Ελλάδα χωρίς να γνωρίζει το λόγο' ('Unwanted in Greece without knowing the reason') *Efimerida ton Syntakton* (Athens, 5 April 2020).

ii. *Administrative Detention of Foreigners under Expulsion*

Under the provisions of the Greek Constitution, the individual right of personal safety (*habeas corpus*) not only refers to abuses in the criminal justice system but also covers every administrative provision or measure that leads to deprivation of liberty. For this reason, the systematic approach of articles 5 paragraphs 3 and 6 of Greek Constitution leads to a wide acceptance, on a theoretical level, of the opinion that the guarantees of article 6, especially the provision that no one should suffer from deprivation of freedom without a judicial decision, with the exception of flagrante delicta, refer to every deprivation of personal freedom, irrespective of its imposition within a judicial or otherwise procedure.[75] Given this interpretative approach, it was argued that civil imprisonment in cases of public debtors (the detention of public debtors without a judicial order was used to force people to pay their debt)[76] was unconstitutional. Today, this detention measure falls within the jurisdiction of judicial bodies.[77]

This constitutional provision refers to foreigners too.[78] This implies that all relevant provisions about the detention of foreigners under expulsion both within the framework of article 74 CC, a provision already repealed, and the detention used as a kind of instrument to the implementation of administrative expulsion, were unconstitutional.[79]

The unconstitutionality with reference to both provisions had already been highlighted during the adoption of corresponding bills.[80] This tacit denial by both judges[81] and lawmakers to acknowledge the dimensions of this problem, raises

[75] See e.g., A Manessis, *Ατομικές Ελευθερίες* (*Individual Freedoms*) (Thessaloniki, Sakkoulas, 1982) 178; P Dagtoglou, *Ατομικά Δικαιώματα, τ. Α΄* (*Individual Rights, part A*) 2nd edn (Athens, AN Sakkoulas, 2005) 279 no 373, 377, 406, with further documentation.

[76] Article 9 of legislative order No 356/1974.

[77] Statute No 1867/1989. See also Dagtoglou, above n 75, 290. The constitutionality of this provision is another issue, that cannot be questioned in this article; *cf* Court of first instance of Pirgos' Decision No 66/2005, (2005) *Praxis-Logos Poinikou Dikaiou* 352.

[78] See K Chrisogonos, *Ατομικά και Κοινωνικά Δικαιώματα* (*Personal and Social Rights*) (Athens, AN Sakkoulas, 2002) 203.

[79] See Chatzinikolaou, above n 2, 391 ff; but see Symeonides, above n 3, 357 ff, A Konstadinou, 'Παρατηρήσεις για την κράτηση υπηκόων τρίτων χωρών στην Ελλάδα' ('Remarks on detention of third-country nationals in Greece') (2014) *Journal of Migration Law* 151 ff.

[80] See (for article 74 para 4 CC) N Paraskevopoulos in L Margaritis and N Paraskevopoulos, *Ποινολογία* (*Penology*) (Thessaloniki, Sakkoulas, 2001) 121–22; Chatzinikolaou, above n 2. For the issue of detention of immigrants under administrative expulsion see Dagtoglou, above n 75, 290; I Kurtovik, 'Μετανάστες: ανάμεσα στο δίκαιο και τη νομιμότητα' ('Immigrants: between law and legality') in Marvaki, Parsanoglou and Pavlou (eds), above n 10, 163, 175.

[81] According to a circular by the Supreme Court's Public Prosecutor 913/1984, (1985) *Poinika Chronika* 279, the administrative detention of the foreigner under administrative expulsion is a prerequisite in order to achieve the implementation of this administrative measure. Moreover, Athens' Administrative Court of first Instance (Decision No 1676/2003, Case-Law of Athens' Administrative Court of first instance 2001-2003, 2004, 175) argued that this administrative measure was constitutional. According to this decision

> this measure is taken in order to make sure that the expulsion measure will be imposed. In any case, there is a special judicial procedure in order to evaluate the legality of the imposed measure. If the court rules in favor of the foreigner, then administrative detention will no longer be imposed.

reasonable questions since no substantial counterargument was ever provided.[82] It is typical that although in the preamble of Common Ministerial Decision No 137954/2000 about the enforcement of expulsion, both articles 5 paragraphs 3 and 4 of the Greek Constitution and article 5 paragraph 1 of ECHR are mentioned, there is no mention of article 6 of Greece's project charter.

There is a distinguishable relationship between the tacit circumvention of the Constitution and the constitutional theory's hesitation to face this problem:[83] even though the protection of individual freedom is not an issue of different theoretical domains, one should at least expect that this problem of great importance that affects vulnerable portions of population,[84] would concern legal theory as much as the problem of civil imprisonment of public debtors.

A more attentive look on both the relevant legislative initiatives and their interpretation – partly from judges and prosecutors[85] – proves that the provision of article 5 paragraph 1 (f) of ECHR was used for diminishing the guarantees provided by the Greek Constitution, that, contrarily to the ECHR, does not recognise foreigners' detention without a judicial order.[86] In this way, we can understand why the absence of article 6 of the Greek Constitution was combined in the Common Ministerial Decision No 137954/2000 with this provision of the ECHR. The Greek Constitution offers increased protection in this field[87] and

[82] See generally D Wilsher, *Immigration Detention* (Cambridge, Cambridge University Press, 2012) xiii and throughout.

[83] Relevant attempts were either sparing (e.g., Dagtoglou, above n 75, 375) or not that clear (e.g., Chrisogonos, above n 78, 202) while the research department of Greek Parliament at the report on statute No 1975/1991 (www.hellenicparliament.gr 106), talked about 'doubtful' constitutionality. See also Th Antoniou, 'Issues and Problems in the Greek Law of Aliens' in H Schermers, C Flinterman, A Kellermann, J van Haersollte and GW v de Meent (eds), *Free Movement of Persons in Europe* (Dordrecht, Martinus Nijhoff, 1993) 125, 139 referring to statute No 1975/1991; *cf* Symeonides, above n 3, 357 ff.

[84] See generally J Bustamante, 'Immigrants' Vulnerability as Subjects of Human Rights' (2002) *International Migration Review* 333.

[85] See A Zygouras, 'Η κράτησις εις την φυλακήν του τελούντος υπό απέλασιν' ('The detention in prison of the migrant under expulsion') (2000) *Poiniki Dikaiossini* 754 ff, G Peponis, 'Η κράτηση στην φυλακή των υπό δικαστική απέλασιν τελούντων αλλοδαπών' ('The detention of migrants under expulsion') (2001) *Poinika Chronika* 94.

[86] Peponis, ibid, argues:

> Indeed, no one can doubt the legality of the detention upon a foreigner under expulsion, since according to article 5 para 1 (f) of European Convention on Human Rights, 'Everyone has the right to liberty and security of person. No one shall be deprived of his liberty save in the following cases and in accordance with a procedure prescribed by law … the lawful arrest or detention of a person to prevent his effecting an unauthorised entry into the country or of a person against whom action is being taken with a view to deportation or extradition'.

See also E Gouli, 'Το νομικό καθεστώς των αλλοδαπών στην Ελλάδα' ('Aliens' legal status in Greece') in 6th Conference of Administrative Judges (Athens, Sakkoulas, 2004) 695, 705, where, wondering whether foreigner's under administrative expulsion detention runs counter to article 6 para 1 of Greek Constitution, the author supports that this administrative measure's legal ground is article 5 para 1 (f) of European Convention on Human Rights; compare D Sideris, 'Διοικητική και δικαστική απέλαση αλλοδαπών' ('Administrative and judicial expulsion of foreigners and political refugees') (1997) *Poinika Chronika* 1233.

[87] See Dagtoglou, above n 75, 281.

further reference to the equally important European Convention is unnecessary and unavailing. The ECHR's provisions can provide important help on the issue of the imposition of expulsion, but they do not provide wider protection than the one already provided by the Greek Constitution as far as detention is concerned. In any case, according to an explicit provision of ECHR,

> Nothing in this Convention shall be construed as limiting or derogating from any of the human rights and fundamental freedoms which may be ensured under the laws of any High Contracting Party or under any other agreement to which it is a party.[88]

In this field, it is easy to realise that the emergency of migration and refugee flows served as an implicit basis for the justification of an exception from such an important individual right, namely the right of *habeas corpus*, that lacks itself adequate foundation. This tendency equally affected the legislator, case-law and legal theory. As already noted, this same tendency is reinforced in the recent bill for asylum, as there is a broad capability for imposing detention to asylum seekers.

IV. Human Rights under Pressure of Criminal Suppression

A. The Imposition of Draconian Penalties to Vulnerable Offenders

An overview of the case-law published over the last two decades proves that even though hundreds of defendants are convicted for migrant smuggling every year, these cases rarely have to do with 'professional slave traders', whose actions were used as a justification for the harsh criminal sanctions. In this respect, it is typical that the criminal justice system rarely succeeds in accessing the significant profits of criminal networks, since most of the time, seizure and confiscation of money is limited to the amount of money that is held by the carrier at the scene of crime. One can reasonably assume that the heads of these criminal networks are usually in neighbouring countries and not in Greece.[89]

An even more important issue is the fact that because of these provisions, there is an open possibility for the imposition of the proscribed harsh criminal sanctions upon immigrants who are being transported[90] or other vulnerable groups, a quite

[88] Art 53.

[89] See the report of Commission SWD (2017) 117 final, REFIT Evaluation of EU legal framework against facilitation of unauthorised entry, transit and residence: the Facilitators Package, 9 and 27. According to a recent report of the daily newspaper *Kathimireni* (24 November 2019) vulnerable 'smugglers' (juveniles, people with severe health problems or drug addicted) are often paid from 400 to 600 euros.

[90] See Chatzinikolaou, above n 37, 95.

common phenomenon in Greek practice. We have already referred to many cases of minor –almost always – aliens who are asked to drive at high speed in order to smuggle foreigners from the borders along the river Evros. This practice has intensified over the last two years mainly because of the 'geographical restrictions' of the EU-Turkey Statement, as those who arrive at the country via the Aegean sea remain on the Greek islands without having real chances of moving to central Europe, and also because of the extremely harsh criminal sanctions prescribed which cannot be imposed to minors.

The victimisation of vulnerable groups with reference to the legislation for the suppression of migrant smuggling is not a recent phenomenon. M Economou's documentary 'The longest run' that was presented at the 18th International Documentary Festival of Thessaloniki describes in a truly credible way the judicial adventure of two minor refugees, who were held in detention for months, after being accused of migrant smuggling, and who were finally mildly punished by Thrace's Court of Appeals.[91]

B. The Tendency of Criminalising the Humanitarian Aid

The prosecution against members of a NGO in Lesvos for the unlawful act of migrant smuggling is another typical example of the fact that strict criminal suppression, despite the fact that it is justified by the need of punishing 'slave traders', covers behaviours with fundamentally different characteristics.[92] The alleged criminal offence had to do with the defendants' communication with people who were on a boat, that aimed at facilitating their arrival to Lesvos.[93] The – doubtful – core of the defendants' criminal responsibility lies in the fact that they did not inform port authorities. The aggravating circumstance of profit-seeking was justified on the grounds of other legal sources of the non-profit organisation's funding, since no one could prove that the defendants asked for a fee in return for providing their help. The case is still pending while it should also be noted that the so-called 'humanitarian clause' set out in article 1 (2) of the Directive 2002/90/EC is not yet incorporated into Greek legislation. Partly relevant to this matter is the modification of article 30 paragraph 6 of statute No 4251/2014 with the putting into force of article 14 paragraph 2 of statute No 4332/2015, a modification that was decided in view of the crisis of 2015 and the alleged 'unclear' field of action of both NGOs and volunteers. According to this provision,

> [the] criminal sanctions are not imposed in cases of rescue of people at sea, transportation of people in need of international protection under international law and

[91] See her relevant article, 'Inside Greece's juvenile prisons', aljazeera.com/blogs/europe/2016/09/greece-juvenile-prisons-160921093814339.html. An official trailer of the documentary is available at www.europeanfilmawards.eu/en_EN/film/the-longest-run.4330.

[92] See also V Mitsilegas, *The Criminalisation of Migration in Europe* (London, Springer, 2015) 53.

[93] See also Carrera, Mitsilegas, Allsop and Vosyliute, above n 25, 113.

> transportation or facilitation of transportation within the country for the purposes of articles 83 of Statute 3386/2005 or article 13 of Statute No 3907/2011 as long as police and coast guard authorities are informed.

It was thus assumed that a necessary precondition for the activation of this clause was the non-profit organisations' compliance with the planning of coast guard authorities.[94] However, this provision does not sufficiently cover every kind of humanitarian aid nor does it correct the broadness of the crimes in question.

Similar situations of use of communications between lawyers and refugees by law enforcement authorities as a threat that might result in prosecution take place in Evros, in cases where NGO lawyers who arrive at the borders to facilitate the asylum application procedures already know the identity of the asylum seekers and their arrival time or are at least aware that the foreigner is kept at the police station.[95]

NGOs' action on this field has recently become the subject of harsh public criticism.[96] Some people are of the opinion that stricter monitoring is necessary. The previous failed attempt of listing NGOs has led to the recent re-introduction of the registration number system in the re-established Ministry of Migration and Asylum, in accordance with statute No 4662/2020. Even though the Greek criminal system does not recognise the criminal liability of legal persons, this wide tendency of putting NGOs' under control and limitation seems to have triggered some investigations about criminal offences, including money laundering, in compliance to respective recommendations of the Financial Action Task Force (FATF).[97] We have already referred above to the recent administrative expulsion of a Danish member of NGO, although he was previously acquitted from the crime of attempt of facilitating unauthorised entry of migrants.[98]

Although no similar convictions have yet been published, and this type of investigation cannot be a priori unjustified in any case,[99] this ever-increasing tendency of putting NGOs under control decreases the chances of humanitarian aid. This situation combined with the frequent victimisation and conviction of

[94] See the recent decision of the Supreme Court No 1464/2019, (2019) *Poinika Chronika* 681, towards the same restrictive direction.

[95] Interview with members of non-profit organisations in Thessaloniki (Thessaloniki, Greece, 3 September 2019).

[96] According to a Panhellenic survey of company Dianeosis (January 2020) 44.9 per cent of people who participated consider NGOs' contribution to humanitarian issues as negative or probably negative. Their opinion was formed on the basis of what is known about their role at Greece's hotspots.

[97] See a relevant news report by Th Koukakis available at www.insider.gr/eidiseis/oikonomia/108986/fintech-mko-kai-metanastes-sto-mikroskopio.

[98] See Agelides and Tessi, above n 74.

[99] A recent press release of prosecuting authorities (www.enikos.gr/society/391142/i-vitrina-ton-diakiniton-itan-mia-mko) referred to NGOs' involvement to an organised network of transporters. The alleged exhibits of the investigation, that took place with Europol's participation, included facilities used for the manufacture of forged documents.

immigrants as migrant smugglers, proves that despite the fact that the criminal framework for the facilitation of irregular immigration is justified on the grounds of punishment of those who exploit immigrants, it reduces directly and indirectly the latter's protection, making them and people who are trying to help them targets of criminal suppression.

V. Conclusions

The immigration and refugee phenomenon in Greece over the last 30 years is related to significant challenges that are caused by the general geopolitical instability of the Southeastern Mediterranean. The location of Greece, at the crossroads of the Mediterranean Sea, that was a major cultural advantage over time, is now thought to be a disadvantage. Greece had to handle severe pressure, that resulted in taking on a disproportionate burden during the last phase of the refugee crisis while lacking administrative experience and adequate infrastructure. These circumstances contributed to the gradual creation of a strict criminal suppression system against irregular migration, that is characterised by unique derogations from fundamental principles of the rule of law in an impressive number of fields of substantive and procedural criminal law and individual rights in general. These exceptions and especially the provision of extremely harsh penalties, without adequate justification, are attempted to be justified by the need to punish organised transportation networks. However, strict penalties are imposed to punish behaviours that do not necessarily relate to these networks. This same tendency of providing derogations from general principles of criminal suppression and challenging fundamental human rights, that seems to be becoming permanent, was expressed at all levels of the national legal system in the past, in the creation of rules, their interpretation and the imposition of the legal framework in the context of everyday practice. Some aspects of this development were not discouraged by relevant European provisions and actions including the Facilitators Package and the recent EU-Turkey Statement and the corresponding application of 'geographical restrictions'. The harshness of criminal suppression and the general strict control migration phenomenon does not seem to have contributed either to the effective criminal control of transportation networks or to the containment of migration and refugee flows. The same draconian legal framework often affects vulnerable population groups, including the people who are being transported and who are being allegedly protected from exploitation, while facilitating criminal prosecution of NGOs members and limitation of humanitarian acts of help.

9

Immigration Detention between Law and Practice in Italy

Managing the Border Through Arbitrary Detention

FRANCESCA CANCELLARO

I. Introduction

This chapter is about the blurred line between law and practice at the Italian border, where – despite the existence of a specific national and European legislation on initial immigration detention – deprivation of liberty has been left to the discretion of border authorities. Even after the *Khlaifia and Others v Italy* judgment,[1] where the Grand Chamber of the ECtHR sanctioned arbitrary detention practices both in reception centres and on-board ships, the situation in hotspots remains seriously critical and the procedure for the execution of the judgment before the Committee of Ministers of the Council of Europe is still ongoing. In addition, de facto deprivation of liberty of undocumented migrants at the border has become all too common. Such deprivation of liberty consists of forced detention taking place on ships, both those owned by military authorities and privately owned by NGOs, after undocumented migrants have been rescued at sea. This is known as the 'closed-ports' policy. The policy in question is essentially based on not granting a place of safety and prolongedly denying disembarkation, which de facto results in depriving the migrants on board of their personal liberty. All of this is not based on any legal provision and not subject to judicial review. Therefore, two instances of potentially arbitrary detention at the Italian border have occurred in recent practice (which the same migrant may be subjected to in rapid succession): the deprivation of personal liberty on the mainland within the immigration centres used as hotspots and that taking place on rescue ships, even before reaching the mainland.

[1] *Khlaifia and Others v Italy* [GC], Application No 16483/12 (15 December 2016).

To address the controversial situation at one of Europe's key borders, this chapter will deal, first of all, with the *Khlaifia* judgment and how its execution procedure has changed both the Italian legal framework on immigration detention and the practices at the border. To this end, both the new rules introduced to regulate hotspot centres and their application are described below. The chapter will then focus on the 'closed-ports' policy, to show that the practice of denying disembarkation to shipwrecked persons rescued at sea results in an illegal deprivation of liberty of migrants and asylum seekers entering the country, in turn resulting in serious violations of fundamental rights.

II. The *Khlaifia* Case

In December 2016, the Grand Chamber of the European Court of Human Rights delivered a seminal judgment on immigration detention.[2] The case concerned the pre-admittance detention and the expulsion of three migrants who arrived in Italy by sea in September 2011, in the aftermath of the 'Arab Spring' in Tunisia. The migrants were intercepted by the Italian coastguard and transferred to the 'Early Reception and aid centre' located on the island of Lampedusa. Despite the facility had a humanitarian vocation according to the relevant law (Law no 563 of 1995, known as the 'Puglia Law'), applicants were de facto deprived of their personal liberty for some days together with hundreds of other foreigners. When the centre was partially destroyed by a fire, migrants were transferred aboard two ships moored in the Palermo harbour, which were also under the custody of border authorities. Finally, they were returned to Tunisia.

The Grand Chamber found that such de facto deprivation of liberty is not compatible with the aim of Article 5 of the Convention, even in the context of a migration crisis. As a matter of fact, the practice of border authorities transformed the Reception Centre of Lampedusa – despite its legal nature – in a detention centre for thousands of migrants and asylum seekers disembarked in Italy. In particular, the Court found: first, a violation of Article 5 § 1, as the applicants had been deprived of their liberty in the absence of any legal basis; second, a violation of Article 5 § 2, as the applicants had not been informed of the reasons

[2] See MR Mauro, 'A Step Back in the Protection of Migrants' Rights the Grand Chamber's Judgment in "Khlaifia v. Italy"' (2016) 26 *The Italian Yearbook of International Law* 289; S Zirulia and S Peers, 'A Template for Protecting Human Rights during the "Refugee Crisis"? Immigration Detention and the Expulsion of Migrants in a recent ECHR Grand Chambers Ruling' (2017) *EU Law Analysis*, 5th January; F Cancellaro, 'Migranti, Italia condannata dalla CEDU per trattenimenti illegittimi' (2017) *Questione Giustizia*, 11 January; P Bonetti, 'Khlaifia contro Italia, l'illegittimità di norme e prassi italiane sui respingimenti e trattenimenti degli stranieri' (2017) 1 *Quaderni Costituzionali* 176; A Giliberto, 'La pronuncia della Grande Camera della Corte Edu sui trattenimenti (e i conseguenti respingimenti) di Lampedusa del 2011' (2016) *Diritto penale contemporaneo*, 23 December.

for deprivation of their liberty; third, a violation of Article 5 § 4 as there was no remedy in the Italian legal system to challenge the lawfulness of such a de facto detention. Moreover, the Court also found a violation of Article 13, taken together with Article 3 of the Convention, as there was no effective remedy to complain as to the conditions of detention.

III. The Execution of the *Khlaifia* Judgment

Following the judgment, the procedure for supervising its execution before the Committee of Ministers of the Council of Europe pursuant to Article 46 of the Convention was opened. The *Khlaifia* case was assigned an enhanced supervision procedure, providing for a series of annual reviews of the measures taken by the national authorities. The execution of the *Khlaifia* judgment seems extremely relevant and topical today because it concerns central issues in migration management and border control, which are far from being resolved.

During the procedure before the Committee of Ministers, Italy submitted six communications between September 2017 and June 2019,[3] which essentially concerned Decree-Law No 13 of 2017 and Law No 132 of 2018.

The former (also known as the 'Minniti-Orlando Decree'), converted into Law No 46 of 2017, was the first legislative response to the *Khlaifia* conviction. For the first time the relevant Italian national legislation established the hotspots, that are first-line reception facilities for rescue and first aid, where foreigners undergo pre-identification procedures and are provided with information and primary care.[4]

Law No 46 of 2017 included Article 10 *ter* in the Italian Consolidated Law on Immigration,[5] which states that

> undocumented migrants located when illegally crossing the internal or external border or arriving on national territory as a result of rescue operations at sea shall be conducted for rescue and first aid necessities to ad hoc crisis points [i.e., hotspots] where fingerprinting and identification operations shall also be carried out … and shall be provided

[3] Communications from the Italian authorities are: DD(2019)671 of 4 June 2019, DD(2019)130 of 5 February 2019, DD(2018)918 of 18 September 2018, DD(2018)718 of 11 July 2018, DD(2018)34 of 11 January 2018, DD(2017)980 of 6 September 2017 (all available at hudoc.exec.coe.int).

[4] The European Agenda on Migration (COM(2015) 240 final), presented on 13 May 2015 by the European Commission, with a view to implementing a comprehensive approach to improve the management of migration in all its aspects, proposed, firstly, the adoption of a new system based on crisis points (hotspots). Under the hotspot approach, arrivals are channelled to a number of selected disembarkation ports where Member States' operators, assisted by staff from European agencies (EASO, Frontex and Europol), may quickly carry out the identification, registration and fingerprinting of arriving migrants and, therefore, just as promptly define their legal status.

[5] Legislative Decree No 286 of 1998, currently the main Italian legal reference in the field of immigration, was originally introduced in 1998; the version currently in force is the result of numerous significant legislative changes that have taken place over the years.

> information on the international protection procedure, the relocation programme in other Member States of the European Union and the possibility of assisted voluntary return.[6]

Furthermore, the same article specifies that the undocumented migrant's reiterated refusal to undergo fingerprinting constitutes 'risk of absconding' for the purposes of detention in the centres referred to in Article 14 of the Italian Consolidated Law on Immigration[7] (CPRs, Detention Centres prior to Repatriation, formerly known as CIEs, Identification and Expulsion Centres, in which those who are to be expelled are detained).[8]

As it appears from their wording, these provisions do not provide a legal basis for deprivation of liberty within hotspots.[9] Nonetheless, the practice of de facto deprivation of liberty has continued within these initial centres.

The report on the visit to Italy carried out by the European Committee for the Prevention of Torture and Inhuman or Degrading Treatment or Punishment (CPT) in 2017 emphasised the lack of legal basis for deprivation of liberty in these centres:

> Noting that several categories of foreign nationals may be prevented from leaving the hotspots, the CPT raises the issue of the legal basis for deprivation of liberty in these centres and related problems regarding the existence and operation of legal safeguards. It formulates several recommendations in this respect, including as regards judicial control over deprivation of liberty, the provision of information about rights and procedures and effective access to a lawyer as well as practical measures to reduce the risk of refoulement.[10]

[6] Unofficial translation provided by the Author. The Italian text reads as follows: 'Lo straniero rintracciato in occasione dell'attraversamento irregolare della frontiera interna o esterna ovvero giunto nel territorio nazionale a seguito di operazioni di salvataggio in mare è condotto per le esigenze di soccorso e di prima assistenza presso appositi punti di crisi allestiti nell'ambito delle strutture di cui al decreto-legge 30 ottobre 1995, n. 451, convertito, con modificazioni, dalla legge 29 dicembre 1995, n. 563, e delle strutture di cui all'articolo 9 del decreto legislativo 18 agosto 2015, n. 142. Presso i medesimi punti di crisi sono altresì effettuate le operazioni di rilevamento fotodattiloscopico e segnaletico, anche ai fini di cui agli articoli 9 e 14 del regolamento UE n. 603/2013 del Parlamento europeo e del Consiglio del 26 giugno 2013 ed è assicurata l'informazione sulla procedura di protezione internazionale, sul programma di ricollocazione in altri Stati membri dell'Unione europea e sulla possibilità di ricorso al rimpatrio volontario assistito'.

[7] The Italian text reads as follows: 'Il rifiuto reiterato dello straniero di sottoporsi ai rilievi di cui ai commi 1 e 2 configura rischio di fuga ai fini del trattenimento nei centri di cui all'articolo 14'.

[8] Law 46 of 2017 merely changed the name of these centres, but not the rules under article 14 of the Italian Consolidated Law on Immigration regulating the administrative detention of the undocumented migrant to be repatriated.

[9] See M Benvenuti, 'Gli hotspot come chimera. Una prima fenomenologia dei punti di crisi alla luce del diritto costituzionale' (2018) 2 *Diritto Immigrazione Cittadinanza* 1–37; C Leone, 'La disciplina degli hotspot nel nuovo art. 10 ter TUI: un'occasione mancata' (2017) 2 *Diritto Immigrazione Cittadinanza* 1–24; L Masera, 'I centri di detenzione amministrativa cambiano nome ed aumentano di numero, e gli hotspot rimangono privi di base legale: le sconfortanti novità del decreto Minniti' (2017) *Diritto penale contemporaneo*, 10 March.

[10] European Committee for the Prevention of Torture and Inhuman or Degrading Treatment or Punishment (CPT), *Report to the Italian Government on the visit to Italy carried out by the from 7 to 13 June 2017* (Strasbourg, 10 April 2018) 8–20.

Moreover, the Annual report of the National Ombudsman for persons deprived of personal liberty drew attention to the fact that – in the absence of a specific legal framework – migrants and asylum seekers suffer prolonged deprivation of liberty, which is not subject to judicial review. This situation was described as 'a void of legal protection'.[11] In its examination of March 2018, the Committee of Ministers found that:

> The information provided by the Italian authorities does not address the main issues raised by this judgment, namely the absence in Italian law of a clear and accessible legal basis for the detention of migrants in initial reception centres, and of judicial review of the decisions taken in this context.

Moreover, the Committee took into account the hotspots by stating that: 'It seems, therefore, that the "hotspots" – conceived as transit centres for very short stays – can in practice become places of detention'.

One year later, Italy passed Decree-Law no 113 of 4 October 2018 (known as the 'Security Decree' or the 'Salvini Decree'), converted, with amendments, into Law No 132 of 1 December 2018. With this regulatory intervention, the use of detention for reasons of immigration law enforcement has increased enormously, both in asylum and in removal proceedings.[12]

First, the maximum time a third country national may be detained within CPRs has changed from 90 days to 180 days (Article 14 of the Italian Consolidated Law on Immigration). Second, asylum seekers may be detained within hotspots to ascertain their identity and citizenship for a maximum of 30 days (Article 6, paragraph 3-bis, of Legislative Decree No 142 of 2015), and, for the same reason, they may be detained within the CPRs for a maximum of 180 days. Third, if there is no availability in the CPRs during the expulsion procedure, irregular migrants may be deprived of their liberty 'in other available facilities' (before the validation hearing) and within 'border offices' for 48 hours after the validation hearing (Article 13, paragraph 5-bis of the Italian Consolidated Law on Immigration).

With reference to this regulatory intervention, in its March 2019 review, the Committee of Ministers acknowledged that a legal basis exists for up to 30 days' detention at hotspots of those who have applied for international protection. However, the Committee found that, in the opinion of the National Ombudsman

[11] *Garante Nazionale dei diritti delle persone detenute o private della libertà personale, Relazione al Parlamento* (Italian Ombudsman for the Protection of the Rights of Persons Detained or Deprived of Personal Liberty, Report to the Parliament) (Rome, 2017) 85–125.

[12] See F Curi (ed), *Il decreto Salvini – Immigrazione e sicurezza. Commento al d.l. 4 ottobre 2018, n. 113 conv. con mod. in legge 1° dicembre 2018, n. 132* (Pisa, Pacini Editore, 2018); M Daniele, 'La detenzione come deterrente dell'immigrazione nel decreto sicurezza' (2018) 11 *Diritto penale contemporaneo*, 95; S Manacorda, 'Il contrasto penalistico della tratta e del traffico dei migranti nella stagione della chiusura delle frontiere' (2018) *Diritto penale e processo* 1389; L Masera, 'La crimmigration nel Decreto Salvini' (2019) *La Legislazione penale*, 24 July.

for persons deprived of personal liberty, issued with a view to the approval of Law No 132/2018, concern was expressed both with regard to the lack of a clear definition of the reasons justifying such detention of asylum seekers and to the margin of discretion still left to the authorities.

Indeed, the grounds for detention are not attributable to the conduct of the asylum seeker (such as refusal to be identified), but to a condition – the lack of a valid identification document – which is common to most people arriving in Italy by sea. Detention is thus a potentially general measure that sanctions the very status of the applicant.

In this regard, the wording used by the legislature, according to which detention may be ordered 'for the purpose of determining or verifying identity or nationality', is the same as that used by Directive 2013/33/EU (which, under Article 8 § 3, provides that 'an applicant may be detained only: a) in order to determine or verify his or her identity or nationality'. The Court of Justice of the EU, called upon to assess the compatibility of this provision with Article 6 of the EU Charter of Fundamental Rights and with Article 5 ECHR on personal liberty, ruled that the broad wording used by the Directive is not contrary to the principles of legality, proportionality and necessity of measures affecting personal liberty. The Court came to this conclusion through the interpretation of Article 8 § 3 in the light of Article 8 § 2 of the Directive, the latter providing that the authorities shall carry out 'an individual assessment of each case', and that detention is prescribed only where 'less coercive alternative measures cannot be applied effectively'.[13]

The ruling of the Luxembourg judges provides important criteria for interpreting the new Italian rules on detention of asylum seekers.

A wording as broad as the one introduced by the Italian legislature will not result in indiscriminately detaining asylum seekers, in violation of Directive 2013/33/EU, only where the national courts called upon to validate the orders of the police authority on the detention of the applicants will rigorously ascertain the real necessity for detention on a case-by-case basis, as well as the inadequacy of less coercive measures.

As it has not yet been possible to assess the practical impact of the new legislative framework, the Committee of Ministers asked Italy for further clarifications on the reasons currently justifying the detention of asylum seekers in hotspots and on its possible extension, as well as on the required information granted to migrants in these centres and on the existence of swift and effective judicial review on deprivation of liberty. The Committee also asked for clarification on whether those migrants who have not applied for international protection can also be detained at hotspots and, if so, under what conditions. Finally, the Committee of Ministers once again referred to the intervention of the National

[13] Case C-18/16 *K. v Staatssecretaris van Veiligheid en Justitie* [2017] ECLI:EU:C:2017:680.

Ombudsman before the Italian Parliament, which maintained that the Italian legal system lacks an effective remedy with respect to the detention conditions in hotspots (Article 13, read in relation to Article 3 ECHR) and asked Italy to account for this shortcoming.[14]

The communication that Italy sent in June 2019 (DH-DD(2019)671) in response to these requests is currently under scrutiny by the Committee of Ministers.

IV. A Test for the Law: The Authorities' Practice within Hotspot Centres

In addition to assessing the current legislative framework, the Committee of Ministers asked Italy for clarifications regarding the practical effects of the reforms. The subject matter of the *Khlaifia* conviction was precisely the illegal practices of detention at the border, which had remained completely impervious to the application of the laws then in force.

Even today, migrants disembarking on Italian coasts, generally as a result of sea rescue activities, are subsequently taken to hotspots where they spend several days or weeks before preliminary identification procedures are completed and their legal status as asylum seekers or economic migrants is determined. Indeed, based on disclosures from the institutional sources of the Italian Parliament[15] and from the reports of the Organisations involved in monitoring the Italian hotspots,[16] the practices of deprivation of personal liberty in these centres showed a worrisome degree of arbitrariness, even after the *Khlaifia* conviction.

[14] *Garante Nazionale dei diritti delle persone detenute o private della libertà personale, Relazione al Parlamento* (Italian Ombudsman for the Protection of the Rights of Persons Detained or Deprived of Personal Liberty, Report to the Parliament) (Rome, 2019) 214.

[15] See Commissione straordinaria per la tutela e la promozione dei diritti umani del Senato della Repubblica, 'Rapporto sui centri di permanenza per il rimpatrio in Italia' (Extraordinary Commission for the Protection and Promotion of Human Rights of the Senate of the Republic, Report on repatriation centres in Italy), Chapter III 'Hotspots in Italy' (December 2017) 31–54. See also Commissione di inchiesta sul sistema di accoglienza, 'Relazione sul sistema di identificazione e di prima accoglienza nell'ambito dei centri hotspot' (Commission of Inquiry into the Reception System, Report on the system of identification and initial reception in hotspot centres) (Doc XXII-bis, no 8, October 2016) 29–56.

[16] See the two reports of ASGI, ActionAid, CILD and IndieWatch: 'Considerazioni a cura del progetto In limine relative all'attuale funzionamento del centro hotspot di Lampedusa alla luce delle violazioni riscontrate dalla Corte nella sentenza Khlaifia e altri c. Italia' (Considerations by the In Limine project related to the current operation of the Lampedusa hotspot centre in light of the violations found by the Court in Khlaifia and others v. Italy) (June 2018) and 'Scenari di frontiera: il caso Lampedusa, L'approccio hotspot e le sue possibili evoluzioni alla luce del Decreto legge n. 113/2018' (Borderline scenarios: the Lampedusa case, the hotspot approach and its possible evolutions in light of Decree Law no. 113/2018) (October 2018). See also, A Massimi and F Ferri, 'L'attualità del caso Khlaifia. Gli hotspot alla luce della legge 132/2018: la politica della detenzione extralegale continua' (2019) *Questione Giustizia*, 12 June.

Specifically, it has been found that Law No 132 of 2018, which introduced the possibility of detaining asylum seekers in hotspots, has remained formally unimplemented.[17] The data received from the Prefectures as at 30 September 2019 not only seemingly shows that the detention of asylum seekers under Law No 132/2018 was never formally implemented, but also that no Prefecture has, to date, identified the premises where detention should occur, as required by law.[18] However, in the face of a lack of *formal* application of the rule, the practices observed reveal that foreign nationals passing through hotspot centres may be detained on a generalised basis for several days during the identification procedures, well before their status is defined, without any particular formalities (for this reason no detention orders are recorded). Furthermore, the length of de facto detention is arbitrary; it depends on circumstantial management by the authorities. The situation does not deviate from what emerged in the *Khlaifia* case (the facts of which date back to 2011), when deprivation of liberty was equally devoid of any formality required by law (absence of formal measures and judicial validation) and its duration depended purely on the authorities' management and organisational choices.

Suffice it to refer, for example, to the case of the 50 people rescued by the *Mare Jonio* vessel of the NGO Mediterranea in March 2019, who were taken after landing at the hotspot of Lampedusa. According to ASGI's reports,[19] these third country nationals had not left the hotspot during their prolonged stay in Lampedusa and the managing body, when asked to provide explanations, replied to ASGI that the lack of any regulatory mechanisms regarding exit and return of the people present from the structure was due to the hotspot being – from their point of view – a closed centre. The case is interesting because it visibly shows how there is still ambiguity as to the legal qualification of hotspots and the rights of people passing through them.

In May 2017, the National Ombudsman had already raised the issue of the unlawful detention at the Lampedusa hotspot, and in February 2018 the Prefect of Agrigento (administrative authority responsible for the hotspot of Lampedusa) had sent a communication to the then managing body requesting that it should equip itself with systems to allow asylum seekers to move freely. More than a year

[17] See the report issued by the Associazione Studi Giuridici sull'Immigrazione (Association of Legal Studies on Immigration, hereinafter ASGI) 'Il trattenimento dei richiedenti asilo negli hotspot tra previsioni normative e detenzione arbitraria' (The Detention of Asylum Seekers in Hotspots between Regulatory Provisions and Arbitrary Detention) (In Limine project, September 2019).

[18] To obtain more information on the state of implementation of the provision introduced through Article 6 of Legislative Decree No 142 of 2015, the association ASGI, as part of the mentioned In Limine project, submitted a series of requests for access to information to the Ministry of the Interior and to the Prefectures of the places where the hotspots are located, which, according to the Ministerial Memorandum of 27 December 2018, are tasked with identifying the premises in which to detain asylum seekers.

[19] See ASGI, 'Hotspot di Lampedusa: si teme che i migranti della Mare Jonio siano detenuti arbitrariamente' (Lampedusa Hotspot: there are fears that migrants from the Ionian Sea will be arbitrarily detained) (In Limine project, March 2019).

after that communication, the systems in question had yet to be implemented.[20] Despite statutory amendments, the border management situation continues to appear systematically guided by a logic that is heavily reliant on practice and contingent political sensitivities. Even though the detention of asylum seekers in hotspots now theoretically has a legal basis, it cannot escape the fundamental guarantees associated with any form of deprivation of liberty: the issuance of a detention order validated by the court; the possibility for the person held in detention to challenge the lawfulness of the detention and receive clear information about his or her condition; access to an effective remedy to complain about the treatment to which he or she has been subjected. However, as seen, even though formally having a legal basis, the practice has not changed.

V. The 'Closed-Ports' Policy and the 'Security Decree-bis'

Keeping in mind the legal framework on pre-admittance detention described so far, it is possible to focus on some cases involving migrants rescued on Italian military vessels and NGO vessels operating in the central Mediterranean, which were denied disembarkation as a consequence of the Italian closed-ports policy. These are cases in which vessels that have rescued migrants at sea, as part of SAR (search and rescue) operations, were not granted the nearest 'place of safety' – as required by international law conventions[21] – but, on the contrary, were denied access to Italian ports in the name of a restrictive policy towards migration flows. This policy emerged in the period between June 2018 and August 2019, a period in which the Italian Government engaged in a real tug-of-war, both with regard to the NGOs, accused of directing migratory flows towards Italy, and with regard to other European States, guilty of leaving Italy alone in disembarking and receiving migrants.

With the stated purpose of translating the closed-ports policy into law, in June 2019 Decree-Law No 53 of 14 June 2019 (the 'Security Decree-bis'), then converted into Law No 77 of 8 August 2019, was passed. The Law contains very strict measures on illegal immigration and public security and represents the latest and most extreme frontier in the process of criminalising NGO sea rescue activities.

Under this Law, the Minister of the Interior – in agreement with the Ministers of Defence and Transport, and having informed the Prime Minister – may issue

[20] ASGI, 'Hotspot di Lampedusa' (March 2019).

[21] The authorities informed of the presence of people in danger at sea must activate rescue operations without taking into account the nationality or legal status of the shipwrecked persons; they must provide them with initial medical care; they must transfer them to a safe place (Annex to SAR Convention, Chapters 1.3.2. and 2.1.10).

measures aimed at prohibiting or restricting entry, transit or stay of vessels (excluding military or non-commercial government service) in territorial waters, where at least one of the following alternative conditions is met: i) 'reasons of public order and security'; ii) fulfilment of the conditions set out in Article 19, paragraph 2, point (g) of the Montego Bay Convention, a rule which in turn identifies, as a hypothesis of non-innocent (or 'prejudicial') passage of a foreign ship across territorial waters, the case in which such a ship carries out 'the loading or unloading of … persons in violation of the immigration laws in force in the coastal State'.[22]

This law provision refers to the contents of the directives previously issued by the Minister of the Interior, as part of the closed-ports policy: directives that are 'general' in scope[23] and further directives addressed to individual NGOs, held responsible for conduct described as 'possible manipulation of international obligations concerning search and rescue'; or even '"mediated" cooperation which, de facto, encourages sea crossings of foreigners that do not have a regular residence permit and objectively favours illegal entry into national territory'.

A study by ISPI (Institute for International Policy Studies) provides data which allow evaluating the administrative measures and the legislative reform referred to above.[24] Between June 2018 and August 2019, 25 'crises at sea' occurred, during which the boats were kept off the Italian coast for very variable periods (from a few days up to more than 20 days) for an average of nine days before reaching a solution that would allow the docking in port and the disembarkation of the migrants rescued.[25] In this context of 'ad hoc negotiations', negotiations were almost invariably delegated to the European Commission, which, after contacting the Member States, notified Italy of the extent of each Member State's availability.

[22] Article 1 amended Article 11 of the Italian Consolidated Law on Immigration, the latter provision containing measures on border controls, introducing the following new paragraph 1-ter: 'The Minister of the Interior, National Authority for Public Security within the meaning of Article 1 of Law No. 121, in carrying out the coordination tasks referred to in paragraph 1-bis and in compliance with Italy's international obligations, may limit or prohibit the entry, transit or stay of ships in territorial sea, except in the event of military vessels or ships on non-commercial government service, for reasons of public order and security or when the conditions set out in Article 19, paragraph 2, letter g), limited to violations of the immigration laws in force, of the United Nations Convention on the Law of the Sea, with annexes and final document, drawn up in Montego Bay on 10 December 1982, ratified by Law No. 689 of 2 December 1994. The measure shall be adopted in agreement with the Minister for Defence and the Minister for Infrastructure and Transport, in accordance with their respective powers, and the Prime Minister shall be informed thereof' (Unofficial translation provided by the author).

[23] These measures, invoking the need for the orderly management of migratory flows, had instructed the authorities responsible for the surveillance of maritime borders to refuse entry to anyone who had carried out 'a rescue activity … improperly, … aimed at the entry of persons in breach of immigration laws'.

[24] M Villa and E Corradi, 'Migranti e UE: cosa serve sapere sul vertice di Malta' (ISPI, 20 September 2019), www.ispionline.it.

[25] At first (especially in 2018) rescued people were taken to other European countries, in particular Malta and Spain. During 2019, on the other hand, 80 per cent of crises ended with the migrants being admitted on Italian soil. At different times and in different ways, the Italian government started negotiations with other European states, asking that some of them take over a share of the disembarked migrants.

Eventually, after these negotiations, 1,346 people disembarked in Italy, and other European countries took charge of 593 migrants, while in the same period (June 2018–August 2019) 15,095 people independently disembarked on Italian soil.

Beyond the political rhetoric, the disembarkation of migrants coming from the central Mediterranean route is only negligibly due to the humanitarian rescue activity that the Security Decree-bis was trying to block: in the vast majority of cases, the disembarkations occurred as a result of arrivals with small boats, which Italy could not stop by closing the ports and keeping them off the coast. In these cases, disembarkation has always been permitted and without negotiation with the other European States.[26]

Regardless of this assessment as to the ineffectiveness of the closed-ports policy in terms of reducing disembarkations, the real issue of this political season has been the resulting sacrifice of the fundamental rights of migrants and asylum seekers stranded on rescue ships. The de facto deprivation of liberty, lasting several days, on overcrowded ships unsuitable to accommodate people in severe psychological and physical conditions (due both to the exhausting voyage at sea and the brutality suffered in Libya) is a breach of the right to personal liberty under Article 5 ECHR as well as of the right not to be subjected to inhuman or degrading treatment under Article 3 ECHR (both from a substantive viewpoint and in terms of the related right to an effective remedy to complain about on-board conditions).

From the point of view of the right to personal liberty, two situations can be distinguished: one in which the shipwrecked persons were forced to remain on board for several days on Italian military vessels (for example the *Diciotti* case dealt with in section V.A), where no doubt exists that the Italian authorities arbitrarily deprived the shipwrecked persons rescued of their personal liberty without any legal basis, and where the similarities with the *Khlaifia* case clearly emerge; and the one in which the shipwrecked persons were forced to remain on board the NGO vessels (see the case dealt with in section V.B), where the resulting deprivation of personal liberty is a direct consequence of the impossibility of disembarking (due to the repeated denial by the authorities), it being at the same time impossible to depart towards other destinations. In the above cases, even though the NGO ships are not under the direct management of the Italian military authorities, the captain has no choice but to stay, waiting in front of the Italian coasts for the port where to moor: the captain of the vessel has the duty to request on behalf of the shipwrecked persons the nearest place of safety, and must also face the delicate psychological and physical state in which the migrants on board are generally

[26] As a result, Italy went into crisis mode and asked for outplacement for only 9 per cent of the disembarked migrants, and that it managed to snatch 'European solidarity' (i.e., outplacement promises) for only 4 per cent of the total disembarked migrants.

in (usually they are not in the condition to leave again, facing a further voyage, sometimes in very rough sea conditions).[27]

In the latter cases, vessels are prisons 'with three walls', with the sea ideally representing the fourth wall. An even more impassable wall. Therefore, given the impossibility for the captain to take the migrants back to Libya (a country that evidently cannot be considered a place of safety) or to knock on the door of states that do not represent the neighbouring port, putting the very safety of the rescued persons at risk, the 'closed-port' policy has caused a deprivation of the shipwrecked persons' liberty which is wholly attributable to government authorities.

A. Deprivation of Liberty Aboard Italian Military Ships and the *Diciotti* Case

The case that first, in chronological order, highlighted the contrast between the principles stated by the ECtHR in the *Khlaifia* case and the closed-ports policy is the *Diciotti* case.[28]

In August 2018, more than one hundred people coming from Eritrea, Somalia and other African countries were rescued at high sea by patrol boats of the Italian coastguard and immediately transferred aboard the larger boat, *Diciotti*. The Italian government granted to *Diciotti* the permission to dock in Catania harbour; however, for several days the Ministry of the Interior refused to let migrants disembark, claiming that Europe, and not Italy alone, should take care of people arrived from Africa by boat. The Minister claimed for responsibility in many public occasions, by saying he was 'proud of fighting to defend the Italian border'.

The two cases – *Khlaifia* and *Diciotti* – have a lot in common. And, more importantly, the *Khlaifia* ruling is relevant when assessing the lawfulness of the Italian Government's behaviour in the *Diciotti* case.[29] First, both cases deal with undocumented migrants who were de facto deprived of their personal liberty for several days aboard a ship, without a detention order. Second, in the *Khlaifia* case, migrants were detained for nine days; almost 10 days had passed before migrants

[27] The crucial role played by the Capitan has been emphasised by the Italian Supreme Court in the decision related to Carola Rackete arrest: Corte di Cassazione, Terza Sezione Penale, 16 January 2020 (judgment issuing), 20 February 2020 (judgment release), No 6626. See also the chapter by S Zirulia 'Is that a Smuggler? The Blurring Line between Facilitating Illegal Immigration and Providing Humanitarian Assistance at the European Borders', in this volume.

[28] Tribunale di Catania, sezione Reati Ministeriali, 7 December 2018 (judgment issuing), 22 January 2019 (judgment release). See F Cancellaro and S Zirulia, 'Caso Diciotti: il Tribunale dei Ministri qualifica le condotte del Ministro Salvini come sequestro di persona aggravato e trasmette al Senato la domanda di autorizzazione a procedere' (2019) *Diritto penale contemporaneo*, 28 January; L Masera, 'La richiesta di autorizzazione a procedere nel caso Diciotti' (2019) *Questione Giustizia*, 29 January.

[29] F Cancellaro and S Zirulia, 'Controlling Migration through De Facto Detention: The Case of the "Diciotti" Italian Ship' (2018) *Border Criminologies*, 22 October.

were released from the *Diciotti* ship. Third, the Italian government has justified its behaviour with regard to the *Diciotti* case by invoking the need to defend Italian borders in a context of emergency caused by the massive arrival of migrants and by the inertia of other EU Member States. However, the Strasbourg Court had already rejected the 'state of emergency argument' as a justification for detention in the *Khlaifia* case. At that time, the Italian Government was dealing with far more remarkable numbers of people migrating from North Africa. In fact, between January and September 2011, 55,000 arrivals were recorded, as opposed to 20,000 arrivals for the same period in 2018.

Since the binding effects of the European Court of Human Rights rulings go beyond the specific individual case, the principles expressed in the *Khlaifia* case also apply to the situation of the *Diciotti* ship. The core principle of the *Khlaifia* judgment is that no human being, with or without valid documents, migrant or asylum seeker, can be deprived of their right to liberty and to the *habeas corpus*. In this light, the conduct of the Italian government in the *Diciotti* case represents, for the first time, a clear political choice to manage migration outside the guarantees of the rule of law. Once again, the use of de facto detention was considered by the authorities as a tool to manage migration flows.

The Tribunal of Catania, Sezione per I Reati Ministeriali (known as the Tribunal of Ministers) requested authorisation from the Senate of the Republic to proceed against Senator Matteo Salvini, for the crime of aggravated kidnapping (Article 605, paragraphs 1, 2, nos 2 and 3, of the Italian Criminal Code), specifically

> for having, in his capacity as Minister of the Interior, abusing his powers, deprived of their personal liberty 177 migrants of various nationalities who arrived at the port of Catania on board the naval rescue unit U. Diciotti of the Italian Coast Guard at 23:49 on 20 August 2018 … A fact aggravated by having been committed by a public official abusing the powers inherent to the duties performed, as well as committed to the detriment of minors.

The criminal offence alleged against Senator Matteo Salvini, in his capacity as Minister of the Interior, is that he abused the administrative duties assigned to him by arbitrarily vetoing the indication of the place of safety, 'thus determining the forced stay of migrants on board the naval unit U Diciotti, resulting in an illegal deprivation of their personal liberty for a legally relevant period of time and outside the cases permitted by law'.

Even though the criminal proceedings were dismissed because the Senate did not authorise the proceedings,[30] the case is particularly significant. First, an

[30] In accordance with Article 96 of the Italian Constitution, in conjunction with Article 9, paragraph 5, of Constitutional Law No 1 of 1989, the Italian Senate may deny the authorisation to proceed requested by the Tribunale dei Ministri, by an absolute majority of its members, 'where it deems, with unquestionable assessment, that the person under investigation has acted to protect a constitutionally relevant interest of the State or in the pursuit of a pre-eminent public interest associated with governmental duties' (Article 9, para 3, Constitutional Law No 1 of 1989).

Italian court acknowledged that the application of the closed-ports policy led to an unlawful deprivation of migrants' personal liberty, which may be considered relevant from the point of view of the European Convention on Human Rights, at least under Article 5 § 1 ECHR. Second, the case showed that the principles of the *Khlaifia* case have yet to be implemented in the current practices at the border; third, this case revealed a strong tension between the political claim of the need to 'defend borders' through coercive measures and the need for such measures to comply the rule of law, so as not to encroach on the arbitrariness and subversion of the fundamental values of the constitutional and supranational order.

The *Diciotti* case is by no means isolated. For example, the Tribunale dei Ministri of Catania has brought another accusation against the former Minister of the Interior Matteo Salvini in relation to the *Gregoretti* case. The case concerns 131 migrants detained for several days on board the military vessel *Gregoretti* in July 2019, after they had been rescued partly by a Sicilian fishing vessel and partly by a dinghy. Although the facts date back to a few days after the approval of the Security Decree-bis, the latter does not apply to the case at hand because military vessels are not affected by this law (see Tribunale dei Ministri: 'in the case at hand, since the facts involved an Italian coast guard ship, and therefore a military ship, the rules contained in the Security decree-bis do not apply'). The Tribunale dei Ministri, on the other hand, held that the Italian State had 'the obligation to complete the procedure with the transfer of the migrants to a safe place' and that 'the failure by the Immigration Department to identify the "place of safety", following precise instructions from the Minister of the Interior, has led to a situation of constraints on board, restricting the freedom of movement of migrants'.

B. Deprivation of Personal Liberty on Board NGOs' Vessels: The *Open Arms* Case

The 'closed-ports' policy, as mentioned, was characterised by the open contrast between the action of the Italian Government and the humanitarian activity carried out by NGOs, which culminated in the numerous episodes in which the disembarkation of rescuers' ships was only allowed after having exhausted negotiations with other Member States for the relocation of migrants. During the stand-off at sea, only the most seriously ill migrants were disembarked, sometimes in extreme situations, one by one, after prolonged suffering. Minors were also treated this way: in fact, in general, only after days of stay on board and upon intervention of the competent Youth Courts, were they allowed to disembark.

Emblematic is the case that involved the *Open Arms* ship of the NGO Proactiva in August 2019, when, following the rescue of more than one hundred shipwrecked persons, the ship was banned from entering territorial waters by the Minister of the Interior under the Security Decree-bis. The Catalan NGO had appealed against that ban to the Administrative Court which, as an interim measure, had ordered the entry of the vessel and annulled the ban.[31] For a further week the ship was then at anchor a mile from the coast, suffering the stormy sea, because the Minister of the Interior persisted in vetoing disembarkation despite the Court's ruling.

Once again, the National Ombudsman had expressed to the highest government authorities a deep concern about the ongoing situation of de facto deprivation of liberty of persons on board the ship and the impact this situation had on the fundamental rights of the persons rescued, in particular on their unstable psycho-physical balance, duly certified by the medical teams on board, to the extent that a condition of 'inhuman or degrading treatment', within the meaning of Article 3 of the European Convention on Human Rights, could be envisaged.

The Prosecutor of Agrigento, assuming that the people on board were victims of the crime of kidnapping, ordered the seizure of the ship precisely to prevent the continuation of the unlawful deprivation of liberty on board.

The Judge for preliminary investigations validated this measure,[32] acknowledging that the more than one hundred shipwrecked persons on the Catalan NGO ship had been forced into an 'illegal and wilful deprivation of personal liberty'. The measure reads as follows:

> An urgent need to issue a measure existed, having regard to the physical and psychological conditions of the persons on board, which emerged from the inspection of 20 August and were described by the technical experts. … There is a prima-facie case to state that the criminal offence of kidnapping by public officials was committed.

While confirming the measure, the judge ordered the release of the vessel and its return to the NGO because 'no need to provide evidence exists and no liability has been found on the part of the crew'.

The *Open Arms* case – still subject to a judicial assessment – is certainly representative of how an unlawful deprivation of liberty can occur even in cases where national authorities do not physically and directly control migrants but, as a result of their conduct, determine a de facto deprivation of liberty, albeit indirectly. In the case at hand, the relevant conduct is manifold: the failure to assign the place of safety requested by the rescuers, the administrative measures denying entry and disembarkation of the humanitarian vessel, even the failure to comply with the decision taken by a court to suspend the entry ban imposed by the government authorities under the Security Decree-bis. Also in this case, the application for authorisation to bring proceedings against Senator Matteo Salvini, at the time Minister of the Interior *pro tempore* concerns the criminal offences of aggravated kidnapping (Article 605, paragraphs 1, 2, and 3, of the Italian Criminal Code) and for refusal to perform official duties (Article 328, paragraph 1, of the Italian Criminal Code).

[31] Decreto del Presidente del Tribunale Amministrativo Regionale per il Lazio, 14 August 2019.
[32] Tribunale di Agrigento, Ufficio del Giudice delle Indagini preliminari, 29 August 2019.

VI. Concluding Remarks

Two years after the *Khlaifia* ruling Italy is still a long way from a real solution to ensure the respect of the fundamental right of personal liberty at the southern border of Europe.

Although the statutory reforms implemented by Italy following the ECtHR's finding of liability are still being examined by the Committee of Ministers of the Council of Europe, many critical issues with regard to the substantive and procedural guarantees granted to migrants can already be addressed.

A main, paradoxical, issue regards the management of the hotspot centres. When these centres were finally brought back, at least on paper, under the control of the judicial authorities, thus apparently setting a limit to the absolute arbitrariness with which the police authorities had until now managed reception in these centres, an unreasonable disparity in treatment between asylum seekers and migrants was established. For asylum seekers, the police authorities may legally order detention at hotspots for identification purposes, subject to confirmation of the measure by the judiciary; for migrants who do not intend to ask for protection and will be expelled from the territory because *sans papiers*, this possibility is not provided under law. The rules on deprivation of liberty at hotspots are much more burdensome for asylum seekers than for economic migrants, without any identifiable reason for this difference. Moreover, in providing that asylum seekers may be deprived of their liberty for identification purposes, without specifying anything else, the law ends up providing for the possibility of detaining all asylum seekers as they usually have no identification documents.

The practice found in the Italian hotspots, on the other hand, has largely confirmed a series of enduring problems relating to the management of these centres: the law on the detention of asylum seekers has continued not to be applied while unlawful detention practices continue to be carried out, whether outside the cases provided for by law (i.e., devoid of any legal basis) or in ways not provided for by law (i.e., without procedural guarantees being acknowledged).

The situation is all the more worrying, if one considers that arbitrary detention practices had been experienced even before migrants and asylum seekers crossed the national land border. The sea border – represented by territorial waters – has thus become a place of detention for several hundred migrants, aboard rescue ships of the Italian authorities or private humanitarian ships of NGOs. Against the backdrop of a Europe-wide inability to manage the situation, a new negotiation practice has thus taken place to the detriment of migrants. Human lives were manipulated to create a further instance of twofold punishment:[33] on the one hand,

[33] The punitive nature of migration enforcement practices is frequently characterised as being outside the field of 'punishment'. Scholars have pointed to the need to expand 'definitional boundaries of the category of "punishment"'. See K Hannah-Moffat and M Lynch, 'Theorizing Punishment's Boundaries: An Introduction' (2012) 16 *Theoretical Criminology* 119–21, pointing out that previous scholarship 'tend to neglect a number of questions about what constitutes punishment in diverse settings and

undocumented migrants knocking on Europe's doors after having been victims of Libyan hell and, on the other hand, their rescuers, guilty of asking Italy and Europe for a place of safety for the shipwrecked persons who, without their intervention, would have joined the ranks of those perished on the central Mediterranean route.

The laws passed in the last two years did not provide new criminal penalties. However, migration has been criminalised de facto, through policies that stigmatise it and an enduring failure to respect fundamental rights.[34]

The Italian situation has also caused alarm at international level. Ten Special Rapporteurs of the United Nations sent a communication to the Italian Government in which they expressed their concern about fundamental rights in Italy and asked, in particular, for clarification on the following issues: the criminalisation of the search and rescue activities of migrants carried out by NGOs in the Mediterranean; the protracted denials of disembarkation in Italian ports of the ships of the same NGOs and of those belonging to the Italian Coast Guard; the harm to the fundamental rights of migrants that may arise from applying the Security Decree (Decree-Law No 113 of 4 October 2018, converted with amendments into Law No. 132 of 1 December 2018).[35] The closed-ports policy has also been the subject of strong criticism from the UN High Commissioner for Human Rights. A communication signed by five Special Rapporteurs highlighted the radical incompatibility of this policy with the obligations arising from the UNCLOS, SOLAS and SAR Conventions on the International Law of the Sea, as well as with the principle of the *non-refoulement.*[36] According to the communication, the increasing trend of prohibiting rescue activities by NGOs and other private vessels in the central Mediterranean Sea poses very serious risks to the fundamental rights of migrants, who are statistically more and more likely to lose their lives in a shipwreck or to be recovered by the Libyan Coast Guard and taken back to a country where arbitrary detention, torture and sexual violence are a tragic daily routine. In addition, just a few days after the entry into force of the Security Decree-bis, the Commissioner for Human Rights of the Council of Europe issued a Recommendation[37] addressed to the 47 Member States of the Council of Europe, which contains regulatory and

are limited in their ability to explain on-the-ground punitive practices, particularly in contexts that challenge traditional understandings of the penal realm'. To this end, the term 'punishment' should be fundamentally adjusted so as to include 'bordered forms of penality': see M Bosworth, K Franko and S Pickering, 'Punishment, Globalization and Migration Control: "Get them the Hell out of Here"' (2018) 20 *Punishment and Society* 34.

[34] See S Carrera, V Mitsilegas, J Allsopp and L Vosyliūtė, *Policing Humanitarianism. EU Policies Against Human Smuggling and their Impact on Civil Society* (Oxford, Hart Publishing, 2019); V Mitsilegas, *The Criminalisation of Migration in Europe. Challenges for Human Rights and the Rule of Law* (Cham, Springer, 2015); K Franko Aas and M Bosworth (eds), *The Borders of Punishment* (Oxford, Oxford University Press, 2013).

[35] Communication of the UN Special Rapporteurs to the Italian Government (AT ITA 2/2018), 21 November 2018.

[36] The UN High Commissioner for Human Rights in the framework of the 'Special Procedures' mechanisms for monitoring and promoting human rights sent a communication to the Italian Government (AT ITA 4/2019) 15 May 2019.

[37] Council of Europe Commissioner for Human Rights, *Lives Saved. Rights Protected. Bridging the Protection Gap for Refugees and Migrants in the Mediterranean* (Recommendation 2019).

practical guidelines to ensure the effective fulfilment of obligations relating to rescue at sea and the subsequent protection of the fundamental rights of rescued persons. Despite reaffirming the States' right to protect border security, the Recommendation points out that this cannot under any circumstances be done to the detriment of the fundamental rights of the persons concerned.[38]

The populist Government (formed by the League and the Five Star Movement, and presided by Mr Conte) fell on August 2019 and was replaced (without new elections) by a new majority formed by the centre-left wing Democratic party and (again) the Five Star Movement, which obtained the confirmation of Mr Conte as prime minister. Whilst the Security decrees have not been repealed or modified yet, some features on the management of the immigration flows have changed: the average number of days spent at sea by vessels transporting rescued persons has halved, from 9.1 to 4.5;[39] on the supranational side, an attempt has been made to reach an agreement with some European states. The agreement of Malta on the relocation of migrants[40] that Italy, Malta, France and Germany have developed and shared with Finland, president-in-office of the European Union, has put a symbolic halt to the closed-ports policy (June 2018–August 2019). This agreement has highlighted a number of key problems which cannot be underestimated: first and foremost, the weakness of the European Union, which is incapable of reaching an agreement through its decision-making instruments and has revealed its inability to clearly support the vital humanitarian role played by NGOs[41] carrying out search and rescue activities at sea.

[38] 'Whilst states have the right to control their borders and ensure security while co-operating with neighbouring countries to this end, this cannot come at the expense of people's human rights whether at sea or on land. Effectively protecting these rights requires the full implementation of member states' obligations, under international maritime law, human rights law and refugee law, which should be read as being consistent with each other' (p 16).

[39] M Villa, 'Migrazioni nel Mediterraneo: tutti i numeri', 21 January 2020, www.ispionline.it.

[40] The Agreement signed on 23 September 2019 in Valletta provides for a *temporary solidarity mechanism on a voluntary basis* for the relocation of migrants arriving by sea. It is planned to activate a fast track system for relocation on the basis of commitments made prior to disembarkation. The transfer shall take place within a maximum of four weeks and shall concern all rescued asylum seekers. The State of destination is fully responsible for the application for protection, reception and possible repatriation in the event of a negative outcome of the asylum application. The document was presented to the Ministers of Justice and Home Affairs (JHA) of the EU Member States at the summit held on 7–8 October 2019 in Luxembourg. The text of the agreement in available online at www.statewatch.org. See S Carrera and R Cortinovis, 'The Malta declaration on SAR and relocation: A predictable EU solidarity mechanism?' (CEPS Policy Insights, No 2019-14 / October 2019), www.ceps.eu.

[41] The agreement (see point 9) provides that the vessels involved in rescue operations must comply with the instructions of the relevant Coordination Centre, must not facilitate the departure of boats with migrants on board from the coasts of North Africa, and must not hinder the search and rescue operations of the Coast Guards, including the Libyan one.

10

Detention as a Tool of Immigration and Asylum Enforcement in the EU

JUSTINE N STEFANELLI

I. Introduction

States have resorted to detention as a means of enforcing immigration and asylum rules for some time. It is primarily viewed as a means of keeping track of migrants and asylum seekers subject to national immigration and asylum processes and ensuring that individuals viewed as posing a risk of criminal behaviour or flight are prevented from either activity. Though it has been primarily within the purview of state regulation, the European Union has entered the arena by prescribing EU-level processes and conditions of detention in the context of immigration and asylum law. As a result, EU standards of detention will apply at the national level when Member States are returning individuals unlawfully present within their territory under the Return Directive, determining under the Dublin system which Member State is responsible for examining an application for international protection, or examining an application for international protection under the Asylum Procedures and Reception Conditions Directives. This is quite a broad set of circumstances under which EU legislation and the case law of the Court of Justice of the EU (CJEU) can influence national practice. This chapter will demonstrate the breadth of such EU influence to date by briefly outlining in section II the history of EU-level regulation of detention in the immigration and asylum context. Subsequently, section III will focus on the use of detention in the asylum context, with an overview of relevant legislative provisions and case law. Section IV will do the same for detention in the context of return procedures, and it will also consider the EU Commission's proposal for a recast version of the Return Directive and highlight several points for concern regarding the protection of fundamental rights. Section V concludes that, although there may be disagreement regarding the quality of EU regulation of detention, it is ultimately positive that the EU has endeavoured to develop a set of clear standards for the detention of third-country nationals.

II. The EU as a Regulator of Detention and Protector of Liberty

Before discussing the legislative provisions currently applicable to detention under EU law, this section will trace the evolution of EU detention regulation from fairly vague to quite detailed in some circumstances. Prior to the entry into force of the Return Directive in 2009 (which will be the focus of discussion in section IV), the EU had not provided for detailed regulation of immigration detention.[1] For example, the Dublin II Regulation allowed a Member State to request an urgent reply from the Member State that the requesting state felt was responsible for examining an application for asylum, if the applicant was held in detention.[2] The original Reception Conditions Directive referred to detention in two places. First, it placed a general obligation on the Member States to ensure that material reception conditions were available for asylum applicants and that such conditions met an adequate standard of living, especially for individuals with special needs, including those in detention.[3] Second, in the context of discussing specific requirements where housing or reception centres are offered, the Directive permitted Member States to deviate from the standards of the Directive in certain cases, including where the asylum seeker was in detention.[4] Finally, in the first Asylum Procedures Directive, detention was mentioned in the context of access to detainees by legal representation and by the United Nations High Commissioner for Refugees.[5]

[1] Directive 2008/115/EC of the European Parliament and of the Council on 16 December 2008 on common standards and procedures in Member States for returning illegally staying third-country nationals ('EU Return Directive'). This chapter will use the term 'immigration detention' to collectively refer to detention used in both the immigration and asylum contexts. Outside immigration and asylum, EU legislation refers to deprivations of liberty in a number of legislative instruments, including the European Arrest Warrant (Framework Decision 2002/584/JHS of the Council of 13 June 2002 on the European arrest warrant and the surrender procedures between Member States, in particular art 12), the mutual recognition of criminal judgment imposing custodial sentences or measures involving the deprivation of liberty (Framework Decision 2008/909/JHA of the Council 27 November 2008 on the application of the principle of mutual recognition to judgments in criminal matters imposing custodial sentences or measures involving deprivation of liberty for the purpose of their enforcement in the European Union [2008] OJ L 327/27), and the mutual recognition of decisions on supervision measures imposed as alternatives to detention (Framework Decision 2009/829/JHA of the Council of 23 October 2009 on the application, between Member States of the European Union, of the principle of mutual recognition to decisions on supervision measures as an alternative to provisional detention [2009] OJ L 294/20). For an excellent overview of the CJEU's jurisprudence on deprivations of liberty in the EU, see L Mancano, *The European Union and Deprivation of Liberty: A Legislative and Judicial Analysis from the Perspective of the Individual* (Oxford, Hart, 2019).

[2] Council Regulation 343/2003/EC of 18 February 2003 establishing the criteria and mechanisms for determining the Member State responsible for examining an asylum application lodged in one of the Member States by a third-country national, Art 17(2).

[3] Directive 2003/9/EC of the Council of 27 January 2003 laying down minimum standards for the reception of asylum seekers [2003] OJ L 31/18, Art 13(2).

[4] ibid Art 14(8).

[5] Directive 2005/85/EC of the Council of 1 December 2005 on minimum standards on procedures in Member States for granting and withdrawing refugee status [2005] OJ L 326/13, Arts 16(2), 21(1)(a).

The Directive also prohibited Member States from detaining individuals solely on the basis that they were asylum seekers and required Member States to offer a possibility for speedy judicial review of their detention.[6]

These early forays into immigration detention perhaps reflected the generally limited role played by the EU at the time with regard to immigration and asylum matters. Apart from the provision in the Reception Conditions Directive allowing Member States to depart from EU standards where detention centres were being used to house asylum seekers, for the most part, EU legislative provisions in this context demonstrated concern for the right to liberty and a desire to ensure that, where detention was employed by the Member States, it was done so on a limited and humane basis. Indeed, the protection of fundamental rights has long been an objective of the EU. The right to liberty as enshrined in Article 6 of the EU Charter of Fundamental Rights (CFREU) is to be interpreted in accordance with the right as protected in Article 5 of the European Convention on Human Rights (ECHR).[7] It is also part of the EU General Principle of respect for fundamental rights that is used by the CJEU in its interpretive process. The right to liberty is not absolute and can be curtailed by national authorities in certain circumstances. Under Article 5 ECHR (and therefore the CFREU as well), the right can be restricted in the context of regulating entry and exit into a State territory – that is, to give effect to national immigration and asylum policy. However, when detention is employed as a restriction on liberty, it must be sparingly used and closely regulated. The Charter goes one step further than Article 5 ECHR to require necessity before restricting the rights it guarantees, including the right to liberty.[8] This safeguard is obvious in the immigration and asylum legislation adopted by the EU subsequent to the instruments discussed above. In these newer, and in some cases, 'recast' instruments, detention procedures and standards are elaborated upon in more detail. The reasons for this are not always clear, but some of the preparatory documents shed light on the matter.

Prior to negotiations for the Return Directive, the Commission's Green Paper on the return policy of 'illegal immigrants' included a discrete section on the role of detention in enforcing removals.[9] Though the Green Paper acknowledged that detention significantly impairs the liberty of the individual, the Green Paper identified two justifications for its use. First, it assists the State in identifying the person

[6] ibid Art 18(1)–(2).

[7] Charter of Fundamental Rights of the EU [2010] OJ C326/91, Art 52. See also D Wilsher, 'Article 6' in S Peers et al, *The EU Charter of Fundamental Rights: A Commentary* (Oxford, Hart, 2014) and S Peers and S Prechal, 'Article 52' in Peers et al (ibid). In some instances, as I have argued elsewhere, the Charter's substantive right to liberty offers more protection than that of the ECHR. See, JN Stefanelli and E Guild, 'The Right to Liberty in the Field of Migration, Asylum and Borders' in M González Pascual and S Iglesias, *Fundamental Rights in the EU Area of Freedom, Security and Justice* (Cambridge, Cambridge University Press, forthcoming).

[8] Charter of Fundamental Rights of the EU, Art 52(1).

[9] European Commission, 'Green Paper on a Community return policy on illegal immigrants', COM(2002) 175 final 14–15.

and obtaining the requisite travel documents. Second, it prevents the person from fleeing prior to removal.[10] The Green Paper suggested that EU legislation should harmonise standards for detention orders, including issues such as the competence of the responsible authorities, preconditions for detention and mechanisms for judicial oversight.[11] The Green Paper also foresaw the development of minimum standards for the conditions of detention and a European time limit on detention.[12] To balance the reliance on detention as a tool of enforcement, the Green Paper also reiterated the applicability of the ECHR and the Charter, and emphasised that return policy must 'be fully respectful' of fundamental rights.[13]

The Dublin system for determining the country responsible for examining an asylum application began its life as an international convention.[14] In 2003, it was replaced by the Dublin II Regulation.[15] Approximately four years later, the Commission published a report evaluating the operation of the Dublin system and a Green Paper on the future of the Common European Asylum System (CEAS).[16] Despite neither document referring to detention at all, the following year, the Commission published a proposal for a recast Regulation (now known as Dublin III) that included a dedicated article on detention.[17] It was felt that specific safeguards and procedures were necessary to ensure that detention was not arbitrary and that it was used only on a limited basis in the Member States.[18] The Green Paper also emphasised that the proposed detention provisions complied with the CFREU, the ECHR and the UN Convention against Torture and other Cruel Inhuman or Degrading Treatment or Punishment.[19] The operation of the detention provisions in practice will be discussed below in sections III.A and B.

[10] ibid 14.

[11] ibid.

[12] ibid.

[13] ibid 10. It should be noted that the Return Directive, even at this early stage, was not without criticism. See, e.g., OHCHR, 'UN experts express concern about proposed EU Return Directive' (2008) www.ohchr.org/en/NewsEvents/Pages/DisplayNews.aspx?NewsID=8440&LangID=E - sthash.vuMAfFKS.dpuf; D Acosta Arcarazo, 'Latin American Reactions to the Adoption of the Return Directive' (CEPS 2009) 3–4.

[14] Convention determining the State responsible for examining applications for asylum lodged in one of the Member States of the European Communities [1997] OJ C254/1, 19 August 1997, signed in Dublin, Ireland on 15 June 1990, and entering into force on 1 September 1997 for the original 12 signatories.

[15] Regulation 343/2003/EC of the Council of 18 February 2003 establishing the criteria and mechanisms for determining the Member State responsible for examining an asylum application lodged in one of the Member States by a third-country national ('Dublin II Regulation').

[16] European Commission, 'Green Paper on the future of the Common European Asylum System', COM(2007) 301 final.

[17] European Commission Proposal for a Regulation of the European Parliament and of the Council establishing the criteria and mechanisms for determining the Member State responsible for examining an application for international protection lodged in one of the Member States by a third-country national or a stateless person (Recast), COM(2008) 820 final, Art 27.

[18] European Commission Green Paper, above n 16, 8.

[19] ibid. The UN Convention was signed in New York on 10 December 1984 and entered into force on 26 June 1987, UN Treaty Series, vol 1465, p 85.

Both the Asylum Procedures and Reception Conditions Directives were recast in 2013. Because detention provisions in the former refer to the latter,[20] the focus here will be on the development of the recast Reception Conditions Directive. In 2007, alongside the CEAS Green Paper, discussed above, the Commission undertook a study on Member State implementation of the first Reception Conditions Directive.[21] Together, these documents highlighted problems with the applicability of the Directive to detention centres and pointed out specific trouble with poor detention conditions in some Member States, varied lengths of detention in the Member States and the practice of some Member States of automatically detaining all asylum seekers.[22] The result was a proposal for a recast directive which stated the Commission's belief that it was 'necessary to address [detention] in a holistic way' and to 'ensure that detention is not arbitrary and that fundamental rights are respected in all cases'.[23] Other goals of the proposal were to make sure that the Member States only detain asylum seekers in exceptional circumstances and that, where detention is employed, it is done so humanely and in a dignified manner. For the most part, as discussed below in section III.C, this was achieved in the adopted directive.

Accordingly, EU regulation of detention in the immigration and asylum context went from being fairly light-touch to being quite detailed in a relatively short amount of time. This is, in my view, a welcome transition, especially when one considers that thousands of people are subject to these instruments and at risk of having their liberty curtailed. The following section will examine the Dublin III Regulation, the recast Reception Conditions Directive and their relevant case law to gain an understanding of how detention under these instruments is being used in practice and what sorts of questions the CJEU has been asked to consider since their entry into force.

III. Detention of Asylum Seekers

A. The Dublin III Regulation

The Dublin III Regulation provides the criteria and mechanisms for determining which Member State is responsible for handling an application for international protection from someone who entered the EU through another Member State.

[20] Directive 2013/32/EU of the European Parliament and of the Council of 26 June 2013 on common procedures for granting and withdrawing international protection (recast), Art 26.

[21] European Commission Report to the Council and the European Parliament on the application of Directive 2003/9/EC of 27 January 2003 laying down minimum standards for the reception of asylum seekers, COM(2007) 745 final.

[22] European Commission Green Paper, above n 16, 5; European Commission Report, ibid, 6–9.

[23] European Commission Proposal for a Directive of the European Parliament and of the Council laying down minimum standards for the reception of asylum seekers (Recast), COM(2008) 815 final 6.

If a Member State requests the Member State of entry to take back the person and take responsibility for the application, the Member State of entry is obliged to do so. The Dublin III Regulation permits the detention of individuals subject to this process in certain circumstances. In particular, Article 28(2) provides for detention to secure the transfer process where there is a significant risk of absconding.

Where someone is detained pending a determination of the responsible Member State, certain time limits apply. For example, a take back request must be made within one month of the application being lodged, and the requesting Member State must ask for an urgent reply, which must be given within two weeks.[24] Transfer must be made within six weeks of acceptance.[25] Thus, individuals subject to a take back request cannot be detained for longer than three months. If the requesting Member State fails to comply with the applicable timeframes, the person must be released.[26] Finally, where a person is detained under the Dublin III Regulation, the Reception Conditions Directive (discussed in section C below) governs detention guarantees and conditions.[27]

B. The CJEU and the Dublin III Regulation

Since the entry into force of the Dublin III Regulation, there have been two CJEU judgments concerning Article 28 on detention. In *Al Chodor*, the Court considered the nature of the requirement in Article 2(n) that a determination of serious risk of absconding under Article 28(2) must be made according to objective criteria set forth in law.[28] Specifically, the referring court asked whether that meant that the criteria must be set forth in legislation and, if so, whether a failure to do so meant that the State had no power to detain under Article 28(2). In that case, the Czech Republic had determined under the Regulation that Hungary was responsible for examining the applications for protection made by Mr Al Chodor

[24] Regulation 604/2013/EU of the European Parliament and of the Council of 26 June 2013 establishing the criteria and mechanisms for determining the Member State responsible for examining an application for international protection lodged in one of the Member States by a third-country national or a stateless person (recast) ('Dublin III Regulation'), Art 28(3), para 2.

[25] The Regulation notes in Article 28(3) paragraph 2 that a failure to reply within two weeks will be treated as an acceptance of the request.

[26] Dublin III Regulation (n 24) Art 28(3), para 4. There is currently a proposal on the table for a fourth version of the Regulation that would tighten up the timeframe in which a final decision on transfer must be made with respect to detained individuals. Proposed Article 29 would bring the overall time period for this decision-making process down from three months to seven weeks. See European Commission Proposal for a Regulation of the European Parliament and of the Council establishing the criteria and mechanisms for determining the Member State responsible for examining an application for international protection lodged in one of the Member States by a third-country national or a stateless person (recast), COM(2017) 270 final. See also, European Commission Directorate General for Migration and Home Affairs Evaluation of the Dublin III Regulation, 4 December 2015.

[27] ibid Art 28(4).

[28] Case C-528/15 *Al Chodor*. See also T Poli, 'Immigration detention and the rule of law: the ECJ's first ruling on detaining asylum seekers in the Dublin system', EU Law Analysis, 5 May 2017 http://eulawanalysis.blogspot.com/2017/05/immigration-detention-and-rule-of-law.html.

and his two minor children. Because they were picked up without documentation, they were judged to present a serious risk of absconding and were detained. The Al Chodors successfully challenged their detention arguing that national law did not set out objective criteria for such a determination, in contravention of Article 2(n). Instead of legislation, the national authorities used case law and administrative practice to make their decisions. The State appealed to the Supreme Administrative Court (*Nejvyšší správní soud*), which referred the case to the CJEU.

The Court's analysis began with an overview of Article 6 CFREU and Article 5 ECHR.[29] It then quickly determined that Article 2(n) requires legislative criteria and set about establishing the appropriate character of such legislation, by reference to the Regulation's twin aims of ensuring that the Dublin system operates effectively and enhancing the protections afforded to asylum seekers subjected to the system.[30] The CJEU considered that the fact that Dublin III included specific provisions on detention, whereas Dublin II did not, indicated an intention to offer greater legal protection to detainees under the new regime.[31] Therefore, the Court stated that any limitation on the right to liberty must be undertaken with regard to the essence of that right and according to the principle of proportionality.[32] It further considered that Article 5 ECHR and its case law required deprivations of liberty to be lawful, meaning not only that there be a legal basis for detention, but that such legal basis must be 'sufficiently accessible, precise and foreseeable in its application in order to avoid all risk of arbitrariness'.[33] One of the ways to ensure against arbitrariness, according to the CJEU, was to subject to 'predetermined limits' any discretion associated with a determination that detention is necessary under Articles 2(n) and 28.[34] This aim therefore requires objective criteria to be set forth in a binding legislative act of general application.[35] The CJEU concluded that national practice did not comply with the requirements of Article 5 ECHR/ Article 6 CFREU and that where no provision in law exists in such circumstances, the power to detain in Article 28(2) is unavailable.[36]

The second case, *Khir Amayry*, concerned the deadlines for carrying out transfers in Article 28 and their impact on the calculation of detention time limits in the context of transfers.[37] The Administrative Court of Appeal for Immigration Matters in Stockholm, Sweden (*Kammarrätten i Stockholm – Migrationsöverdomstolen*) asked the CJEU four questions.[38] The first two concerned whether Article 28 prohibited national law providing that where a person was not detained at the

[29] *Al Chodor*, ibid paras 3–5.
[30] ibid paras 24–28, 33.
[31] ibid para 35.
[32] ibid para 37.
[33] ibid para 38, citing *Del Rio Prado v Spain*, Application No 42750/09 (21 October 2009) para 125.
[34] ibid para 42.
[35] ibid paras 42–44.
[36] ibid para 47.
[37] Case C-60/16 *Khir Amayry*.
[38] ibid para 21.

time the responsible State submits the take back request, but is detained later, that person can later be detained for a maximum of two months absent serious reasons for detaining the individual in question (in which case the person can be detained for a maximum of three months).[39] The third question addressed the recommencement of the transfer process after a failed appeal of the transfer decision. In such circumstances, the referring court queried whether the six-week period starts fresh at that point, or whether the number of days the person had already spent in detention since the responsible State agreed to take him or her back should be subtracted so that the State has fewer than six weeks to effect transfer. Finally, the referring court asked whether the answer to the third question depended on whether the person appealing the transfer decision did not apply for suspension of the transfer pending appeal.

Beginning with the first two questions, the CJEU explained that Article 28(3) clearly states that the deadlines must be respected or the person must be released,[40] but it does not, on its face, indicate whether it is applicable to all instances of detention prior to transfer. Therefore, the Court looked to the purpose of the Regulation and focused on its objective of enabling transfer of applicants to the responsible State.[41] The power to detain, said the Court, is aimed at securing transfer by preventing the person from absconding.[42] The EU legislature's choice of six weeks indicates that that period was considered necessary to effect the transfer and therefore to deduct any time from the six-week period because detention occurred later in the process could potentially harm the State's ability to effect transfer and, hence, the effectiveness of the Regulation.[43] Thus, the Court concluded that the limits in the third subparagraph of Article 28(3) apply only to cases where the applicant was in detention at the time the requested State took responsibility for the application or once suspensive effect is lost and transfer is resumed.[44] Where an applicant was detained after the requested State accepts responsibility, national time limits apply (where they exist).[45] National maximums must comply with the aims of Article 28(3) and Article 6 of the Charter of limiting detention to as short as possible a period and for no longer than reasonably necessary to carry out the relevant administrative procedures with due diligence.[46] The CJEU then held that the Member States may not enact maximums that are 'vastly in excess of six weeks', given the above discussion regarding the assessment that such a period should be sufficient to effect transfer.[47] Thus, the two-month

[39] Or for 12 months where transfer is likely to take longer due to the detainee's non-cooperation or difficulty in obtaining the necessary documents.
[40] *Khir Amayry*, above n 37, para 27.
[41] ibid para 30.
[42] ibid para 31.
[43] ibid paras 32–37.
[44] ibid paras 39–40.
[45] ibid para 40.
[46] ibid paras 41–44.
[47] ibid para 45.

maximum in the Swedish legislation was considered permissible, but periods of three and 12 months were not.[48]

In relation to the third and fourth questions, the CJEU revisited the notion of effectiveness. It acknowledged that Member States would face the same obstacles to transfer once transfer has recommenced following its temporary suspension as they would face attempting to transfer absent such an appeal and should therefore be given the same six-week period in either case.[49] Therefore, the Court held that time already spent in detention should not be deducted when calculating the six-week period following the lifting of suspensive effect.[50] It further held that the answer to the third question does not change depending on whether suspensive effect has been provided by national law or conferred at the request of the applicant because in both cases, the applicant ends up in the same legal position.

C. The Reception Conditions Directive

Though the general rule under the CEAS legislation is that individuals cannot be detained for the sole reason that they are applying for international protection, detention is permitted in certain situations while their applications are pending. In particular, Article 8 of the recast Reception Conditions Directive (RCD) provides six grounds for detention: (a) to determine or verify identity or nationality; (b) to determine elements of the application that could not be verified unless the applicant is detained, particularly where there is a risk of absconding; (c) to decide whether the applicant has the right to enter the territory; (d) where the applicant is detained on the basis of the Return Directive, but there are reasonable grounds to believe that the application for international protection has not been made in good faith; (e) for national security or public order reasons; and (f) under the Dublin III Regulation.[51] It provides additional procedural safeguards, such as requiring that the State undertake its assessment diligently, and that the State provide the applicants with reasons for their decision to detain and a right to have their detention judicially reviewed.[52]

[48] ibid paras 46–47.
[49] ibid para 56.
[50] ibid paras 59.
[51] Directive 2013/33/EU of the European Parliament and of the Council of 26 June 2013 laying down standards for the reception of applicants for international protection ('Reception Conditions Directive') Art 8(3). A proposal for a second recasting of the Reception Conditions Directive has been tabled. It adds an additional ground for detention in cases where an applicant for protection does not comply with an obligation to reside at a particular residence and poses a continued flight risk. It also improves the Directive's provisions on treatment of applicants with special needs. The sections on guaranteed rights and conditions of detention remain unchanged. See European Commission Proposal for a Directive of the European Parliament and of the Council laying down standards for the reception of applicants for international protection (recast), COM(2016) 465 final.
[52] ibid Arts 9(1), 9(3)–(10).

D. The CJEU and the Reception Conditions Directive

At the time of writing, there have been two judgments on Article 8 of the RCD. In *JN*, the Court considered the validity of point (e) of Article 8(3), which permits detention for national security or public order reasons.[53] In that case, JN was detained on that basis in the Netherlands because of numerous criminal convictions.[54] JN challenged his detention, arguing that it violated the second limb of Article 5(1)(f) ECHR because it was not taken with a view toward deportation, but was instead preventive in nature.[55] The Netherlands Council of State (*Raad van State*) asked the CJEU whether detention in such circumstances was permissible under Article 6 of the Charter.

The CJEU's analysis was based explicitly on the Charter and not the ECHR because, in its view, though Article 52 of the Charter strives for consistency between the two instruments, Article 52 should not be applied at the expense of the autonomy of EU law and CJEU judgments.[56] Acknowledging that Article 8(3)(e) is a limitation on the right to liberty as safeguarded in Article 6 CFREU, the CJEU underscored the applicability of the safeguards in Article 52 CFREU – in particular, that any limitations on the exercise of rights in the Charter must respect the essence of the right restricted, be provided in law and be subject to the principles of necessity and proportionality. Limitations must be based on an objective of general interest recognised by the EU (such as public order and national security) or a need to safeguard other individuals' rights.[57]

The Court ultimately held that Article 8(3)(e) satisfied those conditions. First, the CJEU felt that point (e) respected the essence of the right to liberty because it can only be resorted to on the basis of an assessment of the individual's conduct and only in exceptional circumstances.[58] Second, the Court concluded that the objective in point (e) of protecting national security and public order is an objective of general interest of the EU.[59] Third, the Court felt it was axiomatic that detention is suitable and appropriate as a means of ensuring the protection of national security or public order.[60] The fourth and final reason concerned the requirement of necessity. For this, the Court looked to the whole of the RCD and the Explanatory Memorandum to the Proposal for the recast RCD. It considered that the many safeguards in the RCD all pointed toward the fact that detention under the RCD should only be ordered when necessary. The Court referred specifically to, among

[53] Case C-601/15 PPU *JN*.
[54] ibid paras 21–35 (disposition of the facts).
[55] ibid para 34.
[56] ibid paras 45–47.
[57] ibid paras 50–74.
[58] ibid para 52. Note that Article 8(3)(e) does not, on its face, require the circumstances to be exceptional. The CJEU apparently felt that because the RCD provides an exhaustive list of six grounds for detention, its use is necessarily intended to be exceptional.
[59] ibid para 53.
[60] ibid para 55.

other provisions in the RCD, the requirement in Article 8(4) that alternatives to detention must be considered first and the condition in Article 9(1) that detention last only for as long as the grounds in Article 8(3) are applicable.[61]

The judgment in *K* concerned the validity, in light of the CFREU and the ECHR, of the detention grounds in Article 8(3)(a) (to determine or verify identity or nationality) and 8(3)(b) (to enable the authorities to evaluate an application for protection in situations where they may be unable to do so without detention – that is, if the individual presents a risk of absconding).[62] K was detained on the day that he made his application for asylum on the basis that he had been picked up by the authorities in Amsterdam's Schipol Airport with an allegedly false passport, despite the fact that the charges were dropped.[63] The Netherlands Council of State asked the CJEU whether Article 8(3)(a) and (b) were valid bases for detention where a third-country national has a right to remain pending a decision on his application under Article 9 of the Asylum Procedures Directive and whether such detention breached Article 5 ECHR where not imposed with a view toward deportation.[64]

As in *JN*, the CJEU began its analysis with a discussion of the importance of maintaining the autonomy of the EU legal order while striving for coherence with the ECHR. It then went on to rely primarily on its own jurisprudence to conclude that both provisions complied with Articles 6 and 52 of the CFREU.[65] Its reasoning largely mirrored that in *JN*, except for that in *K*, the objective of general interest identified by the Court was the proper functioning of the CEAS, which itself contributes to the overarching EU objective of establishing an area of freedom, security and justice that is open to those who seek refuge in the EU.[66] Detention ordered to ascertain the individual's identity or to ensure that he or she is present during consideration of the application was considered by the Court to be an appropriate means of reaching those objectives.[67] With regard to compliance with Article 5 ECHR, the Court focussed on the decision of the European Court of Human Rights (ECtHR) in *Saadi v UK*, where the ECtHR held that the first limb of Article 5(1)(f) ECHR permits detention to prevent unauthorised entry of asylum seekers as long as the detention is lawful not arbitrary.[68]

[61] ibid paras 56–70.

[62] Case C-18/16 *K*.

[63] ibid paras 17–29 (disposition of the facts).

[64] ibid para 28.

[65] ibid paras 31–49.

[66] ibid para 36.

[67] ibid.

[68] *Saadi v United Kingdom* [GC], Application No 13229/03 (29 January 2008). It should be noted that *Saadi* was later distinguished by *Suso Musa v Malta* (Application No 42337/12 (23 July 2013)), where the ECtHR held that, where a State has conferred a right to remain pending an application for asylum, it may be more difficult to justify detention. Given that the Asylum Procedures Directive requires, in Article 9, Member States to grant such a right, detention under the RCD may have implications for EU consistency with the ECHR under Article 52 CFREU. As this sort of case has not yet come before the CJEU, it is impossible to predict whether the CJEU would emphasise the autonomy of the EU legal order, as it has done in *JN* and *K*, or whether it would find in a manner consistent with the ECHR.

E. Conclusion

CJEU jurisprudence on asylum detention legislation demonstrates a mixed approach. Rights-protecting judgments like *Al Chodor* and *JN* illustrate the strong concern for the fundamental rights of detainees. In these cases, the CJEU engaged in a detailed review of fundamental rights jurisprudence to arrive at its conclusions. This approach can be contrasted with cases where the Court's conclusions are arrived at more as a result of a desire to ensure the effectiveness of the legislation than the rights of detainees. Though the Court does, of course, exhibit a concern for detainees' right to liberty, its decisions in *Khir Amayry* and *K* result from the Court's goal of maintaining the effectiveness of the legislation at issue. In *Khir Amayry*, this is evidenced in the Court's emphasis on the importance of the Member States having enough time to organise Dublin transfers, even if it means the individual will be detained longer than the period allotted in the Regulation. In *K*, the Court uses effectiveness to justify detention of asylum seekers to ascertain identity or ensure presence. The tension between these guiding principles continues in the case law reviewed in the next section.

IV. Detention of Third-Country Nationals Subject to Return

A. The Return Directive

The EU Return Directive was the first EU legal instrument that regulated the detention of third-country nationals in a detailed manner. It has been in force in the Member States since 2010 and is the subject of the majority of CJEU decisions touching on immigration detention. The Directive was adopted to safeguard the integrity of the EU admissions policy and to harmonise return procedures in the Member States.[69] Its aim is to establish a well-functioning and humane removal and return policy for third-country nationals based on harmonised standards and in accordance respect for fundamental rights and dignity.[70] Once a Member State determines that a third-country national is present unlawfully, that Member State is obliged under the Directive to issue a return decision and begin return proceedings.[71] As part of this process, the Directive permits the Member States to detain people in certain circumstances, but only as a last resort after alternatives are considered.[72] Having to consider the suitability of alternatives means

[69] European Commission Green Paper, above n 9, 6–7.
[70] EU Return Directive, above n 1, recital 2.
[71] ibid Art 6.
[72] ibid Art 15(1).

that detention decisions must be made on a case-by-case basis, according to the specific circumstances of the individual. Article 15(1) of the Return Directive sets out an exhaustive list of two grounds for detention in cases where alternatives cannot be applied: (a) where there is a risk of absconding, and (b) where the individual impedes return or removal processes. Once detention has been ordered, it may only continue as long as removal arrangements are in progress and where there is a reasonable prospect of removal.[73] Moreover, removal must be pursued diligently by the State authorities.[74] Perhaps most importantly, the Directive imposes a maximum time period for detention. While underscoring that detention must be as short as possible,[75] the Directive prescribes time periods in two stages. An initial six-month period can exceptionally be extended by up to 12 months where removal has not yet occurred due to a lack of cooperation by the third-country national, or where there is difficulty obtaining the requisite documents from third countries.[76]

B. The CJEU and the Return Directive

Cases concerning the Return Directive fall into two categories. The first category concerns cases dealing specifically with the Directive's detention provisions in Articles 15 and 16. The second category is comprised of cases where the CJEU was asked to consider the extent to which the Member States can criminalise unlawful presence through a prison sentence, home detention or a fine imposed prior to the initiation of return proceedings. This chapter will focus on the first category of cases, as they most closely concern the EU's regulation of immigration-related detention.[77]

[73] ibid Art 15(1), (4).

[74] ibid Art 15(1).

[75] ibid.

[76] ibid Art 15(6). Additional procedural guarantees for detainees are provided by the Directive, including the right to the reasons for their detention, to judicial review and to have the legality of their detention reviewed periodically. See Art 15(2)–(5). As with the Dublin III Regulation and the Asylum Procedures Directive, the Commission has published a proposal for a recasting of the Return Directive in an effort to improve its overall system for returns. The proposal is examined in detail below in section IV.C.

[77] See e.g., Case C-61/11 PPU *El Dridi* [2011] ECR I-3015; Case C-329/11 *Achughbabian* [ECR TBC]; Case C-430/11 *Md Sagor* [ECR TBC]; Case C-522/11 *Mbaye* [ECR TBC]. In these cases, the principle of effectiveness is employed by the CJEU to prevent Member States from using criminal detention as a means of punishing unlawful presence. In the Court's view, criminalising unlawful presence in this way impedes the effective functioning of the Return Directive because it interferes with the removal process, which must be initiated as soon as a determination has been made that the individual is unlawfully present in the Member State. Thus, the principle of effectiveness has had, in these cases, an indirect impact on the Member States' use of detention as a means of enforcing immigration law, which has resulted in what is perhaps an unintentional additional safeguard on the right to liberty under Article 6 CFREU. Whereas effectiveness has operated in a positive way in these cases, the principle does not always result in rights-protecting outcomes. See the discussion in section III.B concerning *Khir Amayry* and section IV.B concerning *G and R*. See also V Mitsilegas, 'The Changing Landscape

The first Return Directive case to reach the CJEU was *Kadzoev*.[78] Mr Kadzoev was picked up without identification by the Bulgarian authorities, ordered deported and put into immigration detention until the correct documentation and funds could be obtained.[79] The Bulgarian authorities spent two years trying to return him to Russia, but were unsuccessful. The Administrative Court in Sofia, Bulgaria (*Administrativen sad Sofia-grad*) asked the CJEU for its interpretation of several provisions in the Directive, including: (a) whether to include in the calculation of Kadzoev's detention period under Article 15(5) and (6), (i) the time he was detained pending his asylum appeal, and (ii) the time he spent in detention during the pendency of his appeal against the removal decision; (b) how to determine when removal is no longer reasonably possible; and (c) whether release at the expiry of the maximum period was appropriate in view of the fact that he did not have identification documents, had displayed aggressive behaviour in the past and did not have the means to support himself.

The Court concluded with respect to (a)(i) that the time Kadzoev spent in detention should be included unless a formal decision to detain him under the Reception Conditions Directive had been made. In such cases, the detention is no longer within the scope of the Return Directive and the maximum therefore does not apply.[80] The Court's response to (a)(ii) was more straightforward: because suspension of removal pending judicial review is not a ground for extending detention under the Directive, such a period must be included in the calculation of the maximum.[81] Moreover, the Court underscored the important role played by the maximum in limiting deprivations of liberty.[82]

With regard to (b), the Court considered that Article 15(1) and (5) only permit detention if removal is pursued with due diligence, and specified that it must be apparent to the national authorities that a 'real prospect exists that the removal can be carried out successfully' in light of the length of detention to date.[83] Moreover, the likelihood that the person will be safely admitted to the third State in question plays a key role. That is, even where the State is diligently pursuing removal, where it appears that the third country is not going to admit the individual, detention is no longer permitted, even if the maximum period has not been reached.[84]

of the Criminalisation of Migration in Europe' in Maria João et al (eds), *Social Control and Justice: Crimmigration in the Age of Fear* (The Hague, Eleven International Publishing, 2013); E Herlin-Karnell, 'Effectiveness and Constitutional Limits in European Criminal Law' (2014) 5 *New Journal of European Criminal Law* 267; E Herlin-Karnell, 'An Exercise in Effectiveness?' (2007) 18 *European Business Law Review* 1181.

[78] Case C-357/09 PPU *Kadzoev* [2009] ECR I-11189.

[79] ibid paras 13–29.

[80] ibid paras 41–48.

[81] ibid paras 52–54.

[82] ibid para 56.

[83] ibid para 65.

[84] ibid para 66.

The Court also stressed that once the maximum period of detention is reached, the question of whether there is a reasonable prospect of removal is no longer relevant.[85] Indeed, the Court made it clear that regardless of the factual circumstances, including those described in (c) above, the individual must be released upon expiration of the maximum period of detention.[86] Detention under the Return Directive cannot serve as a substitute for detention based on public order or national security, especially in view of the fact that the maximum is there to limit deprivations of liberty.[87]

Arslan involved the related issue of whether the Return Directive's detention provisions apply to someone who has made an application for asylum under the CEAS legislation.[88] The Court concluded that where a person has made a genuine application for asylum, that person will no longer be subject to the Return Directive and therefore the time he or she spends in detention under the CEAS legislation does not count toward the maximum period in the Return Directive. Whether the application is genuine must be assessed on a case-by-case basis and cannot be adjudicated based solely on the fact that the application was made while the individual was subject to return proceedings.[89] The national court must consider all relevant circumstances to determine whether the application was made solely to delay or jeopardise enforcement of the return decision.[90] In addition, the national court must make a separate assessment regarding the appropriateness of detention under the CEAS framework.[91] Given the Court's previously strong emphasis on the important role played by a maximum period in relation to the right to liberty, this holding is disappointing, but in line with the Court's previous discussion in *Kadzoev*.

In *Bero and Bouzalmate*[92] and *Pham*,[93] the German referring courts[94] asked the CJEU whether the requirement in Article 16 to house detainees in specialised detention facilities applied to Länder (federated State within Germany) where such facilities were not available. Holding in the affirmative, the CJEU stressed the significance of specialised detention facilities in relation to the Directive's aim of ensuring that detention is carried out humanely and with respect for fundamental rights and dignity.[95] In addition, the Court ruled that detainees cannot

[85] ibid para 60.

[86] ibid paras 68–71. See also V Mitsilegas, *The Criminalisation of Migration in Europe: Challenges for Human Rights and the Rule of Law* (Cham, Springer, 2015) 99.

[87] *Kadzoev*, above n 78, paras 56, 68–71.

[88] Case C-534/11 *Arslan*.

[89] ibid para 62.

[90] ibid.

[91] ibid.

[92] Joined Cases C-473/13 and C-514/13 *Bero and Bouzalmate*.

[93] Case C-474/13 *Pham*.

[94] In *Bero and Bouzalmate*, the reference came from the Bundesgerichtshof and the Landgericht München I, and in *Pham*, the reference originated in the Bundesgerichtshof.

[95] *Pham*, above n 93, para 21.

be permitted to waive their right to detention in specialised facilities because the language in Article 16 is mandatory in nature.[96]

Mahdi[97] and *G and R*[98] both addressed fair hearing principles. *Mahdi* concerned the requirement in Article 15(2) to provide detainees with written legal and factual reasons for their detention. The question before the CJEU was whether that obligation also applied to decisions to extend detention under Article 15(6). The Court answered in the affirmative. It emphasised the function of reasons in the greater context of access to justice: providing detainees with written reasons enables them to effectively challenge their detention and provides the reviewing court with the information it needs to engage in a full merits review of the decision to detain.[99] The Court considered that the CFREU requires further written reasons because an extension of the initial decision to detain is just as much a deprivation of liberty as the initial decision.[100] Therefore, without an obligation to provide reasons in the event of an extension, detainees would be unable to challenge their continued detention and would be left without an effective remedy under EU law, which is impermissible.[101] By contrast, the CJEU inexplicably felt that written reasons were unnecessary in relation to periodic reviews under Article 15(3) during the initial period of detention.[102]

The question in *G and R* was whether a failure to give detainees the opportunity to be heard prior to a decision to extend detention required automatic release from detention. The Court's analysis here turned on the impact of that failure on the outcome of the decision. Though the Court recognised the fundamental nature of the right to be heard in the EU legal order,[103] it acknowledged that the right is not absolute. As noted in the discussion of *Al Chodor* and *JN*, above, rights in the CFREU can be limited as long as such limitations are in pursuit of a legitimate public interest objective, are proportionate, and do not impinge on the essence of the right.[104] Therefore, the Court held that the Member States must evaluate the nature of the breach on a case-by-case basis to determine if the breach directly affected the outcome of the extension decision.[105] The Court felt that to hold that every breach must result in the nullity of detention would harm the effectiveness of the Return Directive.[106]

[96] ibid paras 21–22.
[97] Case C-146/14 PPU *Mahdi.*
[98] Case C-383/13 PPU *G and R.*
[99] *Mahdi*, above n 97, para 45.
[100] Ibid paras 44, 52.
[101] Ibid para 46.
[102] ibid para 47.
[103] *G and R*, above n 98, para 32.
[104] ibid para 33.
[105] ibid para 38.
[106] ibid paras 41–42.

C. The Proposal for a Recast Return Directive

At the end of 2018, the Commission tabled a proposal for a recasting of the Return Directive ('the proposal').[107] The Commission's explanatory memorandum explains that because 'migratory pressure on the Member States and the Union as a whole has increased' since the entry into force of the Directive, an update to the legislation is needed. In particular, the Commission cites two significant issues in Member State implementation of the Directive, one of which relates to immigration detention. Specifically, the Commission highlights the inconsistent approach among Member States in their use of immigration detention.[108] In view of that challenge, the Commission extensively amended Article 15 (now Article 18) on immigration detention.

Proposed Article 18 makes four significant changes to Article 15, all but one of which are negative progress. First, proposed Article 18(1) deletes the word 'only' so that the grounds for detention listed in that provision no longer form an exhaustive list. Second, in that same provision, a new ground for detention in subsection (c) is added: 'the third-country national concerned poses a risk to public policy, public security or national security'. That same provision includes the only positive addition to proposed Article 18 and that is an explicit requirement that the Member States set forth the grounds for detention in national law – i.e., effectively a codification of the decision in *Al Chodor*. Finally, proposed Article 18(5) reflects the Commission's belief that inconsistencies in Member States' use of detention have been impeding the effective implementation of the Directive, particularly, where Member States have set detention maximums shorter than the initial maximum of six months in the Directive. The second sentence of the new provision reads, 'Each Member State shall set a maximum period of detention of not less than three months and not more than six months'.

The Commission's explanatory notes for proposed Article 18 offer unconvincing and incomplete justifications for most of these changes. The Commission does not specifically address its decision to omit the word 'only' from the text of proposed Article 18(1). An amendment tabled by the European Parliament added it back in to the provision, reiterating that detention should be used only as a last

[107] Proposal for a Directive of the European Parliament and of the Council on common standards and procedures in Member States for returning illegally staying third-country nationals (recast) ('Return Directive Proposal'), COM(2018) 634 final, 12 September 2018.

[108] ibid 1. The Commission also identified problems with Member State identification of whether an individual poses a risk of absconding and, in that regard, proposed a new Article 6 on absconding with relevant criteria for such determinations. Proposed Article 6 is beyond the scope of this chapter, but suffice it to say that it has attracted criticism from the European Parliament because of its over-breadth and the potential for it to capture nearly all migrants subject to the Directive, thereby requiring their detention. See European Parliament Committee on Civil Liberties, Justice and Home Affairs, 'Draft Report on the proposal for a directive of the European Parliament and of the Council on common standards and procedures in Member States for returning illegally staying third-country nationals (recast), 2018/0329(COD), 16 January 2019, pp 42–44.

resort, after consideration of alternatives to detention.[109] In its impact assessment of the proposal, the Parliamentary Research Service rightly pointed out that, though the proposal retains the requirement that detention decisions be made on a case-by-case basis, removal of the word 'only' 'modif[ies] the tone of the provision, transforming the limiting clause contained in Article 15(1) of the current Return Directive into an enabling clause'.[110]

The addition of a security-based ground for detention is defended by the Commission as being necessary to address 'new risks [that] have emerged in recent years'.[111] The Commission also pointed out that the new provision brings the Return Directive in line with asylum acquis.[112] Indeed, Article 8(3)(e) of the Asylum Reception Conditions Directive permits the detention of applicants for international protection 'when protection of national security or public order so requires'. In its impact assessment, the Parliament remarked that the new provision seems to be a direct response to the judgment in *Kadzoev*, where the Court foreclosed detention based on public order and public safety under the Return Directive.[113] The Parliament comments that even the Commission itself had, apparently until recently, viewed the function of the Return Directive as being specifically related to migration and did not envision it as a tool for safeguarding the public from threats to national security.[114] The impact assessment highlights the potential for conflict with Article 5 ECHR, which does not include public security as a ground for immigration detention. It also warns that by permitting the use of immigration detention as a means of dealing with public security threats (as opposed to, e.g., pre-trial detention), the proposal attempts to circumvent normal criminal processes, including procedural guarantees that are not always available in the context of immigration detention.[115]

The Commission justifies its new provisions on the maximum period of detention based on a perception that shorter periods of detention in the Member States have been 'precluding effective removals'.[116] This justification is rejected by the Parliament which points out that, based on an analysis of available data, 'there does not seem to be a clear correlation between the maximum period of detention established under national law and the effectiveness of return from individual

[109] European Parliament, ibid, 77 (Amendment 106).

[110] European Parliamentary Research Service, 'The proposed Return Directive (recast): Substitute Impact Assessment', PE 631.727 (February 2019), Annex I, p 69.

[111] Return Directive Proposal (n 107) Explanatory Memorandum, section 8.

[112] ibid.

[113] European Parliament, above n 110, 69.

[114] ibid, citing in fn 274 of the Commission's 2017 Return Handbook (N.B. Parliament refers to p 69 of the Handbook, but I believe this was in error and that it meant to refer to p 79, which specifically discusses this issue under the heading 'No detention for public order reasons'.

[115] ibid.

[116] Return Directive Proposal, above n 107, Explanatory Memorandum, section 8.

Member States'.[117] The European Parliament therefore proposed an amendment that would set an absolute maximum period for detention at three months.[118]

No further legislative progress on the proposal has been made public since the Parliament offered its amendments in January 2019. It is clear from those amendments that there is a high degree of disagreement between the two institutions and it is difficult to see how the legislation can move forward without substantial compromise on both sides. The proposal's provisions on detention have clearly moved in the direction of further criminalisation of immigration, which is an unwelcome and disappointing development, especially in light of evidence that some Member States have been rolling back their use of immigration detention.[119] Should this version be adopted, it will be interesting to see the extent to which the Court continues to emphasise the effectiveness of the Return Directive over its concerns for fundamental rights.

D. Concluding Remarks

The CJEU's Return Directive decisions illustrate again the tension between fundamental rights and effectiveness. The Court's judgment in *Kadzoev* sets out strong principles that underscore the exceptional role that detention should play in the removal process. Its decision in *Mahdi* follows that logic by highlighting the role that the right to written reasons plays in guarding against arbitrary detention. Similarly, the judgments in *Bero and Bouzalmate* and *Pham* emphasise that, where detention is ordered, it must be in an environment that is humane and respects human dignity. But even some of these judgments have their downsides. Though *Kadzoev* is largely rights-protecting, the Court's conclusion that time spent in the asylum process should not be counted toward the maximum period of detention in the Return Directive has negative implications for detainees' liberty and extends the overall time in which individuals can be detained under EU law. This is a concern especially because, unlike the Return Directive, there is no prescribed maximum period in the context of the CEAS legislation. By contrast, the Court's judgment in *G and R* is itself an example of the tension between respect for fundamental rights and the effectiveness of EU law, and it demonstrates how effectiveness can operate to limit detainees' rights

[117] European Parliament, above n 108, 79 (Amendment 110). See also European Parliamentary Research Service, 'Briefing: Recasting the Return Directive', PE 637.901 (April 2019) 6 (text in box with statistics from individual Member States).

[118] European Parliament, above n 108, 79 (Amendment 110).

[119] K Groenendijk, 'Book Review: The Human Rights of Migrants and Refugees in European Law, by Cathryn Costello. (Oxford University Press, 2015)' (2017) 54 *Common Market Law Review* 943, 944. See also JN Stefanelli, *Judicial Review of Immigration Detention in the UK, US and EU: From Principles to Practice* (Oxford, Hart, 2020) 3 (fn 13–15).

V. Conclusion

Though EU regulation of immigration detention may, in some cases, be modest, it is important to understand that these legal instruments include many important safeguards with which the Member States are obliged to comply.[120] These safeguards penetrate national legal orders and can raise standards in many Member States. Equally, they may serve to lower standards in Member States that previously provided higher levels of protection. This has been seen, for example, in Member States that increased their detention maximums after the Return Directive entered into force.[121]

CJEU jurisprudence on these instruments demonstrates a strong tension between safeguarding fundamental rights and promoting the effectiveness of EU legislation. The Court is the guardian of the Treaties and EU legislation. It therefore makes sense that the Court has to balance these competing interests when it interprets EU law. Effectiveness as an interpretive aid is not all good or all bad, however. The judgments discussed above illustrate how the principle has the potential to harm or to help immigration detainees.

Despite some stumbles, I suggest that, on the whole, the EU is making a positive contribution to asylum and migration frameworks in the Member States. If one were to keep score based on who, between the Member States and the CJEU, was making more positive strides in this field, the CJEU would be slightly ahead. For example, in *Al Chodor*, the Court condemned Hungary's failure to provide clear, objective legislative criteria to assess the risk of absconding, citing the rule of law as the basis for this requirement. Now we see this requirement in the proposal for a recast Return Directive, which is no bad thing. In *Bero and Bouzalmate* and in *Pham*, the Court rejected Germany's use of prisons to hold migrants subject to return and emphasised the link between specialised facilities and human dignity. However, in other cases, the CJEU has not performed as well. For example, although in *Kadzoev* and *Arslan*, the Court highlighted the importance of the maximum period of detention in the Return Directive, it distinguished between the returns regime and the CEAS framework, allowing for the possibility of prolonged detention in cases where individuals subject to return make a genuine application for international protection. And in the cases of *JN* and *K* under the Reception Conditions Directive, in a sense, no one is the winner. At issue in both of these cases were provisions in the RCD allowing for the criminalisation of applicants for international protection through the imposition of detention as a punishment rather than a tool of immigration enforcement. Rather than seizing on an opportunity to prevent Member States from using immigration detention in

[120] G Cornelisse, 'Case Note Case C 357/09 PPU, Proceedings Concerning Said Shamilovich Kadzoev (Huchbarov) Judgment of the Court (Grand Chamber) of 30 November 2009' (2011) 48 *Common Market Law Review* 3.

[121] European Commission Directorate General for Home Affairs Evaluation on the Application of the Return Directive (2008/115/EC), 22 October 2013, 45.

this way, the Court endorsed the provisions based on the principle of effectiveness. These judgments do not improve the situation for migrants at the national level.

A comparison of the use of detention in the context of returns versus asylum yields a small insight, though a true comparison cannot be made for the simple reason that there have been fewer cases under the asylum framework relating to detention. Leaving that aside, it seems as though the CJEU has been more willing to criticise Member State implementation of the Return Directive and offer fundamental rights interpretations of its provisions than it has in relation to the Member State practice under the Dublin III Regulation and the RCD. As discussed above, the Court's decisions in *JN* and *K* are examples of significant failures of the Court to limit the use of detention. However, the main criticism I have of the Court's approach to these two regimes is its strict separation of the two as manifested by the Court's unwillingness to count time spent in detention pending a decision on international protection in the maximum detention period set forth in the Return Directive. Logically, its approach is understandable – yes, they are two separate regimes and only one of them provides for a maximum period of detention. But it is difficult to understand, especially after the language used in *Kadzoev* when the Court discussed the aim and purpose of having a maximum, how the Court could then turn around and discount asylum-related detention in the tally.

Though there may be disagreement about the appropriateness or adequacy of EU regulation of detention, in my view, it is ultimately better that the EU has tried to provide clear legislative standards for use in all the Member States. The CJEU may get things wrong from time-to-time, but there is room for positive evolution. This is also true in the context of legislative development. We have seen this in practice, especially in the evolution of the RCD. By contrast, we are currently seeing an example of retrograde progress with the proposed recast Return Directive. In any case, it is clear from proposals to recast some of this legislation that the EU is not finished with these instruments and that standards will continue to evolve.[122] The CJEU will undoubtedly continue to think deeply about these instruments, strive to strike a fair balance between their effective application and respect for fundamental rights, and seek to set clear standards for the Member States. These endeavours should be applauded and encouraged, but also guided by scholarly thinking and civil society participation.

[122] See the 2016 proposal for another recast version of the Reception Conditions Directive, above n 51, the 2017 proposal for a Dublin IV, above n 26, and the 2018 proposal for a recast Return Directive, above n 107.

PART III

Who is to Blame? Smuggling, Humanitarian Assistance and Human Rights Violations in the Mediterranean Area

11

Is that a Smuggler?

The Blurring Line between Facilitating Illegal Immigration and Providing Humanitarian Assistance at the European Borders

STEFANO ZIRULIA*

I. Introduction

Reducing illegal immigration by fighting the smuggling of migrants has been one of the main objectives of European border control policies for the five-year period 2015–2020.[1] However, the anti-smuggling measures introduced so far by the European institutions and the Member States, especially in the area of criminal law enforcement, not only have proved inadequate for the purpose,[2] but also – as detailed below – have caused serious collateral damage, characterised by the violation of migrants' fundamental rights and the persons assisting them. Against this backdrop, this chapter focuses in particular on the issue of overcriminalising conduct that, albeit driven by humanitarian purposes, has the effect of facilitating

* The research for this work began in Fall 2018 at the University of Lund, in the context of the LERU Exchange Program for visiting scholars. I am grateful to Christoffer Wong, Vladislava Stoyanova and other Lund's scholars for those inspiring discussions, and for the kind hospitality as well. A first draft of this chapter was presented at the conference 'Managing Migration Through Criminal Law Tools', held at the University of Milano on 3–4 December 2018. My sincere thanks are also due to Valsamis Mitsilegas for his invaluable advice during the drafting of this work.

[1] EU Commission, *EU Action Plan against migrant smuggling (2015–2020)*, COM(2015) 285 final, Brussels, 27.5.2015: 'This first EU Action Plan sets out concrete actions to counter and prevent migrant smuggling … The Action Plan should be seen in the broader context of EU efforts to address the root causes of irregular migration, in cooperation with countries of origin and transit, and prevent the loss of lives caused by smugglers and traffickers' (p 2).

[2] On the multiple weaknesses of the current European system against the smuggling of migrants, see L Achilli and G Sanchez, *What Does It Mean to Disrupt the Business Models of People Smugglers?* (Policy Brief, European University Institute, Issue 2017/09); S Carrera, V Mitsilegas, J Allsopp and L Vosyliūtė, *Policing Humanitarianism. EU Policies Against Human Smuggling and their Impact on Civil Society* (Oxford, Hart Publishing, 2019) 24–54 (especially 42).

the crossing of borders, external or internal to the European Union, by undocumented migrants and asylum-seekers.[3]

On closer inspection, in the Action Plan against migrant smuggling of 2015, the European Commission had already pointed out the need to revise the existing EU legal framework to tackle migrant smuggling with a view to achieving a twofold outcome: 'to ensure that appropriate criminal sanctions are in place while avoiding risks of criminalisation of those who provide humanitarian assistance to migrants in distress'.[4] In 2017, however, the Commission itself took a step back, stating on the contrary that 'at this point in time the Facilitators Package should be maintained in its present form, while the Commission further pursues the implementation of the Action Plan against migrant smuggling, in cooperation with all relevant actors'.[5] As the following analysis shows, the arguments put forward by the Commission in support of this conclusion lend themselves to a number of critical remarks, also taking into account the widespread criminalisation of humanitarian activities throughout Europe, with an alarming escalation that began with the 2015 'refugee crisis'.[6]

First, this chapter analyses the European obligations to criminalise facilitating unauthorised entry and transit of undocumented migrants within the Union and the implementation of these criminalisation obligations in the Member States (section II and III, respectively). The focus will then shift to case law regarding 'criminalisation of solidarity', considering both sea and land borders (section IV). Next, following the illustration of the main critical issues found in the Facilitators package (section V), some possible alternatives will be presented, on the whole aimed at outlining the criminal-law construct of smuggling to conduct not limited to facilitating the entry or transit of undocumented migrants, but rather aimed at obtaining an unfair profit, exploiting to one's own advantage the vulnerability inherent in an 'illegal' status. This result is to be achieved either through a reform of the Facilitators package (section VI), or – lacking the political will to do so – by means of judicial remedies (section VII).

[3] Although this distinction is generally accepted, it is important to keep in mind that a clear line between the category of undocumented migrants (i.e., those who migrate with the primary motive of improving their economic perspectives or to join members of their family) and that of asylum-seekers (those who seek protection from conflicts, persecutions and other risks) cannot always be drawn: indeed, as the United Nation Office on Drugs and Crime (UNODC) recently pointed out, the desire to migrate 'stems from a combination of different political, security and/or socio-economic needs where migration is perceived as a viable path to live in larger freedom from fear and poverty' (UNODC, *Global Study on Smuggling of Migrants* (2018) 37).

[4] EU Commission, *EU Action Plan against migrant smuggling (2015–2020)*, above n 1, 3.

[5] EU Commission, *Staff Working Document – REFIT Evaluation of the EU legal framework against facilitation of unauthorised entry, transit and residence: the Facilitators Package (Directive 2002/90/EC and Framework Decision 2002/946/JHA)*, SWD(2017) 117 final, Brussels, 22.3.2017, 37.

[6] L Vosyliūtė and C Conte, *Crackdown on NGOs and volunteers helping refugees and other migrants* (ReSOMA report, June 2019) 23.

II. The European Obligations to Criminalise the Facilitation of Illegal Immigration ('Facilitators Package')

The obligation for the Member States of the European Union to strike down with criminal penalties the facilitation of irregular immigration derives from the combination of provisions under Directive 2002/90/EC[7] and Framework Decision 2002/946/JHA,[8] according to the double-text approach in use before 2005.[9] These provisions, which as a whole outline the 'Facilitators package',[10] apply to all Member States (with the exception of Ireland and, even before Brexit, the United Kingdom)[11] and non-Member States participating in the Schengen acquis[12] (Iceland, Norway, Switzerland and Liechtenstein).[13]

[7] Council Directive 2002/90/EC, of 28 November 2002, defining the facilitation of unauthorised entry, transit and residence [2002] OJ L 328 (hereinafter Facilitation Directive).

[8] Council Framework Decision, of 28 November 2002, on the strengthening of the penal framework to prevent the facilitation of unauthorised entry, transit and residence [2002] OJ L 328 (hereinafter Facilitation Framework Decision).

[9] The *double-text* (or *cross-reference*) approach was used when, in the run-up to the Court of Justice's ruling of 2005 (Case C-176/03 *Commission v Council* [2005] ECR I-7908), it was still considered that only third pillar instruments (such as Framework Decisions) could provide for incrimination obligations. In this context, illegal behaviour was defined by means of a directive (with the greater binding force characteristic of first-pillar instruments), and the obligation to provide for *criminal* sanctions by means of a framework decision was added.

[10] For a historical and systematic overview of this instrument, see S Carrera, E Guild, A Aliverti, J Allsopp, MG Manieri and M Levoy, *Fit for Purpose? The Facilitation Directive and the Criminalisation of Humanitarian Assistance to Irregular Migrants* (Study Commissioned by the European Parliament's Policy Department for Citizens' Rights and Constitutional Affairs at the Request of the LIBE Committee, 2016) 22–29.

[11] At the time of the adoption of the Facilitators Package, UK and Ireland took part in the adoption and application of both the Facilitation Directive and the Facilitation Framework Decision. However, considering that the Facilitators Package forms part of the Schengen acquis, both UK and Ireland had to be evaluated before implementing the relevant provisions according to Council Regulation (EU) 1053/2013 of 7 October 2013 establishing an evaluation and monitoring mechanism to verify the application of the Schengen acquis and repealing the Decision of the Executive Committee of 16 September 1998 setting up a Standing Committee on the evaluation and implementation of Schengen [2013] OJ L 295. In the case of the UK, the procedure was completed in 2004; subsequently, UK chose to opt-out of the Facilitation Framework Decision with effect from 1 December 2014. In the case of Ireland, the evaluation procedure has not been completed and therefore the package does not apply to that country yet.

[12] The obligation to penalise the facilitation of illegal immigration was originally introduced in order to counterbalance free movement within the European area by tightening external border controls. To this end, Article 27 of the Schengen Convention (Convention implementing the Schengen Agreement of 14 June 1985 between the Governments of the States of the Benelux Economic Union, the Federal Republic of Germany and the French Republic on the gradual abolition of checks at their common borders [1985] OJ L 239): 'The Contracting Parties undertake to impose appropriate penalties on any person who, for financial gain, assists or tries to assist an alien to enter or reside within the territory of one of the Contracting Parties in violation of that Contracting Party's laws on the entry and residence of aliens'.

[13] On the territorial application of the Facilitators package see also the summary *EU measures to prevent the facilitation of illegal immigration*, www.eur-lex.europa.eu (last update 11 February 2019).

The Directive first and foremost requires States to adopt 'appropriate sanctions' against anyone facilitating the entry or transit of foreigners into the territory of a Member State in violation of the relevant immigration legislation.[14] The scope of illegality is expressly extended to cases of incitement, complicity, as well as attempted offences.[15] It is worth noting that 'profit', in exchange for facilitation, is not envisaged as an element making up the offence. In fact, unlike other international tools fighting the smuggling of migrants,[16] the European legislation identifies profit only as an element making up the offence of facilitating an illegal stay,[17] and not instead entry and transit.

The Framework Decision, in turn, provides that the unlawful conduct identified by the Directive shall be sanctioned by penalties that are necessarily criminal in nature.[18] The choices regarding the type, amount and duration of the applicable criminal penalties are left to the States; however, where the conduct is aimed at profit-making, and is also carried out within the framework of a criminal organisation or endangering the lives of migrants, the criminal penalties must be custodial and must be issued for a maximum of no less than eight years of imprisonment.[19]

The European Legislator was aware that such a legislative framework, particularly where it does not provide for profit as an element making up the base criminal

[14] Facilitation Directive, art 1, para 1: 'Each Member State shall adopt appropriate sanctions on (a) any person who intentionally assists a person who is not a national of a Member State to enter, or transit across, the territory of a Member State in violation of the laws of the State concerned on the entry or transit of alien'.

[15] Facilitation Directive, art 2: 'Each Member State shall take the measures necessary to ensure that the sanctions referred to in Article 1 are also applicable to any person who: (a) is the instigator of, (b) is an accomplice in, or (c) attempts to commit an infringement as referred to in Article 1(1)(a) or (b)'.

[16] The reference is to the Schengen Convention (see n 12 above), as well as the Protocol Against the Smuggling of Migrants by Land, Sea and Air, supplementing the United Nations Convention Against Transnational Organized Crime, adopted by the UN General Assembly on 15 November 2000 (Palermo Protocol Against Smuggling). The latter provides for an obligation on the signatory States to criminalise the 'smuggling of migrants' (art 6), to be understood as 'the procurement, in order to obtain, directly or indirectly, a financial or other material benefit, of the illegal entry of a person into a State Party of which the person is not a national or permanent resident' (art 3(a)). The purpose of securing a profit or other material advantage is an element making up the obligation under consideration, the fulfilment of which therefore requires that at least such categories of conduct be punishable; without prejudice to the States retaining discretion to further extend the scope of punishability.

[17] See Facilitation Directive, art 1, para 1(b), requiring Member States to adopt appropriate sanctions on 'any person who, for financial gain, intentionally assists a person who is not a national of a Member State to reside within the territory of a Member State in violation of the laws of the State concerned on the residence of aliens'.

[18] See Facilitation Framework Decision, art 1, para 1: 'Each Member State shall take the measures necessary to ensure that the infringements defined in Articles 1 and 2 of Directive 2002/90/EC are punishable by effective, proportionate and dissuasive criminal penalties which may entail extradition'.

[19] Facilitation Framework Decision, art 1, para 3: 'Each Member State shall take the measures necessary to ensure that, when committed for financial gain, the infringements defined in Article 1(1)(a) and, to the extent relevant, Article 2(a) of Directive 2002/90/EC are punishable by custodial sentences with a maximum sentence of not less than eight years where they are committed in any of the following circumstances: – the offence was committed as an activity of a criminal organisation as defined in Joint Action 98/733/JHA(8), – the offence was committed while endangering the lives of the persons who are the subject of the offence'.

offence of facilitating entry and transit, could have led to the criminalisation of conduct motivated by purely solidarity purposes; the countermeasure adopted was the provision, in the Directive, of the (mere) *possibility* for the Member States of ruling out liability in cases where the facilitation of irregular entry or transit takes place for the purpose of providing humanitarian assistance.[20]

However, as Valsamis Mitsilegas argues in this volume,[21] the scope of these provisions remains too broad, as it imposes upon Member States the obligation to prosecute any form of assistance to what is essentially a violation of administrative immigration law, without requiring at the same to take into account the aim pursued by the facilitator, thus paving the way for the sacrifice of migrants' fundamental rights, beginning from the right to seek asylum.

III. The Implementation of the Facilitators Package by the Member States

The European Commission never initiated any infringement proceedings against EU Member States for failure to implement or partial implementation of the Facilitators package.[22] Indeed, existing criminal law provisions cover a wide spectrum of conduct, basically any conduct likely to facilitate the illegal entry or transit of undocumented migrants,[23] including mere attempts.[24] Some States also issued special provisions for the conduct of falsifying documents or organising marriages of convenience, cases which elsewhere fall within the general case of aiding and abetting or within the framework of the rules on falsification. The extent of the penalties varies a great deal. On the basis of the data collected by the Commission in 2017,[25] some States provide for a custodial sentence or a fine[26] as alternative penalties; other States provide for the possibility of applying them

[20] Facilitation Directive, art 1, para 2: 'Any Member State may decide not to impose sanctions with regard to the behaviour defined in paragraph 1(a) by applying its national law and practice for cases where the aim of the behaviour is to provide humanitarian assistance to the person concerned'.

[21] See the chapter by V Mitsilegas 'The Criminalisation of Migration in the Law of the European Union. Challenging the Preventive Paradigm', in this volume. See also V Mitsilegas, 'The Normative Foundations of the Criminalisation of Human Smuggling. Exploring the Fault Lines between European and International Law' (2019) 10 *New Journal of European Criminal Law* 68; V Mitsilegas, *The Criminalisation of Migration in Europe. Challenges for Human Rights and the Rule of Law* (Cham, Springer, 2015).

[22] EU Commission, *Staff Working Document – REFIT Evaluation* (2017), above n 5, 13–14.

[23] According to the European Commission, the only critical point is the Slovenian legislation, which makes punishability conditional on repeated conduct (ibid, p 14).

[24] The Commission also notes that there are (unspecified) criticalities with regard to the regulations of Belgium, Germany, Finland, Croatia and Romania (ibid, p 15).

[25] EU Commission, *Staff Working Document – REFIT Evaluation* (2017), above n 5, 84–87.

[26] Germany, Estonia, Spain, Finland, Lithuania, Netherlands, Sweden.

both alternatively and cumulatively;[27] other States provide for a custodial sentence alone;[28] finally, other States provide for the two types of penalty cumulatively.[29] As for the length of prison sentences, they range from countries with sentences of up to one year (Belgium, Spain) to countries with sentences of up to eight or 10 years (Bulgaria, Cyprus, Greece, Ireland, Poland), passing through an intermediate range of countries with maximum sentences of between two and seven years.

Contrary to what some reports state,[30] no Member State includes profit-making among the elements making up facilitation of illegal entry, a choice which, in addition, would be incompatible, as we have seen, with European obligations. Exceptions can be found in Ireland[31] (which, however, is not bound by the Facilitators package); and in England[32] (yet, even before Brexit, this is a country that had exercised the opt-out from the Framework Decision).

Only a few Member States have exercised the option granted by Article 1(2) of the Directive through the adoption of ad hoc clauses excluding criminal liability for humanitarian conduct facilitating illegal entry or transit. The broadest formulations are found in Belgian[33] and Spanish[34] legislation, excluding punishability whenever a humanitarian purpose is sought (albeit such purpose shall be 'exclusive' in Spain and only 'prevailing' in Belgium). Intermediate solutions also exist, characterised by exemptions with different scopes of application: Finland considers conduct carried out for humanitarian or family solidarity purposes lawful, also taking into account the security conditions in the migrant's country of origin;[35]

[27] Belgium, Cyprus, Ireland, Luxembourg, Malta, United Kingdom.

[28] Austria, Hungary, Latvia, Poland, Portugal, Romania, Slovakia.

[29] Bulgaria, Greece, France, Croatia, Italy, Slovenia.

[30] For example, a report issued by the European Union Agency for Fundamental Rights (FRA, *Criminalisation of Migrants in an Irregular Situation and of Persons Engaging with Them*, 2014), much cited by subsequent informative and academic writings, wrongly states that 'In Germany, Ireland, Luxembourg and Portugal alone does the law expressly require that facilitation is punishable only if proven to be for profit or gain' (p 9). This statement is only correct for Ireland, which is not bound by the Facilitators package.

[31] See Illegal Immigrants (Trafficking) Act, 2000 (as amended), Sec 2(2), providing that the offence of facilitating illegal entry into the State 'shall not apply (a) to anything done by a person otherwise than for gain, or (b) to anything done to assist a person seeking asylum by a person in the course of his or her employment by a bona fide organisation if the purposes of that organisation include giving assistance to persons seeking asylum'.

[32] See Immigration Act 1971 (as amended), Sec 25(A)(1)(a) and (A)(3), providing that the facilitation of asylum-seekers' entry shall be punished only where committed 'for gain'; moreover, no penalty shall be imposed upon 'a person acting on behalf of an organisation which aims to assist asylum-seekers, and does not charge for its services'.

[33] Loi sur l'accès au territoire, le séjour, l'établissement et l'éloignement des étrangers (Belgian Immigration Law), art 77, para 2. This provision, referring to para 1, which makes it an offence to facilitate entry, stay and transit, establishes: 'L'alinéa 1er ne s'applique pas si'aide est offerte pour des raisons principalement humanitaires'.

[34] Código penal (Criminal Code of Spain), art 318-bis, para 2. This provision, referring to entry or transit facilitation conduct, provides that: 'Los hechos no seran punibles cuando el objetivo perseguido por el autor fuere unicamente prestar ayuda humanitaria a la persona de que se trate'.

[35] Rikoslaki (Criminal Code of Finland), Ch 17, Sec 8, para 2: 'An act which, when taking into account in particular the humanitarian motives of the person committing it or his or her motives relating to close family relations, and the circumstances pertaining to the safety of the foreigner in his

in Greece, the carrier who has transported to State territory persons rescued at sea and requiring international protection is not punishable;[36] Malta's legislation states that 'the principal immigration officer may decide not to institute proceedings on any person who aids or assists any other person in any immediate situation of danger to land or attempt to land or transit through Malta, when such acts have been committed with a view to providing humanitarian assistance';[37] in France, the humanitarian exemption was initially reserved for the facilitation of illegal *stay*, but in 2018 it was extended to facilitating *transit* following the judgment of the Conseil Constitutionnel in the *Cédric Herrou* case;[38] finally, in Italy only humanitarian conduct in favour of undocumented migrants already present on national territory is considered lawful.[39]

IV. Case Studies on the Criminalisation of Assistance and Rescue Activities

On the basis of the rules implementing the Facilitators package in the Member States, bringing (or even attempting to bring) undocumented third-country nationals across both the EU's external borders and internal borders has been the object of various policing measures, even when the aim pursued was solidarity-based.[40] The concept of criminalisation of humanitarian assistance activities is generally

or her home country or country of permanent residence, and when assessed as a whole, is to be deemed committed under vindicating circumstances, does not constitute arrangement of illegal immigration' (translation provided by the Finnish Ministry of Justice: www.finlex.fi/en).

[36] Law No 3386/2005, art 30, para 6: 'The above penalties shall not be imposed in case of rescue of people at sea and in case of carriage of people in need of international protection, as dictated by the international maritime law' (unofficial translation available on the European Database of Asylum Law: www.refworld.org).

[37] Laws of Malta, Ch. 217, Immigration Act, art 32.

[38] Code de l'entrée et du séjour des étrangers et du droit d'asile (CESEDA) (French Immigration and Asylum Law), art L 622-4: 'l'aide à la circulation ou au séjour irréguliers d'un étranger lorsqu'elle est le fait [on behalf of a family member etc.] ou toute autre aide apportée dans un but exclusivement humanitaire'. On the judgment of the Conseil Constitutionnel, see section VII.B. below.

[39] Legislative Decree No 286 of 1998 (hereinafter, Italian Consolidated Law on Immigration), art 12, para 2, provides that 'aid and humanitarian assistance carried out in Italy towards aliens in state of need, however present on the State's territory, do not constitute crime' (unofficial translation available on the European Database of Asylum Law: www.refworld.org). Therefore, this exemption is only applicable to the facilitation of transit and (theoretically) illegal stay (the latter hypothesis, however, requires the intent of *unfair* profit, which is incompatible with the humanitarian purpose).

[40] Among the most up-to-date case studies on the subject, see S Carrera, L Vosyliūtė, S Smialowski, J Allsopp and G Sanchez, *Fit for Purpose? The Facilitation Directive and the Criminalisation of Humanitarian Assistance to Irregular Migrants: 2018 Update* (Study Requested by the PETI committee, European Parliament, 2018) 59–87; Vosyliūtė and Conte, above n 6, 19–31; Expert Council on NGO Law, *Using Criminal Law to Restrict the Work of NGOs Supporting Refugees and Other Migrants in Council of Europe Member States* (2019). For an in-depth account of the development of criminalisation narratives and practices over the period 2015–17, see J Allsopp, 'Solidarity, Smuggling and the European Refugee Crisis: Civil Society and its Discontents' (2017) 3 *Diritto, immigrazione e cittadinanza* 1.

used to refer to wholly distinct situations, ranging from intimidation by the police to convictions for facilitating illegal immigration or other related offences,[41] as well as a series of intermediate situations including arrests, investigations, kidnappings.[42] The focus here will be on the hypotheses in which formal prosecution has been at least initiated by national judicial authorities under offences implementing the prohibition against facilitating illegal entry or transit of migrants. According to a report that took into account the period from the beginning of the refugee crisis in 2015 until April 2019, such cases were recorded in 11 Member States: mainly Italy, France and Greece; and, to a lesser extent, Belgium, Croatia, Denmark, Germany, the Netherlands, Spain, Sweden and the United Kingdom.[43] The investigated persons include members of NGOs, volunteers, activists and ordinary people, migrants' families, journalists, religious and even the mayor of an Italian municipality (Riace). So far, at least 15 convictions have been handed down, with sentences that vary greatly in type and severity (from fines to imprisonment for several years).

A. The Criminalisation of Rescue at Sea Along the Central Mediterranean Route

When humanitarian assistance is provided to migrants attempting to cross the Mediterranean Sea, national criminal law rules are intertwined with international maritime law, in particular with the rules requiring coastal States and ship masters to render assistance to distressed persons and to transfer them to a place of safety (often referred to as POS) within a reasonable window of time.[44] Prior to 2015, the case study on the subject was that relating to the ship *Cap Anamur*, in which the captain of a humanitarian vessel, accused of facilitating illegal entry for having transported 37 nationals from non-Member States rescued in international waters

[41] Indeed, civil society actors have been investigated or prosecuted not only for facilitating illegal immigration, but also for terrorism related-offences, money laundering and even environmental crimes with regard to the disposal of waste from rescue missions: see Expert Council on NGO Law, *Using Criminal Law to Restrict the Work of NGOs* (2019), above n 40, 27.

[42] This broad notion of 'policing' humanitarian activities is adopted by Carrera, Mitsilegas, Allsopp and Vosyliūtė, above n 2, 5.

[43] Vosyliūtė and Conte, above n 6, 23.

[44] These are, principally, Article 98 of the Montego Bay Convention on the maritime law (UNCLOS, 1982); Regulation No 33(1) of Chapter V of the Annex to the International Convention for the Safety of Life at Sea (Conv. SOLAS, 1974); Chapters 1.3.2. and 2.1.10 of the Annex to the International Convention on Maritime Search and Rescue (Conv. SAR, 1979). For an analysis of the complex web of international regulations behind the concept of 'duty to save life at sea', see F De Vittor and M Starita, 'Distributing Responsibility between Shipmasters and the Different States Involved in SAR Disasters' (2018) XXVIII *Italian Yearbook of International Law* 77, 77–95; with specific reference to search and rescue operations carried out by NGOs in the Mediterranean, see Council of Europe Commissioner for Human Rights, *Lives Saved. Rights Protected. Bridging the Protection Gap for Refugees and Migrants in the Mediterranean* (Recommendation 2019).

to Italy, was acquitted by the Court of Agrigento for having acted in accordance with the duty of rescue.[45] Beginning from 2016, after the end of the Mare Nostrum operation, some NGOs are trying to fill the protection gap left by the States;[46] since then, the transport of rescued migrants to the European territory led to the opening of investigations against the crews, many of them in Italy.[47]

The first in chronological order has been the case of the ship *Iuventa*, flying the Dutch flag and owned by the German NGO Jugend Rettet, which at the time of writing is still under seizure for the crime of facilitating illegal entry (Article 12 of the Italian Consolidated Law on Immigration)[48] according to a decree issued in 2017 by the Judge for Preliminary Investigations (Giudice per le Indagini Preliminari, GIP) of Trapani.[49] The particularity of this case is that, according to the public prosecutor, migrants from Libya were not rescued, but rather were the subject of 'agreed handovers' between the traffickers and crew members of the NGO, in different occasions in 2016 and 2017.[50] For this reason, according to the GIP, the legal justification for the fulfilment of the duty of rescue at sea, enshrined in the International Conventions on maritime law, could not be invoked. From this viewpoint, the crew of the *Iuventa* did not simply lend assistance – supposedly – to

[45] Tribunale di Agrigento, 7 October 2009 (hearing), 15 February 2010 (deposit). The Court found that the commander had correctly assessed the factual situation and acted in accordance with international law, in particular by excluding Libya as a place of safety and consequently heading towards Italy, since it was the closest POS to the salvaging location.

[46] From October 2013 to October 2014, the search and rescue operation Mare Nostrum rescued over 100,000 shipwrecked people. It was replaced by Operation Triton, led by EU's border agency Frontex, which deployed fewer vessels, much further from Libya (where most shipwrecks occur) and whose priority was border surveillance rather than search and rescue. In July 2015, the EU naval force (EUNAVFOR MED) was launched: under the name of Operation Sophia, it conducted anti-smuggling operations leading to the arrest of smugglers and destruction of vessels. Search and rescue missions were thus mainly left to the NGOs, such as Save the Children, Médecins Sans Frontières and smaller ones (Jugen Rettet, Proactiva Open Arms, Sea Watch, Mediterranea etc). For more details on operation EUNAVFOR MED-Sophia, see S Carrera, S Blockmans, JP Cassarino, D Gros D and E Guild, *The European Border and Coast Guard. Addressing Migration and Asylum Challenges in the Mediterranean?* (CEPS, 2017) 31–37; E Cusumano, 'Migrant Rescue as Organized Hypocrisy: EU Maritime Missions Offshore Libya between Humanitarianism and Border Control' (2019) 54 *Cooperation and Conflict* 3.

[47] On case law concerning policing civil society conducting SAR activities, see European Union Agency for Fundamental Rights, *NGO Ships Involved in Search and Rescue in the Mediterranean and Criminal Investigations – 2019 update* (2019); Carrera, Mitsilegas, Allsopp and Vosyliūtė, above n 2, 104–15.

[48] The scope of the offence is very broad as it encompasses, inter alia, any intentional act directed to procure the entry of a third-country national into the State's territory, or into the territory of another State, in breach of the laws of the State concerned on the entry or transit of aliens. Conversely, the 'humanitarian clause' provided for this offence has a very narrow scope (see n 39 above). For a recent comprehensive analysis, see A Spena, 'Migrant Smuggling: A Normative and Phenomenological View from Italy' in V Militello and A Spena (eds), *Between Criminalisation and Protection. The Italian Way of Dealing with Migrant Smuggling and Trafficking within the European and International Context* (Leiden, Brill, 2019) 5, 5–41.

[49] Tribunale di Trapani, Ufficio GIP, 2 August 2017 (www.questionegiustizia.it, 18 September 2017).

[50] The evidence file consists of photographic documents and wiretaps, as well as the report of an undercover agent. An interesting counter-investigation of the authorities' version is provided by Forensic Oceanography and Forensic Architecture in their study on the *Iuventa* case (www.blamingtherescuers.org/iuventa).

persons in danger, but participated in activities designed to secure the entry into Italy of undocumented migrants who did not have title to do so lawfully. The findings of the GIP were confirmed during the review and before the Italian Supreme Court, which, however, ruled on procedural matters alone.[51]

A second significant case involves the crew of the *Open Arms* ship, flying the Spanish flag and belonging to the NGO Proactiva Open Arms, based in Barcelona. On 15 March 2018, three overcrowded dinghies had been sighted in Libyan SAR waters. Given that the Libyan Coast Guard had formally taken charge of the rescue operations, the Italian Coast Guard had ordered the NGO not to intervene. The order was based on the 'Code of conduct for NGOs undertaking activities in migrants' rescue operations at sea', drawn up by the Italian Government (with the support of EU Interior Ministers meeting in Tallinn on 6 July 2017) to prevent NGO activities from feeding new corridors of illegal immigration.[52] Although Proactiva Open Arms (unlike Jugend Rettet) had signed the code, in this case the crew had disregarded the order and carried out the rescue of over two hundred people, having arrived before the Libyans at the scene of the incident. The following day, once arrived near the coast of Malta, Open Arms had handed over to the authorities of that State two people whose lives were in danger, but had not followed the instructions given by the Italian Coast Guard (and also by the Spanish Coast Guard, which intervened because of the flag), according to which the Maltese should have been asked for permission to disembark the other passengers too. On the contrary, the NGO had sailed onwards to the Italian coast on its own initiative, where it was finally authorised to dock at Pozzallo. The Catania Preliminary Investigations Judge[53] had initially ordered the seizure of the ship due to it having facilitated illegal entry, ruling out the justification of the duty of rescue at sea, in view of the violation of the Code of Conduct, defined by the same judge as an 'appendix' to the supranational law of the sea. Furthermore, the presence of Libyan patrol boats excluded, from the judge's viewpoint, the inevitability of danger, which is a requirement of 'necessity' under the Italian penal code.

The same GIP of Catania, however, ruled out the existence of a criminal organisation (falling within its remit as district judge), with the consequence that

[51] Corte di Cassazione, Prima Sezione Penale, 23 April 2018 (judgment issuing), 13 December 2018 (judgment release), No 56138 (www.italgiure.giustizia.it/sncass). The judgment concerns jurisdiction, the applicability of Italian criminal law, the protection of the third-party owner of the seized ship.

[52] The Code provides, inter alia, that subscribing NGOs undertake commitments such as: 'not to enter Libyan territorial waters, except in situations of grave and imminent danger requiring immediate assistance and not to obstruct search and rescue by the Libyan Coast Guard …; not to make communications or send light signals to facilitate the departure and embarkation of vessels carrying migrants …; commitment to cooperate with the competent MRCC, executing its instructions and informing it in advance of any initiative undertaken independently because it is deemed necessary and urgent; commitment to receive on board … judicial police officers for information and evidence gathering with a view to conducting investigations related to migrant smuggling …'. For an overview of this document see E Cusumano, 'Straightjacketing Migrant Rescuers? The Code of Conduct on Maritime NGOs' (2017) 24 *Mediterranean Politics* 106.

[53] Tribunale di Catania, Ufficio GIP, 27 March 2018 (www.questionegiustizia.it, 31 March 2018).

territorial remit for the criminal offence of facilitating illegal entry alone passed to the GIP of Ragusa.[54] The latter also denied that fulfilling the duty of rescue justified the conduct held in the case at hand, but for a different reason, namely because the dinghies, albeit overloaded, were in a good state of buoyancy and the weather conditions were stable; there was, therefore, no imminent danger of shipwreck. The same judge, however, considered that the *Open Arms* crew had acted in a state of necessity, to remove the migrants from the danger of being intercepted by the Libyan Coast Guard and taken back to a country where, admittedly, no safe ports exist, and indeed migrants are subjected to serious and documented human rights violations.

The legal justification of fulfilling a duty to rescue has been more recently acknowledged in the case of the Dutch-flagged vessel *Sea Watch 3* of the German NGO Sea Watch. The case came into the spotlight for the manoeuvre of forced entry into the port of Lampedusa conducted by Captain Carola Rackete. The Judge for Preliminary Investigations in Agrigento[55] only ruled on the arrest of the vessel's captain for the offence of resisting or obstructing a public officer (Article 337 of the Italian Criminal Code) and resisting a warship (Article 1100 of the Italian Navigation Code), for colliding with an Italian patrol boat while docking in port. However, the captain is also under investigation for facilitating illegal immigration, and some of the arguments developed by the GIP measure potentially extend to such conduct.

Summing up the facts, the migrants had been rescued in the Libyan SAR area on 12 June 2019, as the *Sea Watch 3* vessel had arrived at the site of the event before the Tripoli Coast Guard (which had formally taken over coordinating the rescue). The dinghy at the scene was in a precarious condition, no one on board was wearing a life jacket and the fuel level was not high enough to reach any place. Once the rescue was completed, the captain requested the assignment of a POS to several maritime authorities, receiving a response from Libyans indicating Tripoli. Rackete replied that Libya could not qualify as a safe port and asked for an alternative POS; in the meantime, she headed north in the direction of the nearest POSs, i.e., Italian and Maltese ports, repeating her request to dock. On 15 June the Italian Minister of the Interior ordered an entry ban on *Sea Watch 3* as implementation of the Decreto Sicurezza-bis, which had just come into force.[56]

[54] Tribunale di Ragusa, Ufficio GIP, 16 April 2018 (www.questionegiustizia.it, 19 April 2018).

[55] Tribunale di Agrigento, Ufficio GIP, 2 July 2019 (www.penalecontemporaneo.it, 3 July 2019).

[56] Legislative Decree No 53 of 2019 (so called *Decreto Sicurezza-bis*) introduced two fundamental amendments to the Italian Consolidated Law on Immigration. First of all, by introducing paragraph 1-*ter* into Article 11, it conferred on the Minister of the Interior – in agreement with the Ministers of Defence and Transport, and having informed the Prime Minister – the power to issue measures aimed at prohibiting or restricting entry, transit or stay in territorial waters of ships (excluding military or non-commercial government service), where at least one of the following conditions is met: i) 'reasons of public order and security'; ii) 'fulfilment of the conditions set out in Article 19, paragraph 2, lett (g) of the UNCLOS Convention', a rule which in turn identifies, as a hypothesis of non-inoffensive (or 'prejudicial') passage of a foreign ship into territorial waters, the case in which such a ship carries out 'the loading or unloading of … persons in violation of the immigration laws

In the following days, the ship was stationed close to Italian territorial waters, forwarding medical reports on the health situation on board, and reiterating the POS request. Two subsequent evacuations of persons in need of medical treatment were carried out. On 26 June the *Sea Watch 3* entered Italian waters and headed towards Lampedusa, disregarding the halt of the Guardia di Finanza patrol boats and invoking the state of necessity; it stopped near the Port waiting for instructions on where to moor. This further stalemate lasted for a few days, during which the ship was searched by the border police. On the night of 29 June – having ascertained that a political solution was nowhere in sight, that the interim measures sought before the Regional Administrative Court of Lazio and the European Court of Human Rights had not been successful, and that one of the doctors on board had said that people's reactions were no longer predictable – the captain of *Sea Watch 3* started the engines and headed for the commercial quay in the port of Lampedusa; during the docking operation, she bumped into a Guardia di Finanza patrol boat acting as border police on that stretch. In relation to such conduct, as mentioned above, Rackete was arrested for the offences of resisting or obstructing a public officer (Article 337 of the Italian Criminal Code) and resisting a warship (Article 1100 of the Italian Navigation Code).

However, the GIP of Agrigento rejected the requests of the Public Prosecutor's Office to validate the arrest and apply the precautionary measure of prohibition to reside in the province. The GIP recognised on the one hand that States are free to regulate entry flows into their territories (Article 19 of the UNCLOS Convention);[57] on the other hand, it stressed that this power is limited by the duty to provide first aid to ships in distress and rescue shipwrecked persons (Article 18 of the same Convention). With regard to the latter, the judge stressed that all coastal States must cooperate to ensure that rescue operations are completed (SAR Convention), as quickly as possible, by taking the shipwrecked persons on board and conducting them to a safe port. This duty of rescue concerns not only States but also ship masters (Article 98 UNCLOS Convention): it follows – here the findings are ideally linked with those of the *Cap Anamur* case – that the final segment of the suspect's conduct, for which Captain Rackete has been charged for the offence of resisting or obstructing a public officer, is also the result of fulfilling the duty of rescue.

in force in the coastal State'. The wording reproduces at legislative level the contents of the ministerial instructions which in the previous months had been issued by the Italian Minister of the Interior within the 'closed ports' policy. Second, the *Decreto Sicurezza-bis* introduced paragraph 6-*bis* into art 12 of the Italian Consolidated Immigration Law, which provides, in case of violation of the prohibition against entering territorial waters, an administrative fine between EUR 10,000 and 50,000, as well as the confiscation of the vessel in case of repeated conduct. The law converting the decree (Law No 77 of 8 August 2019) significantly increased the fine (which now ranges between EUR 150,000 and 1 million) and provided for confiscation to be applied following the first violation, with immediate seizure.

[57] This provision, as recalled (see previous fn), acknowledges that the States may prohibit harmful passage, including disembarking persons in violation of national immigration rules.

The appeal lodged by the Public Prosecutor against the decision of the GIP of Agrigento has been eventually rejected by the Court of Cassation in January 2020.[58] For the first time in Italy, a high criminal court has expressly stated that the duty to rescue shipwrecked people does not end with their transfer on board the assisting ship, as it encompasses the accessory obligation upon the Capitan to disembark them in a 'place of safety'. The principle follows from point No 3.1.9 of the Annex of the SAR Convention,[59] under which the Contracting Parties are obliged to cooperate with each other to promptly determine a safe place where people may be accompanied. With regard to the notion of 'place of safety', the Court has noted that the SAR Convention itself refers to the 'Guidelines on the Treatment of Persons Rescued at Sea' adopted by the Maritime Safety Committee of the International Maritime Organisation, according to which:[60]

> A place of safety (as referred to in the Annex to the 1979 SAR Convention, paragraph 1.3.2) is a location where rescue operations are considered to terminate. It is also a place where the survivors' safety of life is no longer threatened and where their basic human needs (such as food, shelter and medical needs) can be met … Even if the [assisting] ship is capable of safely accommodating the survivors and may serve as a temporary place of safety, it should be relieved of this responsibility as soon as alternative arrangements can be made.[61]

In the light of these provisions, the Court of Cassation not only has confirmed the decision of the judge of Agrigento (which had denied the Libyan territory the status of POS), but has also stated, as a matter of law, that the assisting vessel cannot be considered a final POS. In support of this conclusion, the Court of Cassation has also referred to the 1951 Geneva Convention, stating that the right to apply for international protection cannot be exercised on board the ship; as well as to Resolution of the Parliamentary Assembly of the Council of Europe on 'The interception and rescue at sea of asylum seekers, refugees and irregular migrants',[62] according to which 'it is clear that the notion of "place of safety" should not be

[58] Corte di Cassazione, Terza Sezione Penale, 16 January 2020 (judgment issuing), 20 February 2020 (judgment release), No 6626 (www.sistemapenale.it, 24 February 2020). On this judgment, see also S Zirulia, 'La Cassazione sul caso Sea Watch: le motivazioni sull'illegittimità dell'arresto di Carola Rackete' (www.sistemapenale.it, 24 February 2020).

[59] This provision was introduced by the 2004 amendments to the Annex of the SAR Convention, aimed at enhancing the cooperation between States. It reads as follows: 'Parties shall co-ordinate and co-operate to ensure that masters of ships providing assistance by embarking persons in distress at sea are released from their obligations with minimum further deviation from the ships' intended voyage, provided that releasing the master of the ship from these obligations does not further endanger the safety of life at sea. The Party responsible for the search and rescue region in which such assistance is rendered shall exercise primary responsibility for ensuring such co-ordination and co-operation occurs, so that survivors assisted are disembarked from the assisting ship and delivered to a place of safety, taking into account the particular circumstances of the case and guidelines developed by the Organization. In these cases, the relevant Parties shall arrange for such disembarkation to be effected as soon as reasonably practicable'.

[60] Resolution MSC.167(78) of 2004.

[61] No 6.12 and 6.13.

[62] Resolution No 1821 of 21 June 2011.

restricted solely to the physical protection of people, but necessarily also entails respect for their fundamental rights' (no 5.2.), including the right to apply for asylum.

There are at least three reasons why the judgment of the Court of Cassation in the Rackete case could be a turning point in the development of the Italian jurisprudence on the limits between rescue activities and facilitation of irregular immigration. To begin, as already noted, this is the first case in which the Court of Cassation (i.e., the highest Italian jurisdiction on issues of interpretation of the law) has addressed the justification of fulfilment of a duty in the light of the international law of the sea, extending its scope to conducting rescued people to a safe port, even when the identification of the latter does not depend on an assignment by the coastal States (which have often proven reluctant to grant it), but on an assessment of the ship's Captain.[63] Second, the judgment is particularly important because, by establishing the illegality of the arrest, the Court stated that the legitimacy of the Master's conduct was perceptible ex ante by the border authorities, which are trained precisely to deal with rescue operations in accordance with the law of the sea: this finding is likely to prevent future arrests in similar cases and, more fundamentally, the opening of new investigations against NGO members, thus also reducing the chilling effect of rescue activities which unfortunately goes hand in hand with repressive initiatives. Finally, by considering it justified a conduct that consisted in forcing the blockade of entry into territorial waters and hitting a patrol boat that was obstructing the docking manoeuvre, the Court of Cassation assigned a sort of 'right of resistance' to whoever, acting in accordance with the law, opposes the conduct of the public forces that might jeopardise the fundamental rights of persons, including (given the explicit reference to the Geneva Convention) the right to seek asylum.

B. Other Cases of Criminalisation of Humanitarian Assistance

Outside the case studies on rescue at sea, numerous situations occurred in which aid for entry into the European Union, or transit from one Member State to another, was provided for humanitarian reasons. However, whereas migrants trying to cross the Mediterranean Sea aboard unstable and overcrowded boats invariably amounts to distress, thus entailing – as the Court of Agrigento also acknowledged in the *Sea Watch* case – the existence of the duty of rescue and transport to a place of safety, situations likely to occur on land are much more varied and, above all, cannot be placed within a similar framework of topic-specific international conventions.

[63] Remarkably, this is the same position expressed by the Council of Europe Commissioner for Human Rights: see *Lives Saved. Rights Protected. Bridging the Protection Gap for Refugees and Migrants in the Mediterranean* (Recommendation 2019) 29–30.

Here, too, cases where humanitarian assistance may easily be traced back to justifications and exemptions generally accepted in all European systems, certainly exist. For example, if someone travelling in winter over the Alpine passes, at the Italian-French border, comes across a migrant in obvious need because he or she lacks adequate clothing and footwear, or because he or she is lost, or because he or she is an unaccompanied minor, then the duty to help or at least necessity would almost certainly apply.[64] The same logic could arguably be extended to justify the aid given to family members or asylum seekers exposed to imminent risks in their countries of origin.[65]

However, generally applicable legal excuses do not seem as easily applicable outside the above instances. And yet, recent cases emblematically demonstrate how the humanitarian purpose may coexist with situations devoid of any real danger to persons, or at least where the risk is not as imminent as in the cases described so far. Situations of this kind, where aid has been given on the basis of family relationships or pure solidarity, have occurred between the internal borders of the Union, specifically between Italy and France[66] and between France and

[64] 'Traverser la frontière: une nuit avec des migrants qui tentent de fuir l'Italie de Salvini', *Le Monde*, 21 February 2019.

[65] Whereas in some countries, such as England, aid given free of charge to asylum seekers is excluded from the scope of punishment, elsewhere such conduct is often prosecuted. In Greece, for example, the following cases were singled out: 'A French citizen was arrested in August 2015 while trying to smuggle out his Syrian family in Greece. He was sentenced to seven years in prison by the court of first instance and he has now been acquitted by the Greek Tribunal of Patras in March 2019. Two young volunteers are still under investigation on grounds of human smuggling, money laundering and sabotage. They were accused of joining the NGO Emergency Response Centre Inter-national (ERCI), described as a criminal organisation with a perpetual action group of more than three persons, with internal and hierarchical structure, acting with intent of facilitating entry of refugees flows from Turkey to the Northeast Aegean Islands (Lesvos and Samos) with illegal methods and procedures. ERCI was accused of money laundering because, despite its non-profit status, it accepted donations of physical objects and payments by private individuals or other collective bodies. … This investigation started in 2018 and involves a total of 37 individuals. In April 2019, the prosecutor decided to press extra charges including fraud' (Vosyliūtė and Conte, above n 6, 27).

[66] Two well-known cases occurred on the Alpine border between the Italian municipality of Claviere and the French municipality of Montgenevre. In the first, seven young people of different European nationalities were sentenced in the first instance to six months' imprisonment (suspended sentence) for having helped twenty or so undocumented migrants enter French territory, hiding them in a pro-migrant demonstration held on 22 April 2018 (Tribunal de Grande Instance de Gap, 13 December 2018, available on www.gisti.org). In the second case, a French man, mountain guide by profession, was sentenced in the first instance to three months' imprisonment (suspended sentence) for having accompanied three undocumented migrants to France on the evening of 6 January 2018: his version of the facts, according to which he had encountered the undocumented migrants during one of the patrols he used to carry out to check whether anyone required aid, was not considered reliable by the judge, according to whom the meeting had been set up beforehand (Tribunal de Grande Instance de Gap, 10 January 2019, available on www.gisti.org). Shifting the focus further south, in addition to the well-known case of Cédric Herrou and Pierre-Alain Mannoni (see section VII.B. below), one can recall the case of an Italian volunteer from an association in support of migrants, sentenced on appeal to six months' imprisonment (suspended sentence) and a five-year ban on staying in the region where the facts took place, for having transported a family of undocumented migrants from Ventimiglia to Menton in a van (Cour d'Appel d'Aix-en-Provence, 6 June 2018, www.gisti.org).

England;[67] among Hungary, Austria Germany;[68] between Denmark and Sweden;[69] between Greece and other countries.[70] Such conduct has been prosecuted, either by the authorities of the State of departure, by way of illegal facilitation of transit or entry into another State; or by the authorities of the State of destination, by way of illegal facilitation of entry.

An Italian case that was also much discussed abroad is that of the Mayor of Riace Domenico Lucano. According to the judge for the preliminary investigations of Locri,[71] in 2017 Lucano tried to organise a marriage of convenience between an Italian woman of Ethiopian origin and her brother, residing in Ethiopia and intending to emigrate: the purpose of the marriage was to obtain the entry into Italy of the man through a procedure of family reunification, as Italian law allows reunification between spouses and not between siblings. However, the manoeuvre was discovered both by the Ethiopian authorities (which arrested the young man) and by the Italian ones, which accused the Mayor of Riace of facilitating illegal immigration, a criminal offence for which, as already mentioned, it is not necessary for illegal entry to actually occur. Although the aim pursued by Lucano was solidarity-based and not economic in nature, yet this element, as previously

[67] An example could be the well-known case of the British volunteer who attempted to transport a four-year-old Afghan girl from the 'Calais Jungle' (a migrant and refugee camp in northern France) to the United Kingdom, at the request of the girl's father, who wanted her to join relatives in Leeds. The volunteer, discovered by the French authorities, was tried for illegal transit aid, and acquitted on the basis of the humanitarian justification under art L 622-4 CESEDA (Tribunal de Grande Instance de Boulogne-sur-Mer, 14 January 2016, www.gisti.org).

[68] On this point see for example L Fekete, F Webber and A Edmond-Pettitt, *Humanitarianism: the Unacceptable Face of Solidarity* (London, Institute of Race Relations, 2017) 12–13: 'When, in August 2015, Angela Merkel waived the normal Dublin criteria and opened Germany's southern border with Austria to enable Syrian refugees to come to Germany, Berlin-based refugee support Peng Collective called for a convoy of refugee helpers ("Fluchthelfer.in") to collect refugees from Austria and bring them to Germany, and over 700 people responded. Border controls were re-introduced in September, and Bavarian police arrested a number of "border crossing helpers" who gave people lifts from Vienna to the German border, or within Germany, for migrant smuggling or for the lesser offence of abetting illegal entry. Helpers' found themselves handcuffed, strip-searched and detained in "container cells" at the German-Austrian border for up to thirty-one hours. Activists in the "convoy of hope", around fifty cars which travelled to Hungary to bring refugees to Germany, were also reportedly arrested on suspicion of smuggling. More than 700 'smugglers' were reported to be in detention during the weekend of 12–13 September 2015, although how many of them were humanitarian and how many opportunists making money is impossible to know'.

[69] See Fekete, Webber and Edmond-Pettitt, ibid, 14: 'Most weeks since September 2015, police have detained a handful of people driving across the Øresund bridge from Denmark on suspicion of smuggling, prosecuting around half of them. The police say most cases they deal with are of asylum seekers already living in Sweden picking up family members from Germany. But, an unnamed young man was sentenced to three months in prison [in August 2016] for bringing a family with two children, whom he met at a gas station in Denmark, across the bridge to Sweden. He wanted to help the children and took no payment, but the Swedish authorities do not consider bringing people from Denmark 'humanitarian', as Denmark is safe, so the sentence was not reduced or suspended'.

[70] See Fekete, Webber and Edmond-Pettitt, ibid, 14, reporting that, in 2014, 'a journalist and two other Sveriges Television (SVT) employees were arrested and charged with facilitating illegal entry after helping a 15-year-old Syrian from Greece to Sweden'.

[71] Tribunale di Locri, Ufficio GIP, 26 September 2018, pp 69-122 (www.questionegiustizia.it, 3 October 2018).

pointed out many times, is insufficient to rule out criminal liability. Indeed, as a result of this and other accusations made against the Mayor for offences against the public administration, the entire 'Riace system', known throughout Europe as a virtuous and advanced model of integration, became surrounded by an aura of suspicion that seriously damaged its reputation. The judgment of the GIP of Locri, ordering the precautionary measure of house arrest against Lucano, was set aside by the Italian Supreme Court.[72] In April 2019, however, the Public Prosecutor's Office requested and obtained the indictment, also for facilitating illegal immigration.

Compared to shipwrecks or to other cases of people found in imminent danger, where there is no doubt that the conduct of the rescuers is lawful on the basis of general justifications provided by all European legal systems (fulfilment of duty or necessity), marking the threshold of criminal responsibility is much more complicated with regard to the cases which have been examined in this paragraph. In the absence of concrete dangers to life and limb, in fact, it is ultimately up to the discretion of legislators to identify the threshold of lawful actions, by deciding whether to introduce a humanitarian clause and how to define its scope of application. In other words, what appears to be just a matter of law in rescue cases, here is primarily a question of criminal policy relating to the definition of measures to combat irregular immigration. Emblematic, in this perspective, is the Riace case, where the conduct allegedly committed by the Mayor was motivated by the need to compensate for the absence of reunion mechanisms between siblings, excluded from the scope of family reunification rules. It is indeed up to the legislator to determine if and to which extent the interest in the protection of borders can 'tolerate' that type of disobedient conduct. As seen above, few European States have adopted indulgent approaches, by introducing humanitarian clauses of a wide scope (Finland, Belgium, Spain).[73] At the same time, however, the legislators' discretion must not be beyond arbitrariness. Without prejudice to what will be said below with regard to the supranational obligations arising from the Charter of Fundamental Rights of the European Union, a clear bulwark against arbitrariness is to be found in the legal system's consistency. This quality seems indeed to lack in those systems – such as the Italian one – where, on the one hand, illegal entry itself in punished as misdemeanour,[74] while aiding and abetting the (same) illegal entry is severely punished by means of imprisonment. Indeed, whenever the latter conduct is not accompanied by any other element which increases harm or

[72] Corte di Cassazione, Sesta Sezione Penale, 26 February 2019 (judgment issuing), 2 April 2019 (judgment release), No 14418 (www.italgiure.giustizia.it/sncass).

[73] For example, the Tribunal Supremo Español (Resolución No 261 of 6 April 2017, www.poderjudicial.es) considered that a case of bogus marriage celebrated between relatives in order to obtain a residence permit fell within the scope of the Spanish humanitarian clause, which, as seen above, is very broad.

[74] Italy is one of the Member States where illegal entry and stay of third-country nationals amount to criminal offences. On the limits encountered by Member States in introducing this type of offences, see the chapters by V Mitsilegas and J Stefanelli in this volume.

culpability (such as unjust profit, criminal organisation etc), there is no apparent reasonable justification for the increased penalty, which thus could be considered in breach of the *ultima ratio* and proportionality principles.

V. The Unsustainability of the European System to Combat the Facilitation of Illegal Immigration

As already mentioned at the beginning of this chapter, in 2017 the European Commission excluded the need and opportunity to reform the Facilitators package. The reasons provided by Brussels may be summarised as follows: (i) transactions between smugglers and migrants take place mainly outside European territory and through untraceable money transfers, with the consequence that making the punishability of facilitating irregular entry conditional on the establishment of the purpose of making a profit would in most cases jeopardise the success of the investigations;[75] (ii) insufficient evidence exists as to the opening of investigations and the imposition of sentences on persons who have provided humanitarian assistance to undocumented migrants;[76] (iii) only a small proportion of civil society actors interviewed expressed the fear of being sanctioned because of the humanitarian activity they carry out, in the face of the increase in social activities in favour of migrants precisely where migratory pressure is particularly strong;[77] (iv) national legislation usually includes grounds for exemption for conduct carried out when in a state of necessity or in performing a duty to rescue, and in any case the implementation of the package could not result in the criminalisation of humanitarian activities, incompatible with the Charter of Fundamental Rights, the principle of non-refoulement and further international obligations on Member States.[78]

On the whole, as Valsamis Mitsilegas also argues in this volume,[79] these considerations do not appear convincing or comprehensive, for many reasons. Starting with profit-making, in no way does its inclusion among the elements making up the criminal offence determine, from an evidentiary standpoint, the necessity of identifying the cash flow, since it is merely tied to volition ('specific intent' or purpose-oriented wilful misconduct), the demonstration of which

[75] EU Commission, *Staff Working Document – REFIT Evaluation* (2017), above n 5, 8–9. The Commission's interest in (also) targeting conduct outside the European area is linked to the nature of the offence in question, which structurally proceeds from the outside to the inside of the borders; this interest is reflected in Article 4 of Facilitation Framework Decision, which requires States, inter alia, to establish their jurisdiction with regard to the infringements committed in whole or in part within their territory.

[76] EU Commission, *Staff Working Document – REFIT Evaluation* (2017), above n 5, 21–22.

[77] ibid, 22.

[78] ibid, 22, 30, 35.

[79] See the chapter by V Mitsilegas; see also Mitsilegas, above n 21, 79–81.

may be easily provided through other evidence.[80] Furthermore, the Commission overlooks the fact that the most effective investigative techniques in this field are precisely money-focused ones, making it possible to track down and target the strongest criminal networks, driven and fuelled by profit.[81]

The further arguments put forward by the Commission may also be easily refuted. Beyond the consideration that the problem of overcriminalisation was already apparent in 2017,[82] in more recent years, as seen previously, numerous investigations have been launched due to facilitation of illegal entry and transit, which worsened the framework in action of the criminalisation of solidarity: to date, therefore, the question really may no longer be considered merely theoretical. Moreover, recent studies show that the variety of regulations in force in the Member States, accompanied by an increase in policing initiatives,[83] spreads fear among civil society actors and uncertainty as to the boundaries of their lawful action, with the consequent chilling effect of solidarity initiatives.[84] Additionally, the case history mentioned above shows that the grounds for exemption of a general nature are insufficient to prevent humanitarian activities from being at least seriously hampered by investigations, arrests and seizures. Finally, the international instruments for the protection of fundamental rights mentioned by the

[80] In addition to accounts from migrants, the United Nations Office on Drugs and Crime mentions the following indicators: 'lack of any familial or other relationship between the smuggler and the smuggled; the fact that previous migrants have paid; that the accused has offended previously or is living well beyond his legitimate means; or that the conditions of smuggling are so poor they cannot be humanitarian in motivation' (UNODC, *The Concept of 'Financial or Other Material Benefit' in the Smuggling of Migrants Protocol*, Issue Paper, 2017, 67).

[81] UNODC, *The Concept of 'Financial or Other Material Benefit'* (2017), ibid, p iii: 'Smuggling of migrants has become a very profitable business generating significant proceeds that can be disrupted by "following the money", as for other forms of organized crime. – Migration-focused measures risk not fully addressing the challenges presented by migrant smuggling as a form of serious organised crime, to the potential benefit of criminals and to the detriment of migrants'.

[82] S Carrera and others, above n 10, 40–60; R Landry, *The 'Humanitarian Smuggling' of Refugees. Criminal Offence or Moral Obligation?* (Oxford Refugee Studies Centre, Working Paper Series no 119, 2016) 8–11.

[83] The concept of 'policing' is to be understood in a broad sense, as illustrated above (n 42).

[84] The point is widely addressed in Carrera, Mitsilegas, Allsopp and Vosyliūtė, above n 2, 64, 74–79, 84, 93. On the subject of regulatory uncertainty, a civil society operator working for a government service providing social advice declared that 'you feel as a social worker you have to be an immigration lawyer' (ibid, 97). On the adverse effects of anti-smuggling law on third-party rescue at sea, see T Basaran, 'Saving Lives at Sea: Security, Law and Adverse Effects' (2014) 16 *European Journal of Migration and Law* 367. With regard to a case where a small boat left Tripoli with 72 people on board and after two weeks at sea drifted back to Libya with only nine survivors, it has been reported: 'No one went to the aid of this boat, despite a distress call logged by the Italian Maritime Rescue Coordination Centre, which pinpointed the boat's position. There were also a number of alleged direct contacts between the boat in distress and other vessels, including a helicopter that dropped biscuits and water, but never returned, two fishing vessels, both of which refused to provide assistance, and a large military vessel which came into close contact with the boat, but ignored obvious distress signals' (*Lives Lost in the Mediterranean Sea: Who is Responsible?*, Parliamentary Assembly Committee on Migration, Refugees and Displaced Persons, Council of Europe 2012). With regard to another shipwreck, a UN policy officer reported that 'there were 76 ships in the area of rescue. The call centre called them all, and within one minute there were only six ships left on the radar screen. All the others switched off their radar signal' ('Mediterranean Migrants: EU Rescue Policy Criticised', *BBC*, 12 November 2014).

Commission could come to the fore, if anything, in order to review the legality of the Facilitators package and the national rules implementing it (see section VII below).

Targeting conduct aimed at facilitating illegal entry and transit for humanitarian reasons entails further collateral damage. The fact that smuggling migrants is nothing more than the black market of mobility for economic migrants and asylum seekers represents a long-standing certainty; a market that is all the more flourishing where the possibilities for persons to legally enter and stay in States of transit or destination are limited.[85] The overreaching scope of European anti-smuggling legislation is contributing to this black market becoming increasingly dangerous and strong.[86] On the one hand, the dwindled rescue activities, directly affected or in any case daunted by policing activities, translate into greater risks for people trying to reach their destination illegally. On the other hand, the purely securitarian approach to the protection of borders leads to the weakening of solidarity mechanisms at civil society level, and, at the same time, to a strengthening of the better equipped criminal networks, which remain the only channels capable of providing the 'services' requested by undocumented migrants,[87] moreover employing increasingly risky methods.[88]

[85] R Koslowski, 'Economic Globalization, Human Smuggling and Global Governance' in D Kyle and R Koslowski (eds), *Global Human Smuggling: Comparative Perspectives* (Johns Hopkins University Press, 2001) 338: 'Ironically, as States tighten border controls and asylum policies, they have indirectly prompted more people to get into the smuggling business – increased restriction drives up the costs of illegal migration and increases the profit of human smuggling'. For an overview of the multiple profiles of smugglers worldwide and regionally, see UNODC, *Global Study on Smuggling* (2018) 43–54.

[86] See JC Hathaway, 'The Human Rights Quagmire of "Human Trafficking"' (2008) 49 *Virginia Journal of International Law* 37: 'Because of the increasing sophistication of document checks and border controls, refugees – like all other would-be entrants – must increasingly turn to smugglers (and, if poor, often to traffickers), in order to secure the requisite documents, or otherwise to find ways to get across the border'. As noted by a member of the Palermo Public Prosecutor's Office, the choices aimed at containing the migratory flows adopted in almost all the Western Countries have determined, at the same time, an ever-increasing investment of resources by organised crime, with the effect of transforming criminal groups operating in this sector into actual 'service agencies' and giving life to an illegal 'governance' over migratory flows, which often enjoys complicity in institutional, military and paramilitary environments of the Countries of origin and transit (C Ferrara, 'First Jurisprudential Applications on Trafficking in Human Beings', www.giustiziainsieme.it, 5 October 2019).

[87] See J Brachet, 'Manufacturing Smugglers: From Irregular to Clandestine Mobility in the Sahara' (2018) 676 *The Annals of the American Academy of Political and Social Science* 16, 16–35, arguing that 'smugglers appear as directly manufactured by the migration policies that were drafted to control them'; see also A Triandafyllidou, 'Migrant Smuggling: Novel Insights and Implications for Migration Control Policies' (2018) 676 *The Annals of the American Academy of Political and Social Science* 212, 215, claiming that 'the increased restrictions and police violence at the border and in transit lead to the transformation of such loose networks to more professionalized, organized and, indeed, criminal networks'. The thesis of the 'iatrogenic effects of prohibitionist border policies', is shared, amongst others, by L Weber and M Grewcock, 'Criminalizing People Smuggling. Preventing or Globalizing Harm?' in F Allum, S Gilmur, *Routledge Handbook of Transnational Organized Crime* (Abingdon, Routledge, 2011) 379.

[88] As reported by Carrera, Mitsilegas, Allsopp and Vosyliūtė, above n 2, 29–30, 70, one of the consequences of increasingly securitised border-control measures might be the deployment of more life-endangering practices by smugglers. A significant example of how not all methods to facilitate illegal immigration are equivalent is given by Landry, above n 82, 17: 'In the summer of 2015, for

The last argument supporting the option to keep the Facilitators package unchanged is the 'pull factor' one, i.e., the idea that by restricting the area of punishability, and consequently making all the conduct facilitating illegal entry and transit without profit legal, a greater number of undocumented migrants would flock, thus increasing illegal flows rather than curtailing them.[89] However, such an argument is empirically groundless. A 2017 study, for example, showed that the end of the Mare Nostrum operation in no way led to a decrease in departures, as could be expected according to the pull-factor theory, but only to an increase in deaths.[90] This finding is supported by a 2019 study that highlighted the absence of correlation between the presence of NGO ships along the central Mediterranean route and the numbers of daily departures, the latter being affected by other factors, mainly weather-related.[91]

VI. Proposals for Reform

Having ascertained that the current regulatory framework of criminal law enforcement relating to the smuggling of migrants is unsustainable, the next step is reflecting on the possible reforms, outlining proposals that may be useful to overcome the critical issues highlighted. First, we will focus below on reforms that national legislative bodies may immediately implement, i.e., without disregarding

example, at the same time that Hungarian taxi drivers were smuggling refugees across the border from Bulgaria through relatively safe means and for a standard fare, 71 refugees – among them a baby girl and three young boys – suffocated in a 7.5 tonne vehicle along the route from Hungary to Germany'. On the subject, see more generally Hathaway, above n 86, 34: 'Simply put, the agreement of states to criminalize smuggling and to strengthen border control efforts, coupled with inelastic demand for border crossing by mostly less-than-wealthy persons, will logically create the conditions within which traditionally benign form of smuggling are transmuted into the clearly rights-abusive practices characteristic of trafficking'.

[89] This argument has become a recurrent commonplace in the European debates on immigration. One of the first documents arguing the existence of a (albeit unintentional) causal link between rescuing activities and departures of boat migrants is the Frontex *Risk Analysis for 2017*, stating that SAR missions too close to territorial waters of Libya 'influence smugglers' planning and act as a pull factor that compounds the difficulties inherent in border control and saving lives and sea' (p 32). In 2019, the pull factor argument was used, for instance, by the Italian Minister of the Interior Salvini as a justification for the 'closed ports policy' (on which, see the chapter by F Cancellaro, 'Immigration Detention Between Law and Practice in Italy. Managing the Border Through Arbitrary Detention', in this volume): some of the Ministerial Decrees issued between March and May (all available at www.interno.gov.org) explicitly refer to SAR activities as 'aimed at the entry of people in violation of immigration laws' (18 March 2019); 'possible instrumentalisation of international obligations in the field of search and rescue' (4 April 2019); or 'mediated cooperation [implied: with smugglers] which, in fact, encourages the crossing by sea of foreign citizens without residence permit and objectively facilitate their irregular entry into the national territory' (15 April 2019).

[90] E Steinhilper and R Gruijters, 'Border Deaths in the Mediterranean: What We Can Learn from the Latest Data' (2017) *Border Criminologies*, 8 March: 'these results strongly suggest that SAR operations reduce mortality risks (or conversely, the absence of SAR operations leads to more deaths), and has little or no effect on the number of arrivals'.

[91] E Cusumano and M Villa, *Sea Rescue NGOs: a Pull Factor of Irregular Migration?* (Policy Brief, European University Institute, Issue 2019/22).

European criminal law obligations. Subsequently, the changes that seem necessary upstream, thus reducing the scope of the Facilitators package, will be analysed.

A. Reforms at National Level

The critical aspects highlighted above might be remedied by all Member States introducing a humanitarian clause exempting from liability the widest possible range of humanitarian conduct, along the lines of the clauses already found in Spain, Belgium and Finland (see section III above). Under the 2002 Directive, this is certainly an *optional* choice for national legislative bodies. However, it can be doubted whether a legal framework penalising humanitarian conduct addressed to third-country nationals is still compatible with the Charter of Fundamental Rights, which, since 2009, has acquired the same legal effectiveness as the Treaties (Article 6 TEU). Specifically, the inviolability of human dignity (Article 1 CFR), the rights to life and personal integrity (Article 2, 3), the right to asylum (Article 18), non-discrimination on grounds of nationality (Article 21) come into play. Beyond any possible supervening illegality of the Facilitators package itself (see below), Member States could be regarded, bound as they are by the Charter in the context of implementing EU regulation (Article 51 CFR), as being now *obliged* to introduce a humanitarian clause.

Some authors observed that the sweeping introduction of such a clause would not in any case produce definitive effects, since its presence would not exclude the 'de facto criminalisation' resulting from investigations, precautionary measures and criminal proceedings (regardless of their outcome).[92] However, this latter issue could only be definitively resolved by decriminalising any facilitation of illegal entry,[93] a solution that is incompatible to date, not only with European but also international incrimination obligations. On closer inspection, however, precisely because they are capable of affecting the outcome of proceedings, the humanitarian clauses should, in the medium or long term, also condition, upstream, the decisions of the law enforcement agencies with regard to the illegal phenomena on which to concentrate their investigative resources.

Additional wiggle room currently already available to Member States, which would at least reduce the impact of criminalisation, concerns the scope of penalties. At present, Member States invariably provide for custodial sentences (alternative to or in combination with fines, or on their own) even in relation to

[92] Landry, above n 82, 19–20. For this reason, the introduction of the exemption was proposed not as a 'defence', but as a 'bar to prosecution' (see Carrera and others, above n 10, 64). This distinction, however, does not bear legal relevance in all legal systems (for example, in Italy it would still be framed as a legal excuse).

[93] This solution was proposed by Landry, above n 82, 21–23, according to which the wrong attributable to smugglers, stripped of the elements of border violation, 'would likely fall under a pre-existing section of criminal law [such as] exploitation to operating an unlicensed or unseaworthy vessel to reckless endangerment to murder …'.

basic cases of facilitation (i.e., those where the conduct simply consists of aiding illegal entry or transit). However, Framework Decision 2002/946 requires States to provide for 'custodial sentences with a maximum sentence of no less than eight years' only where the offence is 'committed for financial gain' and at least one of the listed aggravating circumstances occurs (i.e., the activity is carried out by a criminal organisation or by putting the lives of migrants at risk). Therefore, arguing by contrast, in the absence of such conditions, not only is it possible to provide for custodial sanctions of a maximum length of less than eight years; but rather, more pointedly, even non-custodial penalties may be provided for. Such a solution, after all, would also be more in line with the limited offensiveness of the conduct. The latter indeed amounts to nothing but a participation in the unlawful crossing of the border, so that the general principle of proportionality (also reaffirmed by Article 1(1) of the Framework Decision) would entail penalties similar to those provided for in respect of the facilitated undocumented migrant. Given that, according to the unequivocal case law of the Court of Justice of the European Union, the mere condition of illegal immigration cannot be punished by imprisonment,[94] even in relation to basic cases of facilitation, for the sake of consistency of the system, fines alone should apply to these cases.

B. Reforms at European Level

Certainly, optimal results would be achieved where a radical reform of the Facilitators package (to be conveyed into a single directive adopted under Article 83 TFEU) were to be carried out, as all the authors who have dealt with the subject envision.

The first possible change is to introduce a profit-making purpose among the elements making up the criminal offence, thus returning to the original wording of the Schengen Convention and aligning the European rules with those of the Palermo Protocol Against Smuggling (see section II above). The Commission

[94] This was famously established by the Court of Justice of the European Union in the judgments *El Dridi* (Case C-61/11 PPU [2011] ECR I-3031) and *Achughbabian* (Case C-329/11 [2011] ECR I-12709), which found the criminal offences of illegal immigration in force in Italy and France, respectively, incompatible with the Return Directive (Directive 2008/115/EC of the European Parliament and of the Council of 16 December 2008 on common standards and procedures in Member States for returning illegally staying third-country nationals [2008] OJ L 348), as the custodial sentence they provided for risked jeopardising the attainment of an effective policy of removal and repatriation. Clearly, however, against this backdrop, the two judgments also took account of the reduced offensiveness of the conduct in question, as the opposite outcome reached by the Court of Justice itself in the subsequent *Celaj* judgment (C-290/14 [2015] OJ C 292, 1.9.2014) unequivocally demonstrated, which found that Italian legislation providing for the imposition of a prison sentence on an illegally staying third-country national who, after having been returned to his country of origin in the context of an earlier return procedure, unlawfully re-enters the territory of that State in violation of an entry ban was compatible with the Return Directive.

itself, moreover, recognises that the target of anti-smuggling measures is fighting criminal organisations acting for profit;[95] and the reasons why a money-focused investigative approach would be a win-win have already been underlined (see section V above).

The introduction of mere profit-making purpose, without further specification, does not seem sufficient. The request for money or other advantage does not automatically entail that the 'service' offered is devoid of any humanitarian purpose.[96] The Danish fishermen who, during the Second World War, helped thousands of Jews flee to Sweden, asking for remuneration proportionate to the days of work they lost and the risks they were facing could represent an example here.[97] Who could argue, apart from Nazis, that those fishermen deserved severe penalties? Nowadays, similar reasoning could be extended to all those providing aid in return for payment to asylum seekers in search of protection, who often have no means of escaping other than illegally.[98] Exempting such persons from liability, therefore, requires more than providing for profit-making purpose among the elements making up the criminal offence.

The profit-making provision should therefore be accompanied by an obligation on the Member States (and not merely an option) to introduce a humanitarian clause, exempting all conduct based on solidarity reasons, according to the Spanish, Belgian and Finnish models. On this point, the new directive should be worded as clearly and precisely as possible, for at least two reasons: on the one hand, this would reduce the discretion of the Member States in the implementation phase, avoiding discrepancies between one legal system and another, and reducing the uncertainties in its application (in order to avoid any chilling effect on members of civil society); on the other hand, and above all, once the term for transposition has elapsed, it would make it possible to invoke its direct effect before the national courts in the event of failure to transpose it into national legislation or unfaithful implementation within the national framework.

Finally, a more radical and effective solution than those proposed so far is represented by the transition from the current description of the punishable

[95] See EU Commission, *EU Action Plan against migrant smuggling (2015–2020)*, above n 1: 'The Agenda set the goal to transform migrant smuggling networks from "low risk, high return" operations into "high risk, low return" ones'; 'Ruthless criminal networks organize the journeys of large numbers of migrants desperate to reach the EU. They make substantial gains while putting the migrants' lives at risk'; 'Migrant smuggling is a highly profitable business, with criminal networks thriving on the low risk of detection and punishment'; 'the difference [between smuggling and trafficking] is that in the former, migrants willingly engage in the irregular migration process by paying for the services of a smuggler in order to cross and international border, while in the latter they are the victims, coerced into severe exploitation which may or may not be linked to a crossing of a border'.

[96] In this regard see S Watson, 'The Criminalization of Human and Humanitarian Smuggling' (2015) 1 *Migration, Mobility and Displacement* 39, 44: 'the distinction between altruistic and financial/self-interested motivations that sustain the categories of smuggler and humanitarian is problematic'; Landry, above n 82, 8: the 'for-profit/humanitarian binary is problematic, as it rests on the premises that acts for gain cannot be humanitarian and acts not for gain cannot be criminal'.

[97] The case is reported by Landry, above n 82, 15.

[98] A recent example is represented by Hungarian taxi drivers transporting refugees coming from the Eastern Europe borders, asking for the standard fare in return (see n 88 above).

conduct in terms of 'facilitating illegal entry' to a more meaningful description in terms of 'smuggling of migrants'. The latter should be worded in terms of aid to illegal entry by *exploiting* the vulnerability of undocumented migrants and asylum-seekers in order to gain an *unfair* advantage. Such a solution would have the advantage of aligning the description of the conduct with the criminal-political aim that the anti-smuggling measures should pursue: i.e., – recalling the words of the European Commission – targeting 'ruthless criminal networks [which] organize the journeys of large numbers of migrants desperate to reach the EU [and] make substantial gains while putting the migrants' lives at risk'.[99] This way, resources and investigative efforts could also be more easily directed towards the objective – recently mentioned anew by the Commission itself – of conducting 'highly complex crossborder and international anti-smuggling operations'.[100] Moreover, the criminalisation of 'smuggling' instead of 'facilitating' would help ward off the misleading idea that aiding *sans papiers* with a humanitarian aim operates as a mere 'exemption' to an otherwise criminal conduct. This conviction fuels current attitudes of distrust and suspicion towards humanitarian activities and should be overcome in favour of a culture that recognises the importance of human solidarity also within the legal framework, drawing the necessary consequences in terms of distinguishing between lawful and unlawful conduct.

VII. Challenging the Legality of Legislations Criminalising the Assistance to Undocumented Migrants and Asylum Seekers

Although the need to reform the Facilitators package has received renewed attention in recent times, legislative measures such as those described above do not

[99] EU Commission, *EU Action Plan against migrant smuggling (2015–2020)*, above n 1, 1. This is consistent with the Preamble of the Palermo Protocol Against Smuggling, in which the signatory States declared themselves 'concerned by the significant increase in the activities of organized criminal groups in smuggling of migrants and other related criminal activities set forth in this Protocol, which bring great harm to the States concerned; also concerned that the smuggling of migrants can endanger the lives or security of the migrants involved'. Undeniably, however, the aims of European anti-smuggling instruments are nowadays cloaked in ambiguity. On point, see Mitsilegas, above n 21, 81, pointing out that 'the main purpose behind the criminalization of human smuggling by certain legislators is really the prevention of migration flows towards their territory', and more in general underlying a certain 'ambiguity regarding the concrete aims behind the criminalisation of human smuggling' (p 85). It is worth pointing out, although the subject goes beyond the scope of this chapter, that such underlying ambiguity was also reported with regard to criminalising human trafficking, the aims of which seem rather about protecting European borders than vulnerable victims: see C Lernestedt, 'What Does the Trafficker Do Wrong and Towards What or Whom?' in R Haverkamp, E Herlin-Karnell and C Lernestedt (eds), *What Is Wrong With Human Trafficking? Critical Perspectives on the Law* (Oxford, Hart Publishing, 2019) 140.

[100] EU Commission, *Progress Report on the Implementation of the European Agenda on Migration*, COM(2019) 481 final, 16 October 2019, 14.

yet appear on the agenda; on the contrary, clear signs of the European legislator's desire to strengthen existing measures to protect external borders exist. Given the continued institutional inertia, the judicial route may be taken after all, invoking before the Court of Justice of the European Union the illegality of the Facilitators package in light of the constraints arising from the Charter of Fundamental Rights, in the context of proceedings instituted under Article 263 TFEU or by seeking a preliminary ruling under Article 267 TFEU. Before examining the illegality aspects that the Court may be seised with, it is worth taking note of the two main case-law precedents that, at global level, led to reworking criminal rules on the smuggling of migrants by making them more restrictive.

A. The Judgment of the Supreme Court of Canada in the *Appulonappa* Case

The first relevant ruling in the perspective adopted here is that handed down by the Supreme Court of Canada in the *Appulonappa* case,[101] which in 2017 found the partial illegality of a criminal offence entirely similar to those in force in Europe as implementation of the Facilitators package. This is the first (and as far as we know, the only) case in which a higher court found that the crime of facilitating illegal entry was illegitimate due to its overreaching scope. This statement, therefore, on the one hand reinforces the idea that the overcriminalisation issue could be resolved by judicial means; on the other hand, it develops certain arguments which, *mutatis mutandis*, could be replicated at European level.

The Canadian Court found that the criminal offence of facilitating irregular entry in section 117(1) of the Immigration and Refugee Protection Act (IRPA),[102] to the extent that it punished with severe penalties (including imprisonment) mere aid to entry (even in the absence of a criminal organisation, profit-making intent or danger to migrants), had to be considered overbroad, as it interfered with

[101] Supreme Court of Canada, *R v Appulonappa* [2015] 3 RCS 754. The case originated in 2009, when a ship carrying 76 Tamil asylum seekers fleeing the civil war in Sri Lanka was intercepted in Canadian waters. Four of them, including Mr Francis Anthonimuthu Appulonappa, were accused of being the trusted persons of the criminal organisation that had organised the trafficking, against payment of between 30,000 and 40,000 dollars for each person transported. Following the conviction reported on appeal, they complained to the Supreme Court about the illegality of the Canadian rule facilitating illegal entry (see following footnote).

[102] At the time of the charges at issue in that case, Section 117(1) of the Canadian *IRPA*, under the marginal note 'Organizing entry into Canada' read as follows: 'No person shall knowingly organize, induce, aid or abet the coming into Canada of one or more persons who are not in possession of a visa, passport or other document required by this act'. Sections 177(2) and (3) provided penalties of fines and imprisonment (up to 2 years and $100,000 on summary conviction; up to 10 years and $500,000 on conviction on indictment for a first offence; up to 14 years and $1,000,000 for a subsequent offence; up to life imprisonment and $1,000,000 in case of facilitation with respect to a group of 10 persons or more). Section 121(1)(c), under the marginal note 'Aggravating factors' stipulated that committing the offence for profit ('whether or not any profit was realized') was a fact to be considered in sentencing.

conduct that bore no connection to the law's objectives. Taking into account, on the one hand, a number of national and international regulatory indices (in particular the Palermo Protocol Against Smuggling and the 1951 Convention relating to the Status of Refugees) and, on the other hand, the evolution of Section 117 IRPA as well as its drafting, the Court concluded that: i) 'the true purpose of s. 117 is to combat people smuggling'; (ii) 'the meaning of people smuggling excludes mere humanitarian conduct, mutual assistance or aid to family members'; (iii) therefore, 'section 117 violates the Charter by catching these categories of conduct outside the provision's purpose' (paragraph 34). The constitutional parameter that came to the fore was Section 1 of the Canadian Charter of Rights and Freedoms (incorporated into Part I of the 1982 Canadian Constitution), which legitimises the compression of fundamental rights (in this case, the personal freedom of the accused) only where amounting to a 'reasonable measure in a free and democratic society'.[103] According to the Court, the justification provided by the Canadian State for introducing such a wide-ranging criminal offence, namely the fear of creating 'unacceptable loopholes', was insufficient: 'Section 1 of the Charter does not allow rights to be limited on the basis of bare claims, but requires the Crown to provide a demonstrable justification for inconsistencies with Charter rights' (paragraph 82). In conclusion, the Court found that Section 117 was overbroad 'in relation to three categories of conduct: (1) humanitarian aid to undocumented entrants, (2) mutual aid amongst asylum-seekers, and (3) assistance to family entering without the required documents' (paragraph 84); with the consequence, in terms of remedies, that this provision has to be read down 'as not applicable to persons who give humanitarian, mutual or family assistance' (paragraph 85).

B. The Judgment of the French Conseil Constitutionnel in the *Cédric Herrou* Case

The scope of the French judgment is much narrower than the one just examined, but it is nevertheless important with a view to seeking legal tools to assess the legality of the Facilitators package. The question of legality concerned the humanitarian clause in Article L 622-4 CESEDA, in so far as (according to the wording in force at the time) it limited immunity to aiding the *stay* of undocumented migrants, thus excluding assistance provided not only during *entry* into the national territory, but also mere *movement within it*. The question had been raised by the Cour de cassation with two identical judgments, issued on the same day in two different proceedings,[104] both relating to events in Val Roia, which in recent years has

[103] The whole provision reads: 'The Canadian Charter of Rights and Freedoms guarantees the rights and freedoms set out in it subject only to such reasonable limits prescribed by law as can be demonstrably justified in a free and democratic society'.

[104] Cour de cassation, Chambre criminelle, 9 May 2018, affaires nos 17-85736 and 17-85737 (www.egifrance.gouv.fr.).

become one of the routes migrants attempting to pass from Italy into France employ: in one case the accusation was that of facilitating stay and movement; in the other, it also included facilitating entry (this is the case concerning the activist farmer Cédric Herrou, which received a lot of press attention).[105]

The two referrals were dealt with jointly by the Conseil Constitutionnel, which only partially upheld them.[106] The reasoning behind the judgment revolves around the question of whether the legislature, in limiting the scope of application of Article L 622-4 to the sole aid to stay, reasonably balanced ('une conciliation équilibrée') the principle of *fraternité* and the protection of public order, both constitutionally enshrined. The judges' reply was that the rule was unlawful in so far as it did not extend immunity to aiding the movement of undocumented migrants already on French territory; but not in so far as it excluded aiding illegal entry from its scope: this is because only in the first case it amounts to conduct not giving rise to a new instance of illegality, just as in the case of aiding residence. By Law of 10 September 2018, the French legislature amended Article L 622-4 CESEDA accordingly, by adding aid to movement within the French territory as conduct liable to be justified in light of humanitarian purposes.[107]

C. Implications for European Legislation

Some passages in the reasoning developed in the judgments just examined may also be developed, *mutatis mutandis*, within the EU legal framework.

Starting with the judgment of the French Conseil Constitutionnel, it is necessary to focus on the argument that, in terms of balancing border protection with *fraternité*, aid to movement within the national territory is no different from aid to stay; therefore, regulating such instances differently would be unreasonable. Similar considerations could be developed with reference to Article 1(1) of Directive 2002/90/EC, in so far as it distinguishes between facilitating movement (provided for in letter a): 'to enter or *transit across*', emphasis added) and facilitating stay (provided for in letter b): 'to reside'), considering the former illegal even in the absence of profit, and therefore implicitly more serious. Here, obviously, *fraternité* could not act as the legality parameter, which is not included in the Treaties; nonetheless, a similar counterbalancing function with respect to the need to protect borders could be served by the principles enshrined in the Charter of Fundamental

[105] Mr Herrou was sentenced to four months' imprisonment (suspended sentence) by the Court of Appeal of Aix-en-Provence (judgment of 8 August 2017, www.gisti.org) for facilitating entry, movement and even illegal stay (the judges considered that his purpose was political and not humanitarian). The question of constitutional legality was raised by the Cour de cassation by order of 9 May 2018 (www.gisti.org).

[106] Conseil Constitutionnel, Décision No 2018/717-718 QPC, 6 July 2018.

[107] The Cour de cassation subsequently set aside the verdict against Herrou and referred the case back to the Court of Appeal of Lyon (Cour de cassation, Chambre criminelle, 12 December 2018, affaire No 17-85736, www.egifrance.gouv.fr).

Rights of the European Union, namely the human dignity of migrants (Article 1) and the right to personal liberty of those who aid transit through national territory, risking imprisonment (Article 6). On the basis of the above arguments, the Directive should be found unlawful, in so far as it provides for stricter treatment for the non-profit-making facilitation of illegal transit across a Member State's territory, unreasonably sacrificing the interests protected by Articles 1 and 6 CDFEU.

More radical results would be achieved by transmuting, within the European legislative context, the reasoning developed by the Canadian Court, on the basis of Article 52(1) of the EU Charter of Fundamental Rights. This provision states that limitations on the exercise of the rights and freedoms recognised by the Charter itself must comply, inter alia, with the principle of proportionality: this requires, according to the settled case-law of the Court of Justice, 'that acts of the EU institutions be appropriate for attaining the legitimate objectives pursued by the legislation at issue and do not exceed the limits of what is appropriate and necessary in order to achieve those objectives'.[108] The test therefore requires at least two steps: first, the objective pursued by the legislature by passing given legislation must be assessed; second, the tight hold on fundamental rights brought about by the legislation in question must measure up to the pursued objective. Given that the alleged objective of the European legislature in adopting the Facilitators package was (and still is) to combat the smuggling of migrants,[109] the choice to punish any conduct of facilitation of irregular entry or transit appears completely disproportionate, as it results in *a sacrifice of the fundamental rights of the accused persons* (the right to personal liberty under Article 6 CFR, stifled by the criminal penalty) *and of the migrants themselves* (the right to human dignity as per Article 1; to life and physical integrity as per Articles 2 and 3; to private and family life as per Article 7; to apply for asylum as per Article 18; to non-discrimination on the basis of nationality as per Article 21 CFR) *which goes far beyond that strictly functional to fighting criminal organisations*. Indeed, the legislature ends up including within the scope of the penalty also behaviours that, due to being non-profit making and driven by humanitarian purposes, clearly have nothing to do with those meant to be targeted, since their offensiveness merely amounts to having contributed to violating the administrative requirements of access to the territory and movement within it. From this point of view, the reasoning proposed here may be superimposed on that followed by the Canadian Supreme Court: the regulatory flaw amounts to forcing unreasonable sacrifices compared to the objectives pursued; at the same time, the need to avoid gaps in protection of borders does not, on its own, constitute a reasonable justification for suppressing fundamental rights.

Finally, the breadth of the legal construct provided by the Facilitators package appears incompatible with the principles of legality of criminal offences and penalties (Article 49 CFR). National legislators are called to make it punishable

[108] Joined Cases C-293/12 and C-594/12, *Digital Rights Ireland Ltd* [2014] OJ C 175, para 46.
[109] See section VI.B. above.

as 'facilitating illegal immigration' a spectrum of conduct ranging from the international organisation dealing in smuggling, all the way to the individual citizen occasionally aiding a person in need. As a result, domestic criminal law implementing the European provisions confer quite a wide-ranging margin of appreciation to the judiciary and the law enforcement authorities; this may eventually undermine the foreseeability of the acts which will make people criminally liable for assisting undocumented third-country nationals.

VIII. Concluding Remarks

In the years that have elapsed since the refugee crisis began, at least 1262 undocumented migrants died in shipwrecks in 2019, 1314 in 2018, 2853 in 2017, 4581 in 2016, 3149 in 2015, 3165 in 2014.[110] As stated above, a statistical correlation exists between on the one hand, the increased risk of death while crossing the Mediterranean (i.e. the relationship between the number of departures and the number of casualties) and, on the other hand, the curtailment in search and rescue activities carried out by civil society, the latter due to States' preventive and sanctioning measures as well as from the chilling effect that those measures produce. Moreover, risks to the lives and physical integrity of migrants may also arise along land borders, for example when they cross Alpine borders on foot or hide on board transport means; even in these cases, targeting rescuers or discouraging humanitarian assistance may result in further tragedies. But that is not all. Stifling aid to entry into or transit through the European area, without further filters other than that of administrative irregularity, is also likely to suppress further fundamental rights such as the right to seek asylum or the right to preserve family ties, given the limited possibilities of satisfying them through the channels recognised by the Member States' legal systems. As we have seen, these sacrifices are maladjusted and disproportionate to the criminal policy objectives pursued.

[110] Data reported by the Missing Migrants Project (www.missingmigrants.iom.int), estimated on the basis of International Organisation for Migration, national authorities and media sources. The Project presentation page refers the main challenges of collecting data on missed migrants, which may lead to their underestimation: 'Data on migrant fatalities are challenging to collect for a number of reasons. First, because the majority of deaths are of migrants travelling by irregular means, they often occur in remote areas chosen because of a lack of legal routes. As a result, bodies are not always found quickly, if it all, and deaths may not be systematically reported to authorities. Furthermore, when deaths occur at sea or in other bodies of water, many of the deceased may not be recovered, and without passenger lists, the precise number of missing is unknown. In addition, the involvement of criminal actors, border guards, and others in the process of irregular migration might make survivors fearful of reporting deaths, and some deaths may even be actively covered up. Data on migrant deaths and disappearances are also challenging to collect as consistent reporting by states on the deaths of non-nationals in transit, or nationals who have died while in transit abroad is very scarce. Few official sources collect and publish data on migrant deaths. Often incidents come to light through media sources, which may have incomplete and infrequent coverage'.

Against this backdrop, this paper proposed and envisioned reforms of existing legislation both at national level (within the limits allowed by the Facilitators package) and, above all, at European level, with a view to limiting the obligation to criminalise to conduct exploiting the weak position of migrants in order to make an unfair profit; without these reforms, as explained above, there would be no alternative but to refer the question of the Facilitators package's legality before the Court of Justice as soon as possible.

Fears that restricting the scope of criminal law would end up favouring criminal organisations dealing in smuggling are groundless, as pointed out, but also fail to overcome the objection that, on the contrary, criminal law would gain in terms of enhanced targeting, and therefore overall effectiveness. On the contrary, the absence of regulated access routes for people on the move is profoundly damaging to the fight against smuggling, because it creates the conditions for its propagation. Then again, for any unreasonable limitation of widespread conduct, and to a greater extent conduct innate to human nature (such as migrating), a corresponding black market arises. That is why it is all the more urgent that institutions take action to implement what the Commission already recognised in 2015: 'Smuggling networks can be weakened if fewer people seek their services. Therefore, it is important to open more safe, legal ways into the EU'.[111] As Cesare Beccaria acknowledged with regard to the smuggling of goods (but the argument, *mutatis mutandis*, may be extended to this field of investigation), 'This crime is not infamous in the public opinion …; This crime is owing to the laws themselves'.[112]

[111] EU Commission, *EU Action Plan against migrant smuggling (2015–2020)*, above n 1, 2. Concordantly, see the report of the European Union Agency for Fundamental Rights (FRA, *Legal Pathways to Europe needed to help curb human smuggling*, 25 October 2019).

[112] C Beccaria, *'On Crimes and Punishments' and Other Writings* (Cambridge, Cambridge University Press, 1995) 87–88.

12

Reversing the Perspective

Criminal Responsibility of Italian Authorities for Human Rights Violations in Libya?

LUCA MASERA

I. A Provocative Viewpoint: The Criminal Liability of Italy's Top Leadership for the Crimes Perpetrated in Libya against Migrants

In this intervention, I would like to 'reverse the perspective', as indicated by the title of my contribution. So far, we have seen how criminal law represents a tool used increasingly more to *punish irregular migrants* or those who facilitate their migration, if not actually to punish whoever endeavours to save the migrants in danger at sea. Now we want to check whether criminal law might also become a tool to *defend migrants* from the serious offences that during the migratory process are inflicted on them, often – as we will see – with the complicity of Italian and European authorities.

My approach is deliberately and explicitly *provocative*, and we will soon discover why. Before doing so, however, I would like to clarify the concrete scenario tackled in this intervention. The international community and the public opinion have known for years that the detention centres where migrants are kept in Libya are infernal places: both the 'regular' centres managed by the Libyan Cost Guard (LCG) and, more generally, by the authorities of the internationally recognised Libyan government, and, more so in fact, the irregular centres managed by the various militias operating in the country. The most atrocious tortures are run-of-the-mill daily occurrences; various commentators, to express the utmost seriousness of the situation, have stated that the conditions prevailing inside them recall those of the most atrocious places in history, the Nazi concentration camps.[1]

[1] Out of various contributions on the tragedies of Libyan concentration camps, see especially M Veglio (ed), *L'attualità del male – La Libia dei lager è verità processuale* (Torino, Seb27, 2018).

We are going to see it better in the first part of this intervention: the centres for migrants in Libya are currently among the worst places in the world where you might happen to be detained. Despite the fact that such reality has been known for years, the Italian government, beginning in particular with 2017, has identified in the collaboration with Libyan authorities (especially with the LCG) a decisive element of its own migratory policy. Supporting the LCG by technical and financial means, besides logistical and operational ones, is a constant of Italian policy in recent years. This strategy had a massive launch in 2016–17 under the Gentiloni government, particularly during Minniti's term as Minister of Internal Affairs, as he was responsible for the code of conduct applicable to NGOs, which explicitly laid down that NGOs were under a duty to support the LCG in migrant refoulement activities;[2] and it continued on an even more explicit note under the first Conte government and Salvini's ministry.

Here is, then, my provocation. Our authorities know that the Libyan detention centres, where the LCG sends back the migrants rescued at sea, are hellish places, where the worst atrocities are committed. Nevertheless, they fund and support the rescue operations at sea whereby the migrants who have finally managed to escape from those centres are restored by the LCG to the hell they came from. Can we posit an issue of criminal liability against our top leaders for *complicity* in the crimes of which the migrants are victims in Libya?

The question is seemingly provocative, since the policy of collaboration with Libyan authorities in controlling migrations is far from a circumstance denied or passed over in silence by our governments, and its implementation has in fact been greeted with extreme favour by the EU institutions as well.

The political reasoning is clear and explicit, at both Italian and European level. The result to be obtained at all costs is the reduction in the number of migrants setting out from Libya for the Italian shores. Until 2012, ships of the Italian military navy were conducting refoulement operations directly, intercepting migrants' vessels on the high seas and taking them back to Libya: after the 2012 *Hirsi* judgment by the ECHR,[3] this practice is no longer possible. The only possibility left after 2012 is for the Libyan authorities themselves to run the rescue operations and take the migrants back to Libya. Surely, the Italian and European authorities are pretty well aware of the situation of detention centres in Libya, and there are always official occasions on which they undertake to improve living conditions in such centres. However, according to our authorities, there are at present no other places where the migrants repelled at sea might be brought back, and it is not the

[2] On code of conduct for NGOs approved on summer 2017 summer, see F Ferri, 'Il Codice di condotta per le ONG e i diritti dei migranti: fra diritto internazionale e politiche europee' (2018) (1) *Diritti umani e diritto internazionale* 189.

[3] The reference is obviously to the very well-known judgment by the Grand Chamber of the European Court of Human Rights, 23 February 2012, *Hirsi Jamaa v Italy*, where the ECHR held that the Italian praxis of intercepting with military ships the vessels heading from Libya, sending migrants back, was illegitimate as being in conflict with the *non refoulement* principle (article 3 of the ECHR) and with the prohibition of collective expulsions (article 4 Prot 4 ECHR).

responsibility of Italy and Europe if the Libyan authorities are unable to ensure to detained migrants fulfilment of even the most basic rights.

This discourse boasts a very wide support at the level of public opinion, and is more or less the common opinion of European governments on the issue of how to govern the Libyan flows of migrants. The support for the LCG's ability to carry out rescue operations at sea is necessary for precluding the intervention of NGOs, so that migrants can be sent back to Libya and the migrant flows to Europe reduced. No politician in Italy who aspires to some kind of electoral following could nowadays assert that, although helping Libyans manage rescue operations at sea has drastically reduced the number of new arrivals, that should be stopped, as the Libyan detention centres migrants are sent back to are atrocious places. The argument of the need to block the flows has such a powerful resonance in the political debate that the issue of human rights protection is doomed to certain defeat. First arrivals must be contained, and only then, if at all, should the issue of human rights in Libya be tackled: currently, these priorities are not in discussion, in Italy or in Europe.

Is it thus possible that the activities in support of Libyan authorities, while boasting so much consent, nevertheless configure a case of criminal liability on the part of our institutional leaders? Let us indeed de-contextualise the issue, and let us shelve aside, for a moment, politics and current affairs. There are torture centres managed by authority of government X, and another government Y, which is well acquainted with the situation of these centres, provides X with aids and means for it to run them: is it so far-fetched to ask ourselves whether the members of government Y could be held liable for what happens in those centres?

My intention is to try to articulate some thoughts on this point. We will begin with a short analysis of the state of detention centres in Libya, analysing the crimes we can identify there, and the proceedings currently underway against those who directly manage the centres. We will then look at the possible scenarios for liability on the part of the Italian authorities: first vis-à-vis the jurisdiction of the International Criminal Court, and second vis-à-vis the internal criminal jurisdiction. We will not deal instead with the profiles relating to any international liability of the Italian State for what happens in Libya, before the ECHR or other international venues: a profile we do not have enough room to analyse here, even though it obviously has many points where it intersects with the problems we are about to tackle.

II. The Situation in Libya: The Criminal Liability of Libyan Agents or Agents Acting Directly in the Libyan Centres

The conditions of detention centres in Libya have been for years at the centre of attention among NGOs and international human rights organisations: there are countless reports, and it would be pointless to list them here.[4] So exceptional is the situation that, since the end of 2017, the UNHCR has embarked on a temporary programme of evacuation from such centres of the most highly vulnerable subjects, transferring them to Niger and subsequently installing them in European countries. A programme that in any event involves but a few hundreds of migrants, compared to the thousands and thousands blocked inside the Libyan centres.

I would like to focus now on the investigations and on the criminal proceedings that involve the liability of the authors of crimes perpetrated against migrants in Libya. As for the international jurisdictions, starting from the end of 2016 the Prosecutor's office at the ICC has launched a preliminary investigation into the violent acts perpetrated against migrants in Libya. As we know, Libya has not signed the Rome Statute and is accordingly not subject to the jurisdiction of the ICC. Nevertheless, the Security Council referred the situation in Libya to the ICC Prosecutor on 26 February 2011 through Resolution 1970 (2011): this referral confers jurisdiction in the Libya situation on the ICC. Concerning the ICC's jurisdiction over the crimes committed in the Libyan camps against migrants, it is therefore necessary to find a link between such crimes and the situation that in 2011 led the Security Council to refer the case to the ICC. A link that can be proved by highlighting the fact that the crimes of which migrants are victims are still the consequence of the lawlessness that has arisen in Libya since 2011, and that the authors of such crimes are the same armed groups that gave birth to the 2011 conflict.[5] In any event, at the time we are writing these notes (May 2020), there is still no news of any proceedings officially opened by the ICC Prosecutor's office with regard to the events of interest here.

More developments took place at the level of internal jurisdictions. As regards Italy, in particular, there have been two important judgments that inflicted extremely heavy punishments on the persons held to be liable for the atrocities committed in separate Libyan camps. It is worth remembering that the jurisdiction of our courts for offences (like those examined here) perpetrated abroad by a foreign citizen against foreign citizens is founded on the dual requirement, laid down by Article 10 of the Italian Criminal Code, of the presence in Italy of the wrongdoer and the request to prosecute by the Minister of Justice.

In December 2017, the Criminal Court (Corte d'assise) of Milan sentenced to life imprisonment – for the crimes of multiple and aggravated murder, kidnapping

[4] See, lastly, the very harsh December 2018 report by the High Commissioner for Human Rights of the United Nations, significantly titled *Desperate and Dangerous: Report on the human rights situation of migrants and refugees in Libya*.

[5] For a more in-depth discussion on such issues, see in particular A Whitford, 'Challenges to Bringing a Case before the International Criminal Court in Relation to Alleged Crimes Committed against migrants in Libya' and C Meloni, 'Legal Responsibility before the International Criminal Court in Libya', both of them available in the volume that gathers the texts of the reports delivered at the international Conference held in Tunis on 15 and 16 March 2019, titled *Violations of Human Rights after the Libyan Route Shutdown: Legal Liability of the Italian and Libyan Governments and Possible Legal Solutions*, available on www.asgi.it.

and sexual violence – a Somali citizen identified by several of his fellow countrymen in his role as co-manager of a Libyan detention camp (the facts dealt with in the judgment relate to a period covering the second half of 2015 and the first months of 2016).[6] The description that emerges from the tale of the 17 wronged persons leaves us breathless. In a shed near the Libyan city of Bani Walid, more than 500 persons were detained in horrific hygienic and health conditions, exposed daily to physical violence and sexual abuses. The accused was tasked with inducing the detainees, through the most atrocious tortures, to obtain from their families the money needed to release them and continue their journey to Italy (around 7000 dollars); inside a 'torture chamber', the accused daily raped and tortured his victims, many of whom eventually died of the violence they were made to suffer. The life sentence was later confirmed by the Criminal Court of Appeal (Corte d'assise d'appello) of Milan, which reiterated the reasons for ruling that the testimonies of the victims were reliable, and the accused's liability for the atrocities he was charged with can be established beyond any reasonable doubt.[7]

In June 2015, moreover, the Criminal Court (Corte d'assise) of Agrigento had sentenced to 10 years in jail, for the crime of conspiracy (*associazione a delinquere*) and reduction into slavery, a person held liable for terrible acts of violence against a group of migrants waiting to leave for Italy.[8] The picture that emerged at this trial is consistent with the tragic tales of victims at the proceedings held in Milan, thereby confirming the systematic character of the atrocities the migrants detained in the several concentrations camps of Libya are subjected to.

To sum up, therefore, the responsibilities of Libya's governmental authorities are the target of a preliminary investigation by the ICC; whereas at an internal level, already on two occasions the seriousness of what is taking place at the detention centres in Libya has been established, resulting in heavy sentences against the persons identified as culprits.

Let us check now whether and to what extent we can postulate a liability of the Italian authorities, in the form of complicity, for the offences that are committed in Libya's detention camps for foreigners.

III. Liability before the ICC and its Complementarity with National Jurisdictions

The issue of the possible liability of Italian authorities before the ICC for complicity in the crimes against humanity committed by the Libyan authorities has been

[6] For an analysis of that decision see Veglio, above n 1: the contributions available in the volume take the cue precisely from such decision, providing a more comprehensive interpretation of the state of Libya's detention camps.

[7] The text of the decision by Milan's Criminal Court of Appeal (Corte d'Assise d'Appello di Milano), filed on 12 June 2019, is available on www.asgi.it.

[8] Corte d'Assise Agrigento, 9 May 2015, www.asgi.it.

the specific focus of an interesting work published in April 2018 by Flavia Pacella,[9] a young jurist who worked for a short period at the ICC offices.

According to the author, the scenario we could possibly envisage as regards the Italian authorities before the ICC is a form of responsibility for *complicity for aiding or abetting* (Article 25 § 3 letter c of the Rome Statute). The Italian leaders would be liable for complicity in the crimes against humanity perpetrated by the LCG and by the other Libyan authorities in charge of the detention centres.

Let us leave aside the issues relating to *proof* of actual cooperation by Italian authorities with the Libyan ones, and let us assume as proven the actual collaboration of our authorities with the Libyans; let us also assume as proven the awareness on the part of our authorities of the crimes committed in the detention centres. Based on this, and given the patent relevance of the Italian contribution to the activities of the LCG, it is not so difficult to establish the *actus reus* of the complicity towards the Italian authority that facilitated the execution of the crime committed by Libyans.

Far more complex, instead, is in our view the discourse about the subjective element of the offence, the element of *mens rea*, which presupposes under the Statute that the accomplice has acted 'for the purpose of facilitating the commission of such crime' (article 25 § 3 letter C) or 'in the knowledge of the intention of the group to commit the crime' (article 25 § 3 letter D, ii). Pacella puts forward an interpretation of this subjective requirement that makes is subsumable under the Italian category of *dolus eventualis*, essentially requiring a) the conscious will to facilitate the Libyan authorities; and b) the awareness that in the normal course of events serious crimes would be committed against migrants.

The issue seems indeed to be more complex. In the interpretation of *mens rea* put forward by Pacella, no account is taken of the possible defensive argument that the Italian authorities do not consent at all (at least according to official statements) to the use of their own resources for the perpetration of any crime. On the contrary, according to the Italian government the activities aimed at improving the conditions of migrants in Libya would testify to the will of hindering, rather than facilitating, the criminal activities against them. No doubt that, in hypothetical proceedings against Italian leaders for complicity in the crimes committed in Libya, the problem of the *mens rea* would be a topic for far-reaching discussion. This subject deserves, however, an in-depth analysis not in abstract terms, but rather in the light of the probative evidence that would concretely emerge during any such proceedings, so we do not deem it useful now to dwell on it further.

The thesis of the liability on the part of Italian (and European) authorities for *complicity in crimes against humanity* that take place in Libya was also dealt with in depth in an important document drawn up as part of a project of legal clinics

[9] F Pacella, 'Cooperazione Italia-Libia: profili di responsabilità per crimini di diritto internazionale' (2018) *Diritto penale contemporaneo*, 6 April.

from the Paris University of Sciences Politiques, presented in June 2019 at the ICC Prosecutor's Office.[10]

It is quite a detailed communication (the document runs into nearly 250 pages), which reconstructs the policies deployed in recent years at European level as regards management of rescue operations at sea on behalf of migrants' vessels heading from Libya, and as regards the collaboration by European and Italian authorities with Libyan ones. The document identifies in particular two scenarios in which we might conceive an Italian and European liability. The first such scenario relates to management of rescue operations and to the progressive European disengagement following the brief parenthesis of the (Italian) *Mare Nostrum* operation, a disengagement that prevented the implementation of an effective system capable of avoiding the thousands of deaths that occurred over these years along the Libya-Italy route. The second scenario relates to the European policies of 'Border Externalisation', which, starting in particular from 2015, have aimed to strengthen the operational ability of Libyan authorities to prevent migrants' departures to Europe, resulting in a drastic increase in the number of foreigners held in the Libyan detention camps.

In respect of both scenarios, the document deems it possible to envision a criminal liability for crimes against humanity on the part of European and Italian authorities that consciously decided not to set up an effective system of rescue operations at sea, thereby contributing with their omissions to the occurrence of shipwrecks and deaths at sea (first scenario); and that collaborated and keep on collaborating with Libyan authorities to prevent departures for Italy, by so doing contributing to the atrocities to which migrants are subjected in the detention camps (second scenario).

We cannot here reconstruct the multiple arguments that in the opinion of the drafters of the communication allow to consider as proven all the definitional elements of the crime against humanity, as described in Article 7 of the ICC Statute (in particular the element of 'a widespread or systematic attack directed against any civilian population', and the element of the 'knowledge of the attack'). The document reconstructs quite thoroughly any legal or political act by which the European and Italian authorities have implemented the policies in aid and support of Libyan authorities preventing migrants' journeys to Europe.

As for the identification of the individual persons who might be held liable for such crimes before the ICC, the text does not actually spell out 'names and surnames' of any possible accused. The tone of the arguments makes it however clear that in hypothetical proceedings, all the heads of state and government that at European Council level have contributed to the formulation of the Union's

[10] The document (signed, besides the students of the Paris legal clinic, by advocates Omer Shatz and Juan Branco) is freely accessible on the Internet (see e.g., www.statewatch.org/news/2019/jun/eu-icc-case-EU-Migration-Policies.pdf).

migratory policies would stand trial, together with a further and independent liability attaching to the Italian Prime Minister and the Minister of Internal Affairs, who through separate initiatives from the European context have concluded a series of bilateral agreements with Libyan authorities responsible for running the detention and torture centres.

We can only refer to the perusal of the aforementioned contributions for a more extensive exposition of the issues regarding the possibility of holding European and Italian authorities liable for crimes against humanity committed in Libya. We would like now to focus our attention – particularly as regards the liability of Italian authorities, which is the specific matter of this work – on a *preliminary issue*, which is only briefly hinted at both in the 2018 work and in the 2019 communication, although, in my view, it is of the utmost importance: the issue of the relationships between the Italian criminal courts and the ICC.

As we know, such relationships draw inspiration from the *principle of complementarity*, which under Article 17 of the ICC Statute enjoins on the Court, before proceeding to examine a case, the verification of a series of requirements. The requirement of specific interest here is the one set out under the letter (a) ('the Court shall determine that a case is inadmissible where: (a) The case is being investigated or prosecuted by a State which has jurisdiction over it, unless the State is unwilling or unable genuinely to carry out the investigation or prosecution'). For the ICC not to decline jurisdiction over the matter, therefore, it is necessary to direct attention to the internal legal system, in order to check whether or not the national criminal justice system is capable of ensuring a reliable ascertainment of facts and responsibilities.

The abovementioned works essentially argue that the current lack of any pending proceedings in our criminal courts means that the Italian State has expressed its intention not to consider the conduct of Italian authorities in support of the LCG as triable in a criminal case, and any such case must therefore be deemed to fall under the jurisdiction of the ICC.

I do not find this conclusion entirely convincing. It is indeed true that the Italian criminal prosecutors have not ostensibly launched any investigation against the Italian authorities for complicity in the crimes committed by the LCG at sea and in the detention camps in Libya. It is however similarly true that, as far as I am aware, such problem has never been explicitly brought to the attention of the State prosecutors with a formal request (complaint for complicity in the crimes of the LCG), hence Italian prosecutors, quite simply, never had a chance to take a position on this point. It is furthermore obvious that this kind of crimes can be prosecuted *ex officio*, and that, therefore, no formal complaint is necessary for the Prosecutor's Office to launch investigations. Nonetheless, it seems to be precisely because of that complementarity which ought to inspire the relationships between the ICC jurisdiction and the national ones, that it would be preferable to formally involve the Italian prosecutors in the case, before bringing it to the attention of the ICC prosecution. Although the likelihood of opening a criminal proceeding is limited, the Italian prosecutors would at least be enabled to spell out the reasons why the collaboration of Italian authorities with Libyan ones could not be punished, in spite of the terrible acts of violence ascribable to the latter.

There is moreover no shortage of cases, including very recent ones, in which the Italian prosecutors have hypothesised criminal responsibilities of the Italian authorities for facts associated with migratory flows from Libya.

Let's think about the trial (currently pending before the Criminal Court of Rome) for manslaughter and failure to provide assistance concerning a military ship that arrived too late to rescue the shipwreck survivors of a boat heading from Libya, at a time when tens of castaways had already drowned (the trial relates to the shipwreck which, on 10 October 2013, had caused the death of more than 200 persons, at least 60 of whom children). The persons accused of such crimes are the captain of the ship and other subjects (military and civilians) occupying top positions, who, by delaying with their conduct the rescue operations, contributed to the occurrence of the disaster.

The most famous case is the one known as the '*Diciotti* case', concerning the former Minister of Internal Affairs, M Salvini (the facts of the case date back to August 2018). The media, including the foreign ones, closely followed the case, and the space is too narrow here to account for it in detail. Put in a nutshell, the Court of Ministers (Tribunale dei ministri) of Catania (the competent body to investigate crimes allegedly committed by a Minister in the discharge of his functions) took the view that the decision by Minister Salvini to prevent for five days the disembarkation of the migrants on board the military ship *Diciotti*, at anchor in the port of Lampedusa, realised the crime of aggravated kidnapping: an extremely serious offence, punished with imprisonment up to 15 years. The Italian Constitution (Article 96) stipulates, as regards ministerial crimes, that the Court must request the authorisation to prosecute from Parliament (the Senate for Salvini, as the Minister is a Senator as well), which may deny the authorisation when the offence has been committed 'for the sake of pursuing an overriding public interest in the exercise of a governmental function' (Article 9, § 3, law no 1/1989, a constitutional law that governs the procedure applicable in the event of ministerial crime). The Senate, by a vote dated March 2019, denied the authorisation to prosecute, holding that the blockage of migrants had occurred as part of the Government's strategy to forcefully raise at European level the problem of the redistribution of migrants who land from Libya on Italy's shores. So the Minister, by his conduct, had pursued the overriding public interest in a reduction of the migratory pressure on Italy.[11]

In August 2019, a very similar case to that of the *Diciotti* occurred, the case of the *Open Arms* ship, which had assisted a number of migrants adrift in international waters. A decree issued by the Minister of Internal Affairs applying the

[11] For an analysis of the opinion of the Senate Immunity Council, which was then approved by the Senate assembly, see L Masera, 'Il parere della Giunta del Senato per le immunità nel caso Diciotti. Alcune riflessioni in attesa della decisione dell'assemblea del Senato' (2019) (1) *Diritto, immigrazione e cittadinanza*.

new rules introduced in June 2019 through the so-called security decree-*bis* (*Decreto sicurezza bis*, Decree law no 53/2019, converted into Law no 77/2019) had prevented the *Open Arms* from entering Italian territorial waters. The decree had been appealed against before the Administrative Court (TAR Lazio), which had provisionally suspended its legal effect, holding that it was in conflict with the rules of international law that govern rescue operations at sea. Despite that, the Minister of Internal Affairs had refused to authorise the disembarkation of the migrants, who had been forced to remain on the ship anchored in the port of Lampedusa, in utterly distressful health and psychological conditions due to the overcrowding on the ship and the length of the stay (altogether, from the rescue to the disembarkation the migrants remained for more than three weeks on board the *Open Arms*). Faced with the aggravation of the health and hygiene conditions, the Prosecutor of Agrigento had ordered the immediate disembarkation of the shipwreck victims, in the belief that the Minister's prohibition against them disembarking was in conflict with both domestic and international law, and amounted therefore to the offence of refusal to perform official duties (Article 328 of the Italian Criminal Code). The judge for the preliminary investigations subsequently confirmed the Prosecutor's decision, stressing the fact that the matter had many points in common with the *Diciotti* case, and adumbrating therefore the possibility of charging the Minister with the offence of kidnapping as well.

In the coming weeks, we will able to see how this case is going to develop, as well as whether the criminal judiciary will also take steps with regard to the many similar incidents of orders prohibiting disembarkations issued by the Ministry of Internal Affairs in breach of international law.[12] For the purposes of our argument, these events show in any case that the Italian judiciary enjoys sufficient independence to prosecute even the highest governmental authorities whenever it is of the view that they have committed serious crimes. Sure, the constitutional mechanism which, in the event of ministerial crimes, requires the authorisation to prosecute on the part of Parliament, makes it harder to open a criminal trial against a Minister, exposing the proceeding to the vagaries of political decisions. Despite that, the control of legality carried out by the criminal judiciary over the executive power, on the issue of managing the migratory flows as well, is a serious and independent control, complying with the standards of a State subject to the rule of law.

For this reason, in conclusion, it seems to me that – concerning the issue of interest here, the complicity of Italian authorities in the atrocities perpetrated in Libya – it would be appropriate to submit the case to the national criminal authority, before approaching the ICC. Such a solution seems to me the one most in line with the spirit of the complementarity clause that regulates the relationships between the ICC jurisdiction and the national criminal jurisdictions. So, let us

[12] On 12 February 2020, in relation to the case of the Gregoretti ship blocked for days in the port of Lampedusa in July 2019, the Senate granted the authorisation to prosecute the former Minister Salvini for the crime of kidnapping: see P Gentilucci, 'Il rebus politico-giuridico della nave Gregoretti – Una bussola per i futuri governi' (2020) (2) *Giur. pen. web.*

now try to imagine the scenario an investigating judge would have to face if he wanted to argue the criminal liability of our institutional leaders for the atrocities in Libya.

IV. The Liability before the National Criminal Justice System and the Problem of the Legal Qualification of the Fact

Let us assume as a well-established fact that the Italian authorities (especially the Prime Minister and the Minister of Internal Affairs who in recent years have concluded the agreements with the Libyans, M Gentiloni and M Minniti until June 2018, then M Conte and M Salvini) had funded the LCG while knowing the atrocities whose perpetration the LCG was contributing to and still contributes to in the Libyan detention camps. Without having the pretence here to analyse all the intricate issues a public prosecutor who decided to open an investigation on these facts would have to face, I would limit myself here to focus attention on a profile I regard as particularly important, being preliminary to any further discussion.

The first, major difficulty that would arise at internal level is to identify the *qualification* of the facts *under criminal law*. As we know, Italy has ratified and implemented the ICC Statute, but had not introduced in the internal legal system the offences corresponding to the crimes described in the Statute. For the Italian criminal law, the species of 'crimes against humanity' does not exist; the crimes that can be charged against the Libyans (and thus ascribable to the Italians for complicity) are those provided in our criminal code: kidnapping, sexual violence, murder, torture, reduction into slavery, conspiracy. Therefore, in the event of a criminal trial against the Italian authorities, complicity in crimes against humanity could not be held against them, and what they could be charged with is the participation in the common offences the Libyan authorities have been responsible for.

The lack of the species of crimes against humanity makes it much harder to formulate the charge. Crimes against humanity are by their nature 'macro-crimes', wherein what is charged is not the single episode, but rather the overall situation framing the individual facts: it is thus a crime that, precisely because of its macro-nature, can be more easily held against the leaders of a State or an organisation, as it does not require proof of a personal contribution by them to a specific criminal episode. At the internal level, a corresponding species of offence is lacking, which means that any conviction would have to be for specific offences: complicity in those specific acts of sexual violence, committed on date X in place X and by the material authors Y and Z; complicity in the murders perpetrated by X against Y and Z; kidnapping of X, Y and Z; and so on.

It is clear that put in these terms it is truly hard to conceive the liability of the leaders of the Italian government. What could be ascribed to our leaders (perhaps, and in any event with difficulty) is the conscious collaboration with the LCG, knowing the crimes committed by the latter. However, it seems to me practically impossible to think of proving, on the standard of proof beyond any reasonable doubt applied in a criminal trial, their conscious contribution to a specific criminal episode perpetrated by the Libyans.

I see two possible ways out of this problem. The first would be to imagine a liability for complicity in sexual violence, kidnapping, etc, without indicating any specific episodes for which complicity has been proven. The reasoning would be as follows: the Italian leaders helped the LCG, though aware of the very serious crimes being committed in the centres managed by the latter; the Italian leaders could thus stand trial for complicity in these crimes, even without proof of any contribution to a specific episode. Would this reconstruction be compatible with the principle of the personal nature of criminal liability, and with the principle of the strict determination of the charge? Perhaps yes, but we are dealing with a far from straightforward issue. We would have to argue that, once the operational and financial support of the LCG has been proved, as well as the awareness of the crimes it is responsible for in the detention camps for migrants, we might then allege the liability of Italian authorities even without proof of their direct involvement in a specific criminal episode. Still, it would be a novel legal principle for Italian jurisprudence, which would undoubtedly arouse many negative reactions within the community of criminal law academics and defence lawyers.

A second solution, which I think is simpler, would be to assume the complicity of Italian authorities not in the individual offences perpetrated by the Libyans, but purely in the offence of conspiracy (*associazione a delinquere*), by article 416 of the Italian Criminal Code. An offence which, as we know, does not require proof of complicity in the specific criminal facts committed by the agents. We could then postulate a criminal association run by the LCG and by the other subjects that manage the centres; and a complicity of Italian authorities in such an association, which the Italians certainly do not take part in, but whose activity they support through their collaboration.

It would essentially be a case of applying in the specific instance the category of *external support in a criminal association* (*concorso esterno in associazione a delinquere*), developed by Italian judges particularly in relation to the scenario of external support in Mafia-style association. It is to this legal category that our judges referred when they condemn politicians whose collaboration with Mafia exponents had been established. In the absence of proof linking the politician to specific criminal episodes carried out by the Mafia group, the charge would be that of criminal association: article 416-bis of the Italian Criminal Code, which describes the special offence of participation in a Mafia-style criminal association (*associazione di tipo mafioso*). The politicians proved to have colluded with the Mafia were not convicted of actual participation in the Mafia-style association (a requirement for which our judges require proof of the subject's stable inclusion in the group's criminal activities), but of having provided from the outside, by virtue of their own political-institutional role, a significant contribution to the activity of the criminal group.

In the case of Libya, which is what interests us here, we could attempt to develop a similar argument. The Italian authorities that collaborated and collaborate with subjects responsible for atrocious crimes are neither accountable for the individual offences committed by the Libyans nor definable as participants in the criminal association set up for the purpose of managing the detention and torture camps. They could however be convicted of external support in the criminal association ascribable to the Libyans, just as the politicians colluding with the Mafia have been convicted of external support in Mafia-style association.

However somewhat bizarre it might prima facie appear, this solution nevertheless seems to be more capable of expressing the disvalue of the conduct reproached to the Italian authorities. The charge against them is not so much their voluntary participation in specific criminal episodes the Libyans engaged in, but the fact that they entertained a collaboration relationship with authorities suspected of having perpetrated and continuing to perpetrate terrible crimes against migrants. As the species of crimes against humanity is absent from the Italian criminal law system, external support in a criminal association seems to me the juridical characterisation best fitting the need to express the sense of criminal charge against Italian authorities.

V. Conclusions

In the Libyan detention camps, a tragedy of horrific proportions is taking place. For years, thousands of migrants have been the victims of inhuman suffering, the women systematically raped, the men and children tortured and killed. The testimonies of what is happening in those camps are by now countless, and yet the Italian (and European) authorities keep on collaborating with the authors of such atrocities. All that matters are to block or in any event reduce the migratory flows to Italy, and the manner in which such result is pursued is seemingly quite indifferent.

Faced with such a flagrant breach of the most basic rights of thousands of people, the question of who is responsible for such infringements cannot be eluded. No doubt, the direct authors of the acts of violence in the Libyan camps must respond for the crimes therein committed. However, we cannot ignore the fact that the authorities running those camps (at least the governmental ones) only have means and money to perform their criminal activities because Italy and Europe continue to fund them, in the name of combating illegal immigration.

Asking ourselves whether criminal liability might be imputed to the Italian (and European) authorities as well for what is happening in the Libyan camps is thus a question we criminal law theorists cannot shy away from. So far, as we have seen, the issue has been tackled from the viewpoint of international criminal law, by envisioning a liability on the part of Italian and European authorities for complicity in the crimes against humanity perpetrated at sea and in the Libyan detention camps. The recent communication from the Paris legal clinic to the ICC Prosecution seems to us to be an excellent contribution, on top of that well documented, from which we can draw an initial, interesting analysis of the many complex issues that rise to the fore from that perspective.

In my intervention I have likewise sought to envision the possible internal law scenarios, reflecting on which qualification might be the most apt to penalise the conduct of the Italian authorities in the absence, in the Italian criminal law system, of species of offences corresponding to the crimes against humanity featuring in the ICC Statute.

Realistically, there is an extremely low likelihood of criminal proceedings being instituted against the Italian (and European) authorities for the atrocities of the Libyan camps. As far as the ICC is concerned, we have seen earlier that the ICC Prosecution has not formally opened an investigation even against the Libyan militias that materially run the torture camps. To imagine that, for the same facts, the Prosecutor's Office wants instead to prosecute the top Italian and European institutional leaders frankly seems utterly unlikely, not so much for legal reasons, but first and foremost on political grounds. We are in fact quite familiar with the difficulties that, since its foundation, the ICC had to cope with when discharging its mission. Investigating precisely the leaders of those European countries, which are among the few to support the ICC politically and financially, would be a very risky operation for the legitimisation of the Court.

As for the internal criminal jurisdiction, we have remarked that the lack of the species of crimes against humanity complicates the legal qualification of the facts, without overlooking the obstacle represented, in the event of ministerial crimes, by the need for the judiciary to request Parliament's authorisation to prosecute. If it is possible that the judiciary will take steps, as in the *Diciotti* case, in relation to offences perpetrated through specific episodes of breach of migrants' fundamental rights, it is far more difficult to imagine an investigation being opened against our highest governmental authorities for complicity in the tortures committed in Libya. Faced with such a broad and general charge, an outcry would surely be raised by people accusing it of being a political trial due to the judiciary's determination to encroach on exclusive prerogatives of Government and Parliament: it is unlikely that the judiciary would want to adopt such a radical choice in opposition to political power.

Taking note of the fact that criminal proceedings are unlikely to be opened against Italian and European authorities does not however void of meaning the reflections herein put forward. A document like the communication sent by the Parisian legal clinic to the ICC Prosecutor will quite likely result in no formal investigation being opened, yet it has the very great merit of explicitly asserting on solid juridical grounds the terrible responsibilities of European authorities for what is happening in Libya. This is precisely our task as jurists, leaving behind a testimony that what Europe is doing in Libya is against national and international law and should result in an ascertainment of the liability, criminal as well, on the part of those who took such decisions. Politics will almost certainly prevent the opening of criminal proceedings, but as jurists, we can say that we have not failed in our professional and ethical responsibilities.

INDEX

absconding risk
detention where 61, 196, 216, 217, 218, 219, 221, 223, 227–228, 227n
***Achughbabian* case** 41, 42
***Adil* case** 153
***Affum* case** 42–44, 45
***Al Chodor* case** 216–217, 222, 227, 230
Aliverti, A 39–40
Alpert, GP et al 160
***Appulonappa* case** 36–37, 260–261, 263
Arab Spring 88–89, 148, 194
***Arib* case** 43–44, 45
***Arslan* case** 224, 230
asylum/asylum seekers
Common European Asylum System 110–114, 214, 219, 221, 225, 229
detention as enforcement tool 211–231
EU Asylum Dactyloscopy Database 110–111
EU Asylum Procedures Directive 111, 211, 215
EU Asylum Support Office 112
EU policy 28, 63, 104, 105, 110–114
Geneva Convention 248
Greece 171–172, 184–188
Italy 63, 89, 208
must be outside country of origin 14
Palermo Protocols 18
reception centres 63, 194–201, 212
Reception Conditions Directive 111, 112, 114, 198, 211–216, 219–222, 219n, 224, 228, 230–231
right to seek 248, 256
security of refugee status 115
status categorisation 104
United States 58
Austria
deportation 121
internal EU borders 250
migrants in criminal justice system 90
authorised entry, overstaying *see* **overstaying**

Balkan route 171
Barbagli, M 86
Beccaria, C 265
Beck, U 147–148
Belgium 90, 240
deportation 121–122, 129
humanitarian assistance 251, 256, 258
Bell, D 93
***Bero and Bouzalmate* case** 225–226, 229, 230
biometric data
European Asylum Dactyloscopy Database 110–111
European Dactylographic System 107, 110–112, 111n, 112n, 143
Italy 195–196, 195n
refusal to undergo fingerprinting 196, 198
boat seizures 32, 243, 243n, 244
Bonnet, F and Caillault, C 157
border control
see also irregular entry/border crossing; sea, migrant crossings
carrier sanctions 13–15
cost 69, 70
country of departure, in 14
creation of new borders 9
detention 49
ethnicity as selection criteria 142–143, 149, 153–163
EU, generally 60, 104, 112, 121, 142, 160–161, 235–265
EU internal borders 38–44, 236, 241, 249–250
extraterritorialisation 14–16, 19
human trafficking 142
Italian – French border 249, 249n, 261–262
Italy 193–211
law enforcement authorities 70–71
nationality as selection criteria 157–163
Netherlands 141–143
passport fraud 142
privatisation 14–15, 19
UK – French border 249–250, 250n
United States 126
walls and fences 70
Bosworth, M et al 149
Bowling, B 123

Bowling, B and Westenra, S 146
Bulgaria 240

Canada
Appulonappa case 36–37, 260–261, 263
Charter of Rights and Freedoms 261
Immigration and Refugee Protection Act 260–261
***Cap Anamur* case** 242–243, 246
Carrera, S 162
carrier sanctions 13–15
***Cédric Herrou* case** 33, 241, 261–262
central Mediterranean route 242–248, 255
Chae Chan Ping v United States 74, 75
Charter of Fundamental Rights 30, 32, 110, 213, 217, 220–221, 226, 251–252, 260, 262–263
proportionality principle 217, 220, 252, 263
children *see* **minors**
CLANDESTINO project 105
Colombia
deterritorialization 98
colonial occupation
border claims following 9
confiscation measures
boat seizures 32, 243, 243n, 244
European Union 27
generally 72
proceeds of crime 177, 188
profits of human smuggling 177, 188
vessels, confiscation 246n
consular protection
principle of 12
trafficking victims 21
Conte, G 210, 268, 277
Convention against Torture 10, 214
Convention against Transnational Organized Crime *see* **Palermo Convention**
Convention Concerning Decent Work for Domestic Workers 11
Convention on the Elimination of All Forms of Racial Discrimination 160
Convention on Migration for Employment 10
Convention on the Rights of Migrant Workers and their Families 10–11
Coronavirus pandemic 141, 143, 162
country of origin
asylum must be sought outside 14
consular protection, principle of 12
of smugglers and traffickers 18
Cressey, D 93–94
criminal conviction
EU border control 142
as grounds for detention 220
as grounds for removal 51–59, 74–75, 126–127, 136–139
immigration law consequences 48, 52–59, 64, 73–74, 78–79
ne bis in idem principle 74, 75
reato comune 52
criminal law
Engel criteria 74, 79
exclusionary nature 151
fundamental principles 72
migrant crime, generally 81–83, 267
migrants in justice system 87–92
post-release deportation of prisoners 127–128
reporting mechanism 88
criminalisation of facilitating migrants/migration
see also facilitating unauthorised entry, transit and residence; human smuggling
attempt to facilitate 27–29, 238, 239
complicity in migration 27–28, 32, 238
EU Facilitators Package 26, 29–34, 44–45, 106, 191, 236–265
EU law 25, 27–34, 44–45, 235–265
EU sanctions regime 27, 27n, 28, 238
financial or other material benefit 27, 27n, 29, 34, 39, 238, 238n, 241, 252–253, 253n, 257–258
Greece 172–191
humanitarian assistance 30–34, 37–38, 235–265
instigating/inciting migration 27–28, 238
international law 27, 34–38
Italy 201–210, 267–280
legality of legislation 259–264
money laundering 190
organised crime, framed as 34–38, 45
Palermo Protocol 27, 34–38, 257–258
preventive rationale 30–34
proposed reforms to system 252–265
prosecution of NGOs 31–32, 37–38, 189–191, 242–248, 243n, 249n
search and rescue operations 31–34, 202–203, 209–210, 242–248
criminalisation of immigration law
criminal convictions, immigration law consequences 48, 52–59
custodial measures *see* custodial measures

Europe 50, 53–54, 59, 60–63
generally 149–151
global trend 47–79
immigration breached 48, 49–52
Italy 49, 50
parallel legal system, creation 48, 70
penalties and proceedings 48, 59–79
subsidiarity, principle of 49–50
United States 49, 51–52, 54–59, 64–70

criminalisation of irregular entry/border crossing
EU, within 38–44, 236
exiting territory 42–43
generally 12, 22–23, 38–44, 165–191, 267
Greece 165–191
Italy 50
malum in se 39
national legislation 38, 40–42, 45
precautionary criminalisation 39
re-entry, irregular 38–44, 49, 51
Schengen area and 38, 42–44, 45, 143–149
United States 51–52, 64–70

criminalisation of irregular transit
generally 38–44

criminalisation of migrants/migration
ad hoc instrumentalism 151
crimmigration, use of term 149–151
deportation powers 123–124
deterritorialization and 98–99
effect on labour standards 19, 22–23
ethnic profiling 86–87, 153–163
EU law, generally 25–26, 44–45, 73, 97–99, 101
generally 11, 20, 122–124
Greece 188–191
human rights and 22–23
human smuggling 38–40
irregular transit 38–44
Italy 209
judicial decision-making process 151–152
objectives 12
'othering' and xenophobia 81–83, 93
over-criminalisation 25, 26–30, 34, 44–45
overrepresentation of migrants in justice system 87–92
Palermo Protocols 11, 12–16, 27, 35–36
perceptual shorthands 152
preventive rationale 25, 26, 38–40, 44
ratchet effect 87, 88
reporting mechanism 88
Spain 119–124, 130–139
statistics for reported crimes 85–86
status crimes 86, 88, 99
stereotyping 157–163
stigmatisation of migrants 39, 50, 209
structural discrimination 87
symbolic criminalisation 45, 50, 72
transnational criminal law 11, 12, 13
UN Convention against Transnational Organized Crime 11
United States 93, 99, 123–126
unlawful presence 223, 223n, 230

custodial measures
generally 48
Greece 172–184
immigration offences 59–71, 72, 238, 239–240, 257
Italy 54
overrepresentation of migrants 88–89
symbolic cases 185
United States 51–52, 56, 64–70

Cyprus 240

data protection
information and intelligence sharing 22

Davis, A 98–99

demonisation
of humanitarian assistance 25, 30–31
of migrants 25

Denmark
migrants in criminal justice system 90
Swedish border 250, 250n

deportation/removal
criminal record as grounds 51–59, 74–75, 125–127
crimmigration thesis 122–124
deportability thesis 121
deportation gap 120–124, 127
deportation turn 122
detention during proceedings *see* detention
Dublin system 110, 111, 112–114, 211–219, 231, 250n
enforcement rates 120–121
European Union 61, 73–74, 121–122, 213–214
fundamental rights and 214
generally 71
Greece 121–122, 166, 170, 184–188
Italy 49, 51, 52–54, 61, 62–63, 121
resources required by 20, 123–124, 125
Return Directive *see* Return Directive
Spain 61, 119, 121–124, 130–139
targeted migrant groups 124
undocumented migrants 49, 64

United Kingdom 121, 124, 127–129, 136, 139
United States 49, 51, 52, 54–59, 64–69, 74–78, 123–127, 136–137

destination country
carrier sanctions 13–15

detention
Charter of Fundamental Rights 220–221, 226
CJEU jurisprudence 220–222, 223–227, 229, 230–231
criminal convictions as grounds 220–221
criminalising unlawful presence 223, 223n, 230
deportation proceedings, during 50, 60, 213–214, 216, 217, 219, 222–231
Dublin III Regulation 216, 219, 231
ECHR 73, 79, 194–195, 217, 228
effectiveness principle 223n
enforcement tool, as 211–231
European Union 61–63, 73, 107, 109, 211–231
extension 226
generally 48, 60, 70, 71, 213
Greece 170, 186–188
grounds for 213–214, 219, 222–223, 227–228
identification purposes, for 61, 63, 199–200, 208, 219, 222, 224
Italy 50, 51, 52, 62–63, 72–73, 193–211
Italy's closed-ports policy 193, 194, 201–210
judicial review 219
keeping track of migrants 211
legal representation, access to 212
length 197, 200, 214, 215, 216, 217–219, 222, 224–225, 227–229, 230
Libyan detention centres 267–280
necessity, requirement of 220–221
opportunity to be heard 226
personal freedom, restriction 73, 79, 193–211, 213, 217, 220–222, 223, 225
preventive measure, as 220–221
proportionality principle 73, 198, 217, 226
purpose 211
reception centres 193, 194–201
Reception Conditions Directive 111, 112, 114–115, 198, 211–216, 219–222, 219n, 224, 228, 230–231
Return Directive 219, 222–231
risk of absconding 61, 196, 216, 217, 218, 219, 221, 223, 227–228, 227n
ships used as detention centres 193, 194
specialised facilities 225–226
undocumented migrants 49, 61, 136, 217
United States 51–52, 56, 64–70, 74–75, 125, 126
written reasons to be given 226

deterritorialization
migration and 98–99

***Diciotti* case** 203, 204–206, 275–276, 280

Dines, N and Rigo, E 89

discrimination
direct and indirect 161
ethnicity as selection criteria 86–87, 142–143, 149, 153–159
European Union law 160–161
Global Compact on Migration 20n
nationality as selection criteria 157–163, 256
Palermo Protocol on human trafficking 13
structural 87

domestic workers
Convention 11

drug offences
by migrants 58, 58n, 59, 76–77, 86, 127
fight against trafficking 71

Dublin Convention 110, 111, 112–114, 211–219, 231, 250n
CJEU cases 216–219, 222

due process
Global Compact on Migration 20
United States 69

Economou, M 189

***El Dridi* case** 40–41, 42, 45, 50, 52

Emergency Response Centre International 249n

equality, principle of 72

ethnicity
ethnic profiling 86–87, 155–157
perceptual shorthands 152
protection of minorities 20n
as selection criteria 86–87, 142–143, 149, 153–163

Eurodac 107, 110–112, 111n, 112n, 143

European Committee for the Prevention of Torture 196

European Convention of Human Rights
see also fundamental rights
administrative expulsion 187–188
collective forced returns 73
personal freedom, restriction 73, 79, 193–211, 213, 217, 220–222
prohibition on retroactive application 74

European Court of Human Rights
case law 71, 72–74, 78
Khlaifia and Others v Italy 73, 79, 193–199, 200, 203, 204–206, 208
European Union
see also individual countries
2015 migration crisis 102, 107, 143, 149, 162–163, 170–172, 236
accelerated procedures, proposed 104
Action Plan against migrant smuggling 236
Action Plan on return 105, 107
administrative detention 62–63
administrative immigration law 3, 4, 28, 39
Agenda on Migration 105, 112
Area of Freedom, Security and Justice 42–44, 45, 106, 221
asylum policy 28, 63, 104, 105, 110–114, 211–231
Asylum Procedures Directive 111, 211, 215
Asylum Support Office 112
autonomy of member states 143, 144–145
birth rate 94–96
Border and Coastguard Regulation 108
border control 60, 104, 112, 121, 142, 143, 148–149, 160–161, 235–265
categorisation of migrants 102, 103–104
Charter of Fundamental Rights *see* Charter of Fundamental Rights
Citizens' Rights Directive 130
Common European Asylum System 110–114, 214, 219, 221, 225, 229
confiscation measures 27
Coronavirus pandemic 141, 143, 162
crime control checks 142
criminal conviction, immigration law consequences 53–54
criminal law consequences for immigration law breaches 50, 72–73
criminal sanctions 25, 73–74, 238
criminalisation of humanitarian aid 30–34, 235, 239
criminalisation of immigration law process 60–63, 72–74
criminalisation of migration 25–26, 44–45, 73–74, 97–99, 101
cross-border crimes 45
current migration trends 102, 104–105
Dactylographic System (Eurodac) 107, 110–112, 111n, 112n, 143
demographic transition 94–97
deportation gap 120–124
deportation/removal 61, 73–74, 121–122
detention 61–63, 73, 107, 109, 211–231
detention as enforcement tool 211–231
detention standards 211
discrimination on grounds of nationality 160–161
Dublin Convention 110, 111, 112–114, 211–219, 231, 250n
enforcement tool, detention as 211–231
entry bans 109–110
entry refusal 60
Entry-Exit System 107
EU citizens, deportation 130, 136
EU-Turkey Statement 171, 172, 189, 191
Europol 112
Facilitation Directive 26–29, 26n, 106, 106n, 189, 237–241
Facilitation Framework Decision 26–27, 26n, 175, 237–241, 257
Facilitators Package 26, 29–34, 44–45, 106, 191, 236–265
family reunification 102
Frontex 60, 105, 112
hotspots *see* hotspot policy
human rights obligations 30, 73–74, 213
human smuggling, criminalisation 25–38, 44–45, 106, 235
immigrant numbers 102
immigration policy, generally 101, 105–110
inability to reach agreement 210
Integrated Return Management Application 107–108
internal borders 38–44, 143, 144, 145–147, 153, 162, 236, 241, 249–250
international law compared 27, 28–30, 34
irregular entry and stay 38–44, 101, 102, 104–110
legal entry 102, 104–105
Lisbon Treaty 27, 30
migrants in justice system 89–92
migration flows and stocks 102–103, 105
Migration Partnership Framework 108
migration routes 102, 171, 242–248
monitoring forced return 107
national legislation 38, 40–42, 45
national security 143, 163
open borders concept, generally 142, 143–149
Operation Sophia 13
outplacement promises 203n
over-criminalisation 25, 26–30, 34, 44–45, 235
overstaying 105

- Palermo Convention 34
- penalty regime 27, 27n
- preventive rationale 25, 26, 28, 29, 30–34, 39–40, 44
- prosecutions under 25
- re-entry bans 61
- reception centres 63
- Reception Conditions Directive 111, 112, 114–115, 198, 211–216, 219–222, 219n, 224, 228, 230–231
- refugees 102
- repatriation orders *see* deportation/removal *above*
- Resettlement Framework 112, 112n
- residence permits 73, 102, 104, 105
- Return Directive *see* Return Directive
- Return Handbook 107
- return procedures, proposed changes 104
- returns policy 106
- Schengen area *see* Schengen area
- securitisation, open borders and 147–149
- securitised criminalisation 25, 45
- solidarity and fair sharing principle 111, 143
- Tampere European Council 106, 110
- Travel Document 107
- Treaty on the Functioning of the European Union 101, 106, 111, 115, 160–161
- undocumented migrants 28, 61, 63, 64, 99, 236
- visa termination 104, 105
- voluntary departures 61, 107, 109–110, 115–116
- vulnerable persons 62

exploitation of migrants
- human smuggling 12, 15, 20n, 71, 176
- human trafficking 71
- migrant workers 12, 15, 71
- sexual exploitation 71

expulsion *see* **deportation/removal**

facilitating unauthorised entry, transit and residence
- central Mediterranean route 242–248, 255
- criminalisation *see* criminalisation of facilitating migrants/migration
- endangering lives of migrants 27n, 238, 257
- EU Facilitation Directive 26–29, 26n, 106, 106n, 189, 237–241
- EU Facilitation Framework Decision 26–27, 26n, 175, 237–241
- EU Facilitators Package 26, 29–34, 44–45, 106, 191, 236–265
- EU law 25, 27–34, 44–45
- freedom of association 32
- hostile environment, creation 30–34
- human smuggling *see* human smuggling
- human trafficking *see* human trafficking
- humanitarian assistance *see* humanitarian assistance
- marriages of convenience 239, 250–251
- mutual assistance among refugees 36–37
- Palermo Protocol 27
- penalty regime 239–241, 257, 263
- preventive measures 30–34
- proposed reforms to system 252–265
- search and rescue operations 31–34, 202–203, 209–210, 242–248
- third country, in 31
- undocumented migrants 28

Fakhoury, T 149

family members
- aiding 249, 249n
- Palermo Protocols 35
- reunification 102, 250–251

Federici, S 82

financial offences
- generally 72

financial transactions
- human smuggling 27, 27n, 29
- international cooperation to trace 22

fingerprinting *see* **biometric data**

Finland 90, 240
- humanitarian assistance 251, 256, 258

Fong Yue Ting v United States 77

forced labour or servitude
- expulsion, threat of 19
- Forced Labour Conventions 17
- migrants held in 15, 19
- prohibition 17

France
- *Achughbabian* case 41, 42
- *Affum* case 42–44, 45
- *Arib* case 43–44, 45
- *Cédric Herrou* case 33, 241, 261–262
- demographic transition 95
- deportation 121–122
- detention centres 63
- entry refusal 60
- facilitating illegal stay or transit 241
- *fraternité* ruling 33–34, 262
- Italian border 249, 249n, 261–262
- migrant population 95
- migrants in criminal justice system 90, 92

overseas territories 63
removal orders 61
returnees 109
Schengen area 148
UK border 249–250, 250n
free travel areas 9
freedom, individual and personal
right to 73, 79, 193–211, 213, 217, 220–222, 223, 225, 263
freedom of association
fundamental right 32
fundamental rights
asylum, right to seek 248, 256
Convention against Torture 10, 214
criminalisation of migration 22–23, 48
data protection 22
defence, right of 73
ECHR *see* European Convention of Human Rights
ECtHR case law 71, 72–74, 78
EU Charter *see* Charter of Fundamental Rights
EU General Principle 213
EU obligations 30, 73–74
EU Return Directive 62, 73–74, 108
forced labour or servitude *see* forced labour or servitude
freedom of association 32
Global Compact on Migration 20–22
Greece 187–191
human dignity 34, 256, 263
human traffickers/smugglers 17
individual and personal freedom 73, 79, 193–211, 213, 217, 220–222, 223, 225, 263
inhuman or degrading treatment 17, 73
international 32
Libyan violations 245, 267–280
life and personal integrity 256
Lisbon Treaty 30
migrants 10–11, 17, 48, 72, 116, 193–211, 235, 248
non-discrimination on grounds of nationality 256
non-refoulement 10, 209, 252
Palermo Protocols and 16–19, 20, 23
privacy 22
refugees 10
Return Directive 62, 73–74, 108, 222, 229
smugglers 17
torture *see* torture, prohibition
Universal Declaration of 10
***G and R* case** 226, 229
Gallagher, AT and David, F 35
Gallo, Z 88
gender
Global Compact on Migration 20
victims of gender-based violence 20n
Geneva Convention 248
Gentiloni, P 268, 277
Germany
demographic transition 95
deportation 121
internal EU borders 250
migrants in criminal justice system 90
net migration 95
Global Compact for Refugees 11–12
Global Compact for Safe, Orderly and Regular Migration
access to justice, facilitating 22
children 20
Common Understanding 20
consular protection 21
due process 20
gender responsiveness 20
generally 11–12, 115
guiding principles 20
human rights and 20–22
human smuggling 20–21
human trafficking 20–21
international cooperation 20, 21–22
legal status 20
monitoring migration routes 22
national sovereignty 19, 20
non-signatories 19–20
Objectives 20–22
Palermo Protocols and 19–22, 23
proposed actions 20–21, 22
rule of law 20
screening, assessment and referral 21
Shared Responsibility 20
sustainable development goals and 20
temporary residence 22
training in anti-trafficking measures 22
Unity of Purpose 20
vulnerable persons 20–21, 20n, 22
globalisation
catastrophic theory of progress 84, 97–98
migration a defining feature 20, 94, 96–98
neoliberal revolution 95
'refugeeisation' of workforce 89, 99
Greece
2015 migration crisis 170–172
administrative detention 170, 186–188

administrative expulsion 166, 184–188
administrative procedure 168–169
assisting unauthorised entry 172–179, 189–191, 249n
asylum legislation 171–172, 184–188
asylum system 184–188
Balkan route 171
Code of Criminal Procedure 165–166, 184
concurrence doctrine 168, 175, 179–182
conditional release 165
Criminal Code 165–166, 174, 180, 186
crimmigration 165–191
deportation 121–122, 166, 170, 184–188
ECHR 187–188
emigration from 166–167
EU-Turkey Statement 171, 172, 189, 191
felonies 165, 169–170, 173–179
Financial Action Task Force 190
financial crisis 166, 169
habeas corpus right 186, 188
hindering police investigation 172
human rights, pressure on 187–191
human smuggling 167–168, 169, 170, 171, 172–184
human trafficking 177–178
humanitarian assistance, criminalising 179, 189–191
mass unauthorised entries 167–169, 176–177
migrant workers 168, 169
migrants in justice system 90
misdemeanours 165, 170, 179–180
overcrowding of irregular immigrants 169
prosecution of NGOs 37–38, 189–191
refugee camps 171
refugee status 184
removal orders 61
residence permits 168
sentencing regime 166–191, 240
transportation within 171
unauthorised entry or exit 170, 173–178, 184–188

***Gregoretti* case** 206
Guia, MJ et al 146
Guild, E and Acosta, D 105
Gurguchiani v Spain 74

Harcourt, B 87
Herrou, Cédric *see* ***Cédric Herrou* case**
Hirsi Jamaa v Italy 73, 268
hostile environment 30–34
hotspot policy
biometric data 195–196, 195n
EU, generally 63, 112, 193–201, 208
Italy 4, 63, 193–201, 195n, 208
human rights *see* **fundamental rights**
human smuggling
see also human trafficking
attempt, criminalisation 27–29, 238, 239
carrier sanctions 13–15
central Mediterranean route 242–248, 255
complicity, criminalisation 27–28, 32
country of origin of smuggler or operation 18–19
criminalisation, generally 13, 18–19, 21, 38–39, 71, 167–168
criminalisation in EU law 25–38, 235–265
criminalisation in Palermo Protocol 34–38, 178, 257–258
definition in EU law 28
definition in international law 28, 261
Dutch measures against 153
EU Action Plan against 236
EU policy 25–38, 106, 235–265
expansion of measures against 12
exploitation and abuse, persons subject to 20n
expulsion following 19, 22
facilitating *see* facilitating unauthorised entry, transit and residence
financial or other material benefit, for 27, 27n, 29, 34–38, 39, 176–179, 238, 238n, 241, 252–254, 253n, 257–258
forced labour or servitude, migrants held in 15, 19
fundamental rights of smugglers 17
Global Compact on Migration 20–21
Greece 167–168, 169, 170, 171, 172–184
instigation, criminalisation 27–28
international cooperation measures 21–22, 29
international law 28, 30, 34
meaning 13
minors used as perpetrators 171, 189
organised crime, framed as 34–38, 45
over-criminalisation 25, 26–30, 34, 44–45, 235
Palermo Protocol *see* Palermo Protocols
penalties and sanctions 21, 25, 27, 27n, 238, 239–241
preventive rationale of criminalisation 38–40
R v Appulonappa 36–37, 260–261, 263

reporting, enabling 19, 22
seizure and confiscation of profits 177, 188
sharing information and intelligence on 21, 22
training anti-smuggling officials 17, 22
human trafficking
see also human smuggling
attempt, criminalisation 27–28
border controls, generally 142
complicity, criminalisation 27–28, 32
country of origin of trafficker or operation 18
criminalisation, generally 13, 18–19, 21, 71
expansion of measures against 12
exploitation of migrants 71
expulsion following 19, 22
facilitating *see* facilitating unauthorised entry, transit and residence
financial or other material benefit, for 27, 27n, 29, 34–38, 39
forced labour or servitude, migrants held in 15, 19
fundamental rights of traffickers 17
Global Compact on Migration 20–21, 22
Greece 177–178
instigation, criminalisation 27–28
international cooperation measures 21–22
meaning 13
minors 13, 16
Palermo Protocol *see* Palermo Protocols
penalties and sanctions 21, 27, 27n
reporting, enabling 19, 22
screening, assessment and referral 21
sharing information and intelligence on 21, 22
trafficking within same state 13
training anti-trafficking officials 17, 22
US, admission denied to traffickers 58
victims of, assistance or protection 16–17
women 13, 16
humanitarian assistance
see also facilitating unauthorised entry, transit and residence
criminalising 30–34, 37–38, 179, 189–191, 201–210, 235–265
family members 249, 249n
hostile environment against 30–34
internal EU borders 249–250
Italy's closed-ports policy 193, 194, 201–210, 267–280
justifications for 249
Palermo Protocols 35
prosecution of NGOs 31–32, 37–38, 189–191, 242–248, 243n, 249n
refugees, protection 89
search and rescue operations 30–34, 63, 102, 103, 201–203, 209–210, 242–248
stigmatisation 25, 30–31, 209
unaccompanied minors 249
Hungary
deportation 121
internal EU borders 250
removal proceedings 61

Iceland 237
identification
checks in country of departure 14
detention for purposes of 61, 63, 199–200, 208, 219, 222, 224
fraud, border controls 142, 153
generally 63, 219, 224
refusal to be identified 61, 196, 198
returnees, of 107
US, identification in 64
immigration law
administrative 3, 4, 28, 39, 48, 49–50
anti-terrorism measures 55, 60, 64, 71
breach *see* immigration law breaches
confiscation measures
see also confiscation measures
criminal convictions, immigration law consequences 48, 52–59, 64, 73–74
criminalisation *see* criminalisation of immigration law
deportation *see* deportation/removal
detention *see* custodial measures; detention
irregularity, creating 103, 105–110
misleading terms, use of 71–72
national security issue, as 71
organised crime, fighting 71
parallel legal system, creation 48, 70
political choices, based on 48, 71, 101
preventive rationale *see* preventive rationale
symbolic criminalisation 45, 50, 72
immigration law breaches
border controls *see* border control
criminal law penalties 48, 59–71
criminal record, where 48, 52–59
global trend towards criminalisation 47–79
removal following 49
immunity, granting 35–36
imprisonment *see* **custodial measures**
indigenous peoples
Global Compact on Migration 20n

inequality, rising 97–98
inhuman or degrading treatment
prohibition 17, 73
Inter-American Court of Human Rights 74
international cooperation
Global Compact on Migration 20, 21–22
information and intelligence sharing 21, 22
necessity for 9
International Covenant on Civil and Political Rights 160
travel industry, carrier sanctions 14
International Criminal Court
Libyan human rights violations 269–270, 271–277, 280
International Labour Office
labour rights and migration 9–10
International Labour Organisation
Domestic Workers Convention 11
Forced Labour Conventions 17
Migration for Employment Convention 10
international law
compliance 33
EU law compared 25, 28–30, 34
EU repatriations 62
human smuggling 28, 34, 36–37, 261
law of the sea 31–33, 206, 209, 246
preventive rationale 26
Ireland 89–90, 237, 240
Irish immigrants to US 93
irregular entry/border crossing
see also border control and individual countries
criminalisation *see* criminalisation of irregular entry/border crossing
custodial sentences 59–71, 72, 238, 239–240
EU, generally 38–44, 101, 102, 104–110
EU Return Directive *see* Return Directive
exploitation *see* exploitation of migrants
Greece 165–191
irregular re-entry 38–44, 49
irregular transit 38–44, 153–155
malum in se 39
mass unauthorised entries 167–169, 176–177
Palermo Protocols 35–36
Schengen area 38, 42–44, 45
selection criteria for checks 142–143, 149, 153–159
irregular status
convertibility 115
generally 114–115
Italy
asylum seekers 63, 89, 208
attempted human smuggling 29
birth rate 94, 96
border control 193–211, 249
Border Externalisation policy 273
central Mediterranean route 193, 194, 201–210, 242–248, 255
closed-ports policy 193, 194, 201–210, 255n, 267–280
Code of conduct for NGOs 244, 268
collaboration with Libyan authorities 268–269, 272–275, 277–280
Consolidated Act on Immigration 50, 195–199, 243
CPT Report 196
Criminal Code 270, 276, 277–280
criminal prosecution non-mandatory 51
criminal record as grounds for denied entry 53
criminal record as grounds for removal 52–54
crimmigration 49, 50, 195–211
demographic transition 94, 95, 96
deportation 6, 49, 51, 52–54, 62–63, 121–122, 196, 197
detention 50, 51, 52, 62–63, 72–73, 109, 193–211
Detention Centres prior to Repatriation 62–63, 196–197
Diciotti case 203, 204–206, 275–276, 280
dolus eventualis 272
El Dridi case 40–41, 42, 45, 50, 52
emigration from 83–84, 93
entry refusal 60
facilitating entry, transit and residence 242–251
fingerprinting 195–196
forcible returns at sea 72–73
French border 249, 249n, 261–262
Gregoretti case 206
Hirsi Jamaa v Italy 73, 268
hotspot policy 4, 63, 193–201, 195n, 208
humanitarian assistance 241
illegal entry or stay 49, 50, 195–196, 251
Italians First policy 94
Khlaifia and Others v Italy 73, 79, 193–199, 200, 203, 204–206, 208
Lampedusa 194–195, 200, 245–246
Libyan human rights violations, liability 267–280
migrant population 95

migrant workers 89
migrants in criminal justice system 88–89, 90
military ships, detention on 204–206
Minniti-Orlando Decree 195
Open Arms Case 31, 32, 206–207, 244–245, 275–276
prison and emigration rates 84
prosecution of NGOs 31–32, 242–248
Puglia Law 194
re-entry after removal 49, 50
reception centres 63, 194–201
'refugeeisation' of workforce 89, 99
refugees 89
removal orders 50, 61
residence permits 53
return rate 109
Richmond Yaw and Others v Italy 73, 79
Schengen area 148
Sea Watch case 31–32, 245–248
Security (Salvini) Decree 89, 99, 197–200, 209, 210
Security Decree-bis 201–203, 206, 209, 210, 245, 245n, 276
statistics for reported crimes 85–86
undocumented migrants 63, 89, 193, 195–198, 208–209
validation hearings 197
voluntary departures 54

Iuventa 243–244

***JN* case** 220–221, 222, 230, 231
Jordan v De George 57–58
judiciary
decision-making process 151–152
***Jugend Rettet* case** 31–32, 243
Juncker, Jean-Claude 108

***K* case** 221, 222, 230, 231
***Kadzoev* case** 224–225, 228, 229, 230, 231
Kanstrom, D 75–76
***Khir Amayry* case** 217–219, 222
Khlaifia and Others v Italy 73, 79, 193–199, 200, 203, 204–206, 208

labour rights and standards
criminalisation of migration and 22–23
forced labour or servitude 15, 19
migration and 9–10, 15
trafficking of workers 13
Legomsky, SH 71, 75
Leun, J van der and Woude, M van de 123
Libya
Coast Guard 244, 245, 267–269, 277
collaboration with 268–269, 272–275, 277–280
human rights violations 245, 267–280
migration from 5, 72–73, 148, 203–206, 209, 243–248
Liechtenstein 237
Lombroso, C 82, 83
Lucano, Domenico 250–251

McClean, D 35–36
McLachlin J 37
***Mahdi* case** 226, 229
Malta 241, 244
Malta Agreement 210
marriages of convenience
EU Facilitators Package 239, 250–251
Martino, A di et al 36
Marx, K 82–83, 98
***Melki/Abdeli* case** 153
Merton, RK 94
migrant workers
Domestic Workers Convention 11
exploitation 12, 15, 71, 176
families 10–11
Forced Labour Conventions 17
forced labour or servitude 15, 19
Greece 168, 169
ILO Convention 10
Italy 89
Recruitment Convention 11
'refugeeisation' of workforce 89, 99
Rights Convention 10–11
trafficking 13
migrants/migration
categorisation 102, 103–104
crime by migrants 81–94
criminalisation *see* criminalisation of migrants/migration
deterritorialization and 98–99
economic migrants 89
endangering lives of migrants 238, 257
ethnic profiling 86–87, 155–157
facilitating *see* criminalisation of facilitating migrants/migration; facilitating unauthorised entry, transit and residence;
friction caused by 9
globalisation and 20, 94, 96–98
measuring 102–103
migrant workers *see* migrant workers

- migrants in justice system 87–92
- migration flows and stocks 102–103
- migration policy *see* migration policy
- national borders, migration within 81–82
- negative narratives surrounding 105
- perception as temporary phenomenon 103
- race and migration 92–94
- relocation, Malta Agreement 210
- rising inequality increasing 97–98
- statistics for reported crimes 85–86
- status crimes 86, 88, 99

migration flows
- measuring 102–103
- policy focus on 105

migration routes
- Balkan route 171
- central Mediterranean route 242–248, 255
- monitoring 22

migration stocks
- impact of EU legislation 103
- measuring 102–103

Minniti, M 268, 277

minors
- Global Compact on Migration 20
- human smuggling, used in 171, 189
- trafficking, Palermo Protocol 13, 16
- unaccompanied 20n, 249

Mitsilegas, V 239, 252

Montego Bay Convention 202, 202n

Morton, J 123–124

Motomura, H 150, 151

Muller, C 93

national culture
- protection 149, 163

national security
- detention on grounds of 219, 220–221, 227–228
- immigration law and 71, 94, 149, 163

nationalism
- migration and 94, 98

nationality
- creation of new states 9
- determination 219

neoliberal revolution 95

Netherlands
- Aliens Decree 153, 154
- Aliens Law 153
- border control 141–143, 153–163
- deportations 121–122
- Dutch approach to article 23 SBC 153–163
- European Union law 160–161
- migrants in criminal justice system 90
- Mobile Security Monitoring 153–163
- Royal Netherlands Marechaussee 142–143, 153, 154–163
- Schengen area 142–143

non-government organisations
- humanitarian assistance by 30–34

non-refoulement
- Convention against Torture 10, 209
- principle, generally 252

Norway 129, 237

***Open Arms* Case** 31, 32, 206–207, 244–245, 275–276

Operation Mare Nostrum 243, 243n, 255, 273

Operation Sophia 13, 243n

Operation Triton 243n

organised crime
- Convention on Transnational *see* Palermo Convention
- fighting, generally 71
- financial or other material benefit, for 34–38, 39, 238, 238n, 252–254, 253n, 257–258
- human smuggling framed as 34–38, 39, 44, 45
- human trafficking *see* human trafficking
- Palermo Protocols 11, 34–38, 39, 44

overstaying
- European Union 105
- generally 18
- precautionary criminalisation 39–40
- United States 65

Pacella, F 272

Padilla v Kentucky 76–77, 78

Palermo Convention
- EU ratification 34
- generally 11, 29, 34
- Protocols *see* Palermo Protocols

Palermo Protocols
- asylum and 18
- criminalisation of migrants 12–19, 35
- diminution of space for 12
- discretion of Member States 35
- EU ratification 34
- financial or other material benefit 27, 29, 34–38, 39, 238n, 252–254, 253n
- Global Compact on Migration 19–22, 23
- human rights and 16–19, 20, 23
- human smuggling/trafficking 11, 12–19, 22, 23, 27, 34–38, 44, 178, 238n, 257–258, 261

humanitarian or family assistance 35
interpretation 34
irregular entry 35–36
minors 13, 16
mutual assistance among refugees 36–37
objectives 13–14, 23, 36
organised crime, smuggling framed as 11, 34–38, 39, 44, 45
protection of migrants 36
refugee protection, effect on 23
relationship with migration 12–16, 23
temporary residence permits 19
training anti-trafficking/smuggling officials 17
women 13, 16

Paris Commune 82
Parisi, R 87
Park, RE 84, 94, 97
passport fraud 142
people smuggling *see* **human smuggling**
***Pham* case** 225–226, 229, 230
Piketty, T 97
Poland 240
deportations 121
entry refusal 60
removal proceedings 61
Portugal 61, 90
Pratt, A and Thompson, SK 159
preventive rationale
anti-terrorism measures 55, 64, 71
EU law, generally 25, 26, 30–34, 39–40, 44
immigration law, generally 72, 147, 152
preventive detention 220
risk, generally 147, 152
privacy, right to
information and intelligence sharing 22
***Proactiva Open Arms* case** *see* ***Open Arms* Case**
profiling *see* **ethnicity**
proportionality principle
Charter of Fundamental Rights 217, 220, 252, 263
detention 73, 198, 217, 226
sentencing 27n, 28n, 238n, 252, 257
public order
detention on grounds of 219, 220

R v Appulonappa *see* ***Appulonappa* case**
Rackete, Carola 32, 245–248
Reagan, R 95
Refugee Convention 10, 14
refugees
see also asylum/asylum seekers
2015 crisis 170–172, 236
access to protection 23
Arab Spring 88–89
carrier sanctions 13–15
Convention on Status of Refugees 261
criminal record affecting status 52
definition 14n
EU-Turkey Statement 171, 172, 189, 191
European Union 102
Global Compact for 11–12
Greece 171, 184
humanitarian assistance *see* humanitarian assistance
international law 33
Italy 89
mutual assistance 36–37
Palermo Protocols and 23
refugee camps 171
'refugeeisation' of workforce 89, 99
smuggling *see* human smuggling
status categorisation 104, 115
undocumented 14
United States 58
refusal of entry
criminal record as grounds 52, 53
generally 49–50
religious minorities
protection 20n
removal *see* **deportation**
residence permit
non renewal or revocation 53, 114
removal of immigrants with 73
Return Directive
aim 222
CJEU jurisprudence 73, 223–227, 229, 230–231
common standards and procedures 107
detention during proceedings 219, 222–231
entry bans 109–110
entry into force 212, 222
EU law, generally 38, 40–44, 45, 106–110, 211
fundamental rights and 62, 73–74, 108, 222, 229
illegal entry 43
illegal stay 43, 107
margin of discretion 109–110
national provisions and 50
possible unwarranted effects 106–110
recast, proposal for 108–109, 114, 227–229
Richmond Yaw and Others v Italy 73, 79
risk
language of 146–149
preventive rationale 147, 152

risk assessment
ethnicity based immigration checks *see* ethnicity
immigration controls and 147–149
Romania 61
rule of law
Global Compact on Migration 20
Rumbaut, R 91

Saadi v UK 221
Salvini, M 89, 99, 197, 205, 206, 268, 275, 277
Sampson, R 91
Scalia J 77
Schengen area
arrest on leaving 42
article 23 checks 144–145, 153–163
autonomy of member states 143, 144–145
compensatory measures 143
Coronavirus pandemic 141, 143, 162
crimmigration 38, 42–44, 45, 143–149
European Dactylographic System 143
generally 1, 26, 106, 162–163
identity controls 153
internal and external borders 43–44, 45
intra-Schengen checks 143, 144, 145–147, 153–163
Netherlands 142–163
open borders concept 142, 143–149
participating non-Member States 237
preventive measures 147
re-introduction of border controls 43, 148
Schengen Borders Code 43, 142–143, 144, 145, 146, 153–159
Schengen Information System 107, 110, 143
securitisation of EU 147–149
sea, migrant crossings
boat seizures 32, 243, 243n, 244
duty of rescue 32–33, 244–247
forcible returns at sea 72–73
high seas 31
IMO Guidelines 247
international conventions 31–33, 201, 209, 246
Italian-Libyan collaboration 268–269, 272–275, 277–280
Italy's closed-ports policy 193, 194, 201–210, 255n, 275–276
Malta Agreement 210
migrant deaths 102
military ships, detention on 204–206
Montego Bay Convention 202, 202n
NGOs 243n
Operation Mare Nostrum 243, 243n, 255, 273
Operation Sophia 243n
Operation Triton 243n
place of safety, transfer to 193, 201, 203–209, 242, 245–248
SAR Convention 209, 246–247
search and rescue, criminalisation 31–34, 202–203, 209–210, 242–248, 255, 255n
UK – French border 249–250, 250n
***Sea Watch* case** 31–32, 245–248
securitisation
EU open borders and 147–149, 163
EU preventive rationale 25, 45
as grounds for detention 227–228
national security issues 71, 219, 220–221, 227–228
securitised criminalisation 45
Spain 134
US preventive rationale 55–56
Sellin, T 94
Sessions v Dimaya 78
sexual violence, victims of 20n
Sklansky, DA 71, 151
Slovenia 90
smuggling *see* **human smuggling**
Social Darwinism 84
socio-economic considerations
generally 71
sociology
catastrophic theory of progress 84, 97–98
Chicago School 84, 91, 94
crime and, sociological debate 83–85
migration and crime 83–85
Positive School 83
sociology of deviance 89
South Africa
deterritorialization 98
sovereignty 19, 20, 48
Soviet Union
fall, border claims following 9
Spain
administrative removals 134, 135
crimmigration 119–124, 130–139
deportation gap 120–124
deportations 121–122, 129, 130–139
detention centres 63
documented foreigners 130
entry refusal 60
EU citizens, deportation 130, 136
express deportations 135
Foreigners' Law 130
Gurguchiani v Spain 74
humanitarian assistance 251, 256, 258
irregular residence 130, 135

migrants in criminal justice system 90
qualified deportations 131–132
removal orders 61, 119, 130–139
security 134
SEDEX 132
sentencing regime 240
undocumented migrants 119
Spena, A 28, 29, 39
stay
illegal 49
overstaying 18, 39–40
Steffensmeier, D et al 152
Stevens J 77
Stumpf, J 48, 122, 123, 146, 150, 151
subsidiarity principle 49–50
subsidiary protection status
criminal record affecting 52
sustainable development
Global Compact on Migration 20
Sutherland, E 85, 94
Sweden
Danish border 250, 250n
deportations 121, 129
migrants in criminal justice system 90
removal proceedings 61
Switzerland 237
Syrian Civil War 170–172
Szpunar AG 43

tax offences 72
temporary residence permits
Global Compact on Migration 22
Palermo Protocols 19
terrorism, preventive measures against
immigration law as 55, 60, 64, 71
language of risk 146–147
United States 55, 64, 125
Thatcher, M 95
third country
assistance given in 31
Thomas J 78
Tillyer, R and Hartley, RD 152
torture
non-refoulement 10, 209, 252
prohibition, generally 17
UN Convention against 10, 214
trafficking *see* **human trafficking**
transnational criminal law
Convention against Transnational Organized Crime 11
human smuggling 13, 15
Palermo Convention 34
trafficking 13, 15
travel industry
carrier sanctions 13–15
regulation 13–14
Tunisia 148, 194
Turkey
EU-Turkey Statement 171, 172, 189, 191
failed 2016 coup d'état 185
February 2020 opening of border 172, 185

undocumented migrants
carrier sanctions 13–15
deportation 49, 61, 136
detention 49, 193, 217
economic migrants 89
European Union 28, 61, 63, 64, 99, 236
fake documentation 99
Italy 63, 89, 193, 195–198, 208–209
refugees 14
reported crimes by 87–88
Spain 119
United States 59, 64–69, 99
United Kingdom 89–90, 92, 237
deportation gap 129
deportation quotas 129
deportations 121, 124, 127–129, 139
detention centres 63
enforcement rate 129
entry refusal 60
French border 249–250, 250n
harm protocols 128, 129
humanitarian assistance 240, 240n, 249n
prisoners, post-release removal 127–128
removal orders 61
Saadi v UK 221
UK Border Force 128
UK Borders Act 128
UK Immigration Enforcement 128
United Nations
communication to Italian government 209
Conventions *see individual* Conventions
Global Compacts *see* Global Compact for Refugees; Global Compact for Safe, Orderly and Regular Migration
High Commissioner for Refugees 212
international cooperation, necessity for 9
Sustainable Development Goals *see* Sustainable Development Goals
Universal Declaration of Human Rights 10
United States
287(g) agreements 126
aggravated felony 59, 59n, 64, 65n, 125
anti-terrorism measures 55, 64, 125

Antiterrorism and Effective Death Penalty Act 125
appeal system 68, 76
apprehension and arrest 56–57, 64–65, 76
asylum seekers 58
Board of Immigration Appeals 66, 68
cancellation of removal 66
Chae Chan Ping v United States 74, 75
conditional parole 64
Criminal Aliens Program 126
criminal law guarantees 74–78
criminal record as grounds for removal 51–52, 54–59, 74–75, 78, 125–127, 136–137
criminal record as grounds to deny entry 57–58, 64
crimmigration 64–70, 74–78, 93, 123–127, 150
custodial sentences 51–52, 59
Customs and Border Protection Agency 55, 56, 64
Department of Homeland Security 55, 69
deportation *see* removal *below*
deportation gap 123–124, 127
detention 51–52, 56, 64–70, 74–78, 125, 126
discretionary powers 64, 65
discretionary relief 66, 76
documented immigrants 125
drug offences 58, 58n, 59, 76–77, 127
due process 69
Electronic Monitoring Programs 64
enforcement operations 64–70
European immigrants 93–94
expedited removal 64–65, 65n
fake documentation 65, 99
federal law 57
Fong Yue Ting v United States 77
foreign convictions 57–58, 64
fraud convictions 57–58, 65
Global Compact on Migration 19
health as grounds to deny entry 57
human trafficking, participation in 58
illegal entry or stay 49, 51–52, 56–57, 58, 64–65
Illegal Immigration Reform and Immigrant Responsibility Act 124–125
immigration bond 64
Immigration and Customs Enforcement 55, 56, 64–69, 123–124
Immigration and Nationality Act 57, 66, 67, 68, 78, 126
incarceration rate 137, 137n
indefinite detention 69
ius soli principle 92
Jordan v De George 57–58
judicial review 66–67, 68, 74
migrants in criminal justice system 90–92
moral turpitude 57–58, 59, 78
national security 55–56, 57
ne bis in idem principle 75
Obama administration 56, 77, 137
overstayers 65
Padilla v Kentucky 76–77, 78
Performance-Based National Detention Standards 69
plea bargain system 51–52, 58, 66, 76–77
Plenary Power Doctrine 74
police and enforcement agencies, collaboration 126
post-entry control 126–127
re-entry, illegal 49, 51
re-entry bans 65
refugees 58
removal, generally 49, 51, 52, 54–59, 64–68, 74–78, 123–127
removal hearings 65–68, 75–77
removal orders 64–69
returns, extended border control 126
Secure Communities Program 126
Sessions v Dimaya 78
suspension of removal 66
Tammany Hall system 93
targeted migrant groups 124, 126–127
Trump administration 52, 55, 56, 69
undocumented immigrants 59, 64–69, 99, 125
United States v Russell 77
unlawful entry 51
voluntary departures 51, 64, 66
United States v Russell 77
Universal Declaration of Human Rights 10

vulnerable persons
European Union 62
Global Compact on Migration 20–21, 20n, 22

Weber, L and McCulloch, J 143, 150–151
women
Global Compact on Migration 20
trafficking, Palermo Protocol 13, 16
Wonders, N 122–123
Wright, R 93

Zirulia, Stefano 32

www.ingramcontent.com/pod-product-compliance
Ingram Content Group UK Ltd.
Pitfield, Milton Keynes, MK11 3LW, UK
UKHW021918271025
464394UK00006B/166